MAKING ENEMIES

MAKING
Enemies

War and State Building in Burma

MARY P. CALLAHAN

Cornell University Press

Ithaca and London

Cornell University Press gratefully acknowledges receipt of a subvention from the University of Washington, which helped in the publication of this book.

First published 2003 by Cornell University Press

Printed in the United States of America

Library of Congress Cataloging-in-Publication Data

Callahan, Mary P. (Mary Patricia) 1961–
   Making enemies : war and state building in Burma / Mary P. Callahan.
      p. cm.
Includes bibliographical references and index.
   ISBN 0-8014-4125-0 (cloth : alk. paper)
   1. Burma—Politics and government—1824–1948. 2. Burma—Politics and government—1948– 3. Burma—Armed forces—Political activity. I. Title.
   DS529.7.C35 2003
   322'.5'095910904—dc21   2003007602

Cloth printing   10 9 8 7 6 5 4 3 2 1

Contents

Maps

Tables

Preface

Have you collected all the facts you need?
>Col. Ye Htut, director of the Defence Services Historical Research
>Institute, as I completed my research in May 1992

You don't need to see the files on what happened after 1962. The Commission for Compiling the Facts of Myanmar History—no, I mean the Authentic Facts of Myanmar History, you know what it's called—is writing that book. You can buy it.
>Col. Ye Htut, responding to my February 1993 request
>to see military archives materials from the 1960s

My understanding of the accidents and forces that turned Burmese citizens into enemies (or at least potential enemies) of the state is a deeply personal one, rooted in a bewildering moment in November 1991 when the military junta gave me a research visa to study the history of the army. For a few years before that, I had tried unsuccessfully to obtain such a visa, first contacting government officials through the Burmese embassy in Washington, D.C., and then making overtures to friends-of-friends-of-friends who were reputed to hold some power and insight. Nothing worked. I gave up, and in October 1991 I went off to London in pursuit of plan B, a study of colonial warfare that could be researched in the comfortable, climate-controlled India Office Library. In early November, as I moped through musty colonial files, Robert Taylor returned to his perch at London's School of Oriental and African Studies after a brief trip to Burma. He phoned me to say that I should try one more time to get the research visa; he was optimistic and better yet had a fax number for one of the half-dozen fax machines in Rangoon. We faxed off my visa request, which consisted of a curriculum vitae and a research proposal to study the "history of the *tatmadaw*" (Burmese for "armed forces"), and a week later the Burmese embassy called to tell me to fetch my visa. Skeptical—surely this was a hoax—I booked no plane reservations and took my time getting over to the embassy. A few days later on my lunch break from the India Office Library, I sauntered in, and a foreign service officer stamped an entry visa into my passport. Astonished, I bolted out the front door of the embassy and hopped a taxi to the inexpensive travel agencies in Earls Court, where I bought a ticket on the first flight possible to Burma. There was still a chance that this visa was a mistake, and I wanted to get there before the mistake registered on any general's radar screen.

When I got to Burma, I realized that there were still many permissions to obtain, and although most eventually were granted, I never understood why I got what I got and why other things were denied me. I was assigned two liaison officers, from the Ministry of Agriculture of all places. The officers were accomplished entomologists, and their careers in pest control made them tireless promoters of my cause. Nonetheless, they were very nervous, and when they took me to a new installation, archive, or library to start the negotiations over my access to treasures therein, my liaisons always whispered my research topic. "*Tatmadaw tha-maing* [history]," they murmured, prompting a startle reflex from the guards or bureaucrats at the gates. At the main military archive where I spent most of my time, I was never given access to the stacks or file storage. Nor did I have any sense of the organizing principle for the piles of catalogs and indexes that the archivists gave me. When I requested files by file numbers, sometimes I got everything I asked for, sometimes nothing. Sometimes files not included in my list or even in the indexes materialized on my desk. The files withheld were said to be "out," and none of them ever came back "in" during my six months' research stay in 1991–92. When asked where they were, the archivists and file clerks said, "*Ma thee bu* [I don't know]." As the time on my visa began to wind down, I asked the archive director for permission to photocopy files I would not have time to get to; he replied, "Make a list." And when I did, he rejected about 10 percent of the list. There was no pattern, no common degree of sensitivity among those denied, no pattern of innocuousness to those released for photocopying. In fact, he let me spend all the time I wanted reviewing and taking notes on the files he crossed off the photocopy order. When I asked why I could make notes on the files but not copy them, he answered, "It simply cannot be permitted that you get everything you ask for."

Over the last several decades, many outside observers of Burmese politics have imputed method to the madness of interactions like these. I now believe those interpretations overstate the logic, unity, and integrity of Burmese history and the state. Early in my research career in Burma, I came to embrace the ambiguity and contingency of both day-to-day life and the history of military rule. Why did I get a visa in 1991? My theory is that it all started with the power of scarce technology. I suspect that the minister of agriculture, Lt. Gen. Chit Swe, happened to have a personal assistant or clerk who picked up my visa application out of a fax tray and—since faxes were so few and far between in 1991—assumed this must be a document of enough power and significance to place it on cabinet minister Chit Swe's desk. For either personal reasons (he considered Robert Taylor, who gave me the fax number, a friend) or political reasons (he was reputedly part of a junta faction that promoted openness to the outside world), Chit Swe got me on the agenda of the very next junta meeting, and my visa got approved. At no point did Chit Swe or any senior official send orders to any archive or library to accommodate or assist me, or even to warn them I was coming. The regime was busy with other, more pressing concerns, and I had the impression that the fact that I was a young woman made my study of the *tatmadaw* distinctly unthreatening.

Each time my entomologist-liaisons and I showed up at a new venue for research, the guards at the entrance gates bristled at my presence. For a few days we would drive to the new place every morning, and every morning the guards would turn me away. Finally, for no apparent reason, I would get through the gate one morning, and then have to start negotiating my presence all over again with those who actually oversaw the files and sources inside the gate. The mere fact that I was there and showed up every day seemed to make librarians and archivists both nervous (they might show me something that later would get them into trouble) and secure (since no other white researcher had appeared in decades, I could not have gotten this far without the backing of some really big big-shot). At times—such as when I turned in my photocopying request at the military archives—it became important for an official to have denied me some of what I asked for. If I later caused trouble, the official would have evidence that he or she had recognized I was a threat and kept me from seeing too much. The politics of my research were dangerous to many of these professionals, precisely because of the absence of clear rules for the research game.

There may have been a logic to the arbitrary cut-off date of the period I was permitted to research, which stopped at 1962. If so, it still escapes me. When I began my research stay in November 1991, Burma was recovering from the deleterious consequences of the policies initiated in 1962, when the military took power for what would become the longest haul in modern world history. After the latest incarnation of military rule was established in 1988, some senior generals started courting foreign investors, pushing for a liberalization of the economy and publicly criticizing the mistakes made in the 1960s and beyond. The regime has been vested in distinguishing itself from the misguided,

army-backed regime that ruled from 1962 to 1988. While this period is one
in which the army waged a brutal counterinsurgency campaign against ethnic and political opponents—a history that has never been fully exposed—
this in itself was not sufficient reason to give me a blanket denial of access to
post-1962 records. Certainly, if some counterinsurgency bloodbath needed
to be covered up, archivists could tell me particular battle records happened
to be "out." But a cover-up seems unlikely, especially because the strategy
and combat in counterinsurgency during this period are actually things that
senior officers are very proud of. Most of the generals running the country
today were promoted because of their service in these campaigns.

Why then wasn't I granted access to any materials beyond 1962? As the
second epigraph to this preface notes, the army archives' director told me
that a commission of mostly retired historians was taking care of that for
me, and their official history was indeed published in a multivolume set in
the mid-1990s. When I went back to Burma a few years ago, I again asked to
see documents from the post-1962 period, and again was rebuffed by the
same director. "You have all the facts," he told me, pointing to his copy of an
official history of the Socialist era (1962–88). For him, history and histori-
ography are rooted in a singular unproblematic truth, whose production he
happened to oversee. One simply collects the facts from his archive as a
geologist collects rock samples or an entomologist collects data on insect
populations. The facts are compiled, cataloged, and then displayed in an objective, scientific manner. This is not to say that this colonel did not understand the possibility that "facts" could be interpreted differently, but any
divergence from the official history was a matter of falsehoods, not of alternative views that had any validity. If official historians had produced the au-
thoritative history, why should I need to look at the files?

And even more simply, I came to understand that somehow, the closing
off of some set of records had become routine in our negotiations over my
research. To read into the inaccessibility of post-1962 records some grand
scheme for obfuscating the "truth" or "facts" of history requires one to assume that Burma's leading generals believe there is anything to cover up.
Most army leaders do not think twice about documents and papers in a
stuffy archive; they do not think that allowing access to the documents
could impact their hold on political authority or their personal gain. These
leaders, as I argue in this book, are not politicians who might sense the un-
tapped power filed away in the archives, but war fighters who find paperwork tedious and unmanly. These are soldiers who wage battles, count up
the casualties, reassess strategy and tactics, and—most important—move
on. Like the 10 percent of the archives' files I was not permitted to photocopy in 1992, the post-1962 records were simply out of the bargain I had
unknowingly negotiated with the archive director.

A Note about Sources and Names

Every social scientist who writes about militaries laments the difficulties of conducting research on these secretive institutions. I believe I had access to nearly all the official documentation that exists on warfare and state building during the colonial and early postcolonial period. The India Office Library and Public Record Office in London are stacked with well-indexed and accessible files from the colonial and World War II eras. Collections of official records from the early years of independent Burma, however, are much thinner. This was neither a paper-generating nor a paper-collecting military in the 1950s, despite British admonitions to the contrary. This was an army on the run within a state on the verge of collapse.

When internal conditions had stabilized a bit, the *tatmadaw* set up the Defence Services Historical Research Institute in 1955. A few staff officers collected scattered copies of internal military correspondence and reports, but came up with only the relatively small number (perhaps several hundred) cited herein. Thus, it is difficult for the researcher to know exactly how to interpret the documents that are on deposit in the military archives. Is the existing documentation representative of the paperwork generated or filed during this period? Probably not. Are there other documents on file at other government repositories? Probably not. Where did the rest of the paperwork go? Probably much of it was shredded or recycled, and even more of it was destroyed when insurgents ransacked army headquarters upcountry. Was documentation even important to understanding the *tatmadaw* of the 1950s? Again, probably not.

Given these limitations, what follows is at best a tentative attempt to understand the internal dynamics of a military. To augment internal army documentation in the postwar era, I consulted British Services Mission, military attaché, embassy, and intelligence reports on file at the Public Record Office in Kew, England. These documents are filled with inaccuracies and disinformation, but read carefully they provide insight into at least the British view of *tatmadaw* developments. To a lesser extent, I consulted U.S. attaché reports and official records of the Australian embassy in Rangoon. I also combed Burmese newspapers, magazines, autobiographies, diaries, fiction, and secondary sources for insights. Master's theses written by students at Rangoon and Mandalay universities helped to fill in missing pieces of the military politics puzzle.

Finally, I conducted interviews with former army officers, politicians, journalists, communists, socialists, leftists, rightists, guerrillas, civil servants, murderers, extortionists, diplomats, students, and spies over the course of the last decade in Rangoon, Mandalay, Pegu, Maymyo, London, Canberra, Bangkok, Chiang Mai, Los Angeles, and Washington, D.C. In trying to understand the events of the past, I found that interviews present particular problems of accuracy and research value. But many of these interviews provided useful details and points of view. Most of all, they gave me a feel for the adventure, danger, promise, and disappointments of wartime and postwar Burma. The interviews, like the archival documentation, represent far from an ideal sample. Many former communists, socialists, and army officers from the 1950s were either dead or in jail. In the political climate of the 1990s, others who were alive and free were unwilling to talk to an American asking questions about the *tatmadaw*. In some cases, a Burmese friend conducted interviews of reluctant subjects on my behalf; in other cases, even that was impossible. Many of my interview subjects requested anonymity. We agreed to use an identification tag—such as "former field commander" or "former staff officer"—that would tell the reader enough to evaluate the information being presented but would protect the interviewee's identity.

The issue of whether to use "Burma" or "Myanmar" as the name of the country is even more complicated than the usage of interviewees' names. In 1989, the ruling junta officially renamed the country "Myanmar." Its stated purpose was to replace the British-given name, "Burma," with one more authentic and dating back to precolonial days. The junta appears to be harkening back to twelfth-century Old Burmese inscriptions, wherein "Myanmar" was the written term for the domain of the kings at Pagan and, later, at Pegu and Mandalay. There is some conceptual slippage here, given that for most of these eras, a king's domain was defined by claims not over territory but over scarce labor and populations. Under the military regime that took power in 1988, the political unit called "Myanmar" has come to refer only to territory. There is also linguistic inventiveness at play here. In modern Burmese language usage, "Myanmar" has been the romanization of the formal literary term for the modern-nation state since independence in 1948, while "Bama/ Bamar" (from which "Burma" is derived) has been the spoken or colloquial language equivalent for the sovereign domain of the government, that is, the name of the country. To the regime's dismay, many countries in the world, including the United States, have refused to embrace the name change because of claims about the illegitimacy of the junta. The usage of "Burma" is often seen as implying a critique of the military junta, while usage of "Myanmar" suggests a more favorable view of the regime. Given the controversy over the name, I have chosen to use the term "Burma" throughout this book when I refer to the country, and "Myanmar" when it occurs in a name of a government agency. This choice is intended to reflect less a political stance than a recognition that there remains controversy over the issue.

Throughout this project I have relied extensively on colleagues and friends for support, advice, and direction. Benedict Anderson, Elizabeth Angell, Vincent Boudreau, Kyaw Yin Hlaing, Takashi Shiraishi, and Robert Taylor read early drafts of the entire manuscript. Two anonymous readers provided invaluable commentary on how to sharpen my arguments. Roger Haydon at Cornell University Press patiently and generously guided revisions of this manuscript from its roughest genesis to the final product; the editing of the final text by Cathi Reinfelder was nothing short of masterful. Patricio Abinales, Donna Amoroso, David Chandler, Elizabeth Kier, Bertil Lintner, Joel Migdal, Elizabeth Remick, and Martin Smith offered feedback on parts of the manuscript. My research was kindly facilitated by entomologists, linguists, historians, archivists, and librarians, including Ben Abel, Patricia Herbert, U Thaw Kaung, U Myat Soe, U Pe Thein, Daw Ni Ni Myint, Daw Tin Phone Nwe, Daw Ah Win, U Nyan Tun, U Tun Aung Chain, Daw Khin Khin Myint, Daw Khin Hla Han, Dr. Myint Kyi, Dr. Saw Rock Top, Dr. Naw Angelene, Ma Monica, Daw Ohn Kyi, Dr. Myo Myint, Maj. Kyaw Zaw, Col. Ye Htut, Commander Hla Shein, U Zaw Zaw, Ma Thanegi, Daw Heather Morris, U Ye Win, San San Hnin, U Saw Tun, John Okell, U Kyaw Hlaing, and U Thet Tun.

Funding for this research came from the Social Science Research Council, Cornell University International Studies Center, the Cornell Southeast Asia Program, the Mellon Foundation, the University of Washington Southeast Asia Center, and the Jackson School of International Studies. For their generosity and support, I am especially grateful to Jackson School directors Resat Kasaba, Martin Jaffee, and Jere Bacharach, to Tom Gething and Marjorie Muecke, directors of the Southeast Asia Center; and to Resat Kasaba and Daniel Chirot, directors of the International Studies Center. The University of Washington Graduate School provided a generous subvention to aid publication. I am grateful to Ian Carter, for creating and allowing me to use the ICMyanmar font, and to Virgil Gloria, for his assistance with all things technical.

My greatest inspiration in all my work on Burma has been and continues to be Dr. Khin Zaw Win.

My deepest gratitude and admiration goes to Jim Powers, whose unwavering support makes everything possible. I dedicate this book to him and our son, Sammy.

MARY P. CALLAHAN

Seattle, Washington

Abbreviations

ABPO	All-Burma Peasants' Organization
ABRO	Army of Burma Reserve Organization
ADA	Arakan Defence Army
AFO	Anti-Fascist Organization
AFPFL	Anti-Fascist People's Freedom League
ALFSEA	Allied Land Forces, Southeast Asia
Amb.	Ambassador
ASEAN	Association of Southeast Asian Nations
AYRG	Army Young (Officers') Resistance Group
BAA	Burma Area Army
BDA	Burma Defence Army (renamed BNA in 1943)
BIA	Burma Independence Army
BNA	Burma National Army
BRNVR	Burma Royal Naval Volunteer Reserve
BSM	British Services Mission
BSP	Burma Socialist Party
BSPP	Burma Socialist Program Party
Burif	Burma Rifles
CAS(B)	Civil Affairs Service (Burma)
CCS	Consumer Cooperative System
CIA	Central Intelligence Agency
CO	Commanding Officer
CPB	Communist Party of Burma
DDSI	Directorate of Defence Services Intelligence
DIG	Deputy Inspector General
DSA	Defence Services Academy
DSC	Defence Services Council

DSHRI	Defence Services Historical Research Institute
DSI	Defence Services Institute
DSP	District Superintendent of Police
EAYL	East Asia Youth League
ECO	Emergency Commissioned Officer
FO	Foreign Office
GSO	General Staff Officer
HQ	Headquarters
IOR	India Office Library and Records
KNDO	Karen National Defence Organisation
KNU	Karen National Union
KMT	Kuomintang
MEC	Myanmar Economic Corporation
MPB	Military Preparations Bureau
MPS	Military Planning Staff
NAAFI	Navy, Army, and Air Force Institutes
NCO	noncommissioned officer
NDC	National Defence Committee
NLD	National League for Democracy
OSS	Office of Strategic Services (U.S.); Office of Strategic Studies (Burma)
OTS	Officers' Training School
PBF	Patriotic Burmese Forces
PLA	People's Liberation Army
PPG	People's Peace Guerrillas
PRC	People's Republic of China
PRO	Public Record Office
PRP	People's Revolutionary Party
psywar	psychological warfare
PVO	People's Volunteer Organisation
SAC	Supreme Allied Commander
SEAC	Southeast Asia Command
SLORC	State Law and Order Restoration Council
SOE	Special Operations Executive
SPDC	State Peace and Development Council
UMEH	Union of Myanmar Economic Holdings, Ltd.
UMP	Union Military Police
UN	United Nations
UTC	University Training Corps
WO	War Office

MAKING ENEMIES

Introduction

Protest started at around 10 A.M. at the sports center across the street [from the Rangoon University Central Library, where I was working]. Chants of "de-mo-ca-ra-cy" actually didn't sound much different from the previous day's cheers during a volleyball match. Librarians told me the Department of Higher Education called and told them to confine me to the manuscript room (opaque windows), turn up the noisy air conditioner and not let me near the fracas. By 11:30, there were no more cheers and the rumor was that the campus had been sealed. How many demonstrators? Someone had ventured across the street and guessed no more than fifty. Why today? [Imprisoned opposition leader] Aung San Suu Kyi was awarded the Nobel Peace Prize in Oslo today.

At 12:30, a librarian told me that one gate had been opened so staff could go home and that he would escort me off campus. When we exited the library, the sports complex was silent. In fact, all was silent. The street was empty. As we neared Convocation Hall, we saw our first soldiers. Young, darker skinned than most Burmans, and agitated. But much more agitated when they saw my white face. Silence became cacophony; the young soldier boys scurried about, brandishing their rifles, shouting for reinforcements, and blocking our path to the gate. We stopped, my escort negotiated firmly, and a colonel muscled his way through the teenagers with big guns. He blanched at the sight of me, looked toward the gate, and then back in the direction of the sports center. Then at me. "Get out. Get out," he screamed (in English) from the bottom of his gut. I did.

Since I left it only a few hours earlier, University Avenue had become a parking lot for war toys. Armored Personnel Carriers, barbed-wire road blocks, troop trucks, weapons trucks. Also four or five menacing dark blue trucks, the sides of which had high, tiny windows with bars over them—used for prisoner transport. Soldiers and police everywhere in a rainbow of different uniforms. Across the star-shaped intersection with Prome and Insein roads, more soldiers. Hledan market, tea shops and all businesses closed. It was a war zone.

My research diary, December 10, 1991

Coming as it did on the day after I received permission from the military government to conduct research on army history, my first close encounter with the *tatmadaw* (Burmese for "armed forces") was surreal. That fifty unarmed students, shouting "de-mo-ca-ra-cy," could provoke a massive joint forces campaign made no sense. But as events unfolded during my research stay in 1991–92 and as the army let me delve into its early history, the reasons for this apparent overreaction became more clear. Contrary to what I had learned in the scholarly literature, the tatmadaw is not a "political movement in military garb."[1] Instead, the soldiers and officers who deployed to the university that December, as well as the generals running the regime over the last several decades, are war fighters who are not adept at politics. But they are war fighters, first and foremost.

That insight guides this book. Unless seen in the light of its war-fighting focus, the Burmese tatmadaw looks like an incomparably efficient team of power-hungry, illiterate, shameless, vicious lunatics. To most outside observers, it seems that the generals routinely and capriciously mount methodical, brutal campaigns of repression against their own citizens, who occasionally mount massive and heroic attempts to defend themselves. Despite the generals' extensive overseas education, training, and service and despite international pressures—the suspension of most international economic aid, the imposition of an arms embargo, the ban on U.S. visas for senior junta leaders, and the ban on new investment in Burma by U.S. citizens—the military regime remains brutally and smugly in power in Rangoon.

Given the costs involved, true politicians would not undertake this kind of combat against their citizenry. War fighters, however, might do just that. This book explains how these war fighters have managed to maintain a stranglehold over political power for the last four decades. Prevailing explanations hold an exceptionally authoritarian culture and the cunning of one dictator responsible for four decades of military rule. In this book, I argue that the origin of this unusually durable and equally unpopular form of rule is found in the discrete historical circumstances that established a state predicated on, constructed around, and ultimately held hostage to organized violence. As in other societies, war and crisis in Burma created institutions with staying power, and in this case created relations between state and society that have been and continue to be what Charles Tilly calls "coercion-intensive."[2] This state was forged in the British colonial period, when the population mapped into the new political unit materialized as threats to colonial commerce rather than as potential citizens. During World War II, warfare transformed this coercion-dominant relationship between state and society. As the British colonial state disintegrated overnight, there emerged a dizzying array of nonstate organizations of violence, wherein coercion was the currency of politics and the weakened state became only one of numerous entities with claims on violence, territory, resources, and people. This dispersal of power and guns throughout the Japanese-occupied territory set postcolonial Burma up for the decades of civil warfare to follow. In this book, I examine how critical periods of state building and transformation in wartime situations turned populations and citizens into potential enemies of the state, and how the tatmadaw eventually became the arbiter of who would be called an "enemy" and who could claim citizenship privileges.

At the heart of my book is a study of the genesis of the baffling configuration of state-society relations that place unchecked coercion and repression at the center of modern Burmese politics. I argue that warfare creates the conditions under which elites and social forces negotiate, create, revitalize, reorganize, and rethink the patterns and practices of governance. Based on extensive archival research and interviews, the main chapters of this book analyze how critical periods of state building and transformation in wartime situations created the particular coercion-intensive institutions that dominated relations between the Burmese state and society throughout the twentieth century. The epilogue considers how these periods of institutional genesis, decay, and renovation in the colonial period, the Japanese occupation, and the first fourteen years of postcolonial rule influenced the subsequent four decades of military rule.[3] The book concludes that the relationship between state building and warfare is a recursive one that has tangled up Burmese state and society in such a way as to produce the most durable incarnation of military rule in history. The generals who sent the young soldiers and tanks to the University of Rangoon campus in December 1991 are products of this historical process. For these generals, the students shouting "de-mo-ca-ra-cy" in the sports center can be no more accommodated or ignored than the well-armed insurgent armies that the tatmadaw has fought and imagined itself fighting since its inception. In twentieth-century Burma, warfare created state institutions that in many situations cannot distinguish between citizens and enemies of the state.

This book is fundamentally an argument for contingency. The coercion-intensive behavior of Burma's postcolonial state is not simply a function of colonial inheritances continuing to enslave postcolonial populations, nor does it necessarily result from the militarist legacy of the Japanese occupation. Other postcolonial, postoccupation nations were able—with varying

Map 1. Burma (cities, towns, and geographical features mentioned in text).

degrees of success and over varying amounts of time—to dismantle top-heavy, repressive colonial and occupation state apparatuses and establish institutions more responsive to new citizenries. Why does the colonial legacy of repression in the particular form of long-running military rule prevail in Burma and not in other former British colonies, such as India or Malaysia, or other former occupation sites such as the Philippines? Like other colonies marching toward independence, Burma erupted in antistate insurgency in the early postwar period. But unlike the states that adopted accommodating, "hearts-and-minds" political solutions to incorporate rather than annihilate domestic opposition, independent Burma found itself in a geostrategic bind just as national leaders launched similarly accommodationist strategies of counterinsurgency. As the Cold War threatened to swallow up Burma, military and civilian leaders had few choices but to reinvigorate and redeploy the colonial security apparatus to hold together a disintegrating country during the formative period of postcolonial state transformation. For both civilian and military leaders in the 1950s, political counterinsurgency strategies—such as power-sharing arrangements or institutional reforms allowing more inclusionary politics—were swept off the agenda when the United States began training Chinese Kuomintang (KMT) soldiers in Burmese territory for their eventual counterattack against the People's Republic of China. When political appeals to the United States and to the United Nations failed, the military took the helm of a barely functioning state apparatus and gradually found itself responsible for law enforcement, economic regulation, tax collection, census taking, political party registration, food distribution, magazine publishing, and so forth. The move of the military into nonmilitary affairs was neither smooth nor uncontested, and the subsequent forty years of military domination was not a foregone conclusion until well into the 1960s. The military solution to internal crises crowded out other potential state reformers, turning officers into state builders and citizens into threats and—more characteristically—enemies.

Alternative Explanations: Culture, Cunning, and Rupture

The use of culture to explain Burmese political and social phenomena has its roots in the precolonial period, when Portuguese and American missionaries scouted the territory for converts by making character assessments. Early reports were mixed, some holding that the Burmese were dishonest and subject to "gross idolatry" and "wicked inclinations," while others considered the indigenes courteous, virtuous, and kind.[4] Throughout the colonial period, British bureaucrats identified negative and positive aspects of indigenous character to account for both social calamity and vitality. In postcolonial Burma of the 1950s, the research agenda continued its reliance on "all embracing categories of culture, identity and personality."[5] In 1962, Lucien Pye tried to explain economic and political stagnation in Burma by showing how local child-rearing practices led to paranoid and dysfunctional national character.[6] As recently as 1999, Mikael Gravers reinvigorated claims about Burmese paranoia to explain antidemocratic societal tendencies.[7]

Most of these cultural explanations have in common a serious methodological flaw: Generalizations about national character, culture, and personality are based on contacts with a handful of Burmese who communicate in a Western language and whose representativeness of cultural traits surely have to be suspect. There have been few serious anthropological analyses of culture and subculture conducted in the country, which renders most characterizations speculative and imaginative at best. Even John S. Furnivall's brilliant critique of British rule in *Colonial Policy and Practice* relies on an idealized, paternalistic vision of a fallen culture and society.[8] In fact, Edmund Leach's work, which constitutes the most compelling anthropological analysis of Burmese communities, rejects culture as the cause of political, social, and economic developments and argues for ecology as a more significant explanatory variable.[9]

One manifestation of Burmese cultural pathology has been portrayed as the cyclical emergence of a cunning, Chakravarti ("world-conqueror") leader who wields absolute power throughout the realm and is answerable to no one.[10] In the rush to explain the deviance of Burma's postwar history, scholars have focused and continue to focus on former dictator Gen. Ne Win as an incarnation of this ruler concept, depicting him as the glue that has held the Burmese armed forces and the post-1962 government together. Throughout the civil wars, economic collapses, and political debacles of the entire post–World War II period, observers have attributed the unusual power of the military regime to Ne Win's charisma, his formative experiences as a student politician, his ruthlessness, his *awza* (awe-inspiring power), his *hpon* (charismatic power "demonstrated by courage, skill in battle, physical and . . . sexual prowess"),[11] and his ability to *yeh-ti-ya-cheh-deh* (tempt fate). According to this view, Ne Win's path to power, from youth onward, has been his destiny. In this view, Ne Win single-handedly made Burma the deviant case it is today.

No one could possibly dispute the central role that Gen. Ne Win has played in modern Burmese politics. However, one problem with attributing all outcomes to Ne Win is that the historical evidence is spotty at best. In fact, Ne Win's prominence resulted in large part from activities and developments that occurred within the army and the Burmese polity in the 1950s, over which he had little control or influence. Moreover, the Ne Win–centered theory suggests that the state is a neutral tool that can be deployed toward whatever end an effective leader may choose. While Ne Win did deploy state violence and institutions craftily in some cases, the nature of both state and society limited greatly what he could accomplish.

The most historically inaccurate aspect of both "cultural" and "cunning" explanations lies in the necessary assumption of a rupture in patterns of state-society relations at independence in 1948. If pathological elements of Burmese culture or the extraordinary cunning of Ne Win are held to explain the unusually coercion-intensive history of postwar Burmese politics, the state must have started fresh with a tabula rasa after the British departed in 1948. Only under that condition could the colonial structuring of state-society relations be said to be fully replaced by uncorrupted, "truly Burmese"—and thus, truly pathological—forms of social and political relations. Edward Said has pointed out the theoretical folly of such an argument: "Imperialism is repeatedly on record as saying, in effect, You are what you are because of us; when we left, you reverted to your deplorable state; know that or you will know nothing, for certainly there is little to be known about imperialism that might help you or us in the present."[12]

The rupture argument is also counterintuitive at a basic empirical level. The framers of the Burmese Constitution of 1947 were British-trained barristers, and the document that structured politics at the national level was a reinvigoration of the governing arrangements set up by the colonial regime a decade earlier. More fundamentally, the government's activities—tax collection, criminal investigation, disease inoculation, customs inspection, and census taking—were all undertaken by bureaucrats who had worked for the British colonial regime and who relied on the same methods they had used prior to independence.

To date, only Robert Taylor's analysis in *The State in Burma* has challenged prevailing explanations of Burmese exceptionalism, culture, and historical rupture and portrayed them as products of ahistorical blinders that underemphasized the continuity of patterns of state-society relations over several centuries. Taylor rejects the assumption that a state is purely a function of and determined by cultural and social forces, without any reverse influence. Instead, he stresses the consistency (rather than historical rupture) of state dominance over social and economic relations in society from as early as the eleventh century Pagan dynasty onward, and he explains variations in state strength and weakness vis-à-vis its internal challengers. He argues that the post-1962 period of army rule is one in which the military attempted to reassert the power of the central state by force, "eliminating its rivals through the power of the law while ensuring that the institutions permitted to exist are dependent upon the state . . . and are therefore unable to organize effective opposition to it."[13]

However, in focusing on macrohistorical issues of state-society relations,

Taylor cannot explain how and why the military rather than some other national- or local-level institution accumulated the resources, clout, and skills to assert the power of the central state, or how the gulf came to exist between the paternalist military and its citizenry of potential enemies. By complementing a careful examination of intra-army developments during the 1950s with a comparatively informed, macrohistorical analysis of the impact of warfare on state formation, this book takes Taylor's approach one level of analysis deeper into the institution that arguably has had the greatest impact on postcolonial Burma—the military. Contrary to standard interpretations of Burmese authoritarianism, I argue that the military regimes of the postwar era do not result from culturally or cunningly produced "political movement[s] in military garb."[14] In fact, postwar Burmese regimes have been made up of war fighters who never mastered the art of politics enough to win a single election. In spite of electoral defeat and widespread domestic and international reprobation, military rule endures. The crucial factor explaining the durability of military rule against domestic and international forces is the historical relationship between war and state formation that emerged over the last century.

The Relationship between War and State Building

Although warfare debilitates fragile states, war also builds states, as the scholars of European absolutism have demonstrated.[15] In the Burmese case, unlike that of Europe, warfare built a state thoroughly beholden to war fighters. This suggests a variation in outcome worth exploring. Why does war making sometimes lead to coercive, autocratic government dominated by war fighters, as in Burma, and sometimes to democratic or representative government led by civilians, as in England and France? The lessons of early state formation in Europe suggest that an important determinant of democratic development in France and England was the monarch's dependence on social forces with control over the resources necessary to wage war. In mobilizing these resources, kings not only built modern bureaucracies of tax collectors but also provided institutional mechanisms that allowed the taxpayers to have input on decision making. In some instances, the road was rocky and greater central demands for resources led to rebellions or civil wars. Ultimately, however, in England and France, the demands of the increasingly dangerous international environment ultimately led to the co-development of state bureaucratic apparatuses and constitutional, representative frameworks of governance. The lessons of comparative history suggest that negotiation and bargaining between state builders and social constituencies are crucial to the development of responsive, representative governing institutions.

While the discrete historical conditions that led to the emergence of national states in Europe were not replicated precisely anywhere in the non-European world, the analytical tools derived from studies of European war and state formation can usefully inform the study of non-European warfare, state building, and transformation. The key analytical distinction that must be made in such a comparatively informed analysis lies in the character of the warfare waged by colonial states and the legacies of that warfare for postcolonial state-society relations. Modern states in Africa and most of Asia were established via warfare directed not against enemies one could identify as "external" but instead against populations mapped into an arbitrary—though nonetheless durable—political unit. Colonial states went to war against populations they designated as "internal." This kind of warfare was conducted by legions of European officers and non-European soldiers recruited from conquered populations. The increasingly repressive colonial state required little or no social cooperation or accommodation from local populations. In the early stages of imperial aggrandizement, European trading companies arrived in Asia and Africa with their private armies, demanding trading privileges at ports, squashing any serious commercial or political threats and competition, and ignoring most of the population. Later, it was the armies attached to European states that performed these duties. While Kalevi J. Holsti is correct in asserting that "[t]he original purposes of colonialism . . . never included state-making,"[16] the garrisoning of large numbers of government troops in the conquest of Africa and the expansion into and pacification of the interior regions of Southeast Asia in the nineteenth century established de facto military administration. In the process, most of the population met the modern state in the form of an unintelligible, gun-wielding soldier, not in an encounter with a tax collector who might negotiate in a comprehensible dialect.

Not surprisingly, military administration did not guarantee omnipotence, and threats to the colonial state and capital were frequent. In rare instances they came from other imperial armies, but more commonly the threats came from local populations in the form of such wide-ranging activities as cattle thievery, highway banditry, trade unionization, peasant rebellions, student protests, and hunger strikes. To defend against these threats, colonial regimes in some cases attempted to control local populations by co-opting traditional, indigenous rulers via "indirect rule"; in other cases, the regimes opted for "direct rule" by deploying their own bureaucrats and soldiers and enlisting the services of a minority group whose loyalty to the regime could be ensured by their numerical weakness vis-à-vis the majority of the population. Across these two forms of administration, colonial states incidentally materialized and developed into what Karen Rasler and William Thompson call "nonaccommodating governments."[17] When local populations threatened the order necessary for successful colonial commerce and authority, the state's response rarely entailed any attempt to win the support of allies or resource providers among the populace. Instead, colonial regimes repressed, coerced, arrested, exiled, and executed murderers and nationalists, robbers and monks, and cattle thieves and student strikers. The formation of modern, bureaucratic states in much of the colonial world thus established "a command relationship [between state and] civil society, reflected in its laws, its routine, its mentalities, even its imagery."[18]

It is important to note that there were breaks in this command relationship, such as in the throes of World War I. At that point, colonial regimes became army recruiters, tasked with filling out the ranks of the European armies that had been depleted in the trenches in Europe. For example, in India, the British government's first-ever discussion of India's transition to self-government came during World War I. In return for access to more recruits for the war efforts in Europe, British army officials opened negotiations with Indian nationalists and pledged political reforms toward independence. In the post–World War I period, Indian nationalists were disappointed with the limited nature of the reforms that resulted from these promises, but nonetheless this represented the first real steps toward accommodating the wishes of Indian elites—in this case, nationalist leaders who had substantial leverage over potential recruits. In comparative perspective, it is no surprise that accommodation of Indian social forces came as a result of wartime mobilization negotiations.

When indigenous elites took over national states at independence, they started not with a tabula rasa but with the rickety yet repressive architecture of colonial states, which was often at odds with their anticolonial ideological programs. A central hypothesis of this book is that the nature and conduct of warfare in the years surrounding the transfer of power from a colonial to a postcolonial regime determined how much power the military would wield in the array of organizations that would constitute the postcolonial state for decades to come. The existence of ongoing, continuous civil warfare—which erupted in most of the postcolonial nations of South and Southeast Asia—did not necessarily privilege the military vis-à-vis civilian contenders for national power. However, states adopted different strategies for fighting and ending civil wars. These strategies were determined by the institutions and resources inherited from the colonial regimes, the sources of nonstate or social power existing in the territory, and the intrusions of the Cold War. When insurgency first erupted in post–World War II Asia, most states first pursued a purely military strategy to wipe out antistate movements. However, in Malaysia, the Philippines, and parts of India, governments quickly abandoned the purely coercive, military approach, opting for accommodationist strategies to co-opt and incorporate opposition and seeking to win the hearts and minds of the populations that otherwise might support antistate insurgents. In postcolonial Indonesia and Burma, states experimented with accommodation but never really budged from the military approach.

In postwar South and Southeast Asia, counterinsurgency efforts were the primary force driving the construction and reconstruction of postcolonial states. In the period of the 1950s and 1960s, national leaders devoted scarce resources and talent to the development of policies and institutions that could eliminate internal threats. States like Malaya, the Philippines, and India, which pursued a combination of political and military counterinsurgency strategies, saw concurrent bureaucratization, centralization, articulation, and empowerment of both nonmilitary and military institutions. States such as Burma and Indonesia pursued mainly military strategies, and consequently saw the development of powerful centralizing militaries and the concurrent withering of the civil services bequeathed by the departed colonizers. Moreover, in both of these cases, the armies—not civilian bureaucracies—began experimenting with and institutionalizing political counterinsurgency strategies to co-opt internal populations. In Burma and Indonesia, this state-making process created two parallel structures of governance that processed and regulated national economic and social life. One limp structure of governance lay in the civilian realm, the other more robust structure lay in the military bureaucracy.

What determined the kind of counterinsurgency solution these states adopted? While this question calls for a program of research beyond the scope of this book, it is nonetheless possible to formulate one explanation based on variation across the Asian cases. In cases in which civil strife was accompanied by the arrival of global warfare threatening the state's claims over domestic territory, the institutionalization of accommodational arrangements between states and social forces was derailed by the prioritization of national security interests above all else. For example, India and Indonesia both inaugurated their postcolonial regimes in the midst of internal, civil warfare; in the former case, against Muslim separatist groups, and in the latter case, against communists and regional separatists. However, in India in the 1950s, the state found compromise solutions that either accommodated the interests of antistate forces or marginalized these groups. In Indonesia in the late 1950s, just as political opponents appeared willing to work through state institutions rather than against them, the U.S. sponsorship of rebellions in the outer islands ultimately led to a concentration of state power within the military.[19] In Burma, a similar covert operation by the U.S. Central Intelligence Agency (CIA) in the northeastern frontier region led the postcolonial Union government to abandon the newly forged alliance between leaders of socioeconomic forces and state managers and instead to elevate army modernization as the top national priority.

The Study of State-Building Processes

This book is fundamentally an analysis of the genesis of political institutions in warfare and the consequences of such origins. In accordance with Joel Migdal's warning that "[i]t is far from inevitable that state leaders achieve predominance for the state,"[20] I attempt to retrace the path of the Burmese state from its precolonial, decentralized, highly personal character to its contemporary centralized, impersonal, and militarist nature. I begin with an assumption that such an historical-institutional analysis is of more than antiquarian value. In her analysis of state formation and popular movements in nineteenth-century Mexico, Florencia Mallon writes: "As the products of previous conflicts and confrontations, institutions have embedded in them the sediments of earlier struggles. Uncovering these helps us understand not only the history of how they were formed, but also their present character and future potential."[21]

Moreover, this book attempts to account for the unusual endurance record and strange policies of Burmese military rulers over the last four decades by applying the comparative insights gained from the studies of militaries, states, and societies across Asia, Africa, Latin America, and Europe. This analysis is theoretically and comparatively informed, but also attempts to be faithful to the complexity and curiosity of Burmese politics by offering a rich, detailed, empirical narrative. For example, references to such basic theoretical concepts as "the state" and "the military" do not involve assumptions of unitary institutional coherence but instead are treated as empirical questions. Ayesha Jalal notes in her analysis of the polities that emerged on the Indian subcontinent: "Neither the administrative bureaucracy nor the military are institutional monoliths immune from internal jockeying for position between their different arms. Nor is the state viewed as omnipotent or completely distinct from society. The domain of the state is seen to be one of accommodation and contest by innumerable and contending sites of power embedded in society at the regional and sub-regional levels."[22] In attempting to understand the unusual array of relations between state and society in postcolonial Burma, this book views the armed forces as one of several sites of power embedded and grounded firmly in discrete historical struggles over national, regional, and local power and resources.

My attention to empirical detail is framed by basic definitions of the major theoretical concepts employed. *State building* and *institution building* refer to the processes in which state actors and institution managers organize resources and personnel so as to extend the geographical and functional "reach of the state" or institution.[23] The geographical extension of the state or an institution occurs when policies adopted in the national administrative center can be and are implemented by centrally designated, locally based organizations in territory beyond that center. The functional extension of the state or an institution occurs when state actors and managers take on and successfully carry out new tasks not previously undertaken or implemented.

Moreover, I assume an analytical distinction between state building and nation building. *State building* involves the creation of concrete, identifiable administrative and political institutions. *Nation building* is the process by which a population develops a sense of community or connection that becomes the basis of individual and group political identity, which in turn influences individual and group political behavior. The common analytical conflation of these two processes is a result of the transformation of state-building activities in the post-Napoleonic era into more purposive recipes for forging legitimate structures of command and control over people, resources, and land. In the modern era, state builders often attempt to forge a national identity in order to succeed in their activities. I assume that the relationship between these processes is an empirical question.

War and State Building in Burma

Since the arrival of a prefabricated, relatively rationalized bureaucracy in Burma in the nineteenth century, the state has been continuously at war with the population mapped into its territorial claim. Prior to the advent of British colonial authority, armed conflict was common, but the nature of political organization limited the impact of warfare on most individuals' lives. In precolonial Burma, regimes were centered in the capital city, and their authority diminished with geographical distance from the center. During the seventeenth and eighteenth centuries monarchs of the restored Toungoo and Konbaung dynasties had somewhat more geographically extensive claims over people and resources than their predecessors in the Pagan and Ava kingdoms. Nonetheless, no precolonial state ever exercised the capacity to control the daily lives of individuals in the uniform, centralized manner of the bureaucratic, impersonal, and rationalized states that arrived with colonial rule. Burmese kings ordered local officials to conscript soldiers and resources during wartime, but "the further from the centre the more difficult it was for officials to convince their subordinates of the state's sanction for their demands."[24] Military commanders in Konbaung Burma "operated much more in the sense of private entrepreneurs rather than as state officials." This system had almost no "clear-cut command structures [emanating] from the political centre downward," and locally based unit commanders had considerable autonomy in recruitment, operational practices, and discipline.[25] Moreover, given the vastness of territory and the limitations of central power in distant regions, the soldiers of the king's army tended to desert in hard times. The army was required to grow its own food, and although this tied soldiers to their royally allotted land in good times, frequent droughts, famines, and wars led to flight in both peacetime and war.[26] Therefore, precolonial Burmese armies often consisted of slaves captured in previous battle campaigns. Shortfalls in state revenue were normally resolved by recourse to war and conquest against neighboring kings, rather than by developing internal taxation processes that might have led to the kind of state formation that was occurring simultaneously in Western Europe.

From the first Anglo-Burmese War (1824–26) until Britain's hasty escape from Burma in early 1942, the arrival of the modern state brought not only the file cabinets and clerks of European bureaucracies but also the guns and soldiers to enforce the sanctity and security of commerce and administration. Even though Britain's governance in Asia appeared relatively less brutal than its colonial activities in sub-Saharan Africa, the colonial state in Burma was nonetheless built by armed force and relied frequently on an extensive security apparatus to maintain its inexpensive, putatively laissez-faire form of governance. Since many indigenous people in what is today called "Burma" met the modern state for the first time at the end of a rifle, this security apparatus had a huge impact on the population's expectations of a modern government and the government's requirements of the population. But this interaction did not guarantee unlimited state mastery over territory or people, or even over categorizations of peoples as subjects, enemies, or slaves. In fact, from the first pacification campaigns in the early nineteenth century through to the suppression of popular rebellions in the 1930s, the colonial state inspired in Burmese society forms of resistance—such as the development of martial organizations—that mirrored the structure of colonial security forces and redefined enemy status as one of colonial collaboration. Moreover, beyond the territory straddling the roads, telegraph wires, and railroads, the colonial state barely existed.

Chapter 1 examines the construction of the colonial security apparatus within the broader colonial project. During the colonial period, the state was built by default; no one in London or Calcutta ever mapped out a strategy for establishing governance in Burma. Instead of sending in legal, commercial, or police experts to establish law and order—the preconditions of the all-important commerce—Britain sent the Indian Army, which faced an

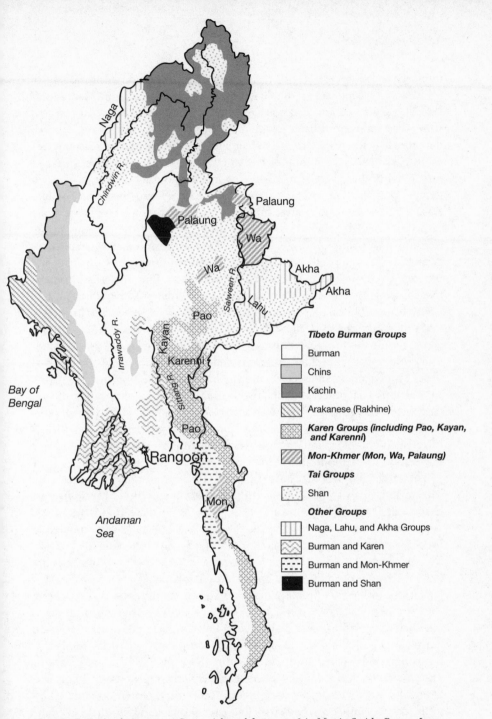

Naga

Chindwin R.

Palaung

Palaung

Wa

Akha

Wa

Akha

Salween R.

Lahu

Pao

Irrawaddy R.

Kayan

Karenni

Sittang R.

Bay of
Bengal

Pao

Rangoon

Mon

Andaman
Sea

Tibeto Burman Groups

Burman

Chins

Kachin

Arakanese (Rakhine)

Karen Groups (including Pao, Kayan, and Karenni)

Mon-Khmer (Mon, Wa, Palaung)

Tai Groups

Shan

Other Groups

Naga, Lahu, and Akha Groups

Burman and Karen

Burman and Mon-Khmer

Burman and Shan

Map 2. Burma's ethnic groups. *Source:* Adapted from map 2 in Martin Smith, *Burma: Insurgency and the Politics of Ethnicity,* 2d ed. (London, 1999); also consulted, "Ethnolinguistic Groups of Burma/Myanmar," in David I. Steinberg, *Burma: The State of Myanmar* (Washington, D.C., 2001); "Distribution of the Hill Tribes of Burma," in Bisheshwar Prasad, *The Reconquest of Burma* (Calcutta, 1958–59), vol. 1, p. 49.

intensity and range of guerrilla resistance never anticipated. More and more soldiers were deployed to the central regions of Burma from Madras and Bengal, only to be attacked constantly by unidentifiable bands of resisters who were indistinguishable from the noncombatant population. Consequently, early forays into the establishment of law and order increasingly became based on conceptions of the population as enemies to be pacified rather than subjects to be incorporated into or even ignored by the newly defined political entity. The character of armed administration in colonial Burma had a disproportionate impact on how that population came to be regarded, treated, legalized, and made into subjects of the British empire. Administrative simplifications along territorial and racial lines resulted in political, economic, and social boundaries that continue to divide the country today. The residents of central Burma—the ethnic majority Burmans (constituting 50–65 percent of the national population), the Christian minority Karens (at least 7 percent of the population), other smaller groups of lowlanders, and the small numbers of Indian and Chinese residents—had no contact with the juridically distinct "frontier" or "excluded" areas, where other ethnic groups resided and remained largely forgotten by the colonial state.[27] Bureaucratic and security mechanisms politicized violence along territorial and racial lines, creating "two Burmas" in the administrative and security arms of the state. Despite proclamations of laissez-faire colonial policies in Burma, this geographically and functionally limited state nonetheless established durable administrative structures that precluded any significant integration throughout the territory for a century to come.

The rather frail colonial state collapsed almost overnight under the pressure of the Japanese invasion in the early months of 1942, the subject of chapter 2. During the following three years of Japanese rule, "Burma . . . became a series of little republics, as the central state's authority extended to little more than the capital."[28] In the early, heady days following the occupation of Rangoon, various Japanese military agencies vied for power over the natural resources and transportation routes that had made Burma a target of Japanese expansion. Given this chaotic competition at the center, young Burmese nationalists were able to take over abandoned state institutions at the district, township, and village levels. The conduct and nature of warfare during this period shifted to ongoing, uncoordinated guerrilla combat in the countryside, while Burmese elites in the capital city plotted ways to mold guerrillas into national soldiers. For the increasingly powerful Burmese nationalist movement, upcountry social forces represented potential allies in the fight against first the British and later the Japanese. In this war, Rangoon-based elites increasingly came to view the population as partners to be wooed and courted, not enemies to be pacified and crushed. By the end of the Japanese occupation, these upcountry allies provided nationalists the cover they needed to organize the anti-Japanese resistance. Chapter 3 explains how that armed resistance was conducted and overseen by the Allies. This process created politically incompatible centers of power and institutionalized highly decentralized, centrifugal forms of control over violence that carried over well into the postcolonial era. In a sense, anti-Japanese warfare attained its goal—to destroy the state—but it also doomed state-rebuilding efforts in the early postwar years.

Nonetheless, in the postwar period, some aspects of the top-heavy, order-obsessed security apparatus of the prewar colonial era were restored successfully, first in the return of British rule from 1945–48 (covered in chapter 4) and then again under Burmese rulers when civil war erupted at independence in 1948 (chapter 5). As might be expected, the citizenry of independent Burma often responded to the government's repression by invoking colonial- and Japanese-era forms of resistance to limit and constrain the power of the central state and army. At first, powerful local leaders who had achieved prominence in the Japanese resistance forced political and economic accommodations from the faltering central government. When civil warfare threatened the capital in 1949, army field commanders cut deals up-country with local social forces to mobilize weapons, resources, and soldiers in order to save the state. However, just as internal threats diminished and the emboldened local leaders began to cooperate with and work within national political institutions such as the army, parliament, and national political parties, the Cold War erupted in Burmese territory. The advent of this qualitatively different kind of warfare shattered the fragile balance achieved between the newly accommodating state and center-phobic social forces, and reestablished the conditions under which social forces and the citizenry became potential enemies in the eyes of the state.

From bases inside Burma, units of the defeated Chinese KMT, armed and trained by U.S. intelligence operatives, planned and carried out operations against the People's Republic of China starting in 1951. Burmese government and army leaders quickly surmised that these campaigns might lead Communist China to invade Burma in its war against the KMT. While the undisciplined, unreliable troops of Burmese political bosses upcountry probably saved the Union government from armed internal opponents in the 1948–50 period, the KMT crisis prompted tatmadaw leaders to build an army capable of defending the country from more threatening, global kinds of warfare. This meant abandoning the loose, decentralized structure of the anti–civil war forces of 1948–50 and establishing a bureaucratized, European-style standing army. Chapter 6 examines this process.

Timing is the crucial issue here. Just as national leaders started dismantling the security-obsessed colonial state during the 1948–50 civil war and replacing it with structures and processes that integrated social forces into national decision making, the civilian and military leadership of the country felt compelled to reinvigorate the colonial security apparatus and pursue purely military solutions to all problems of domestic unrest. After Burmese diplomatic initiatives failed to end the U.S.–backed KMT operation, the tatmadaw undertook its most significant structural transformation into a war-fighting machine. Notably, improvements in civilian bureaucratic capacities did not keep pace with the transformation of the army, and over the next decade this uneven development across sites of power within the national state led to military aggrandizement of resources, responsibilities, and powers in traditionally nonmilitary realms. Chapter 7 explains how warriors became state builders in the late 1950s.

How was this reinvigoration of the state apparatus—at least in the military realm—possible? Drawing on the experiences of absolutist states in Western Europe, Youssef Cohen, Brian Brown, and A. F. K. Organski might suggest that the tatmadaw's victory in the 1948–50 civil war laid the foundations for greater centralization by establishing the sovereignty of the center once and for all.[29] However, the world had changed by the mid-1950s, and the resources that army leadership deployed to effect this institutional transformation did not come from domestic sources, newly tied in to the center as a result of a Rangoon victory in the civil war. Instead, the tatmadaw looked overseas for the funding and tools for state rebuilding. Given the insecurity of Burma's geographical position in the Cold War, army leaders began wooing arms manufacturers and superpower rivals, the enthusiastic suitors who pursued most new nations in the early postwar period. Purchasing missions comprised of War Office, army field command, and navy and air force staff traveled around the world and brought back fighter-bombers from Israel, advisors from Italy to establish the first ammunition factory, and counterintelligence trainers from the United States.

Although this pattern of seeking sellers and assistance from wide-ranging overseas sources mimicked Prime Minister U Nu's neutralist foreign policy, there was a significant difference in military external relations vis-à-vis those of civilian leaders. While key tatmadaw leaders had influence over Nu's foreign policy, those same army leaders acted independently when buying arms in the world market and negotiating programs of military assistance. There was little or no oversight by civilian politicians. Moreover, during this period, army leaders—and not civilian Home Ministers, permanent secretaries, or political party leaders—were frequently courted by British, Yugoslav, Czech, and U.S. arms manufacturers and dealers, who paid for many of the purchasing and study missions that inspired army leadership to expand military influence in domestic, nonsecurity realms.

In response to the threat of total warfare posed by the KMT crisis, the tatmadaw initially took charge of managing all aspects of the impact of the

Cold War on internal military affairs in the 1950s by means of these overseas treasure hunts. By the end of the 1950s, however, the army's vista had
broadened, and it soon displaced weaker state agencies and financial interests in regulating the impact of the world economy on the entire national
economy. This displacement occurred when the army's Defence Services
Institute expanded to take over major import-export operations for the whole
country. The tatmadaw's effectiveness and domestic autonomy in these activities contrasted with the failures of the economic arms of the government
bureaucracy and the ruling political party (the Anti-Fascist People's Freedom League [AFPFL]), and suggests yet another early source of the army's
growing strength among the institutions that constituted the postcolonial
state in Burma.

The redeployed, colonial-vintage security apparatus was restored as the
core of the Burmese state in the 1950s, bringing with it not only the time-
tested tools of colonial warfare but also the accompanying weaknesses and
flaws in state-ness and nation-ness that have plagued the territory since it
was first unified by the British as a modern, bureaucratic, border-conscious
state. Cold War dynamics and military rule provided the motive, manpower,
and firepower to take state violence further out to the countryside than had
the British and to label, quarantine, and disempower large portions of the
population as "enemies." However, military rule never solved the problem
of reforming a state with little capacity to exert authority throughout its territory and little skill to integrate geographically dispersed minority groups
that have spent centuries fighting for autonomy from central interference.

These problems have plagued Burma throughout the entire postcolonial
era and contribute to the stalemate in elite-level politics that today pits the
army against both centrally based and territorially more distant critics arguing for more accommodating, responsive governance. On the surface, the
1990s showed some movement away from rigid, coercion-dominant state-
society relations in ethnic minority regions located near the country's external borders. In these areas, the military regime concluded quite generous
cease-fire agreements with all but four of the two dozen armed insurgent
groups battling Rangoon. This effort might be viewed as a step toward enduring reconciliation and compromise or at least as an unprecedented commitment by the tatmadaw to a nonmilitary, explicitly political solution to an
internal political crisis.[30] However, these arrangements are nothing more
than temporary, ad hoc answers to complex, centuries-old structural problems of state building in the regions beyond central Burma where most of
these insurgent groups operated and where many of Burma's most ex-
portable resources lie. As many observers have noted, the cease-fires have
broken down in a number of regions. Additionally, the agreements have
provided former insurgent groups with the authority to retain their arms, to

police their territory, and to use their former rebel armies as private security forces to protect both legal and illegal (i.e., drug-related) business operations. This authority, however, is due to run out when the junta's hand-picked National Convention completes its new constitution. At that point, it is difficult to imagine that the Rangoon regime will be successful at persuading ethnic and drug warlords to turn in their weapons without extensive concessions, to which Rangoon is unlikely to commit in the public forum required by the new constitution.

Notably, this is a problem not only for the military junta but also for any future regime, democratic or otherwise. It would be virtually impossible for a democratic government to collect taxes or implement social or economic restructuring in, for example, the Kokang regions, where local elites are profiting greatly from noninterference by Rangoon. And without access to revenues generated by the extraction of resources such as gems or teak in these regions, how would a democratic regime be able to finance programs to alleviate the suffering of populations throughout the frontier regions who are trying to claw their way out of two generations of warfare? In these regions, remote from the Rangoon-centered struggles between the regime and the opposition led by Aung San Suu Kyi, warfare has built a relatively brittle and fragile state. The residues of that warfare and state-building process will continue to limit the power of Rangoon-based elites, whether of a military or a democratic persuasion.

1

Coercion and the Colonial State, 1826–1941

Normally, society is organised for life; the object of Leviathan was to organise it for production.

John Furnivall, *The Fashioning of Leviathan*, 1939

In its pursuit of efficient production and unfettered commerce, the British colonial state in Burma established a coercion-intensive political relationship between state and society that hardened into durable institutions and practices. Organizing society "for production"—in the words of British colonial bureaucrat, scholar, and Fabian socialist John Furnivall—was far from simple. First the East India Company and then a succession of unimaginative governors-general engaged in a variant of state building that never paid for itself, never accommodated any local interests, and never hesitated to call in firepower when the profits of European firms were threatened. From the nineteenth century on, Burma was a territorial and administrative appendage to India, serving as a buffer zone between French Indochina and India. As such, Burma was never a priority in British imperial policy. At best, the British built a skinny state, aimed at letting commerce flourish (which it did) and at making the colonial state pay for itself (which it never did) by taxation of land and some commerce.

In order to promote commerce and minimize overhead costs, British colonizers had to pacify the Burmese population following the three Anglo-Burmese wars. The agents of pacification—the soldiers of the Indian Army—had no way to communicate with locals and little information about

21

the terrain or the unexpectedly dangerous enemy. Soon they came to see little distinction between new subjects of the Raj and new enemies of the Raj. In these campaigns, the "internal security" goal of British and Indian soldiers was to eliminate resistance to British rule. By the early twentieth century, internal security—still maintained by foreigners—gradually became equated with crime control as rising rates of violent property crimes threatened the interests of British capital. With the emergence of the second wave of the Burmese nationalist movement after World War I came a new state conception of internal security, which placed responsibility for quashing criticism and potentially seditious acts with the armed forces. This meant that murderers and nationalists, robbers and monks, and cattle thieves and student strikers, all came face to face with the colonial state at the barrels of foreigner-held rifles.

The British never entirely achieved pacification, and the skinny state was filled out with the coercive muscles of British and Indian army units. However, the state's coercion-intensive relationship with Burmese society did not remain rigid and static throughout the colonial period. Changes in the missions, character, and makeup of the colonial armed forces—as well as reforms of every other aspect of colonial governance—came out of negotiations and compromises between colonial officials and Indian nationalists in India proper, and not out of any attempts to create channels of input from significant social forces in the colonial province of Burma. As colonial officials increasingly identified most political and social forces in Burma as criminal, some critics from within the colonial regime began to recognize the difficulty and futility of ruling the province in such a single-mindedly coercive manner. Just as state-society relations in India were becoming more inclusive and more open to accommodation with Indian elites after World War I, the British began a fifteen-year process of severing Burma from India because this was the one part of the colony where political reforms were unthinkable. The separation process sustained the command relationship between state and social forces but also required a revamping of the security forces, which politicized violence along ethnic lines.

Transplanting the British-Indian Colonial State

In the nineteenth century, diplomatic tensions and commercial competition between France and Britain over the natural resources available in Southeast Asia and over the security of Britain's flagship colony in India led to Britain's three-stage, gradual takeover of all territory now considered part of "Burma." In the three Anglo-Burmese wars of 1824–26, 1852, and

1885–86, British-Indian troops dispatched from Madras and Bengal defeated the armies of the increasingly weak Burmese kings of the Konbaung dynasty. None of these wars were waged with a coherent, expansionist vision of a future "British Burma," and the state that was established by default in post-1886 Burma was an appendage to the colonial regime in India. The government of India paid the bills for the expensive battles in Burma, and its model of administration and the bureaucrats to run it were conscripted from India and transported to Burma following the proclaimed victory of the Indian Army in 1886. The British never *built* a colonial state in Burma; they merely packed up some components of administration in India and shipped them to the new territory.

Unlike in British colonies in Africa, state building was never explicitly a military enterprise in Burma. There was never a military governor. Colonial administration sailed over from the other three provinces of India, complete with English-speaking, mostly civilian Indian personnel to operate it. There were no significant armed European competitors for control over Burmese territory as there were in Britain's African colonies; the British and Indian army garrisons established after the final annexation were strictly instruments of internal security rather than of foreign policy. In a sense, the British-Indian state hit Burmese territory running. It was comprised of a relatively professional, modern, tested bureaucracy, developed over a century of experience in India and well-suited to the needs of the Bombay-Burma Trading Corporation and other powerful commercial interests seeking a rapid establishment of law and order and an expansion of business opportunities in resource-rich Burma.

After 1886, colonial rule brought to Burmese society unprecedented changes, most of which benefited British and other foreign commercial interests at the expense of the majority of indigenous peoples. Many historians point to Chief Commissioner Charles Crosthwaite's implantation of the Indian system of local administration in Burma as one of the most important causes of the destruction of the social and cultural fabric of late-nineteenth-century Burma.[1] Crosthwaite's Village Act was passed as an instrument of martial law during the pacification campaign (1886–90) in villages throughout Upper and Lower Burma. The Act broke up traditional local-level administrative organizations, which Crosthwaite saw as giving rise to banditry and organized resistance to British rule. The traditional, nonterritorial ties of the indigenous social unit (called the *myo*) of central Burma were replaced by the Indian administrative and territorial grid of the village. The new village system led to a gradual but steady increase in centralization and government involvement in the daily lives of the indigenous people. As Furnivall wrote, "Even up to 1900 the people saw little of any Government officials, and very few ever caught more than a passing glimpse of a European official. By 1923 the Government was no longer remote from the people but, through various departmental subordinates, touched on almost every aspect of private life."[2]

If Furnivall is right, by the 1920s, the British had constructed a modern bureaucratic state in Burma. Along the way, a whole class of traditional local officials were eliminated, destroying centuries-old social ties at the *myo* level. In the process, state building via the Village Act paved the way for a longer-term trend of lawlessness and disorder. From the turn of the century onward, Burma became the most dangerous place in the empire. Rangoon boasted the highest murder rates for any colonial city.[3] The destruction of local authority did not *cause* these increases in violent crime, which more probably resulted from the dislocations experienced with the intrusions of the modern capitalist economy in precapitalist, agrarian Burma. Nonetheless, the construction of modern authority eliminated traditional social controls and curbs on lawlessness—not the effect Crosthwaite intended by enacting the Village Act.

Coercion and the State in British Burma

As we can see from the above consideration of the Village Act, the organization of Burmese society "for production," in Furnivall's words, required from 1885 (and arguably, from 1826) all the way through to 1942 a form of governance that one historian likens to martial law.[4] The political and military roles played by units of the British-Indian army in the early years following the third annexation institutionalized an unequal relationship between military and civil authorities—in favor of military authority—that would greatly influence the development of future military and civil institutions in Burma.

Resistance and Rebellion

This military-dominated setup did not come out of any coherent British or British-Indian plans to build a state around coercion. The postconquest role of British-Indian troops was never much considered by any civilian or military authorities plotting the conquest from India. While British-Indian forces faced little effective resistance from the Burmese king's army in the final annexation, the British occupation of Upper Burma in late 1885 sparked disturbances throughout the region and triggered a new round of resistance, dacoity (armed robbery carried out by a gang), brigandage, and rebellion in Lower Burma. By mid-1886, "a truly formidable rebellion had enveloped the country," and the government of India deployed upward of

16,000 reinforcement troops to back up the original expeditionary force.[5] Ten military outposts were set up throughout Upper Burma to attempt to control local resistance. The resistance lacked centralized leadership and was comprised largely of small rebel groups and a handful of locally popular "pretender-kings" hoping to reestablish indigenous rule. Even so, the violence spread through every district of Upper Burma, most of Lower Burma, and "[i]n many plains villages of Burma practically every household had some male member fighting with a rebel gang."[6] A regimental history of the Third Gurkha Rifles, whose units served in the campaign, blamed the expedition commander's "error of judgment" in allowing "the disbandment of King Thebaw's [sic] army. . . . [H]undreds of Burmese soldiery were allowed to disperse, *with their arms*, all over the country."[7]

At the outbreak of violence in December 1885, British-Indian troops shot anyone caught pillaging or with firearms; they also burned villages where they encountered any resistance and conducted public floggings of alleged rebels. Another Indian army regimental history defended these ruthless tactics, given the Indian Army's lack of expertise in guerrilla warfare:

> In practically all engagements with the enemy we had to fight an invisible foe. The dacoits waylaid our troops as they came up the river in boats or by road marches, poured forth a heavy fire upon the advancing forces as they got within range. Not only was it difficult to locate the enemy in their hidden lairs, but our men laboured under the vast disadvantage of having to force their way through the close undergrowth of an unknown forest, whilst the enemy knew all the ins and outs of their tangled labyrinths and were able to keep concealed. . . . Our only means of punishment was to burn these villages.[8]

These harsh tactics backfired on the British. Villagers responded to the repressive measures by banding together to attack military posts. Eventually, Gen. Prendergrast of the expeditionary force ordered an end to summary executions and village burning. Later, the ten military posts were expanded to twenty-five. Detachments patrolled actively between posts, breaking up larger bands of rebels into smaller units. By February 1887, 40,500 British and Indian troops were fighting in Burma. In some areas of Upper Burma, they had established armed garrisons every ten to fifteen miles.[9]

By 1890, British-Indian troops had extinguished much of the rebellion, breaking up most large bands of rebels and forcing all pretender kings into hiding. Order was maintained in Upper Burma by 30,000 troops and Indian police; another 5,300 were assigned to Lower Burma. The cost of the annexation and subsequent pacification campaign, originally estimated to run £300,000, rose to £635,000 in 1885–86 and to more than twice that amount in 1888.[10]

As order was restored to most of Burma, the British sent the majority of Indian Army troops back to India, lifted martial law, and created a civilian administration to manage village and colonial affairs. However, both British and Indian army troops were garrisoned in Burma throughout the first half of the twentieth century. In 1938, there were 10,365 army troops in Burma. Of these 4,713 were British (led by 358 British officers), roughly 3,000 were Indians, and nearly 3,000 were indigenous Karens, Chins, and Kachins.[11]

Pacification and Internal Security

What did these soldiers do in Burma? Beginning with the pacification operations and continuing throughout the colonial period with the armed forces' suppression of threats to commerce and order, the function of Indian and British army units was primarily internal security. As in other British colonies where early interaction between the populace and the military was coercive and repressive in nature, colonial security policies "left a deep rift in army-society interaction."[12] From the start of the pacification campaigns, the first contact between much of the population of rural central Burma and the colonial state was carried out by the forty thousand British-Indian army troops in Burma. In those first years following annexation in 1886, Indian Army units also pressed Burmese villagers into service for public works projects, such as the construction of roads and railways.

Following the third pacification period in the 1890s, the reduced, peacetime contingent of the armed forces served in two roles: first, as territorial forces, defending the frontier areas which were considered the major strategic threat in the territory; and second, as a backup to civil and military police charged with maintaining law and order in both the frontier and the central regions.

In terms of defending the freshly drawn borders of the colony, the British-Indian army arrived in the frontier areas as a pacification force, just as it had in the central regions. After the third Anglo-Burmese war, some *sawbwas* (traditional leaders) in ethnic Shan areas acquiesced to British plans to establish indirect rule in the hilly northeastern regions. In exchange for retaining their local authority over law and order within their domains, the cooperating sawbwas granted British concerns free trade and commerce in their regions. However, local leaders in the Chin and Kachin hills organized fairly extensive resistance to British overtures in the aftermath of the third war. Most local leaders in these regions had been nearly autonomous under the Konbaung state, aside from occasional demands for tribute. Thus British intrusions were not appreciated. Eventually, the British were able to convince most Chin and Kachin leaders to accept British authority in return for a promise not to interfere with local politics and customs and not to undermine the local chiefs' powers to tax their subjects. (See map 3 for a view of how the British administered central and frontier regions in Burma.) When a few local leaders refused to grant British demands, the British-Indian army conducted punitive raids on their areas.

The army's ongoing role in the internal affairs of the frontier regions was minimal from the conclusion of the pacification period through the 1930s. As Taylor argued, "During much of the British period, the central state's authority in more remote areas amounted to little more than periodic 'flag marches' in which the symbol of state supremacy was displayed and the promise of punishment for unruly behavior was made."[13] Occasionally, British-Indian troops were called on by the British representative in a Shan state to put down a popular rebellion sparked by a tax increase or other repressive measure undertaken by one of the sawbwas. However, most of the colonial period was characterized by relative peace in the hill regions, and whatever conflicts arose between villages and tribes were usually resolved peacefully, given the threat of punishment by British-Indian troops. With the approach of World War II, the Shan states, in particular, emerged as a region of strategic threat in the colony. For centuries, these regions had been vulnerable to invading armies that attacked the Irrawaddy basin. In the buildup of forces preceding the war, Britain developed a more extensive territorial defense of the hill regions, allowing Shan sawbwas to recruit their own military forces and deploying more than ten thousand other Frontier Force troops in the frontier areas.

Nonetheless, the significance of this expansion should not be overstated. Throughout the colonial period and until the Japanese invasion, British officials did not perceive any imminent threat to the borders of Burma. Hence, according to a 1938 Colonial Office assessment of the armed forces in Burma, "the primary role of the Army in Burma" throughout the colonial era was not border defense but instead "Internal Security."[14] As far as the British-Indian army was concerned, Burma was a military backwater, and as such received little consideration in army policy reviews even after the war in Europe had begun.

Responsibility for internal security in the central plains and delta regions was the main occupation of the military. In these regions, most of the residents were ethnic Burmans, although there were other smaller ethnolinguistic groups who lived there, including Karens and Anglo-Burmans.[15] Formally this responsibility was divided between police and military units, but the British were never able to establish a functional police force in Burma. During the pacification campaign that followed the second Anglo-Burmese war, the British raised indigenous local police forces to maintain law and order in the villages and towns. At first, the British attempted to identify a traditional village leader who could take over police duties and chose the *kyedangyi*, the largest taxpayer who traditionally assisted the *thu-*

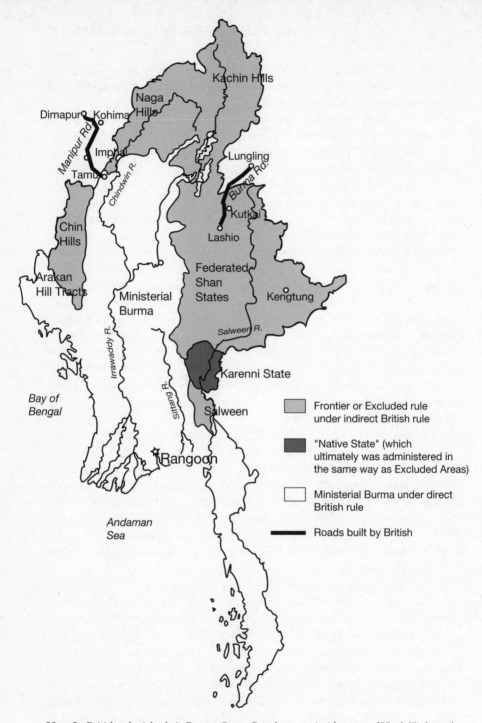

Map 3. British colonial rule in Burma. *Source:* Based on map inside cover of Hugh Tinker, ed. *Burma, the Struggle for Independence, 1944–1948: Documents from Official and Private Sources*, vol. 2 (London, 1983–84).

gyi (headman) with revenue collection and police responsibilities. In a typical British colonial practice, the kyedangyi was appointed as an unarmed and initially unpaid constable. By the 1880s, the anti-British rebellions had undermined the authority of the kyedangyi and the British had great difficulties recruiting local police officers despite offers of attractive salaries. Nonetheless, the British managed to reorganize local administrative units under Crosthwaite's Village Act, and from about 1890 on, made the new state-appointed headmen of the amalgamated village units responsible for maintaining order. In fact, the annual reports of the colonial provincial government in Burma placed the summary of "village affairs" in the section headed "police administration."[16]

Later, the British gave up this police conscription system at the local level and tried to centralize law enforcement administration. The deputy commissioner of each district was assigned a district superintendent of police (DSP), about half of whom were British or Indian, while the other half were mostly Anglo-Burmans and Karens from Lower Burma. Under the DSP were locally recruited town and village constables, most of whom were unarmed until the late 1930s when the administration authorized each village to hold two or three firearms to ward off bandits. Furnivall found in the annual administration report of 1931–32 great praise for the increasing effectiveness of the appointed village officers in processing criminal cases. But he notes also a considerable increase in crime rates, concluding with irony: "The greater efficiency of the machinery for dealing with crime was ineffective to prevent the growth of crime."[17]

Because Burma was "consistently the most criminal province in the empire"[18] throughout the twentieth-century colonial period, the response of the British-Indian government was to authorize frequent enlargements and reorganizations of the more centralized civilian police force. As Official British historian and former colonial officer F. S. V. Donnison noted: "The accepted treatment was to strengthen that part of the administration whose task it was to combat the criminal, but this cure proved to be no cure for the disease—it was scarcely a palliative."[19] Another former civil servant observed: "The population was growing rapidly, but crime grew more rapidly. Between 1900 and the outbreak of war in 1914 the population increased by about 15 percent, the number of police rose from one for every 789 people to one for every 744, but crime increased by 26 percent."[20] In areas with higher-than-average crime rates, the "punitive police" reinforced civilian police. Under the Police Act, collective penalties were imposed over localities by quartering a unit of this Indian-dominated, armed police force. The local community would pay their upkeep in additional land taxes. Still, crime rates continued to increase. From 1911 to 1921, the population increased by about 9 percent, but the increase of major crimes "ranged from

31 percent in the case of murder to 109 percent in the case of robbery and dacoity."[21]

The corruption of the "ill-educated, ill-paid policemen" became a favorite target for nationalist politicians in the early 1920s, both because of the sorry state of the civilian police forces and because "of the political control exercised by the police."[22] One of the first acts of the Legislative Council established under the new 1923 constitution was an attempt to clean up the civilian police force by increasing pay to qualified officers and terminating the contracts of corrupt, unqualified ones. However, the attempt failed miserably when a subsequent increase in robbery and dacoity forced the reinstatement of the fired officers and the relowering of standards.

These failures to establish effective local policing set the pattern of law enforcement that persists to today: When local affairs get unruly, the state sends in the military. The ineffectiveness of the civilian police led to the deployment of units of the British-Indian army and the expansion of the military police in times of trouble. The military police was established in 1886 for use in the final pacification campaign and grew to nine battalions by 1935.[23] Unlike the civilian police force with its indigenous recruits, the military police consisted almost entirely of Indians, with British officers in command positions usually assigned from the British-Indian army appointments. They were the only police force to regularly carry firearms in Burma. John Leroy Christian describes these units as constituting something of a strike force, "serving as mobile, well-armed police for duty in case of racial disturbances, riots, disasters, and similar emergencies that cannot be dealt with by local authorities."[24] From about 1920 on, the armed forces and the military police were called out to put down communal, nationalist, or labor uprisings at least once a year. The most prominent of these disturbances—the Hsaya San peasant rebellion of 1930–32—led to the immediate deployment of military troops, supported by administrative units operated by civilian police. Reinforcement troops came from India, and by June 1931, the British governor had sent in roughly 8,100 Indian and British army troops to fight the small, geographically dispersed groups of unarmed peasants. Three months later, six more Indian battalions and one more British battalion arrived from India, bringing British military strength to more than ten thousand. Additionally, levies of Karens were raised and armed to fight against Burman rebel bands in the delta.

Beginning with the pacification campaign of 1885–90, the coercive organizations of the colonial state played a significant role in organizing Burmese society for production. British colonial definitions of "crime" and "internal security" brought murderers, cattle thieves, robbers, rebels, Buddhist monks, labor organizers, and starving, scavenging peasants into a legal system that treated them all similarly, and for the first time ever, as enemies of the state. Facing these enemies, the colonial state relied heavily on the armed forces and police to control nearly all forms of criminal and political behavior throughout the colonial period. Even though widespread nationalist-oriented political mobilization did not occur until the 1920s, the population of Burma had had extensive experience with the military arm of the colonial state beginning in 1886 given the frequent deployment of armed force to fight colonially defined crime. One of the "residues of the colonial state" that shaped the nature of postcolonial state-society relations is this prominent role of the military—vis-à-vis other state institutions—in controlling individual and social behavior.[25]

Clearly, armed force played a significant role in the governance of colonial Burma. The British state, which has long been characterized as laissez-faire in its organization of Burmese society for production, did not hesitate to employ coercion when there was any perception of a threat to British commerce and authority.[26] The "laissez-faire" response of the colonial state to the enormous social and economic dislocations that came with the intrusion of the world economy and the commercialization of agriculture in Burma was to attempt to arrest and coerce the victims of these processes. This was undoubtedly a skinny state, barely capable of collecting enough land revenue to pay its police. Beyond the main lines of communication in the central region, this state barely existed. But where it did, it flexed its muscles with little restraint. The slightest challenge to tenuous colonial order provoked automatic deployments of armed force, establishing a coercion-intensive relationship between armed force and the state, and between the state and society, that carried over into the postcolonial period.

The Armed Forces in British Burma: Indigenous Participation

Negotiations between Burmese social forces and colonial state elites occurred only in the ethnic minority "excluded" areas—as the evocative British bureaucratic lexicon labeled them—and were of limited duration and significance. (See map 3.) Nowhere in the colony did the European-style state-building process of contestation, negotiation, accommodation, and compromise unfold. Instead, many of the most enduring changes in the deployment of coercion in Burma came as a result of contestation and negotiation carried out by colonial officials and nationalists in India. The colonial organization of Burmese society for production, extraction, and trade underwent two major institutional modifications under British rule, which were both outcomes of changes in governance in Calcutta and Delhi. From 1885 until 1923, Burma was designated a province of India, added to the existing three provinces, Madras, Bengal, and Bombay. Notably, most of the territory of modern Burma had never been ruled by any sovereign based in India. After the three Anglo-Burmese wars, all major decisions about the new province were made or had to be approved by the governor-general of India.[27]

The first change in the administrative setup came after World War I, when Britain began planning for India's eventual transition to self-government. London's shift in policy was, in part, the result of wartime pledges by British officials eager to entice India to provide more indigenous troops for the British war effort. However, in the minds of colonial officials and Indian nationalists, the prospect of including what they considered the more backward Burma in a future independent India was implausible. Accordingly, Britain began formulating plans to treat Burma differently from the more "advanced" India. On January 1, 1923, Burma became a full Governor's Province under a new dyarchy constitution. The governor of Burma was given a Legislative Council with a majority of seats to be filled by election; additionally, local administrative bodies were to be partially democratized. Most important, as Robert Taylor points out, Burma became a distinct entity in British policy from this time forward: "All of the major decisions regarding Burma from the 1820's to 1920 were made in Calcutta or New Delhi, not London. It was the decision in 1918 [implemented in 1923] not to extend . . . reforms [granted India] to the province of Burma that first caused His Majesty's Government in London to take an active part in shaping Burma. After this event it is possible to write about 'British policy' toward Burma."[28] The separation of Burma from India was completed in 1935, when another new constitution was enacted (effective in 1937) providing for a distinct, separate colony of Burma for the first time ever. It survived only four years.

For our purposes, the significance of the three sets of reforms was that the character of the armed forces gradually became a political issue as Burma gradually emerged as a distinct juridical and administrative entity in British policy. As Burma was being detached from India, British officials and Burmese nationalist politicians realized that the government would not be able to depend forever on the troops of the Indian Army to keep order. By the early 1920s, leaders of the Indian National Congress were agitating to bring all overseas units of the Indian Army back to India proper, where they would be used only for defense of Indian territory rather than in the service of the British Empire.

The question of the availability of the Indian Army for internal and external security purposes in Burma emerged at the same time Burmese nationalists began criticizing British policies that excluded ethnic majority Burmans from the Indian Army. Although some piecemeal reforms were put into place to modify this exclusion at the time of the 1923 constitutional changes, colonial officials never seriously addressed the issue until separation was declared in 1935. According to Donnison: "It was not until after the separation of Burma from India had actually taken place that serious consideration was given to the problems of building up a separate Burmese army. . . . A self-governing Burma would be overwhelmingly Burman, with 12 million true Burmans as against 4 million minority peoples. The majority race would be unrepresented in the military forces of the new state."[29]

This issue of non-enrollment of indigenous Burmese in the armed forces in Burma actually needs to be broken down into two considerations. First, relative to British practices in the other administrative units of India—which was the reference point for indigenous peoples in Burma—participation by *all* indigenous groups in the armed forces in Burma was extremely low. Second, an examination of the development of British policy on nonrecruitment of ethnic-majority Burmans throughout the colonial period shows that this practice was something of a historical accident—rather than a coherently thought-out policy—resulting from the timing of the annexation of Burma and the particular stage of development of the Indian armed forces. In existing historical analyses, the practice of excluding ethnic-majority Burmans has long been characterized as a classic example of British *divide et impera* (divide and rule).[30] It is true that most of the British-recruited levies were members of ethnic-minority groups with long-standing hostilities toward the ethnic-majority Burman race throughout the colonial period, and in fact they dominated the armed forces on the eve of World War II. However, the recruitment of ethnic minorities did not begin in earnest until World War I, and the absence of significant numbers of indigenous troops of any ethnicity before 1914 is at least as important in the development of military institutions as the absence of ethnic-majority Burman troops from 1914–42.

At various points in the nineteenth century, British army and civilian officials considered recruiting indigenous peoples to fight alongside the Indian troops. In 1824, the government of India authorized British-Indian troops to raise a levy of Arakanese to fight the Burmese king's forces in the first Anglo-Burmese War. As early as 1833, Mons were recruited as soldiers to defend Tenasserim, although the British policy that the Mons be paid less than members of Indian units posted there made recruitment nearly impossible, and the unit languished, being formally disbanded in 1849. When the second Anglo-Burmese war broke out in 1852, the question of recruiting local troops was reopened. Commissioner Arthur Phayre raised a light infantry regiment in Pegu comprised at least in part of Burmans; but in 1861, when the threat of war with the Burmese king had diminished, the Pegu Light Infantry and the Arakan Levy were converted into unarmed civilian police.[31] Over the next three decades, British officials made further attempts to enlist

Karens, perhaps because of the increasing success of American Baptist missionaries in converting Karens to Christianity and teaching them English. By 1880, the Karen contingent of the levies had grown, accounting for about three-quarters of the two indigenous companies. At the outbreak of widespread violence throughout Upper and Lower Burma after the third Anglo-Burmese war, the American Baptist missionaries successfully lobbied British officials to recruit more Karens as auxiliaries to put down the rebellion; they were disbanded at the end of martial law. In 1891, a Karen military police battalion was formed, but problems of discipline led to the disbanding of the unit. The few Karens who were allowed to continue service were reassigned across the remaining battalions, which were predominantly Indian.[32]

By the outbreak of World War I, the number of indigenous members of the army and military police in Burma was probably no more than 300; the indigenous population in 1911 was 12 million,[33] giving Burma 2.5 indigenous members of the armed forces for every 100,000 people. While most observers looked back on the early exclusion of ethnic-majority Burmans as the source of great political tensions in the later colonial period, these data suggest that what is more significant about colonial army recruitment is the absence of any appreciable indigenous representation whatsoever in the armed forces. Recruitment policy and practices were not functioning on the basis of a divide-and-rule principle. Instead there was no significant recruitment of indigenous Burmese of any ethnicity.

This nonrecruitment of any indigenous peoples is especially stark in comparison with the British recruitment of Indian soldiers and prompts the question why the British did not consider this to be an important issue in Burma until the World War I era. The explanation is obvious if one considers the makeup of the forces garrisoned in Burma. As Furnivall notes, after a century of development from the earliest guards of the East India Company to battalions "of sepoys, drilled, disciplined and clothed on western lines," the Indian Army was "accustomed to European officers, under European officers accustomed to Indian ways."[34] Each time the government of India decided to raise indigenous forces in Burma, it was because a Burma-based British official had made an appeal to do so based on the projected cost savings of not having to send Indian troops to Burma. In most of the cases, the units were disbanded due to higher-than-expected costs vis-à-vis the availability of cheaper, English-speaking, already-trained Indian forces.

The Armed Forces in British Burma: Divide and Rule

Recruiting for the new, World War I–era units followed the twenty-year-old Indian Army practice of establishing single-race or single-"class" units.[35] When the war ended, the government of India reduced its armed forces throughout its provinces to a peacetime skeleton. Hence, in Burma, as in the rest of India, recruitment was halted for all army and military police units and many of the units formed during the war were disbanded. In Burma, top on the list of units to go were the various Burman-only companies and battalions, easily identifiable given the practice of establishing class-specific units.

Furnivall argues that this policy to exclude Burmans came out of British concerns about arming and training Burmans who might someday be swept up in the growing anticolonial nationalist movement.[36] The British established the Indian Army policy of raising class-specific battalions and companies in the wake of the devastating mutiny in 1857. In India, this recruiting policy enabled the British to keep the "politically conscious classes" out of the army.[37] In Burma, the British had been surprised by the nationwide show of strength in the 1920 students' strike, and there is no doubt that concerns about Burman nationalism led to the policy of formally banning Burmans from the armed forces.

By the time of the 1931 census, the impact of the nonrecruitment policy was clear: the ethnic-majority Burmans were underrepresented in the armed forces (table 1). The Karen, Kachin, and Chin ethnic groups, representing roughly 13 percent of the population, accounted for 83 percent of the indigenous portion of the armed forces in Burma in 1931. The indigenous contingent of the armed forces in Burma was ten times larger than it was on the eve of World War I, but the three thousand new spaces created in the interim provided little access to the ethnic-majority Burmans.

The 1920s policy to dismiss and effectively ban Burmans from the army came along just as the second generation of the nationalist movement was coming of age. Although nationalist politicians were more concerned with the issues of expanding higher education opportunities and of indigenous and especially ethnically Burman representation on the Legislative Council, "[t]he belief was in the minds of Burmans that British policy to dismiss Burmans from the armed forces [deliberately] segregated the races."[38] Ethnic tensions had been on the rise since the early part of the century, and increasing Burman resentment of Indian moneylenders, landlords, tenants, and laborers led to bloody explosions of anti-Indian emotion during the 1920 strike, as well as later in 1924 and 1931. Although various factions of the nationalist movement competed with each other for popular support and disagreed over a number of contentious issues, all were united in their opposition to the occupation of Burmese territory by foreign "mercenary" (i.e., Indian) troops.

Additionally, the Dobama Asiayone (usually translated "Our Burma Association" or "Our Burmese Association"), founded in 1930 in the aftermath of four days of Indo-Burman rioting in Rangoon and moving gradually to the forefront of the nationalist campaign, developed a new target of anticolo-

Table 1. Ethnic Composition of the Armed Forces in Burma, 1931

Ethic Group	No. in Army	Proportion of Army	Proportion of Population
Burman[a]	472	12.30	75.11
Karen	1,448	37.74	9.34
Chin	868	22.62	2.38
Kachin	881	22.96	1.05
Others[b]	168	4.38	12.12
Total	3,837	100	100

Source: Government of India, Census Commissioner, "Census," Rangoon, 1931, quoted in John S. Furnivall, *Colonial Policy and Practice: A Comparative Study of Burma and Netherlands India*, rev. ed. (New York, 1956), p. 184.

[a] The census category "Burman" includes Shans and Mons, in addition to ethnic Burmans.

[b] Includes other indigenous minorities as well as foreigners.

nial, nationalist fervor.[39] It was the indigenous (non-Indian and non-Chinese) ethnic groups that collaborated with the British imperialists. The Dobama's early successes in popular mobilization came in its campaign aimed at repudiating foreign influences in language, clothing, and literature and at affirming the traditions of indigenous Burmese language and clothing.[40] This campaign was not aimed against the British colonial officials or Indian mercenaries, but instead targeted the indigenous people who collaborated with the British, took English names, wore English clothes, ate English food, and served the interests of the British. Kei Nemoto argues that the Dobama Asiayone began defining "our Burma" in opposition to *Thudo-Bama* ("their Burma"). *Thudo* referred to collaborators who did not love their own country, cherish their own literature, or respect their own language.[41] Dobama activists, who often added the honorific title, *thakin* (master), to their names, criticized Karen troops for their participation in putting down the Hsaya San peasant rebellion of 1930–32, the 1936 student strike, and the 1938 general strike.[42] These deployments were seen as evidence of collaboration on the part of Karen and other minority troops and of British attempts to divide and rule Burma.

Political Pocket Armies

With no opportunity to obtain any kind of military training in the armed forces, all the Burman-majority nationalist political organizations began considering how to prepare for the possible use of armed force in their efforts to attain independence from Britain. By the mid-1930s, every major nationalist or religious organization had established its own *tat* (army).[43] According to U Maung Maung, the idea for this kind of organization had been initially discussed by the Young Men's Buddhist Association (one of the earliest nationalist organizations) a decade earlier, "but usually the promoters became ambitious and made requests to the government to open Burman military units to serve in the defence of Burma."[44] The first tat was founded in 1930 by U Maung Gyee, a conservative politician who was a former Legislative Council member for education and later (1940) became the first indigenous Defence Councilor. He set up his Ye-tat (brave or daring tat) to organize and give youths basic military and physical training for the nationalist movement, and he recruited units in both major urban areas and small towns upcountry. In 1935 and 1936, two prominent groups of young, university-affiliated nationalists also created cadet corps to provide paramilitary training: first, the Dobama Asiayone established the Burma Letyone (strength) Tat, and then the university students' union established the Thanmani (Steel) Tat. Older politicians such as U Saw and Dr. Ba Maw also established their own armies, called the Galon Tat and the Dahma (hewing knife) Tat, respectively. Religious organizations also established tats.[45] Prominent Hindus in Rangoon founded the Aryan Veer Dal (Brave Aryan Troops) to coordinate efforts of Hindu Volunteer Corps. In Mandalay, followers of Premier U Pu formed the Thathana Alingyaung (light of religion) tat in June 1940.[46]

What is strange about the tats is that the British allowed them to exist at all. The British colonial government not only allowed these tats to function, but the governor of Burma actually viewed Ye-tat parades on two different occasions. According to British law, none of these tats could carry firearms, but they carried out extensive military drills and war exercises with bamboo staffs. Often wearing uniforms and strutting publicly in formation, these tats provided "protection" at nationalist political demonstrations, workers' and peasant strikes, and elections. Some modeled themselves explicitly and proudly after Hitler's Brown Shirts.[47] Even though their numbers as a proportion of the general population were probably not large, they became a prominent feature of public life.[48] They were particularly visible at National Day celebrations (held on the anniversary of the 1920 students' strike), when they held parades in Rangoon and Mandalay, as well as in towns such as Pakkoku, Shwebo, Myingyan, and Yenangyaung. Although they carried no firearms in public, their military nature should not have been difficult for the British to discern.[49] However, at no point in the prewar period were Burmese nationalists ever arrested for their participation in tats, even though the British Defence of Burma law and public order laws would have authorized such arrests. In the immediate postwar period, Aung San defended the absorption of his anti-Japanese guerrillas into a political army called the People's Volunteer Organisation (PVO) against British criticisms by pointing out that "volunteer corps [like the PVO] existed in this country

Burma Letyone (strength) Tat marching to attend meeting of pro-independence forces under the Freedom Bloc, 1939. P(AN84-13) PII(b), DSHRI.

before the war and they had been allowed to exist without being a danger to established government or law and order."[50]

Why did the British tolerate these tats? One possible explanation may lie in the characteristically imperial optimism that the tats would never turn against the British. To wit, British civil servant Leslie Glass discussed the formation of the tats in his memoirs. Even with the benefit of forty years of postcolonial hindsight, Glass still maintains the tats were no real threat: "Anti-British feeling was not widespread," he writes.[51]

More significantly, the tats were organized during a window of opportunity for such antistate forces under an otherwise repressive colonial regime. After the Hsaya San rebellion, British policy makers began exploring in earnest the necessity for a full separation of Burma from India. As Donnison noted, this was when it became clear to the British that Burmans eventually would have to be recruited for the armed forces of a separated Burma.[52] In the meantime, growing concerns about the threat of coming war in Europe were accompanied by concerns about the practical issues of how to recruit soldiers from throughout the empire for the war effort, as in World War I. Perhaps this was a time when the Burman-dominated nationalist *tats* could be tolerated, with the objective that they might be incorporated into the war effort in the long run. Taylor argues that the British saw the tats "as a means of developing Burma's capacity of self-defense at a time when the British felt that Burmans were not fit for military service."[53] The incorporation of U Maung Gyee's Ye-tat into the British-organized Rangoon Defence Volunteer Force supports this proposition.

Regardless of the reasons the colonial state tolerated the tats, what is clear is that the organization of non- or antistate tats—armed to varying degrees—had at least three important implications for the development of state institutions in Burma. First, these party-affiliated tats found a space to operate under the powerful colonial regime. The space afforded to these nationalist tats by the state never really disappeared in the postcolonial era until after the military coup of 1962. The proclivity of party politicians throughout the twentieth century to form "private," "pocket," or "party" armies is a direct result of the lessons learned by the tats of the 1930s. In fact, 1930s tats were active in the anti-Japanese underground in 1944–45 and in early postwar politics. Some survived intact well into the postwar era and were led by the same prewar politicians and manned by some of the same personnel.

Second, the tats further institutionalized the ethnically demarcated boundaries between "collaborators" and "nationalists." The colonial state had itself rejected ethnic Burman tat members for enrollment in any state armed force on ethnic grounds. By the late 1930s, after more than a decade of outright rejection of ethnic Burman recruitment and several years of operation of nonstate armies (i.e., the tats), Burman nationalists identified membership in the government's armed forces with "collaboration" or "Thudo-Bama." There was little chance that these tats could be persuaded to cooperate with anyone constituting Thudo-Bama in the increasingly threatened security environment of Southeast Asia.

Third, it was in the organization of these tats that military terminology, institutions, and symbols were Burmanized. Ranks, words of command, and marching songs were all translated into Burmese by leaders of the Ye-tat and Letyone Tat. The 1936 constitution of the Letyone Tat—called "The Constitution of the Most Dependable Army of Burma"—included the first extensive consideration of military affairs written in Burmese during the colonial period. One hundred fifty items in Burmese spelled out regulations

regarding membership in the Letyone Tat, as well as discipline, ranks, officers' perquisites, training, communication, and the relationship between the
tat and the Dobama Asiayone.[54]

Too Little, Too Late

When the British finally implemented the full separation from India in
1937 and established for the first time ever a "Burma Command," it was too
late to try to build a numerically significant, integrated army.[55] By the time
the ban against enrollment of Burmans was lifted in 1935, there were few
Burmans who could view military service as anything but "collaboration."
And the existence of the various tats that provided military training for a
possible anticolonial revolution meant that the Burmese and Burman nationalists—unlike their counterparts in India in the same years—did not seriously entertain schemes for infiltrating existing units of the British armed
forces in Burma for later subversion or for the development of tactical and
martial skills.

The creation of the British Burma Army on April 1, 1937, was anticli-
mactic. Units of the Indian Army serving in Burma (including the four battalions of the Twentieth Burma Rifles and detachments of Administrative
Corps and Departments) and the military police were renamed and placed
under the command of the governor of Burma, who served as commander
in chief. The latter authorized the Burma Army to include about six thousand soldiers to serve under five hundred officers. Notably, most of the soldiers and officers came from renamed Indian Army units; few were recruited
from the Burmese population.

If we break down this authorization and look at what Taylor calls the
"core" of the army—the regular forces—we see in table 2 a minimal role for
ethnic Burmans in the all-important infantry forces, which became the
dominant service in the postwar army. Of the 22 officers and 715 indigenous
other ranks in the Burma Rifles infantry battalion, 50 percent were Karen,
25 percent Chin, and 25 percent Kachin; only four officers (18 percent)
were Burmans. There was a plan to add a fifth company of Burma Rifles that
would be all Burman, but the British never got around to raising it. Nearly
all of the Sappers and Miners were Burman.

In addition to this core, irregular units included an Auxiliary Force with a
total of 81 officers, 1,784 other ranks on active duty, and 1,353 other ranks
on reserve duty; auxiliaries were all volunteers of European descent, including British, Anglo-Burmans, or Anglo-Indians. There was also a Territorial
Battalion with four British grade officers and 694 other ranks; personnel
consisted of indigenous volunteers, mostly Karens, though some Burmans
were admitted.[56] The only antiaircraft battalion in prewar Burma was comprised mainly of Anglo-Burmans.[57]

Table 2. Regulars of the Burma Army, 1938

Unit	British Officers	British Other Ranks	Burma Army Officers	Burma Army[a] Other Ranks
Burma Company Sappers and Miners	6	3	6	380
Battalion of the Burma Rifles	13	0	22	715
Animal Transport Company, BASC[c]	1	0	2	123[b]

Source: Robert H. Taylor, "The Relationship Between Burmese Social Classes and British-Indian Policy on the Behavior of the Burmese Political Elite, 1937–1942" (Ph.D. diss., Cornell University, 1974), p. 32, n. 47.
[a] Indigenous members of the Burma Army.
[b] Tentative only.
[c] BASC=Burma Army Supply Corps.

At separation in 1937, the military police was divided into two forces. One was deployed primarily in central Burma and the other—renamed the Burma Frontier Force—was for use mainly in the excluded areas. The former group, still called the military police, consisted of 4,294 men in 1941. Nearly all were Indians, and British and Indian officers seconded from the Indian Army held command authority. The strength of the Frontier Force was 10,073, including 7,376 Indians, with the remainder coming from the hill populations of Burma.[58]

Therefore, although the creation of the Burma Army in 1937 opened up the possibility of access for indigenous people, there was still no serious attempt to involve ethnic Burmans in what British officials considered the core of an army of a future independent Burma. This oversight can probably be attributed to the colonial regime's preoccupation with internal security, which narrowed the vision of army reformers so that considerations of how to establish a "national army"—in which indigenous minorities and the majority-Burmans could function in harmony—were never really entertained. Scholar-bureaucrat Furnivall summed up the British position:

> If the problem of responsible [colonial] government had been conceived in terms of creating a united people to which the Government might [eventually] be made responsible, the question of building up an army would have been recognized as a matter of primary importance, but it was conceived in terms of . . . constructing machinery that, if it could not do much good, could do no serious damage; the military aspect of the problem was disregarded . . .[59]

Furnivall noted that the outbreak of war in 1939 led to a new emphasis by the British to recruit any and all potential troops, regardless of ethnicity. Although some progress was made toward including larger numbers of Bur-

Table 3. Ethnic Composition of the Armed Forces in Burma, 1941

Ethic Group	No. in Army	Proportion of Army	Proportion of Population[a]
Burman[b]	1,893	23.71	75.11
Karen	2,797	35.03	9.34
Chin	1,258	15.76	2.38
Kachin	852	10.61	1.05
Yunnanese	32	0.04	
Chinese	330	4.13	
Indians	2,578	32.29	
Others	168	2.10	
Total	7,984	100	100

Source: "Statement Showing by Class [i.e., ethnicity] the Strength (other than officers) of the Burmese Army and the Frontier Force on 30th April 1941," BOF 66/41; quoted in Robert H. Taylor, *State in Burma* (London, 1987), p. 100.

[a] Population statistics for 1941 are from the 1931 census because the data from the 1941 census was lost in World War II.

[b] The 1931 census category "Burman," includes Shans and Mons, in addition to ethnic Burmans. Taylor does not list the Shans as having any members of the armed forces, which suggests the possibility that Shans were counted among Burmans; otherwise there may have been no Shans in the new Burma Army, and they may have been restricted to membership in the Territorial Army.

mans, the numbers in no way reflected the proportion of Burmans in the colony. Table 3 shows Taylor's breakdown of troops in Burma in 1941.[60]

Referring back to table 1, we can see that the number of troops designated "Burmans" rose from 472 in 1931 to 1,893 in 1941, increasing by a factor of 2.5. At the same time, the number of Karens nearly doubled, rising from 1,448 in 1931 to 2,797 in 1941. The continued higher recruitment of Karens per head of Karen population (vis-à-vis Burman recruitment per head of Burman population) suggests that the colonial regime had not made any significant changes in recruiting priorities and practices.

Conclusion

The transportation of British-Indian rule to nineteenth-century Burma produced a matrix of state institutions that gave primacy to order, coercion, and armed force. In sharp contrast to the earlier mercantilist age of imperialism—during which India was brought into the British Empire—the new imperialism of the nineteenth century produced colonial states throughout Africa and Asia that were able to reorder society for production and commerce at unprecedented speed. However, nowhere was the pace as blinding as it was in the annexation to India of the territory that came to be known as "Burma." The transportation of a century-old colonial system of governance from India to Burma wreaked havoc with traditional, nonstate forms of social control and created the need for internal security forces that would come to control many aspects of indigenous people's lives.

The imposition of Indian administrators and administrative practices in Burma destroyed indigenous social mechanisms that could have cushioned the impact of the rapid insertion into the world economy. The resulting increase in landlessness, tenancy, and indebtedness was responsible for the highest crime rates in the empire, and the government of India's coercion-intensive response to this rising lawlessness was in part responsible for institutionalizing the primacy of armed coercion in Burmese political affairs.

It should not be surprising that the British-Indian state relied on its relatively modern, professional Indian and British armies to combat threats to colonial interests in Burma. The British officials who occupied top administrative positions in the colonial state were nearly all appointed from India, never having previously set foot on Burmese territory.[61] They derived their visions and plans about Asian colonies from their Indian experiences, including a number of communal riots in which armed troops were deployed to restore order. There was never any real consideration of arming substantial numbers of indigenous Burmese. The imperatives of turning a profit in Burma gave these short-term civil servants no incentive to screen, equip, and train the locals, especially when the Indian Army was ready and—most important—cheap to deploy.

In addition to establishing the primacy of coercion in state-society relations, colonial policy and practice also left two other legacies for future incarnations of national authority. First, regimes in twentieth-century Burma have rarely undertaken major policies or initiatives at the behest of or with much concern about the interests of social forces from within the country. During the colonial era, Burma's status as a province of India, which was juridically maintained until only a few years before the Japanese conquest and the subsequent collapse of British rule, made India a pacemaker for political change. As such, colonial policy and practice in Burma was often an afterthought to reforms and innovations proposed for India. Until the 1920s, Burma was often a number of steps behind "the rest" of India. However, after that period, the much skinnier colonial regime in Burma granted much greater political concessions to the Burmese nationalists than to their Indian counterparts. But still, throughout the colonial and wartime eras, both British and Japanese policy toward Burma always derived from colonial policy toward India. Colonial rulers paid little attention to local developments unless they threatened the grander project. Hence, the state built under colonial rule and reinforced during the Japanese occupation was not only run by foreigners but had no real interest in local affairs aside from the maintenance of order necessary to meet imperial objectives.

Second, the colonial state's tolerance of tats had enormous impact over the disposition of violence in the postcolonial era. Because the tats owed their very existence to their exclusion from the state, they were from the outset local militia, never tied into any central chain of command. Organizationally, they constituted networks of individuals not directly under the control of the state. In the postwar era, when political parties tried to organize and build support throughout the country, the postwar generation of tats, like other social actors, became logical constituents for the parties. Soon, the tats became an indispensable part of the political apparatus necessary to accumulate and consolidate power in postcolonial Burma.

2

The Japanese Occupation, 1941–43

Join the navy and see the world, was the invitation to the youth of England in those days when Britannia ruled the waves and the world. *In Burma during the war one joined the army to see the country.*

Dr. Maung Maung, *To a Soldier Son*, 1974 (emphasis added)

Two wartime developments changed forever the nature of state institutions in Burma, particularly the armed forces. First, the Japanese invasion brought about the sudden and complete collapse of the colonial administrative machinery and infrastructure. In the wake of that collapse, the Japanese military needed to mobilize resources immediately for its broader war effort and could not afford to make the population into enemies and objects of coercive pacification. Soon, the Japanese military came to rely on different Burmese groups to prop up its occupation regime than had the British. These newly empowered Burmese elites offered access to those resources in return for political and economic concessions. Indeed, the Japanese regime's dependence inhibited its attempts to reestablish the central state's authority, which at times was undetectable beyond the capital. In fact, during the early months of Japanese rule in 1941, the country disintegrated into an array of autonomous local enclaves. Indigenous Burmans emerged as local state builders in central Burma. They took over abandoned administrative units and created new ones by invoking the hierarchies and resources of their prewar martial organizations, the tats. This decentralization of de facto political power throughout the villages and towns in central Burma established an enduring pattern of political strength—

often backed by force of arms—in the countryside accompanied by paralysis in Rangoon.

The only source of dynamism and growth in administrative capacity from the capital came out of the second prominent development of the occupation: the creation of the first national army in Burma, the Burma Independence Army (BIA). Unlike the prewar army, which was staffed by Indians and a handful of Burmese minorities, the BIA swept into its ranks thousands of ethnic-majority Burmans. Members of the BIA wore uniforms that represented *do-Bama* (our Burma) rather than a foreign power or empire. Their activities were financed and armed by what promised to become a national state, and they received training to defend national territory from foreign incursions. The institutional basis for the idea of a sovereign, territorially defined "Burma" was indigenized for the first time in modern history in the construction of the wartime armed forces. Soldiers joined the army, as Dr. Maung Maung reminisced in the epigraph to this chapter, to see the country, but more importantly to visualize for the first time the possibility of a country stretching to the boundaries drawn by British colonizers.

The Collapse of the Colonial State

One remarkable development of the twentieth century was the speed with which the European colonial Leviathans collapsed at first encounters with Japanese occupying forces. In Burma, the breakdown of the colonial state mirrored the fall of its territory to the Japanese—swift and irreversible. Beginning in December 1941, sixty-four thousand Japanese troops took only five months to drive the thirty thousand British-Indian troops out of Burma. By the end of February 1942, the demise of British rule was clinched when British and Indian units began the one thousand mile retreat to India.

As Gov. Reginald Dorman-Smith and most of his staff prepared to flee Rangoon, state institutions and remaining symbols of British authority in Rangoon either collapsed or were destroyed practically overnight. In a kind of "scorched state" policy, retreating government servants dismantled all institutions designed for social control. The custodians and attendants of the huge central jails at Rangoon and Insein—which were a cornerstone of the law-and-order identity of the British colonial state—deserted their posts after the first Japanese bombing raids in December 1941. By the end of February 1942, so few staff remained at these jails that feeding and caring for the remaining prisoners was impossible. One scholar noted: "The British administrators felt their choice was between starvation of the prisoners or wholesale release. Their humane code called for the release upon the public of five thousand convicts."[1] Similarly, the government mental hospital at

Tadagale released its "criminally insane" patients. Civil servants joined in a "bizarre and melancholy foray" to shoot all the animals in the Rangoon zoo. The university shut down. The British, Indian, and indigenous personnel of the city police, the Port Trust, the hospital, and municipal offices were evacuated. British and Indian soldiers looted the posh Gymkhana Club.[2] By March 7, 1942, the last British forces, including the commanding general of the British Burma Army, fled Rangoon.

The governor's plans to establish an administration at the summer capital, Maymyo, collapsed as the Japanese advance hastened and the retreat of his secretariat was slowed by the increasingly congested flight of nearly four hundred thousand refugees. The advancing Japanese armies eventually drove Dorman-Smith and his administration out of Maymyo, northward to Myitkyina, and over the border into India, where they established a wartime government-in-exile at Simla.

Dorman-Smith initially ordered local indigenous bureaucrats in the countryside to offer assistance to British and Indian forces, and in particular to protect the 350,000 Indian refugees from attacks by Burmans during their escape to India. But as soon as the Japanese air raids started in December 1941, many government staff in district towns abandoned their official positions and often their homes. In January 1942, rumors circulated that the Japanese units in Tenasserim were arresting officials who worked for the British regime, which led to further desertions from local government offices. The exodus stripped the countryside of police, jail attendants, clerks, medical officers, and air raid wardens. By May, not a single colonial administrator was left in Tenasserim (the area first evacuated). Throughout Burma, Guyot estimates that less than one-fourth of the prewar district officials remained at their government posts.[3] In many district towns, not only did the government officials disappear, but the physical evidence of the colonial state (jails, offices, courts, etc.) was torn down by either retreating imperial troops or angry mobs led by BIA units.

Violence and the New State

The Japanese took Burma with astonishing ease and speed. But Japanese penetration into Burma had started at least a decade earlier. As Guyot, Becka, and others have shown, the contacts between Burmese politicians and Japanese government agents that led directly to wartime collaboration began in earnest in September 1939. Japanese intelligence officers operated in Burma under diverse covers (including a dentist, a masseur, and a journalist) and established relationships with a number of Burmese political leaders. Their objective was to foster anti-British nationalism in Burma as part of a general plan to cut off supplies going to China via the 117–mile Burma Road from Rangoon to Yunnan.

The "Thirty Comrades"

By 1941, Col. Suzuki Keiji had emerged at the helm of this intelligence operation in Burma. This "swashbuckling, eccentric character" convinced the Japanese Imperial Army to raise an independence army of Burmese nationalists to aid in the invasion of Burma. By a complicated series of accidents, the young politician Aung San managed to hook up with Suzuki in Amoy, China, in 1940, and from there accompanied the intelligence officer to Tokyo where they planned the establishment of the independence army.[4] Subsequently, Suzuki's Minami Kikan (Southern Agency, in Japanese) arranged to transport a total of twenty-seven other Burmese nationalists to Japan for military training. "The aim was to obtain, not the old politicians, but the youthful activists of the Thakin Party."[5] By July 1941, the "Thirty Comrades" had assembled on Hainan Island for instruction at the San-ya Peasant Training Center.

After their crash course in command, combat, espionage, guerrilla warfare, and political tactics, the trainees were sent to Bangkok in November 1941. There they began raising the BIA with the assistance of Japanese businessmen and intelligence agents based in Siam.[6] Two of the Hainan trainees crossed into Burma on December 3 to recruit anti-British fighters. Additionally, two hundred Burmese living in Siam were assembled in Bangkok to join the struggle for independence, and the BIA was formally placed under the Japanese Fifteenth Army. The latter shipped three hundred tons of military equipment captured from the Chinese to Bangkok for the Minami Kikan's operations, and Colonel Suzuki was named commander of the BIA. Suzuki and his trainees from Burma all took Burmese noms de guerre; Suzuki took the name Bo Mogyo (Captain Thunderbolt).[7]

The Burma Campaign

When Japan's Fifteenth Army launched the invasion of Burma in December 1941, smaller units of the BIA followed Japanese forces into Burma and provided support, including the collection of food and resources in newly occupied areas, the gathering of intelligence from villagers, and the sabotage of British operations. Most important, BIA units immediately started recruiting to fill out the ranks. BIA leaders—mostly former *thakins* (young, anticolonial, nationalist activists associated with the Thakin Party)—tapped into small, secret groups of other nationalists. These groups became loosely amalgamated into an underground, anti-British resistance. Some had been drilling in tats or the University Training Corps (UTC) and providing guerrilla and arms training to their local members.[8]

First BIA flag featuring a peacock (symbol of the nationalist movement), held by new recruits training in Bangkok, 1941. P(AN68-100) PIII(a), DSHRI.

It is important to note that the strengthening of the BIA was never a high priority for the Japanese Fifteenth Army. Leaders of the BIA hoped that their nationalist army could press for immediate independence in Burma at the ouster of the British, but those dreams ended almost overnight as Japanese forces overran the countryside at a blinding pace. In February 1942, as Japanese troops were nearing the Sittang River, Bo Ne Win (who would become the Supreme Commander of the tatmadaw after 1949 and head of the country from 1962–88) and three other BIA officers deployed to the Irrawaddy Delta to organize an uprising. According to Maung Maung, Ne Win carried fewer than a dozen .22–caliber pistols and "barely had time to retrain the principal area commanders [of the underground resistance]" before he was ordered to lead the revolt on February 27. Few of the underground "area commanders" had time to reach their assigned areas, and although a handful managed to train local leaders for the uprising, "virtually

BIA troops arriving at riverbank across from Palaw, February 1942. P(AN74-18) PIII(a), DSHRI.

no revolution, in the proper sense, took place [because] without arms villagers were unable to attack even police stations."[9]

Nevertheless, this early assay at organizing resistance bore fruit. British and Indian military police and civil officials throughout the delta hastily retreated at the first hint of Japanese-supported resistance in their districts. By March 2, Burmese guerrillas were in control of Myaungmya district, and by mid-March, they controlled Bassein. Other towns throughout the delta fell quickly to Burmese guerrillas, many of whom immediately assumed charge of local administrative affairs in the name of the BIA. The guerrillas hoped to preempt Fifteenth Army officers from doing the same. By the end of the campaign in May, there were administration committees staffed mainly by prewar thakins and other young nationalists in nearly every town south of Mandalay.

In her detailed analysis of occupation politics, Guyot notes that the period between January and July 1942 was the first time in over fifty years that a foreign power did not control the country. It was also a time of chaos and ambiguity, with no clear or unified vision of Burma's future emerging from any of the major players. This lack of direction over what to do with conquered territory accounts for the relative ease with which BIA members took over law-and-order duties in the countryside. Prior to 1942, Japanese army, navy, political, and intelligence leaders gave little consideration to the issue of how to administer conquered territory. During the Burma campaign throughout the first half of 1942, a handful of Japanese field and staff officers fought an internal battle over competing visions for post-British Burma.[10] Although BIA-sympathizers in the Japanese command were able to establish a Burmese executive authority based in Rangoon in April, its activities were controlled by Japanese army officials who replaced it outright by direct military administration two months later.

Restoring Order in Burma

The arrival of Japanese military administration was never inevitable in wartime Burma. The Japanese army had only managed to field eighty administrators by the middle of the Burma campaign in 1942, and most of those were concentrated in the Rangoon environs. The initial efforts of Colonel Ishii and the Southern Area Army to establish military administration in February 1942 resulted in a proliferation of Japanese administrative organizations vying for control of varying degrees over Rangoon and the districts. Guyot reports that eight different functionally autonomous army, navy, and intelligence operations attempted to establish order in Rangoon alone.[11]

What little order did prevail throughout the Japanese-conquered countryside was maintained by BIA-backed administrative committees. Guyot argues that despite the rather decentralized, amorphous character of the BIA, its numerous units followed relatively uniform procedures to establish local government upon the collapse of the colonial state. "On arrival in a town, they [BIA units] first quashed the rampant murder and robbery by engendering fear through public executions. They then confiscated all guns in private possession. They finally installed local *Thakin*s as the new government and departed."[12] Many of the thakins who took on governing responsibilities were young—in their early twenties—and denounced the prevailing prewar administrative system. For the most part, however, the administration committees undertook the same tasks as government officials had under the British: "to restore order, reopen trade, raise revenues in the customary manner, through license fees, petty tolls and bazaar rents." As Guyot points out, the collapse of the colonial state and its replacement by BIA administration committees brought about a revolution in personnel, but not necessarily a revolution in policy.[13]

Initially, each local administrative committee operated autonomously, with little oversight or control from Tokyo, Rangoon, or BIA headquarters.

Fifteenth Army leaders grew increasingly concerned about the growing anarchy in the countryside. After the disappearance of twenty thousand police officers in early 1942 and the release of fifteen thousand convicts from the jails, crime grew at unprecedented rates. Murder rates peaked in the first half of 1942 at a rate seven times the already high prewar level, and the rate of dacoity was nearly twenty times the prewar level. According to Guyot, "the rampant nationalist fervor provided a pretext for robbery and even murder. Stealing from warehouses and homes of foreigners was [considered] mere recovery of wealth originally squeezed from the Burmese."[14] Japanese attempts to discipline the young Burmese administrators led to clashes between the BIA-backed administrative units and the BIA, on the one hand, and Japanese troops and Kempetai (military police), on the other.

Eliminating the growing nationalist threat from the countryside became the common objective unifying the various Japanese contenders for control over Burma. The pervasiveness of this threat favored the Southern Area Army's plans to delay Burmese independence and instead institute immediate military administration. It took several months of negotiating, planning, and infighting to work out how to disband the rural administrative committees of thakins. This process involved two preliminary struggles among Japanese and Burmese rivals for control. First, when the Fifteenth Army set out to undermine the thakins' control of the countryside, it needed to find thousands of replacement bureaucrats to staff rural administration as well as government departments in urban areas. When the Japanese began doubting the reliability of the thakins, they gradually moved to recruit those Burmese who had served in the British colonial civil service. By late 1942, the Fifteenth Army had reinstated many prewar government officials in the countryside to local positions of influence. When thakins became marginalized in the districts, they bitterly turned to other kinds of grassroots politics, joining one of three Japanese sponsored organizations: the army, the corporatist political party, or the East Asia Youth League (EAYL). Hence, unlike the British, who deployed cheap Indian officials and soldiers to violently pacify and administer the unruly Burmese, the incoming Japanese colonial officials could not afford to alienate local elites. Instead, the Japanese had to negotiate with indigenous elites to find partners who would prop up their rule.

Second, the greatest threat from these pro-independence administrative committees throughout the country was their linkage—real or perceived by the Japanese military—to the BIA. Military Administration Headquarters in Rangoon wanted to disarm and demobilize those who might use force to reinstate the sacked administrative committee members. Interestingly enough, this attempt at undermining the nationalists had the unintended consequence of forging a national army with a strong sense of corporate identity, an identity that would come to be expressed in a nationwide anti-Japanese movement. In other words, the Japanese attempted to establish a monopoly over administrative and coercive authority throughout Burma by empowering one group of older, somewhat pro-British bureaucrats at the expense of the younger nationalists. However, in the long term, the young castoffs from local administrative committees joined forces with the scaled-down Burmese army to launch the anti-Japanese resistance and to once again destroy the power of the central state.

The National Army

In the chaotic early months of the Japanese conquest and occupation, the BIA emerged as an entity that far outpaced Japanese plans. But it nonetheless disappointed Burman nationalist leaders. Discouraged, they more narrowly refocused their efforts to achieve independence. The BIA survived only seven months (December 1941–June 1942), during which it was Burma's first national, standing army. In creating that army, BIA leaders and Japanese advisors set important parameters for citizenship, definitions of "national security," and visions of nation-ness that carried over into the postwar era.

The Early BIA

Originally conceived by Suzuki as a liberating army, by Aung San as an independence army, and by the Japanese Fifteenth Army as a necessary evil, the BIA developed a viability and vitality of its own, which in many ways far exceeded all three visions. By the end of the Burma campaign in June 1942, there were at least ten thousand (and maybe as many as fifty thousand) members of BIA units scattered throughout Burma.[15] The path of the BIA dictated its composition. Like the prewar British colonial army, the BIA was not an ethnically "representative" army. Nearly all members were of one ethnicity—Burman—who constituted roughly 65–70 percent of the population. As BIA troops marched northward and westward from the Thai border, they swept into their ranks mainly Burmans of Lower Burma. Fully 75 percent of all BIA recruits came from Lower Burma, although Karens of the delta did not enlist nor did the BIA recruit them, probably because of Burman resentments about the overrepresentation of that ethnic group in the prewar colonial army and bureaucracy. By the time the Fifteenth Army deployed BIA columns to Upper Burma in April 1942, the ranks were so swelled with Lower Burma recruits that very little further enlistment occurred.[16] Since the BIA never marched far into the Kachin, Chin, and Shan regions, these populations were not recruited at all.

From its entry into Burma from Siam in December 1941 until occupation of Rangoon in March 1942, the Japanese Army had no line of command operating between its headquarters and any BIA units.[17] The possibilities for a unified command of any degree diminished with the emergence of new BIA units. As Guyot notes, the fission-like nature of BIA expansion meant that at its fringes, "BIA units led by duly-appointed officers [i.e., officers appointed by Aung San] were only one cut above gangs of dacoits using the BIA mantle to cloak their crimes."[18]

Reorganization of the BIA

The rapid growth of the BIA, the increasing crime rates, the frequency of clashes between Japanese and BIA units, and the growing threat to Japanese control over much of the territory outside Rangoon prompted Japanese army authorities to reorganize the BIA into two manageable columns (i.e., divisions) in March 1942, after the occupation of Rangoon. Aung San was named commander in chief, and Bo Let Ya his deputy commander in chief. Colonels Zeya and Ne Win were appointed commanders of the two columns. Eight Japanese "official advisors" oversaw BIA headquarters and each column had three to five such advisors. This field force probably numbered about seven thousand, and incorporated only those men who had arrived in Rangoon by March.

This reorganization of the BIA, even though it was disbanded three months later, was a turning point in the disposition of state violence in Burma. The reconstitution of the myriad of BIA saboteurs, patriots, guerrillas, thugs, and crooks into two institutionalized columns overseen by Japanese and Burmese staff officers had several important consequences. First, it gave the "delayed independence" constituency within the Southern Area Army the channels it needed to pacify the thakins and to contain potential nationalist threats to Japanese military operations. Until this reorganization, the only viable channel for transmitting Southern Area Army orders to BIA units was through Suzuki. After the reorganization, the Japanese army scattered "official advisors" through all levels and tasked them to put BIA soldiers and officers into Japanese-provided uniforms, to count them up, to read them manuals of conduct, to teach them Japanese words of command, and to subject them to varying degrees of discipline. BIA commanders became responsible for the behavior of "their" men, and the Kempetai (military police) grew increasingly prominent in policing this new relationship. It was through these channels that Japanese army officials persuaded Aung San to take unpopular positions in May and June, including his decision to support Japanese plans to dissolve the BIA in June.[19]

The second outcome of the reorganization was the shift in the visions, aspirations, and identifications of BIA leaders. The memoirs and speeches of Aung San and other BIA officers indicate a change in the strategies of these nationalists as a result of the reorganization. They narrowed their plans for immediate independence to a more pragmatic goal: that of maintaining intact an indigenous army and protecting it as much as possible from Japanese meddling. From this point on, Aung San and other BIA leaders remember dedicating themselves first and foremost to army building and protecting the BIA's men.[20] In their views, army building was a necessary prerequisite for eventually remaking the state in an indigenous image.

Japanese authorities used the BIA reorganization to channel indigenous political forces into what became three separate institutional pillars of the occupation-era state. By May 1942, the Japanese had successfully edged out thakin comrades from their positions on administrative committees throughout the countryside and replaced them with former bureaucrats from the British colonial regime, who ultimately dominated all geographical and functional levels of the occupation-era civil service. At the same time Southern Area Army leaders courted the second pillar of the Japanese state—older politicians such as Dr. Ba Maw, who eventually assumed charge of the Burmese cabinet several months later and named himself *anashin* (dictator) in 1943 when the Japanese granted Burma nominal independence. In this early period, the only state institution identified with the younger generation of nationalists was the BIA. Thus we can see, ultimately and probably accidentally, Japanese policy led to a division of indigenous labor within the occupation state, with older politicians running the government established several months later; former colonial civil servants handling administrative affairs in the districts; and the thakins manning the last refuge for their generation of nationalists—the BIA. Had these three pillars been integrated politically, it is possible that the army's leading role in the anti-Japanese resistance two years later might not have materialized and that army dominance in postwar political life may have been precluded as well.

Unintended Consequences

The reorganization of the BIA also had the unintended consequence of diminishing Japanese influence over the army and over Burma in the long run by strengthening the institutional clout of nationalism and by weakening the resource-extraction capabilities of the Japanese army. By establishing a BIA headquarters, designing a flag representing the BIA, appointing Burmese as staff officers, writing a Soldier's Code in Burmese, and organizing two (and later three) field columns of soldiers, the reorganization articulated the structure of the first-ever standing, national army on Burmese soil. The army would become an identifiable institutional basis for nationalist sentiments. Not all nationalists were members of the two columns or the headquarters staff, but all BIA members were preparing to fight for and—more concretely—to march through an identifiable nation. These people joined a Burmese army, not a Japanese one. In their minds, no BIA soldiers were mercenaries, as they considered those employed by the prewar British-Indian army. All were in one way or another "*do-Bama*" or "sons of the soil." Aside from Suzuki, who was transferred out of Burma in June 1942, no one considered "foreign" was ever made a member of the BIA or subsequent incarnations of the national army during the Japanese and postwar eras.

To those in the two BIA columns—who were mostly born and raised in Lower Burma—the reorganization made "Burma" more concrete. In the earlier march through Lower Burma from Siam in early 1942, the goal of the rather loosely connected BIA units was to get to Rangoon; there was little if any consideration of what would happen after the capture of the capital. Once in Rangoon, where it became clear by April that independence would not be immediately forthcoming, the BIA units foundered, and altercations broke out between BIA members and Japanese authorities. The reorganization was designed to give Fifteenth Army Headquarters more control over the BIA units, which were still considered necessary for the conduct of the Upper Burma campaign. Subsequently, the three-month march of BIA columns throughout much of Upper Burma went surprisingly smoothly, considering that few of the Burmese officers or rank and file had ever seen the dry zone beyond Lower Burma, much less the "Burmese" who lived there.

The campaign turned the barely institutionalized BIA—more than any other part of the state—into a school in nation-ness. The two BIA columns and the attending headquarters' staff added up to a standing army of nationals being organized to march northward and fight for, occupy, and administer to parts of "their country." The memoirs of participants in this march north portray a growing sense of common citizenship and comradeship among the members of the two columns, and between them and the residents of Upper Burma. Also evident in these writings are increasingly distinct categories of those who should not be eligible for citizenship or comradeship. These distinctions can be seen in the language used to describe how BIA members followed Japanese troops, skirmished with Chinese forces, and prepared to engage British troops. Herein came a sense that these "foreigners" did not belong on the Burmese soil that they themselves were crossing for the first time in their lives.

Bo Than Daing's two-volume memoir provides examples of both senses of nation-ness among the BIA soldiers. On the one hand, he peppers his day-by-day, blow-by-blow account of his unit's 350-mile march from Rangoon north to Bhamo with travelogue-style description of the foods he encounters—both local delicacies (new and exotic to him) and foods just like he ate at home in Tavoy; through this discovery, he is saying something like: "These people of Upper Burma are 'different,' but we all eat rice." On the other hand, when he writes about skirmishes with Chinese and English troops in Katha, his language emphasizes only difference; all are identified consistently as *"yanthu"* (enemies).[21]

In addition to giving institutional access and fostering ideological commitment to the idea of a territorially defined Burmese nation to thousands who otherwise might have been inclined toward more parochial, local aspirations, another set of more pragmatic, unintended consequences must be mentioned. Prior to the reorganization, the lack of structure in the BIA allowed the nationalists to incorporate a widely varied group of "peasants, intermixed with students, laborers, clerks, hoodlums, lawyers and former monks"[22] into the very public event of marching through and "conquering" Lower Burma. This looseness afforded the Japanese army great economies. During the campaign, it was possible to requisition supplies and restore order by tapping into the variety of networks afforded by this social class mix. The reorganization ended this advantageous fluidity. Indeed, for all of the constraints it placed on BIA leaders and rank and file in their efforts to achieve independence, the reorganization also ended the fluidity and cost-effectiveness of Japanese control over Burma and especially the Burma Road, which Japan intended to use to supply its forces fighting in China. Overnight, the occupation became an administrative project, which grew increasingly expensive with each passing day. Schoolteachers had to be imported to teach the Japanese language, hundreds of Japanese government administrators had to be brought in, and police functions multiplied as war deprivations took a greater toll on the populace and as migration to safer areas increased.[23] The occupation quickly became a project of imperial control, which was far more expensive and complicated than the cooperative rule that Suzuki had planned.

Corporate Identity and New Bases of Unity

The increasing sense of unity and shared national identity that resulted from the reorganization of the BIA in April 1942 continued throughout the next two and a half years under Japanese rule, although with some twists and turns. In July 1942, the Japanese set out to eliminate the unruly elements in the BIA and announced plans to disband it. Japanese recruiters retained only two thousand of the Burmese soldiers and officers in the three infantry battalions for service in the new Burma Defence Army (BDA). The disbandment decision, an outcome of another power struggle among Japanese authorities competing for dominance in Burma, strengthened the hand of the

Southern Area Army. The latter shipped Colonel Suzuki back to Japan and further marginalized the navy from affairs in Burma. However, this move did not end the conflicts within the Japanese administration, although the cast of competitors changed over the next two years. Intraregime conflict would intensify as Japanese fortunes waned in the Pacific theater.

In contrast to the backdrop of continued struggle among Japanese authorities in and over Burma, the tatmadaw—in its three later wartime incarnations—was notable for its increasingly unified sense of identity as a national army and as an institution crucial for the emergence of an independent Burmese nation. Three key developments were responsible for this growing sense of corporate identity in the Burmese army and made possible the army's contribution to the resistance forces that brought down the Japanese regime. The three developments were the inadvertent fostering of unity via downsizing of the army, the creation of a single training institution, and the establishment of a war office.

Size and Identity

First, the Japanese dissolution of the BIA on July 27, 1942, and the decision to allow only two to five thousand to enlist in the newly formed BDA contributed most to the fostering of corporate identity that characterized Burmese military organizations throughout the wartime and postwar era. What is important here is size and concentration. The unwieldy, disorganized, decentralized collection of thousands of thugs, patriots, peasants, and politicians (i.e., the BIA) was replaced by a small group of soldiers and officers, organized initially into only two battalions. All were garrisoned together for a couple of months in Pyinmana, and then later posted to only two or three bases. Thousands (and perhaps even tens of thousands) of BIA members were sent back to their towns and villages in the delta and other parts of central and Lower Burma, while only two thousand of the seven thousand applicants managed to pass medical and other kinds of entrance exams. Those who passed were assembled at Mandalay and Rangoon, and later moved en masse to Pyinmana for orientation.

At the newly formed headquarters in Pyinmana, Japanese advisors allowed Burmese officers including Ne Win and Yan Naing some say in who was accepted into the BDA. Major Ne Win issued a directive to those involved in the examination process that "persons of spurious character" should be excluded. While the Japanese military authorities saw this as their chance to rid the Burmese army of dangerous elements and to reduce overall numbers to a more manageable size, Aung San and other Burmese leaders equally welcomed the reduction. They seized the opportunity to block infiltration by those with interests inimical to their hopes for independence.[24]

Neither the Japanese military advisors nor the Burmese officers realized it at the time, but this small size was the key to the development of the tightly knit, corporate identity of the tatmadaw.[25] Although there were reports of disillusionment and frustration among the five thousand former BIA soldiers who were excluded from the BDA, there is evidence that a new feeling of brotherhood immediately developed among those who were admitted. In the initial orientation process for the BDA in Mandalay and Rangoon, and later in Pyinmana, everyone in the BDA lived together, ate together, drilled together, learned Japanese together, missed their families together, and talked about Burma together. The new battalion commanders and deputy battalion commanders were all Burmese (all former members of the Thirty Comrades) and, more specifically, nearly all were ethnic Burman. While Japanese instructors had ultimate command authority, some of the recruits remember that from the very beginning of the BDA, Burmese unit commanders tried to find subtle ways to protect "their" soldiers from face-slapping and other humiliations imposed by the Japanese teachers.[26]

But this was not simply a case of a negative corporate identity emerging in response to oppression. Instead, a strong, positive sense of collegiality and "us-ness" emerged from the Pyinmana orientation. Almost all of the recruits were between the ages of nineteen and twenty-three, and in each new battalion some soldiers knew each other from old student union ties (either in high school or at Rangoon University) or from involvement in local thakin groups. However, the commonalties of their backgrounds should not be overstated; student politicians from Anglo-vernacular high schools in Rangoon had probably never before met a student politico from Sagaing or Bassein or Tavoy. Instead, they met and formed relationships for the first time in the camps of the new BDA.[27]

Most of the available memoirs of these Pyinmana days speak of the harshness of Japanese training methods and the physical and mental stress on the recruits. However, former BDA recruits also wrote extensively of the fun they had together despite all the stress—and surely these experiences strengthened the growing ties among the two thousand recruits. For example, Bohmu Chit Kaung's animated memoirs of his experiences of the wartime and early postwar years contain fond memories of this training period, including one anecdote about the Burmese junior officer who led bayonet training exercises for Chit Kaung's unit of the Fourth Battalion at Pyinmana: "He would usually conduct our exercises in the place where he was courting a young woman—in the field behind her house. When the young woman came to her window to look out, he usually drew his sword and gave us orders to thrust our bayonets forcefully at the enemy. In this way they fell in love as we became skilled at bayonet warfare."[28]

As the war progressed, BDA numbers gradually expanded, but in such a way that the corporate identity was strengthened rather than weakened by expansion. Over the next year, the BDA gradually grew to eight thousand as Maj. Kyaw Zaw raised the Fourth Battalion and Maj. Aung raised the Fifth Battalion, both in March 1943; Maj. Yan Aung raised the Sixth Battalion that April. After Japan granted Burma nominal independence in August 1943, the army added two engineers' battalions, two antiaircraft battalions, a supply and transport battalion, a motor transport battalion, and one Karen infantry battalion, bringing the BDA to a force of roughly fifteen thousand troops and officers.[29] Additionally, a small number of recruits were sent to Japan for air force and navy training.

Probably unintentionally, the methods the Japanese used to recruit for this expansion provided the tightly knit officer corps of the BDA the opportunity to perpetuate the ties of this emerging corporate identity among the new recruits. With the Japanese authorization for each new battalion came the appointment of a Burmese battalion commander and deputy commander, who usually received general orders to recruit with little in the way of specific instructions.[30] As a result, officers such as Bo Khin Maung Gale and Bo Lun Tin, who did much of the recruiting for the fourth through sixth infantry battalions, went to their home areas in Upper Burma and enlisted new members from their extended families and friends whose reliability and loyalty could be assured.[31] Bo Thein Swe, a Bassein native, went to his home in the delta to recruit for the Third Battalion in 1942.[32]

This growing sense of corporate identity did not eliminate all tensions between various individuals and groups in the BDA. Some of these frictions were personal; others reflected strategic and ideological debates that pitted sympathizers with the Communist Party's virulent anti-Japanese position against sympathizers with the less doctrinaire, more accommodationist position of the prewar People's Revolutionary Party. However, the compactness of the post-BIA army enabled most officers to know each other personally. Among the various factions, there was growing adherence to the notion that the tatmadaw constituted a national army that would defend the territory of Burma.

Officers' Training School at Mingaladon

After March 1943, the officer corps for the new battalions all came from the graduating classes of the Bo Thindan Kyaung[33] (literally translated, "Officers' Training School" [OTS]) in Mingaladon. The first two groups were made up primarily of cadets chosen out of the Pyinmana, Mandalay, and Rangoon training camps of the new BDA. In September 1942, the first batch of OTS cadets enrolled at the newly established facility at Mingaladon, near Rangoon.

As Guyot argues, "The Japanese Army placed its greatest long range hope for controlling the Burmese army upon training its officers" at Mingaladon.[34] However, OTS proved to be an institution that provided space for the army's growing nationalist identity to ferment. Ultimately, OTS served

Cadets from Second Company, First Platoon, first graduating class, Mingaladon Officers' Training School, 1943. P(AN58-485) PIII(b), DSHRI.

as a training ground not for pro-Japanese officers and cadets, as the Japanese military intended, but for politically unified, anti-Japanese cells that formed laterally and vertically among the classes being rushed through the various training programs offered there.

From as early as August 1942—when the selection process for OTS cadets was established by Burma Area Army (BAA) headquarters—Japanese long-term hopes for dominating the tatmadaw were already in danger. Although the Burma Area Army established certain basic criteria for admission, former members of the Thirty Comrades controlled the actual selection of OTS cadets. They chose from the small pool of applicants who had attended the BDA orientation camps. An official history of the tatmadaw reports that the BDA sent Maj. Ne Win, Maj. Yan Naing, Capt. La Yaung, battalion commanders of First and Second Battalions, to select cadets from those posted to Mandalay.

They tested the tenacity and mental toughness of the *yebaws* [comrades]. In this test, the yebaws were lined up on the Sappers-Miners parade ground at Mandalay Hill and told to stand at attention from 7 A.M. until 10 A.M. each morning. During that time, some of the yebaws collapsed on bended knee, others became dizzy. The battalion commanders were able to observe uninterruptedly which yebaws were tenacious and resolute and which were not and which ones could maintain their stance and which could not. As part of this examination method, sometimes the soldiers were served rice without curry, and sometimes were not offered a meal at all, but had to watch when the examiners poured off some undercooked rice from their cooked rice in front of the [hungry] soldiers. They also were required to run the perimeter of the palace moat, to raise their rifles up and down [on command] one hundred times, and to crawl crocodile-style with their rifles over thorny brush and sharp, small stones.[35]

This selection process, which was repeated for later intakes of cadets, was important for three reasons. First, it gave Burmese battalion commanders a chance to observe and evaluate most of the future commissioned and non-commissioned officers of the BDA. Two years later, when army leaders plotted the anti-Japanese resistance, they thus knew something about the psychological and physical endurance of all Mingaladon graduates. Since the first batch to graduate from OTS became the officer corps for the fourth through sixth battalions, resistance planners had a strong sense of which junior officers could be counted on, even if there had been no shared prewar political experiences on which to build linkages.

Second, Bo Min Nyo writes that Ne Win, La Yaung, and Yan Naing ranked mental toughness as the most important attribute for admission to OTS.[36] Having undergone the rigors of Japanese military training at Hainan, these three members of the Thirty Comrades probably were convinced that this trait alone would see trainees through the harsh training and indoctrination by the Japanese instructors.

Third, the process segregated indigenous candidates who might have been pro-Japanese from those more inclined to rebel. The Japanese authorized OTS enrollment to run to three hundred cadets total: two hundred fifty cadets were to be from the BDA, and fifty, who never participated in the BIA or BDA, were to be recommended by the chief of the executive administration, Dr. Ba Maw. While it is unclear what the actual breakdown of those admitted was in terms of BDA cadets (i.e., probably young thakins) versus cadets appointed by Ba Maw,[37] it is likely that this difficult entrance exam faced only by the BDA applicants further set them apart from Dr. Ba Maw's appointees.[38]

Beyond the selection process, Burmese army leaders had little to do with OTS affairs during the seven-month training course of the first graduating class. All instructors and administrators were Japanese. They trained the cadets strictly according to Japanese methods. As soon as the cadets arrived at the school, their heads were shaved. School authorities distributed Japanese clothing, bedding, and books. Once a month, they showed Japanese films, mostly about the heroic adventures of samurai. Japanese OTS officials imposed rigorous dawn-till-dusk study, training, and work schedules. The harshness of these methods was compounded by the insistence that instruction be carried out in the Japanese language. When trainees could not understand or follow orders barked out in Japanese, their trainers struck them in the face, which "went against Burmese tradition. . . . Every day, Japanese *hsayas* [teachers] cruelly slapped faces during military training. No student escaped this treatment."[39]

This adversity probably favored the growth of anti-Japanese sentiment among these cadets. But given that a number of the Burmese resistance leaders who graduated from OTS maintained friendships with their former Japanese instructors over the next forty years, it seems more likely that the camaraderie and friendships forged in the training courses—in the face of adversity, but also in some warmly remembered, pleasant experiences—laid the basis for a positive, shared identity among men from all over central Burma. Colonel Tin Maung wrote about the deep, abiding friendships that he formed with his classmates in the first OTS course, which began on his first night at Mingaladon.[40] Thakin Tin Mya, who conducted secret Communist Party political training throughout Burma during the war, used these friendship connections to organize clandestine discussion groups among OTS cadets.[41] Vertical ties also formed. The OTS nominated some of the first batch of graduates to stay on at Mingaladon as assistants or instructors, and these Burmese officers went to great lengths to help the second and later batches survive the Japanese training methods.[42]

The War Office

When the BDA was formed, the Japanese established the "Military Preparations Bureau . . . under the direct jurisdiction of the Japanese commander in order to execute duties of establishing, developing, and maintaining the . . . Burma Defence Army."[43] This Military Preparations Bureau (MPB), or Hebechoku, was located in Rangoon and was eventually transformed into the War Office. With each set of military reforms over the next two years, the nascent War Office under Aung San became physically and operationally more and more independent of Japanese advisors. In fact, the planning staff at the War Office became autonomous enough that these officers plotted much of the anti-Japanese resistance strategy from there in 1944–45.

Initially, the MPB was set up as a "control unit" to organize, equip, pay, and garrison the troops. One-third of the staff was Japanese and two-thirds Burmese, with the latter proportion expanding over the next two years. The head of MPB was Colonel Fukui (who was also the superintendent of OTS);

the Burmese commander in chief (first Aung San, later Ne Win), the principal of the OTS, and the head of the Burma Area Army Advisory Department all answered to Fukui.[44] In practice, the operation of the MPB proved to be enormously influential in the development of the wartime resistance. Moreover, a decade later, Cols. Maung Maung and Aung Gyi modeled the Military Planning Staff—which systematically reorganized the postcolonial tatmadaw in the early 1950s—on the wartime planning bureau. Structurally, nearly every aspect of the BDA was copied from the Japanese Imperial Army, as the MPB borrowed Japanese battalion organizational styles, training manuals, pay scales, uniforms, and rank insignias.[45]

Perhaps the most enduring legacy of the MPB and later the War Office for the development of the postwar tatmadaw came from the scope of matters considered to be subject to its authority. Bohmu Chit Kaung writes of his experience as a recent OTS graduate assigned to the War Office, where one of the first policies he heard being discussed was how to best operate the military's brothel across Halpern Road from the staff officers' quarters "according to the Japanese system."

> When Burmese tatmadaw leaders were planning the details of the brothel being opened for the Burma army, I was within earshot, and since I was an ordinary junior officer, they spoke freely in front of me.
>
> One senior officer: "About how much time [shall we give our men] with a woman?"
>
> Another: "Let's say a half hour."
>
> "Ha . . . A half hour is too much time—they will do it two times! Fifteen minutes is enough."
>
> "Fifteen minutes is too little. You'd shake your head and the time would be up!"[46]

Chit Kaung's account suggests the extent to which the MPB and later the War Office attempted to structure all aspects of military life.

The modular transfer of the Japanese military structure did not necessarily privilege Japanese army leaders over indigenous officers for control of the army. In fact, the instant-army established with the creation of the BDA instead set up a number of channels that anti-Japanese resistance forces later used for their own purposes. Key members of a rather loose grouping of army officers—which became known as the Army Young Officers' Resistance Group (AYRG)[47]—landed War Office positions by 1943. They used the War Office's resources to publish a series of anti-Japanese pamphlets and to distribute them through the army's field units. According to an official tatmadaw history, the MPB, and later the War Office, "kept records concerning the numbers of recruits, dates of applications, dates and places of examinations for the recruits," as well as ongoing personnel files.[48] Since much of the detailed work still required knowledge of Burmese language, Burmese members of the MPB were sometimes able to manipulate transfers, promotions, and troop dispositions for purposes of strengthening the BDA vis-à-vis the Japanese. The MPB and War Office distributed army uniforms to underground allies, providing disguises that allowed them to attend meetings at the homes of Aung San, Than Tun, and Thakin Nu.[49] Maung Maung and others arranged inspections and other kinds of official trips to army installations around Burma to recruit resistance leaders among field officers while maintaining the appearance of conducting War Office business. Trusted civilians relayed messages and news from the War Office to politicians and other resistance organizers.[50] Additionally, map exercises and strategy planning for the eventual uprising against the Japanese—which these young officers intended to commence as early February 1944, but was held up by the more cautious war minister, Aung San, and the commander in chief, Ne Win—all transpired within the walls of the War Office.

Some of the resistance planning took place outside the offices of the MPB and the War Office on U Wisara Road. Top officers, including Col. Aung San (commander in chief and, later, defense minister) and Maj. Let Ya (Burmese chief of staff at MPB), acquired housing in the lovely colonial mansions of the Windemere and Golden Valley areas of Rangoon. Although some of the junior staff officers rankled at the comfort enjoyed by their higher-ranking colleagues, these homes were located in areas with large trees and high walls, allowing various anti-Japanese military officers, communists, socialists, EAYL members, and other resistance participants to come and go discreetly without raising much suspicion.[51]

Like OTS, this institutional configuration facilitated the development of strong new ties among the Burmese assigned to MPB positions. Although many of the Burmese staff at the MPB/War Office were allied with some strand of the People's Revolutionary Party (PRP; which in 1946 became known as the Socialist Party), there were nonetheless quite a few officers of communist persuasion in both field and War Office positions, as well as a few aligned with still other politicians. When Bo Chit Kaung graduated from OTS in 1944, he was assigned to the War Office and given quarters (*yeiq-tha*) with fellow staff officers on Halpern Road. "In this *yeiq-tha* we had quite a collection of people. There were communist party *yebaws* and PRP Party *yebaws*. There were some who were members of no party and were drunk on sake day and night."[52] Chit Kaung, then a Communist Party member, and his Socialist friends Ko Chit Khaing and Ko Kyi Win, spent long hours at Halpern Road debating Marxist ideology and its implications for the Burmese freedom struggle.[53]

Conclusion

With the collapse of the administrative machinery of the colonial state, the wartime period offered Burmese nationalists opportunities to improvise ad hoc, local solutions to the pervasive crisis of disorder. Once local solutions had achieved any degree of success, the reassertion of central control over local affairs became a task that neither the Japanese, the returning British (from 1945–48), nor the postcolonial Union government could accomplish until well into the 1960s. Furthermore, the local, impromptu administration set up in early 1942 often tapped into existing networks of thakins, students, and other politically active individuals. Their prewar political experience along with their wartime administrative and guerrilla experiences left organizational residues that would privilege local autonomy against the central state throughout much of the postwar period.

The diffusion of authority in the countryside was useful to and encouraged by Japanese military authorities in the early stages of the Burma campaign, but became an administrative headache as the occupation continued. Moreover, in urban areas, Burmese resistance leaders carved out niches inside the Japanese regime (in the MPB/War Office and EAYL) that gave them access to these loose networks, which they used to organize the 1945 anti-Japanese uprising. Not surprisingly, when these same resistance leaders became political and military leaders in Rangoon after independence, they too were confounded by these centrifugal tendencies as local guerrilla groups supported the armed rebel groups or the increasingly autonomous army field commanders and their upcountry allies.

Similarly, Japanese authorities found that their policies had unintended consequences that eventually precipitated their undoing in Burma. Unlike the British, the conquering Japanese could not simply define the local population as "enemies" because they had no Indian Army to beat down resistance. The need for immediate, cost-effective access to resources and the Burma Road necessitated negotiation and compromise with indigenous social forces. Such cooperation proved to be Japan's undoing in wartime Burma. When Japan armed and organized the BIA, a local guerrilla army of between ten thousand and fifty thousand indigenous men, in 1941–42, the imperial military dispensed to cultivators, workers, students, traders, bandits, and others a range of new skills, new outlooks, and new reasons to leave their homes. When Japan's Burma Area Army headquarters attempted to bring this unruly situation under control, they found that disbanding and sending home guerrilla fighters was a far more difficult task than mobilizing them. Displaced guerrillas, uprooted rural families, and urban refugees alike found ways to survive that often undermined Japanese policy and control over the region. Furthermore, once armed, most of these guerrilla groups stayed armed (or at least motivated to rearm). A kind of second generation of the prewar tats, these guerrilla groups reasserted themselves in the anti-Japanese resistance, the postwar anti-British movement, and the postcolonial insurgency.

The creation of the first-ever national army (i.e., the BIA) established a kind of "school" in nation-ness. Marching through and defending regions in Burma that they had never visited before or whose inhabitants they had never seen before gave Burmese soldiers their first lesson in what constituted "Burma." Postcolonial tatmadaw leaders who served in one of these army incarnations typically referred to other army officers as either "one of us" (meaning a member of the BIA or one of its later incarnations) or "one of them." During the occupation, the latter category did not stray far from the Dobama Asiayone's definitions of the 1930s, which targeted indigenous collaborators with the British (not the Japanese) as enemies of the emerging nation.

Missing from both the "us" and the "them" categories was the 30–35 percent of the population who lived in the former Excluded Areas (see map 3). Because Japan's de facto authority never extended far beyond the central regions or former Ministerial Burma, the territorial and experiential segregation of the previous fifty years only deepened. None of the Burmese armies marched through any significant stretch of frontier territory, nor did their territorial authority extend beyond the central regions (see map 4). Still, however, their ideas of where and what "Burma" was included all the territory within the British-drawn boundaries. As will be shown in chapter 3, British and U.S. special forces operated quite freely in the former Excluded Areas of Burma, recruiting residents into anti-Japanese, anti-Burman guerrilla forces and often promising them political independence from the Rangoon-based state after the war ended.

Finally, it should be noted that many scholars suggest that Japan instilled militarist qualities in Burma's nascent military. This Japanese mentoring is said to have set the country inevitably on a path to postwar military dominance of state-society relations. It is true that for decades the Burmese military has shown Japanese legacies, evident in aspects of its training and ceremonial affairs. However, soldiers and officers in the BIA and BDA did not uncritically absorb the lessons of militarism and behave like Japanese robots. Instead they creatively adapted Japanese militarism for their own nationalist purposes and to manage day-to-day crises as they emerged. They appropriated Japanese resources, institutions, and methods to create spaces in which they later launched an effective anti-Japanese resistance.

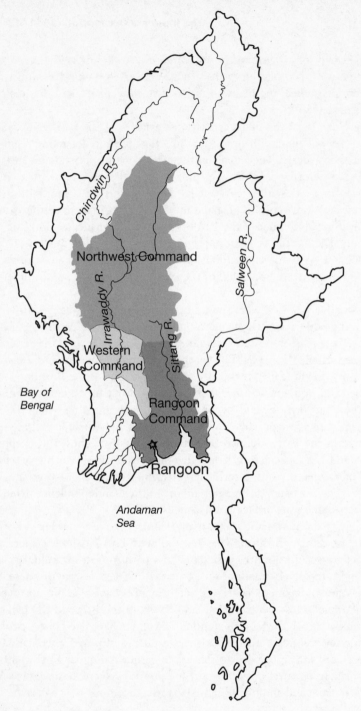

Map 4. Japanese occupation: Burma Defence Army command areas, 1944. *Source:* Based on map in တပ်မတော်သမိုင်း၊ ၁၈၂၄-၁၉၄၅၊ တွဲ ၁ [*Tatmadaw History, 1824–1945*, vol. 1] (Rangoon, 1994), n.p.

3

Resistance and the United Front, 1943–45

When these Burmans become national heroes . . . we shall have largely taken the wind out of their sails by having made it possible to be national heroes with the British rather than against them.

> Admiral Louis Mountbatten, Supreme Allied Commander,
> to British Chiefs of Staff, telegram, March 27, 1945

On the surface, the anti-Japanese resistance of 1943–45 appeared to combine more than a dozen former enemies into a united front never before imagined and never again repeated among Burmese social forces. Many historians point to the resistance as the moment that created the political community that postcolonial Burma claimed as its constituency and its terrain. In fact, this tenuous alliance of former enemies served more to sow the seeds of antagonism and to construct irreconcilable visions of authority and national identity than to lay the foundations for a Burma united for anything beyond the expulsion of the Japanese.

Moreover, during the anti-Japanese resistance of 1944–45, every component of the united front rallied support and resources around idealistic visions of a post-Japanese state that were utterly incompatible with the aims of nearly every other unit of the united front. While only the former British colonial officials in India mapped out an explicit postwar state-building strategy in any detail, every one of the anti-Japanese forces was laying a foundation to realize their particular vision of the post-Japanese state. Success against the common enemy came surprisingly quickly, and the territorially limited indigenous components of the reoccupation forces never had time to pool their resources, integrate their units, or discuss and debate their differing visions in any meaningful way.

The way in which British and U.S. clandestine organizations armed, trained, and indoctrinated indigenous guerrillas in preparation for the second Burma campaign created politically incompatible centers of power, both around the "frontier fringe" and within Japanese-held territory in central Burma.[1] When the motley array of more than a dozen different anti-Japanese forces came together in its very shaky, not-so-united front, the most enduring result was the institutionalization of highly centrifugal, decentralized forms of control over violence that carried over into postwar Burma. Because the conduct of antistate warfare further dispersed power and control over resources, people, and guns, any future state managers would find consolidation of central power extremely difficult. Throughout World War II, state destruction proved easy, which held ruinous consequences for state rebuilders after the war.

The Resistance

Studies of the Japanese occupation era in Burma have been dominated by the debate among various partisans, participants, and historians over which group constituted the decisive force in the successful resistance. The claimants of absolute primacy include Communist Party cadres, the American Kachin Rangers, the British Kachin levies, the Chins, the Socialists, the Indian Army, the British Fourteenth Army, British special forces, the Anti-Fascist Organization leaders, and the young officers in the tatmadaw. The historiographical debate reflects the fundamental incompatibilities among the forces that came together in the anti-Japanese resistance. The debate suggests that the brief unification of more than a dozen different anti-Japanese groups was less significant for the future of Burma than the institutionalization of difference and intolerance among indigenous groups competing for political power over territory in Burma.

Around the Frontier Fringe

After the ignominious British retreat in 1942, the British government of Burma settled in Simla, India, where it continued to claim nominal legal authority over the frontier areas of Burma that had not been conquered by the Japanese. However, it was little more than "a typewriter government"; actual British control over these remote areas was exercised by the regrouping British armed forces.[2] Turf battles developed between civil and military au-

thorities representing the United States and Britain, and these were not resolved until August 1943 at the first Quebec conference. At that point, the
Allies created the more unified Southeast Asia Command (SEAC), which
was headed up by Adm. Lord Louis Mountbatten.[3]

With varying degrees of success, the SEAC brought under a single domain a number of Allied irregular, infantry, and intelligence forces. Shortly
after the 1942 retreat, British forces began recruiting indigenous peoples in
the frontier regions not occupied by the Japanese into irregular units officered by Britons. Donnison wrote that these units were intended "to serve
as a defensive screen and to gain information about the enemy."[4] In Arakan,
the Upper Chindwin, and Naga Hills districts, recruits were formed into
the "V Force," which conducted patrols and collected intelligence in much
of western and northwestern Burma. The Chin levies were raised in the
Chin Hills and were supported by a patched-together battalion of the prewar Burma Frontier Force. Kachin levies were raised in the Fort Hertz (now
Putao) area farther north. United States forces armed and trained Chinese
units in the Hukawng Valley to protect the area of the Ledo railhead, and
the British Special Operations Executive (SOE) Force 136 organized other
Kachin guerrillas in that area as well. Some of these levies from the border
areas had served in the prewar British Burma Army, Frontier Force, or Military Police, and initially, there appeared to be no scarcity of recruits. Meanwhile, British officers secretly organized two thousand Karen levies in 1942
in the eastern hills, and built this resistance force to as many as twelve thousand by the end of the war.[5] Linkages were formed with Karens based in the
Irrawaddy Delta, and by the end of the war, SOE claimed to have a force of
sixteen thousand guerrillas operating in Burma.

Secret Allied organizations proliferated throughout the occupation, and in
the wake of the disastrous Japanese offensive into Imphal in May 1944, a confident Lt. Gen. William Slim, commander of the Fourteenth Army, instituted
a review of the proliferation of intelligence operations in Burma. The review
identified no fewer than twelve different clandestine Allied intelligence or
paramilitary organizations operating in Burma at the time.[6] Among the organizations, none had provisions for information sharing, administrative cooperation, or integration of the twelve different chains of command. Some,
like the British SOE/Force 136, raised resistance forces and conducted sabotage and espionage with almost no SEAC oversight. Robert H. Taylor describes SOE as a "special wartime body not beholden to any established institutions and as an entity that reported directly to the British war cabinet,"
rendering the organization "unusually free" in the conduct of its operations.[7]

In late 1944, Mountbatten authorized SOE to assume command of all secret organizations operating in Burma. Even at this point, though, there was
little communication between civilian authorities, military authorities, and

these clandestine intelligence groups. Taylor accurately portrays the scene as "a complex and murky world of political and military intrigue and ambition that surrounded the various Allied propaganda and espionage organizations."[8] The lack of cooperation among various intelligence authorities operating inside Burma meant that none of them were pursuing anything but the short-term objective of organizing local resistance groups. Maurice Collis wrote: "SOE was concerned only with easing the path for the army by organizing sabotage and rebellion behind the Japanese lines; it left political complications to take care of themselves."[9] Andrew Selth notes that in these frontier areas, there was "considerable confusion and even conflict" over how to treat hill peoples and what to promise them. As the war progressed, demands for local recruits increased. British, U.S., and Chinese regular armies and their paramilitaries all competed for the same recruits. Selth rightly argues that this situation gave rise to misunderstandings among frontier populations that "were to have considerable long-term consequences."[10]

In particular, SOE and other Allied organizations preyed on racial enmity that had existed before and been reinforced during the British colonial period. For example, during his assignment as a psychological warfare officer in Delhi, Calcutta, and Kandy, Leslie Glass wrote propaganda directed at potential recruits in the former frontier regions. The propaganda praised the "loyal" minorities in contrast to the "treacherous" Burmans who were "collaborating" with the Japanese.[11] Cruickshank's official history of SOE concludes that the organization's success in recruiting hill peoples into resistance units "was based as much on hostility to the Burmese of the plains as on loyalty to the British regime."[12] While it is difficult to measure the influence of such propaganda efforts, it is not difficult to conclude that the arming and training of various hill peoples to fight not just the Japanese, but also the Burmans who were cooperating with them, would create further difficulties for future political unity in the territory of Burma. Especially problematic was the propensity of various secret organizations to encourage "their" own levies to dream of political independence.

Inside Japanese Burma: The AFO

In July and August 1944, the Communist Party of Burma (CPB), the People's Revolutionary Party (PRP, later known as the Socialists), and some pro-resistance army officers met first in Dedaye in the delta and later in Rangoon to form a united front, called the Anti-Fascist Organization (AFO). This alliance was the result of spotty, though extensive, secret negotiations among individuals affiliated with each group. The CPB and the PRP both had their roots in small prewar, Marxist, anticolonial cells, comprised initially of about a dozen or fewer cadres. Many cadres were members of both groups in the 1930s.

Although scholars tend to attribute the increasing tensions between these two parties to personality conflicts among party leaders, significant ideological differences also became divisive with the onset of war. The main point of division crystallized around the issue of foreign assistance in achieving national independence. Most of the prewar Marxists who later became CPB leaders eschewed any kind of assistance from Japan. From the beginning of the Japanese campaign in Burma, they started organizing resistance. These nationalists/communists were willing to cooperate with other anti-Japanese forces, including the British. Adherents of the PRP, on the other hand, were among the nationalists who considered Japanese assistance an essential weapon in the battle for independence from the imperialist British. While some in the PRP claim to have realized the duplicitous motives of the Japanese early in the occupation, for the most part these politicians and PRP sympathizers in the army hesitated to organize anti-Japanese resistance but remained determined to block any British attempts to retake political control over Burmese territory. For the PRP, any kind of collaboration with the Allies was taboo.[13]

From the early months of 1942, individual communists flailed around Upper and Lower Burma trying to undermine the Japanese campaign. Within about a year, Thakin Soe emerged as the party leader. In his typically brash, independent style, he took charge of developing what became an extensive network of "underground" cells. The nonetheless skeletal underground had its greatest strength in the delta where Soe spent most of the war. Thakin Soe wrote several tracts that he taught in his small, secret political training courses in towns and villages, and he started training peasant guerrilla units in the delta as early as 1942. He sent his trainees to other regions to organize political training. His right-hand man, Thakin Tin Mya, ran such courses in the shadow of Japanese army headquarters in Rangoon.

The CPB also enjoyed great success at using legal, Japanese-sponsored associations to organize and train resistance fighters. From his cabinet position as agriculture (and later, transport) minister, Thakin Than Tun collected intelligence for Soe and other party members, and hosted clandestine party and resistance meetings at his ministerial home in the Golden Valley section of Rangoon.[14] Even more influential was the party's use of the two corporatist-style mass organizations established by the Japanese: the Dobama Sinyetha Party and the EAYL. Thakin Ba Hein and Thakin Hla Kyway used the offices and programs of the Dobama Sinyetha Party, a Japanese-backed political party, to train and equip members for the resistance forces. The EAYL—the most important organization in this period—absorbed thousands of boys discharged from the BIA, hundreds of young men who had been displaced from the short-lived thakin administrative committees in towns and villages, and thousands of students whose high schools were closed throughout the war. League branches became responsible for street cleaning, air raid warnings, literacy teaching, and mail delivery. Under the cover of these legal EAYL activities, a handful of CPB followers were able to conduct political training courses. Additionally, Japanese leaders sanctioned a program to bring youths from upcountry to Rangoon for three months' training in social work; Thakin Tin Mya organized secret training classes at night to prepare these youths for the coming rebellion. While it is impossible to arrive at an accurate estimate of how many CPB supporters and members were recruited through the EAYL, it is clear that communist-trained leaders of district and local branches at least had opportunities to spread the word among the sixty-five thousand youths registered with the league by 1944.[15]

The strategy of PRP leaders was quite different. Little emphasis was placed on building underground resistance and organizing outside of Rangoon. Instead of constructing and mobilizing social networks to be used explicitly against the state, the PRP chose to work within the state and keep party leadership as safe as possible throughout the war. Then when the British inevitably returned, these cadres would be available to lead Burma in a second anti-British revolution. In line with this, PRP leaders such as Kyaw Nyein and Ba Swe took positions in the Ba Maw government, which gave them legal cover to gather information on Japanese plans and strategy. Ba Swe used his position in the Keibotai (Civil Defence Corps) to stockpile weapons and build a small network of resisters.[16] PRP leaders also had close ties with some of the army officers plotting against the Japanese, and it is certain that they counted on the army to be the core of both the anti-Japanese and anti-British forces.

Resistance activities within the army came in waves. In October 1942, junior officers in the MPB, War Office, and battalion commands—many of whom had been prewar PRP members and maintained ties with party leaders throughout the war—began using army resources to publish and distribute anti-Japanese propaganda. This so-called Army Young Officers Resistance Group gradually expanded its clout within the MPB/War Office, which gave officers such as Maung Maung, Aung Gyi, Khin Maung Gale, and Tin Pe opportunities to build a network of loyal, anti-Japanese soldiers and officers in the tatmadaw. Eventually, in mid-1944, these junior officers convinced the far more cautious Gen. Aung San to prepare the Burma National Army (BNA; as the BDA had been renamed in 1943) for a full-scale uprising.

Preliminary discussions among army officers, CPB members, and PRP leaders did not bring about a workable alliance until August 1944, when an agreement to form the AFO resulted from three days of discussions at the BNA's San-pya (Model) Battalion in Pegu.[17] Aung San was elected president of the AFO, Thakin Than Tun its secretary general, and Thakin Soe its political leader.[18]

Both political parties compromised in formulating the "Leftist Unity" program of the new organization, which established the Japanese "as the main enemy" and allowed for conditional cooperation with the Allies provided that "the democratic Allied Powers" recognized the "provisional freedom Government" of the AFO.[19] Japanese-held territory was divided into ten districts, with a military commander and a political commissar appointed to head up the resistance efforts in each zone. Inside each district, these two officers arranged to hold courses in both "basic military training and political training" for "yebaws, EAYL groups, police groups, the Keibo-tai, etc."[20] Reflecting the united front nature of the AFO, these resistance zones were managed by pairs of military and political leaders, most of which included one who was identified later with the CPB and one who was either explicitly non-communist or else later identified with the PRP and the Socialist Party. Notably, as was the case with the BDA's three divisional command regions (see map 4), these zones did not extend past the edges of what the British had called Ministerial Burma (see map 3).

Inside Japanese Burma: The Minorities

Tensions between the exclusively Burman BIA troops and minorities living in territory the BIA occupied began soon after these troops entered Burma from Thailand. Indians, Chinese, and Shans endured BIA high-handedness. The Karens suffered the greatest harm, especially in Papun and Salween in the east and in other rural parts of the Irrawaddy Delta. In the delta district of Myaungmya alone, BIA troops may have killed as many as eighteen hundred when they destroyed four hundred Karen villages in early 1942. BIA units executed Karen men, women, and children and arrested whole villages simply for being Karen. There were some acts of retaliation by Karens against Burmans, and "what amounted to a race war raged among the Burman and Karen communities," according to Selth.[21]

Many historians point to this outbreak of violence as having irrevocably sealed a split between Karens and Burmans. In the words of one Karen leader, "How could anyone expect the Karen people to trust the Burmans after what happened during the war—the murder and slaughter of so many Karen people and the robbing of so many Karen villages? After all this, how could anyone seriously expect us to trust any Burman government in Rangoon?"[22] Unease among Karen survivors continued well into 1943, although both Burman and Japanese leaders attempted to smooth things over. Two Karens, including long-time Karen nationalist (and former Barnum and Bailey–Ringling Brothers Circus performer) San Po Thin, were brought into Dr. Ba Maw's government in 1943. Eventually, Aung San,

Than Tun, and other Burmese nationalists were able to convince Karen leaders to sanction the raising of a Karen army battalion in late 1944. The 170–man battalion was led by Saw (Hanson) Kya Doe, the only indigenous person to have been trained at Sandhurst in the prewar period. Kya Doe joined only after Aung San, Than Tun, and Ne Win convinced him that Aung San truly intended to turn his army against the Japanese and that the Karen battalion would be all Karen, with no Burmans in command or in the ranks. In the AFO agreement, Kya Doe was assigned command of the largely Karen western portion of the delta during the anti-Japanese uprising, mainly in order to deter another outbreak of communal riots.[23]

British attempts to organize Karen resistance deep inside Japanese-held territory in the delta were successful at the outset of the war, though ultimately tragic. In the Karen Hills and in the delta, a handful of British army officers had remained behind after the retreat of British forces. British airdrops in 1943–44 brought supplies and reinforcements to organize and equip the Karen underground. Japanese authorities discovered these activities, and brutally crushed this cell of the resistance. In the eastern hills, where there was less Japanese control over Karen territory, a more extensive array of Allied-backed resistance forces emerged among Karens and Karenni. By late 1944, a total strength of ten thousand guerrillas operated in the hills running from Tenasserim as far north as Pyinmana. As many as twelve thousand weapons were air-dropped to these guerrillas, who are credited with killing more than twelve thousand retreating Japanese troops.[24]

The contribution of AFO-affiliated guerrillas in Arakan has been overlooked by Burmese and Western scholars. Given its strategic location near the frontier fringe and the Allies' disastrous failure to retake Arakan in 1943, this area was crucial to the success of the 1944–45 reoccupation campaign.[25] Much of Arakan had come under BIA control in early 1942 when Bo Yan Aung's forces occupied the region. Soon after, the Japanese Burma Area Army ordered BIA troops to withdraw, but Bo Yan Aung secretly deposited weapons with Arakanese who had been members of the prewar nationalist movement. In 1943, Arakanese resistance leaders convinced Japanese military leaders in Arakan to arm the growing numbers of volunteer troops, ostensibly to prepare to defend Arakan against the Allies. The Japanese officially raised these troops, known as the Arakan Defence Army (ADA), in the area of Myohaung (now called Mrauk-U) and provided not only arms but also military training. In 1944, ADA leaders persuaded Japanese military authorities to post some ADA units in Palewa, the northernmost part of Arakan, close to the Indian border. From here, Arakanese resistance leader Nyo Tun was able to travel back and forth to India to establish this ADA garrison as a liaison point between the Burmese resistance forces in Japanese-held Burma and resistance leaders operating in

India. This base became the transit point through which underground resistance leaders from Japanese-held territory in Burma were able to sneak out to India for training and later back into Burma from India to prepare for the uprising.[26]

There was one other Japanese-sponsored army raised inside of Burma, in the Chin Hills. Most of the Chin Hills were never occupied by the Japanese, but in the area around Tiddim, the Japanese established an outpost with the intention that this area be maintained under Japanese control in the event of a decision to move on to India. There are few sources on this outpost, but the memoir of Chin leader Vum Ko Hau depicts a sort of mini-BDA established by Japanese authorities in the Tiddim area. Much as in Arakan, the leaders of the Japanese-sponsored, corporatist-style Chin Leaders' Freedom League persuaded the Japanese to organize a "short-term Japanese Military Academy for the Chin Political leaders at . . . Headquarters in Tiddim."[27] And like both the ADA in Arakan and the BDA in central and southern Burma, the indigenous participants in the Chin Defense Army used the privileges, skills, weapons, and legal cover of this institution to organize secretly for the anti-Japanese resistance from mid-1944 onward and did so within some kind of alliance with the AFO.

Tenuous Linkages

The complexity of bringing all of these former enemies together for the second Burma campaign required negotiation and—more important—a series of unauthorized decisions and deliberate choices to overlook conflicting political visions of post-Japanese Burma. Official records and the extensive range of participants' memoirs make it clear that this complicated alliance must be considered remarkable both for the seeming impossibility of its realization and for the way in which it made inevitable the centrifugal nature of postwar politics.

Until mid-1943, nearly all Allied-sponsored political, military, and intelligence operations were united in their distrust of Burmese "collaborators" in the Japanese-sponsored government, army, and political organizations inside of Burma. Most were similarly united in their objective not simply to reconquer Burma and reestablish colonial rule but also to punish the disloyal Burmese. However, in mid-1943, an important development complicated the simple conflation of Japanese and Burmese as enemies of the Allies. Major Hugh Seagrim, one of the British officers who had remained behind in the Karen Hills in the delta, sent a message out to SOE's Force 136 confirming rumors that Burmese nationalists were organizing an anti-Japanese underground resistance and that they probably had Aung San's tacit approval.[28] After many failed attempts to air-drop a wireless transmitter and operator into plains Burma, Force 136 finally managed to get a wireless set into the delta hills and establish contact with Seagrim, who reconfirmed the validity of his earlier report.[29]

At long last, SOE had what it considered reliable evidence of a resistance movement. Cruickshank argues that this finding sparked fears among SOE leaders in India that such an uprising could occur without British oversight. Special Operations Executive urgently expanded its attempt to contact the resistance forces inside Burma proper, with the hope that there was still time to control Burman nationalist sentiment and to use the resistance movement strategically to defeat the Japanese.[30]

This marked a new source of tensions among Allied forces in the China-Burma-India theater. Over the next year, British *civilian* officials, still sore at being chased out of Burma by the disloyal Burmese, tenaciously maintained that there should be no alliance between the Allies and the Burman National Army and AFO. Governor-in-exile Reginald Dorman-Smith and the Civil Affairs Service (Burma)(CAS[B])—both based in Simla, India—became more determined that direct British rule be reinstated in Burma upon the Japanese defeat. They argued that an alliance with the young nationalists planning the resistance inside Burma would give the nationalists too much leverage to advance their demands for postwar independence. Critical of SOE's activities, British civilian authorities at Simla were convinced that SOE's secret agents were grasping at straws. Glass wrote: "After a long period of expensive failure outside Europe, SOE were [*sic*] desperate for any sort of operational success."[31]

Nonetheless, some military authorities—and most important, SEAC Commander in Chief Mountbatten—saw the potential benefits of working with the anti-Japanese BNA and AFO organizations in the second Burma campaign. As Taylor argued, "By the end of 1944, the battle lines for the political conflict were pretty clearly drawn between the governor and CAS(B) officers on the one hand and the BNA on the other, with [SOE's] Force 136 and Mountbatten in the middle, concerned primarily with getting on with the war."[32]

The Allies: Unauthorized Decisions, Ignored Consequences

SOE's unique position outside the established military and civilian chains of command gave the organization a free hand in establishing clandestine linkages with those groups inside Burma considered to be "traitors" and "quislings" by other Allied organizations. The most well known of these linkages came through SOE's liaison with Thakin Thein Pe, one of the prewar nationalists who rejected alliance with the fascist Japanese and published and distributed anti-Japanese propaganda, especially in

Upper Burma, into the early months of the occupation. In May 1942, he and Thakin Tin Shwe escaped to India to try to forge a temporary anti-Japanese alliance with British authorities there. A year and a half later, they were finally introduced to SOE agents in Delhi, who concluded that they were genuinely anti-Japanese and put them to work as liaisons to plains resistance groups inside Burma. In December 1943, Tin Shwe sneaked back into Burma carrying an official message on microfilm to Thakin Soe and other resistance leaders. Tin Shwe returned two months later, bringing Arakanese thakin leader and former BIA member Nyo Tun with him, along with documentary evidence of the AFO's resistance movement. This journey laid the groundwork for building a network of messengers to carry information back and forth between India and Rangoon. The network also provided protection and intelligence for SOE teams to infiltrate along the Arakan coast and set up wireless radio stations for communications.

The opening of these channels marked the beginning of a small, but significant, flow of at least seventy Burmese "collaborators" (i.e., those who appeared to be helping the Japanese) across Arakan, into India, and as far as Columbo, Ceylon, for short-term, SOE-sponsored resistance training. The large number of Arakanese trainees proved important for two reasons. First, Arakanese leader Nyo Tun's involvement was particularly significant, as he was able to revisit Arakan long enough to establish channels for overland communications between SOE/Force 136 and its Burmese liaisons in India, and Burmese nationalists in the plains. Second, these trainees were sent back into Arakan to bring the underground up to speed on Allied plans, and their efforts no doubt facilitated the rapid Allied advance into Arakan in 1944.

In September 1944, these linkages between SOE/Force 136 and the AFO were firmed up when Thakin Thein Pe's proposal to the Supreme Allied Commander (SAC) "for a policy of trust and cooperation" was accepted by the commander of Force 136 without consultation with the SAC's office or the civilian hierarchy at Simla. The acceptance "promised immediate military assistance [to the thakins] and sympathetic consideration for political claims in the future in return for collaboration against the Japanese." Official army historian Donnison further writes: "It is indeed remarkable that official assurances [from the Force 136 commander] which contained such far reaching implications for the future should have been made without consulting the Chief Civil Affairs Officer, and apparently without the approval of the Supreme Allied Commander."[33] Later in November 1944, Colin Mackenzie, the commander of Force 136, went so far as to promise large numbers of weapons and other supplies to the Burmese resistance movement; he never consulted London.[34]

When these unauthorized decisions to establish a formal alliance with the

AFO and BNA (hereafter, AFO/BNA) came to light, civilian bureaucrats at Simla were outraged but could not find a sympathetic ear from Mountbatten and the military. As Allied operations into Arakan and the Chin and Kachin regions progressed in the first two months of 1945, news arrived at Kandy (Mountbatten's headquarters for the SEAC) that the AFO's nationalist rising against the Japanese would begin by the end of March. Cruickshank writes that SOE and Mountbatten were aware of the potential long-term implications of teaming up with the AFO/BNA, but "believed that to accept their help was the lesser of two evils. The alternative might be to fight large numbers of Burmese in addition to the Japanese."[35] While trying to appease his civilian critics at Simla, Mountbatten nonetheless quickly decided to join forces with the Burmese nationalists in order both to keep the resistance under control and to ease the path of Allied forces into Burma. Mountbatten laid out this eleventh-hour decision in a telegram to the British chiefs of staff sent, ironically, on March 27, 1945 (the day the AFO/BNA commenced its uprising):

> While the assistance we may expect from such a rising was not an essential part of my plans [to reconquer Burma] there is no doubt that it will provide a welcome bonus which may well help to speed the capture of Rangoon . . .
>
> Such action by SOE will naturally involve extending a degree of recognition to this rising and there is some danger from civil affairs' point of view that such recognition will give offence to the more respectable elements of the population. But it must be remembered that the more respectable elements[36] have been inactive while the elements who are about to undertake this action comprise the active politically conscious and organised elements in the country—those in fact who are in a position to give trouble or not to give it depending on our present decision.[37]

Mountbatten also wrote in this telegram that he thought the Allies could take "the wind out of their [the AFO/BNA] sails by having made it possible for them to be national heroes with the British rather than against them."[38] Mountbatten also recognized that if he did not authorize the alliance, there would be international recriminations when liberal forces in the United States and Britain learned of Britain's refusal to join together with Burmese nationalists to fight for the liberation of their own country.

It is unclear from Mountbatten's writings whether he really believed the Allies could successfully contain Burmese aspirations for independence after teaming up with the AFO/BNA in the second campaign. However, it is clear that Mountbatten was aware of the political implications of the alliance with the AFO/BNA from its inception. After the war, Burmese nationalists credited Mountbatten with great courage in defending his allied AFO/BNA partners from Dorman-Smith's and CAS(B)'s attempts to disembowel the nationalist organizations in 1945; however, this interpretation overlooks the fact that the Supreme Allied Commander nonetheless insisted that AFO/BNA participants in the anti-Japanese campaign "must work their passage home." The SAC also ordered Force 136 agents working with AFO/BNA groups to make clear that eventually all arms would have to be surrendered and that no promises regarding Burma's postwar political status be discussed "with any isolated section of the community."[39]

This made for an ambivalent alliance, particularly as the regular Allied forces moved into central Burma and came into contact with BNA and AFO cells. In the weeks leading up to and immediately following the revolt of the BNA on March 27, 1945, clandestine Force 136 Jedburgh teams parachuted into central Burma, ignored the ban on discussions of the political future of Burma, and made promises that neither SOE/Force 136 nor any other Allied or British governmental organization intended to keep. According to an unsympathetic British civil affairs officer: "Some Force 136 officers, flushed with success at their popularity with young Burmans, whom they would not have to try to control later, were sure that they knew much more about Burma than any old stager, and opposed the disarming of their young protégés."[40] In an interview with a Force 136 officer who led resistance efforts behind Japanese lines first in Arakan in 1944 and later in central Burma in 1945, Taylor confirmed the rash behavior on the part of Force 136 officers in February and March 1945: "Orders probably were ignored in the euphoria of antifascist collaboration behind Japanese lines."[41]

The decentralized nature of the AFO's resistance plans and the tendency in British histories to understate the role of the Burmese resistance in the anti-Japanese battle makes it difficult to understand the mechanics of how BNA, AFO, Allied land forces, and the wide range of irregular levies worked together in the campaign to reoccupy Burma. Mountbatten wrote in his postwar report on SEAC operations that BNA units did not begin "to operate in regular coordination with our units and formations" until June 1945.[42] There is evidence that relations were contentious from the very beginning, particularly between the AFO/BNA fighters and the civil affairs personnel assigned to trail the Allied land forces in the campaign. In early April 1945, Mountbatten convened a meeting with senior civil affairs' officers in which he issued a stern warning to civil affairs personnel who were ignoring his orders to work side by side with AFO/BNA troops. He later wrote of the meeting: "I was determined that no section of the Burmese people should be able to claim that we were returning to the country in a spirit of revenge or reprisal."[43]

Moreover, irregular forces raised by the dozen or so Allied clandestine operations reported great suspicion of their new allies, the AFO/BNA. Roger Hilsman, a U.S. intelligence officer who had been working since

1943 with Kachin levies under the authority of Detachment 101, Office of Strategic Services (OSS), reported the "trepidation" with which he received orders from headquarters to work with the BNA.

> For both our guerrillas and the command group, the adjustment was strange. We were joined by about a hundred ethnic Burmese wearing Japanese army uniforms with Burmese national markings and armed with Japanese weapons. Their commanding officer was Bo Tha Shwei. Every morning at dawn, he would assemble the company and lead them in calisthenics to Japanese military commands.
>
> No one in our group slept as well as before. The individual BNA soldiers and officers seemed friendly enough, but the Japanese uniforms and drill commands made us nervous. As a test, we decided to send them out on an ambush. They went, they came back a few days later saying that the ambush had been sprung on a Japanese motorized patrol, and that two Japanese had been killed. Our agents confirmed the report. Gradually we came to accept them.[44]

Given the propaganda efforts of the various Allied organizations operating in this theater, which had identified central Burmans as enemies along with the Japanese, it should not be surprising that many did not sleep comfortably in camps shared with their new allies.

The AFO/BNA: Quick Decisions, Convenient Smoke Screens

Force 136 officers were not alone in ignoring long-term consequences in order to forge an alliance with the AFO/BNA. Leaders of the AFO/BNA similarly chose to ignore the implications of the concessions they made in their alliance with the British. In fact, the contours of postwar and postcolonial Burmese political conflict began to take shape behind a smoke screen forged in the weeks and months surrounding the original overture to SOE in 1943 and the March 27, 1945, uprising against the Japanese.

The compromise reached by the CPB, PRP, and BNA leaders to establish the AFO in August 1944 included a caveat that although these indigenous forces would consider working with other anti-Japanese allies to rid Burma of fascism, the AFO would also fight against any force that did not recognize the AFO's "provisional freedom government." Clearly, this was intended to address the concerns of the BNA and PRP leaders who feared the British would simply reestablish colonial rule when the Japanese had been defeated. It also was probably aimed at pressing British authorities to promise concessions toward independence in return for AFO/BNA cooperation in the anti-Japanese campaign.

British authorities from Churchill and the secretary of state for Burma in London to the governor and civil affairs officers in Simla, and Mountbatten, at no point seriously entertained the idea of recognizing any indigenous provisional government at the close of hostilities. In early 1943, Dorman-Smith proposed a gradual move to Burmese independence within the Commonwealth after a seven- to ten-year period of reconstruction and tutelage by his government. This proposal set the general terms of the debate that continued among the prime minister's office, the Burma Office in London, the government of Burma at Simla, CAS(B) officials in India (who were planning reconstruction efforts), Mountbatten's office, and British firms (who were less than eager to take their capital back to a Burma with an uncertain political future). Although a handful of Burmese advisors to Dorman-Smith at Simla suggested this minimum of seven years of restored colonial rule would cause political problems among the Burmese, there was scant high-level discussion of any shorter period of British tutelage.[45]

Given the consistency of the British stance on this issue, it is surprising that there appeared to be no recognition of it by Aung San and other nationalists inside Burma. Why not? The best explanation is that the AFO/BNA leaders, like SOE and Mountbatten, focused on the short-term goal of defeating the Japanese and sidestepped the thorny, longer-term issues of Burma's future. During the establishment of communications and cooperation between SOE in India and the Burmese nationalists in central Burma in 1943–44, there developed a gradual, though probably not consciously fabricated, smoke screen between the two sides through which the new partners perceived the broad outlines of each other's positions and the benefits to be gained by cooperation but avoided seeing clearly the details that did not square with each side's longer-range political objectives.

The key to the development of this smoke screen was Thakin Thein Pe, who, as Taylor rightly argues, set the terms by which each side could work with the other. When the AFO was formed in August 1944, its leaders appointed Thein Pe as AFO liaison to the Allies. Over the next several weeks, he wrote "Toward Better Mutual Understanding and Greater Cooperation," the political treatise that established the smoke screen. According to Taylor, this document "served as the basis of the understanding between the anti-fascist Burmese and the British in India, but also it became a guide to international political conditions for the leaders of the anti-Japanese united front, the Anti-Fascist Organization isolated in Burma."[46]

Heavily influenced by the doctrines of Earl Browder, the U.S. Communist who led his party into a popular front arrangement with the bourgeois Democratic Party to fight fascism, Thein Pe wrote this September 1944 essay in English for Mountbatten. The thesis favorably impressed Mountbatten, as demonstrated in his March 1945 decision to allow SOE agents to arm the AFO. Key to the document's success with SEAC and Mountbatten was the moderate tone of its demands. In calling for independence, the thesis made no mention of the AFO demand of immediate recognition of its provisional government, but instead included a more general statement that "our national aspiration is the complete independence of Burma."[47] Elsewhere, Thein Pe recalled that this tone was deliberate: "I said we did not expect that these aims [of national independence] could be achieved overnight." To Mountbatten, he cleverly wrote: "Have no doubts. We will solve our differences peacefully after the war."[48]

Thein Pe's essay was also directed at his equally cautious AFO audience. The thesis, which was immediately smuggled into Burma and distributed throughout the underground, warned AFO leaders that "even . . . cooperation with reservations" would benefit "no one but the enemy."[49] Taylor argues that the thesis "provided the basic outline of the policy that the AFO, BNA and communist leaders followed" when they undertook their uprising against the Japanese in 1945. Moreover, the document gave AFO leaders insight into international events unavailable to them via other channels.[50]

The dissemination of the "Mutual Understanding" essay on both sides of the Indo-Burmese border likely provided the smoke screen necessary for the two sides to work together. The British effectively ignored the AFO's demand for immediate recognition of its provisional government, while AFO leaders conceded Thein Pe's argument that they needed first to cooperate with other anti-fascist forces and second to pursue what had in August 1944 been formulated as an absolute minimum demand for immediate political independence.

Once the alliance was forged, however, the smoke screen began to clear and the alliance to splinter. In the wake of the successful December 1944–January 1945 Arakan campaign, Mountbatten ordered the disarmament of the indigenous guerrillas who had fought for SOE throughout the campaign. After two months of fighting against the Japanese, Arakanese resistance forces initially wavered, but leaders Nyo Tun and U Seinda persuaded their guerrillas to comply with the British order. Only days after disarmament, CAS(B) officers arrived and began arresting many of those who had worked with SOE in the campaign; those who were not arrested were interrogated and roughed up.[51] A handful of Arakanese political leaders went underground, hoping to link up with the AFO/BNA in the plains to secure assistance in fighting off CAS(B) oppressors. However, they did not reach Rangoon until April 1945, when AFO/BNA leaders had already fully committed their forces to the British.

Additionally, the tensions among civil affairs, Mountbatten, and SOE at headquarters in Kandy, India, and London delayed the delivery of the promised arms to AFO/BNA forces in central Burma. Maung Maung, one of the AFO/BNA leaders based in the War Office as Aung San's aide-de-camp, claims that prior to the March 27, 1945, uprising, the BNA received no arms whatsoever from the British, and the Burmese communists in the underground "received no more than 100 Sten guns and small arms."[52]

The signs of incompatibility had become clear, and despite repeated attempts by Mountbatten and Lt. Gen. William Slim, commander of the Fourteenth Army to arrange a meeting between Aung San and a ranking British officer in the campaign, Aung San balked until May 16, when it became apparent that his troops could no longer hold towns or villages without a struggle against the incoming British troops and civil affairs personnel. During the month and a half before that date, the smoke screen dissipated. As all anti-Japanese forces realized that the campaign would be brief and successful, the AFO/BNA and the returning British rulers began working feverishly to deal with the political implications of their increasingly untenable alliance. With the common enemy vanquished, all eyes turned toward state rebuilding.

Conclusion

The necessarily centrifugal, secret nature of raising the resistance in the shadows of Japanese control tied together loosely the networks of armed guerrillas and soldiers fighting *against* the same enemy but fighting *for* very different visions of the future. The tenuous and decentralized character of the anti-Japanese resistance had at least three lasting implications for postwar, postcolonial Burma. First, the often uncoordinated, clandestine Allied intelligence units operating in Burma's frontiers created and aggravated racial tensions between ethnic-minority levies in both central Burma and the frontier regions, on the one hand, and the Burmans living in central and Lower Burma, on the other hand, for decades to come. Some U.S. and British intelligence officers promised minorities postwar autonomy, power, and independence, none of which they could deliver. Moreover, British SOE agents used extensive anti-Burman propaganda in these regions. The propaganda played on alleged historical grievances but also reminded Karens, Kachins, and Chins that the plains Burmans were collaborating with the treacherous Japanese. It seems likely that in the early days of the tenuous postcolonial Union government, these experiences convinced Karen and Kachin leaders that their former wartime allies in Britain and the United States would support them as they pursued their own vision of postcolonial Burma and prepared to resist violently the Burman nationalists' vision of future Burma.

Second, the way the resistance was organized within the AFO channeled certain members into war-fighting roles and others into noncombat, political roles in Rangoon governmental positions. This division of labor occurred largely along party lines and gave the two major postwar political parties (the CPB and PRP) mutually exclusive bases of power. Specifically, Thakin Soe's communist underground built a fairly extensive following in the Ir-rawaddy Delta and in rural Upper Burma. Most of those who joined the communist rebellion in the postwar period had received guerrilla training through this wartime underground. Meanwhile, those who became identi-fied with the PRP (later renamed the Socialist Party) focused their efforts on using governmental positions and resources to fight the Japanese from within the Japanese regime. Consequently, the postwar Socialist Party had many leaders with governing experience in the capital but very little mass following to rally support for its government during the civil war that erupted in postcolonial Burma.

Finally, the tenuous linkages forged between Aung San's army and the Al-lied military forces eliminated none of the hostility harbored by most British soldiers and civil servants returning to Burma in 1945. The official reports of these British returnees throughout the 1945–48 period refer to Aung San's forces as "quislings" and show how extensively these Britons scrambled to try to imprison, disarm, and demobilize them. On their side, Aung San's men considered the British forces deployed in retaking Burma as "helpful" in ousting the Japanese but not much more. Furthermore, in the 1945–48 British interregnum, they never trusted the British and began making preparations to fight them for independence even before the tenu-ous linkages among resistance forces were formed.

4

Making Peace and Making Armies, 1945–48

My ideal is narrow and limited. I want to see the British Empire preserved for a few more generations in its strength and splendour.

Winston Churchill, 1937

When the Jap [*sic*] War broke out we were left undefended at the mercy of the most ruthless invaders after [the British applied] the "scorched earth" policy most liberally throughout the country. . . . Centuries old monasteries at Bahan, Rangoon, were burnt to ashes . . . and I wonder to whom the poor monks should now apply for compensation. At that time I was Librarian of the Bernard Free Library at the Rangoon Corporation Buildings where drunken British soldiers molested my Assistant, Daw Hnin Mai . . . and we all had no redress . . .

Now the British have come back . . .

U Khant, from letter to Leopold Amery,
former secretary of state for Burma and India, 1945

As in the colonial period, warfare in post-Japanese Burma was imagined, planned, and carried out entirely within the British-drawn borders. After the surprisingly speedy reoccupation campaign in the first six months of 1945, anti-Japanese allies quickly turned on each other, positioning themselves for the coming campaign in which Burma's future would be the prize. In the closing moments of the anti-Japanese campaign and during the first few months after the recapture of Rangoon from the Japanese, no single organization held an unchallenged claim over what

88   *Chapter 4*

remained of an administrative apparatus in Burma. Each component group of the anti-Japanese resistance sought to reconstruct the postwar state according to its own vision. Most of these visions were mutually exclusive.

With no clear heir to the post-Japanese state, what emerged was a random patchwork of competing claims for authority, diffused geographically, functionally, and violently throughout the Burmese territory. Allies-turned-enemies were everywhere, threatening not borders but instead irreconcilable visions of the postwar state. Early in this post-Japanese period, the allies-turned-enemies channeled elite-level conflict into a series of negotiations over the reconstruction of a single state army. All sides brought to the bargaining table conflicting objectives and prepared for war against their former allies in the territory mapped out as colonial Burma.

The three major wartime allies who became peacetime combatants for the reins of the state were (1) the Allied Land Forces, Southeast Asia (ALF-SEA), including the British army and led by SAC Admiral Lord Louis Mountbatten; (2) the British Civil Affairs Service (Burma) (CAS[B]), led by angry former colonial officers and backed by the Governor-in-exile Reginald Dorman-Smith; and (3) the mostly ethnic-Burman nationalist organizations, the Anti-Fascist Organization (AFO) and the Burma National Army (BNA, the new name of the Japanese-sponsored BDA), both led by Aung San.

For the Allied military forces, Burma was neither a destination nor an endpoint, but a stepping stone. From April through July 1945, the soldiers of the British and Allied land forces marched swiftly through Burma and prepared to wage what most expected to be a long, bloody campaign to oust the Japanese from the rest of Southeast Asia. For Mountbatten, moving his troops on to the rest of Asia required establishing order in this staging point. However, as soon as Allied forces cleared major cities and towns of Japanese soldiers in early 1945, the other two principal components of the anti-Japanese alliance moved in to fill the void left by advancing land forces. Immediately, the AFO/BNA guerrillas and CAS(B) agents began trying to disarm, cripple, and destroy each other. Political, often armed struggles erupted in towns and villages in central Burma, where former colonial officials wearing civil affairs uniforms clashed with armed Burmese nationalists. Each group wanted to establish some kind of state authority in the name of either a return to colonial rule (for CAS[B]) or a revolution for independence (for the nationalists). Each of these claimants identified anti-Japanese allies as new political enemies.

Under these conditions, a peaceful resumption of prewar governance was impossible. In fact, peace of any sort was unlikely given that post-Japanese Burma was comprised of a society armed to the hilt, politically mobilized as never before, and facing disastrous economic times. By July 1945, Mount-batten, CAS(B) officials, and Burmese nationalist leaders recognized that a restoration of some degree of law and order was in everyone's interest. Order, they agreed, could be restored only by defusing local power struggles and negotiating a settlement about which armed units were to be the en-forcers of the post-Japanese peace. In other words, peacemaking entailed creating an army of peace enforcers.

Over the next few months, senior military and civilian officials from both Britain and Burma negotiated the shape and constitution of the postwar armed forces. Again, the three major players—Allied military leaders, CAS(B), and the AFO/BNA—took irreconcilable positions. British army leaders attempted to constitute the new military under the control of in-digenous minority officers, while British civil affairs personnel quite inde-pendently worked to disembowel the AFO/BNA. In the meantime, leaders of the latter two groups tried to maintain their forces, armed and intact, be-cause they recognized they might need to fight the British one more time for independence.

During the second half of 1945, all these war fighters forged compro-mises, undermined them, and haphazardly and unintentionally laid down the institutional framework not only for the national army of an indepen-dent Burma but also for the reconstitution of a state based in Rangoon. This process of army and state re-creation produced an unsustainable, bifurcated military structure that defied any strategic or tactical logic, but nonetheless provided an ad hoc solution to the vexing political problem of who was en-titled to defend and pacify Burma. In negotiations over army reconstruc-tion, political ploys, misunderstandings, and calculated tactics produced two armies with two incompatible ideas about what the map of independ-ent "Burma" would look like and which "Burmese" would take charge of it. Anti-Japanese allies spent the early postwar period fashioning two Burmas—one the British would bequeath to those who had stayed loyal to the British throughout the entire war and one the nationalists would claim for those who had fought first against the British and later against the Japan-ese. "Loyalist" Burma would be comprised of mostly ethnic minorities, who lived in territory located both in the central and frontier regions. The other Burma would be dominated by ethnic Burmans, who lived mostly in the central regions.

The haggling over the constitution of postwar, postcolonial Burma played out in negotiations over military affairs. Here, anti-Japanese allies created a nonviable military that brought together a number of incompatible tradi-tions, territories, factions, and fantasies. These contradictions set the pa-rameters for the institutional and political struggles that paralyzed the Burmese state throughout the early years of independence.

Military Administration

The most destabilizing force to reenter Burma after the Japanese occupation was the CAS(B). Founded by the British government in Simla, India, in February 1943, the CAS(B) spent the next two years planning the military administration to be set up after the British invasion of Burma. During the war, leaders of the CAS(B) and the British Burma government-in-exile in Simla (led by Governor Dorman-Smith) opposed the Allied military alliance with the Burmese nationalists in central Burma, considering the latter to constitute what they called the "Burma Traitor Army." This opposition was not simply a refusal to cooperate with a group that had collaborated with the Japanese. More important, as planners for post-Japanese government, the CAS(B) disputed whose Burmese should inherit independent Burma, once it became apparent that some form of independence was inevitable. Would it be Mountbatten's Burmese—the ethnic-majority Burman nationalists in the BNA, AFO guerrillas, and the Thakin Party? Or the CAS(B)'s and Dorman-Smith's Burmese—the "loyalist," mostly ethnic-minority Burmese who had fled to India in 1942 alongside British colonial officials?

Guidance from London was inconclusive. The War Cabinet reluctantly permitted Mountbatten to ally formally with the AFO/BNA at the end of March 1945, but ordered him to warn the Burmese nationalists that their crime of siding with the Japanese in 1941–42 had not been forgotten, though good behavior might earn them forgiveness.[1] The alliance went forward, but not without great ambivalence. Under the command of Maj. Gen. Charles Frederick Byrde Pearce, CAS(B) officials based in India as well as those field officers trailing the regular forces on the Burma campaign worked consistently to undermine the alliance with the AFO/BNA. Although Mountbatten ultimately fired Pearce for this subversion, and the British army eventually reined in the CAS(B), the latter's military administration did much damage during its brief five months of operation by creating new tensions and exacerbating old ones among the British and Burmese vying for control of postwar Burma. In the space of a few months, Pearce and the CAS(B) had launched the postwar battle over Burma's future.

To be fair, the British civil affairs officers who trailed regular Allied forces on the reconquest campaign in early 1945 faced a terribly confusing situation. Most of these officers had been bureaucrats or business officials in prewar Burma and were prepared to resume their duties of three years earlier. Few were prepared for the chaos they met. Gone were many of the old tools of rule: district headquarters had been burned down or bombed in air raids, rice supplies destroyed, town jails dismantled, police forces dispersed, and the all-important perquisites, including social and sporting clubs, had disappeared. Throughout the country, the colonial state had vanished, the economy was in ruins, food was scarce, malaria was on the rise, and there were as many as fifty thousand weapons in private circulation.[2] Into this vortex marched the British officials most bent on revenge.

In the reoccupation campaign, civil affairs officers raced into towns and villages across central Burma, seeking to be the first to establish local administration. In many instances, AFO/BNA guerrillas had remained behind when Allied forces advanced and set up their own local administrative bodies, much as BIA units had in the wake of the Japanese invasion in 1942. Arriving later, the CAS(B) officials often used their sweeping powers of arrest to eliminate these Burmese competitors. One nationalist remembered that in central Burma "CAS(B) started putting us in jail on charges of rape, murder, arson, dacoity. We were called 'traitors.' "[3]

The CAS(B)'s field practices included other harsh measures. On May 1, 1945, the military administration issued its "Currency Declaration," which proclaimed that all Japanese currency was valueless. This demonetization policy hit poor farmers and villagers the hardest. Farmers had already sold that year's rice crop to the Japanese army in December 1944 and had no British or Indian currency with which to buy seed for the planting season. Additionally, the CAS(B) conscripted labor to rebuild villages, roads, and lines of communications. Buildings and paper stocks were confiscated. The CAS(B) established an immediate 6 P.M. to 6 A.M. curfew, price controls on commodities, and restrictions on claiming "enemy and ownerless" property. Despite promises that land revenues would not be collected, civil affairs officers started demanding immediate remissions. As Maung Maung writes, "For the average Burman, the coming of the new 'liberators' was no different from their earlier experiences; both meant effective regulation of his life by outsiders."[4]

When the Allied forces reoccupied Rangoon on May 3, 1945, trailing CAS(B) officers stepped up their pressure on the Allied land forces leadership to break formal ties with the Burmese nationalists in the AFO/BNA and to reestablish linkages with and promote the interests of those indigenous peoples who had sided with the British throughout the war. Pearce waited less than a week after the recapture of Rangoon to demand that Allied military authorities arrest Aung San for trial as a "war criminal" and to declare the BNA illegal.[5] When Mountbatten heard this, he fired Pearce and replaced him with Maj.-Gen. Hubert Rance, a career military officer with no previous experience in Asia but with long-standing personal ties to Mountbatten. However, Rance's appointment came too late to make meaningful accommodation because Pearce's issue of the Aung San arrest order created an irreparable break in relations with the AFO/BNA.

Setting the Agenda for Remaking the Army

Given that each of the major players in central Burma claimed primacy for their own army as the singularly legitimate enforcer of law and order, it is remarkable that these political enemies agreed on broad principles for constructing a postwar army within only three months of reoccupying Rangoon. The early post-Japanese situation was ripe for conflict. There were probably close to one hundred thousand armed soldiers and guerrillas of one army or another in Burma during May–August 1945. Their presence did not restore order but rather inflamed disorder due to the unresolved struggle over who would remain a soldier and who would not, who would carry a gun in the future and who would not, who would enforce what kind of order and who would be subject to those enforcers.

By July 1945, Burmese nationalists and British civilian and military leaders came to a vague but durable agreement about the future organization of armed force: that it would be one comprised of two politically and ethnically homogeneous units, the soldiers and officers of which could not be guaranteed to be loyal beyond the unit. Hardly a textbook design for combat efficiency or for safeguarding national sovereignty, this organizational plan represented a patched-together political solution that in the short term would defuse an explosive situation. In the long term, this structure was unsustainable and made the army the most significant site of post-Japanese political contestation.

Competing Visions of the Postwar Army

How did this two-army, two-Burma compromise position come to pass? In 1944 British political and military leaders began formulating plans for the reoccupation of Burma. At Simla, India, Gov. Dorman Smith and the bureaucrats staffing the government-in-exile of Burma plotted their return to Burma. In 1944, as Allied forces regained control of the frontier regions in Burma with the assistance of Chin and Kachin units, the Simla government began formulating plans to create an army of regulars for reoccupied Burma, in order to be able to wage what was expected to be a long campaign to defeat the Japanese in Southeast Asia. The main objective was to bring these loyal, armed levies under the centralized control of a resurrected British Burma Army. From December 1944 to June 1945, Simla authorized the establishment of eight mostly ethnically demarcated battalions. This was indeed a reincarnation of the prewar army and was made up of indigenous people who constituted the "Burmese" Dorman-Smith intended to inherit political authority when the transfer of power took place.[6]

Geographically, Dorman-Smith's plans were based on the idea of establishing two Burmas after the war. One would encompass the Upper Burma, central plains, delta and southern archipelago areas. This "Burma" would be protected by an army made up of Dorman-Smith's loyal "Burmese"—mostly Karens, Indians and Anglo-Burmans. The other Burma in this plan was the territory around the borders. Authority over this territory would not be transferred to a postcolonial government in Rangoon until the residents chose to become part of that country. The army in these areas would remain British-officered, with the rank-and-file coming from the hill peoples who had worked with the Allies during the war. The British government embraced the two-Burma principle of Simla's plan and formalized it in their White Paper, issued in April 1945.[7]

The View from Inside Burma

The Simla proposal, however, did not square with the logistical, tactical and strategic requirements of the Allied forces inside Burma. During the months from May to August 1945, Allied troops swept through Burma, leaving behind British army detachments and units of the BNA to carry out "mopping up operations" against the Japanese and to assist CAS(B) in restoring order to central Burma. This process required British army and BNA units throughout the country to negotiate terrain and responsibilities, but some British army officials took high-handed approaches when making these arrangements and instead forcibly disarmed nationalist guerrillas at any opportunity.

At Allied headquarters, these activities vexed Mountbatten, who struggled with two difficult, probably irreconcilable strategic objectives at this time. On the one hand, he believed that the AFO/BNA could be useful in further Allied operations against the Japanese; on the other, he wanted to lay the foundation for the disarmament and disbandment of the AFO/BNA without driving them into rebellion. Rightfully so, Mountbatten was convinced that the activities of CAS(B) alienated the guerrillas he was trying to deploy, contain, disarm, and pacify. Despite British attempts to clamp down on information circulation, word spread of CAS(B)'s punitive and oppressive measures in Upper Burma and Arakan, which no doubt accounts at least in part for the unwillingness of AFO/BNA guerrillas to hand over their weapons to civil affairs officers.

Hence, from May to August Mountbatten was in no position to ignore Aung San's frequent complaints and warnings about the way British army and CAS(B) officials treated his soldiers in the BNA. During these confusing months, the top priority for Aung San and other nationalist leaders was not only to maintain the BNA intact but also to weaken the political and military influence of the indigenous minorities suspected of loyalties to the British. Thus, Aung San demanded throughout the months of negotiations over army reorganization that his forces be incorporated as units—rather than as individual soldiers—into the new army. Aung San and other BNA leaders did not want their nationalist followers dispersed across units officered by Britons and made up primarily of indigenous peoples of pro-British and potentially anti-Burman (or at least anti-thakin) inclinations.

With the war continuing throughout the rest of Southeast Asia, Mountbatten, British army commanders, CAS(B) officials, Aung San, and his BNA colleagues met frequently from May through August 1945 to discuss solutions to the irreconcilable differences among armed contenders vying for the helm of the postwar state. CAS(B) and increasingly British army leaders remained committed to bringing the "loyal" armed levies under the centralized control of a resurrected, prewar-style British Burma Army and began collecting soldiers into units.[8] With regard to Aung San's soldiers—whom Mountbatten had declared could not be arrested for collaboration offenses and hence had to be examined for reenlistment into this army—British army recruiters herded some BNA units into holding centers, tried to disarm them, and enrolled few if any in the new army.[9]

Aung San and other BNA leaders had less precise plans for what the postwar army should look like, but they favored arrangements that were like a negative image of CAS(B)'s plan. Broadly, Aung San had written as early as 1941 of the need to construct "powerful Army, Navy and Air Forces [necessary] to defend our country."[10] The nationalists' vision evolved into one of a people's army organized around a strategy of "Total Defence" by a civilian militia of one hundred thousand.[11] This was reaffirmed two weeks after the May 1945 recapture of Rangoon, when the supreme council of the Anti-Fascist People's Freedom League (AFPFL, the new name of the AFO) adopted a resolution to establish the "Burma People's Army" and a volunteer "Home Guard" to "mop up the remnants of Japanese forces, Japanese fifth columnists and to suppress the lawless elements that are disturbing the peace of the country."[12] Conspicuously absent from these plans about the postwar army were any considerations of the people inhabiting the frontier regions of British Burma. Indeed, there was little concern about integrating this "other Burma" into one nation or absorbing the armed populations of this "other Burma" into one army alongside the BNA. What came to dominate Aung San's attention during these months was the necessity of keeping his soldiers together, and his one consistent demand throughout the negotiations was for unit incorporation of BNA forces into the reorganization of the army.

In early 1945, the anti-Japanese allies were utterly at odds over the political and military future of postcolonial Burma. However, given the immediate problem of ridding Burma of Japanese forces, CAS(B) and Aung San had no choice but to compromise on their visions for the future. Neither side won in this struggle. The process of compromise institutionalized two wholly incompatible political blueprints, starting with the creation of the postwar army.

The Two-Wing Solution

As the British army and CAS(B), on the one hand, and the BNA (officially renamed the Patriotic Burmese Forces [PBF] in July) and the AFO (renamed the AFPFL in May), on the other hand, continued to talk menacingly past each other, Mountbatten interceded in July 1945 with a compromise proposal for an army bifurcated into what he called two "wings." At a series of meetings with Aung San and British army and CAS(B) officials, Mountbatten declared that until Burma had achieved Dominion status, the army would have to be placed under the command of a British inspector general. Below this officer, he proposed that the force consist of two wings, one made up of ethnic-Burman soldiers and the other of non-Burmans. The Burman wing would be headed up by a Burman deputy inspector general (DIG), and the minority wing should be headed by a Karen, Kachin, or Chin DIG. The governor would commission these DIGs at the rank of brigadier, and they would be required to swear allegiance to His Majesty.[13] Leaders of CAS(B), the British army detachments in Burma, and the AFO/BNA all embraced this organizational principle, seeing the two-wing solution as an opportunity to build a position of strength within an army that ultimately would shed the unwanted wing when political conditions allowed.

During those July meetings, Aung San proposed a revision to the two-wing policy to establish smaller and thus even more politically homogeneous units in the army under reconstruction. In negotiations with British military officials, he cleverly expropriated the century-old British principle of colonial army organization: that of "class" (i.e., ethnically homogeneous) battalions.[14] At a meeting on July 11 in Rangoon with Major General Rance, Brigadier K. J. H. Lindop, and several other military and civil affairs personnel, Aung San agreed to the Twelfth Army's plan to raise new battalions distributed accordingly: four Burman battalions, two Karen battalions, two Kachin battalions, and two Chin battalions.[15] Most of Aung San's soldiers were of Burman ethnicity, while most of those soldiers whose loyalty to a future AFPFL-led government might be questionable were of other classes. Thus Aung San embraced the proposed class battalions to keep his men together in the four Burman battalions, away from what AFPFL and PBF leaders considered the "mercenaries." Even if the British continued to reject the principle of unit recruitment from the Burmese resistance forces, the principle of defining battalions by ethnic class ensured the possibility of keeping Aung San's soldiers together in the newly defined ethnic-Burman units.

Unfortunately, the two-wing army established in mid-1945 was in fact two armies with two different traditions, two separate destinies being charted, and two different maps of Burma in the minds of their leaders and soldiers. Once in place, this dual track—operationalized in the class principle of organizing battalions—proved nearly impossible to eliminate and, in the long run, almost fatal to the integrity of both the army and independent Burma after 1948. Class-based battalions also provided the first postwar institutional basis for channeling political opponents of the AFPFL into positions from which they could eventually be purged, as happened when Burman staff officers in the early 1950s were able to weed out "rightists" in the army simply by marginalizing the ethnic battalions of suspicious loyalties.

The Kandy Conference: Making an Army, Making Enemies

When the Japanese formally surrendered in August 1945, the allies-turned-enemies viewed these ad hoc compromises on army reconstruction with a new sense of urgency. Gone for good was the common strategic enemy that had held together the loosely united front and tempered the rhetoric and violence of both vengeful returning colonizers and independence-minded nationalist guerrillas. Burma was no longer a staging point for the Allied campaign throughout Southeast Asia but remained a battlefield not only for "mopping up" operations against Japanese stragglers but also for control over the post-Japanese state. Given the continued absence of law and order throughout most of the territory, the crucible for struggles over Burma's future remained the negotiations over the construction of a now truly postwar Burma army.

The mid-August surrender of the Japanese worried PBF and AFPFL leaders, who were concerned that the earlier-than-predicted end of the war against Japan eliminated their most crucial anticolonial bargaining chip: the services of the PBF in the Allies' Southeast Asia campaign. Moreover, after nearly two months of recruiting for the postwar class battalions, British army recruiters had deemed only a handful of PBF personnel eligible for reenlistment, and there was renewed concern that the British would disembowel Aung San's army. As Aung San noted, rumors that "the PBF will soon be disbanded" were rife.[16] Accordingly, a meeting of PBF regional (zone) commanders held on August 12 in Rangoon reasserted the demand for unit-incorporation of the PBF personnel into the new army but also insisted for the first time that the PBF be considered the core of the new army, with indigenous races absorbed into its ranks. The zone commanders did not want to see PBF soldiers scattered across the units of the minority-dominated British Burma Army. They also demanded the appointment of a Burmese Defence Minister when civilian government was restored, and called for meetings to be convened between PBF representatives and British military authorities.[17] A few days later, AFPFL leaders affirmed these resolutions at the Nethurein Conference (August 16–18, 1945) in Rangoon and at a mass meeting of five to six thousand AFPFL followers that followed it on August 19.[18]

For their part, British military officials were no more secure about the post-surrender situation and decidedly unnerved by the sheer numbers attending the Nethurein mass meeting. Contrary to the predictions of CAS(B), the following of the AFPFL and PBF appeared to have expanded dramatically in the months following the recapture of Rangoon. Moreover, in 1945 the potential for anticolonial disruption became more threatening to Mountbatten and British army commanders in Burma the instant Indian nationalist leaders demanded that Indian troops not be used to suppress nationalist movements anywhere in the world. This greatly limited the potential to use the Indian army to put down anti-British rebellions or other disturbances that might follow the forced demobilization of the PBF and the restoration of colonial rule.[19] Accordingly, Mountbatten invited Aung San to his headquarters at Kandy (Ceylon) to try to stave off the anticolonial rebellion that looked increasingly inevitable.

The Kandy Negotiations

The Kandy Conference (September 6–7, 1945) brought together Mountbatten and other Allied forces officials, British army commanders operating in Burma, Aung San and other BNA leaders, Thakin Than Tun and other AFPFL officials, and civil affairs personnel from CAS(B). The objective of Kandy was to flesh out the skeleton of the agreed-on two-wing army. Aung San opened the conference with a prepared speech in which he again called for the incorporation of his soldiers into the new army by unit (not by individual); PBF representation on recruiting teams to ensure fairness in the evaluation of soldiers reporting for reenlistment; and minimum compensation and services to be guaranteed to those soldiers deemed unfit to reenlist and hence demobilized.[20]

Mountbatten ignored Aung San's call for unit recruitment, but he and the other negotiators nonetheless agreed to a military establishment that met Aung San's important objective of keeping his soldiers together in units identified solely as former PBF units. The conference established the following organizational plan for the new army: In the infantry, there would be three Burman battalions made up of PBF recruits only, one Burman battalion made up of non-PBF recruits, two Karen battalions, two Kachin battalions, and two Chin battalions; in the artillery and armor units, there would be one artillery regiment of Burmans, with one battery reserved for Karens, and one armored car regiment.

Mountbatten also offered to address the continued mistreatment of individual PBF personnel in the recruitment process by guaranteeing specific numbers of places in the postwar army to former PBF soldiers. The conference established a standing army of 12,000 men, of which at least 5,200 would come from the PBF; another 200 PBF soldiers would be commissioned as officers.[21] As many as 200 more officers would be taken on for both wings of the army and trained to meet the future requirements of independent Burma. The Kandy Agreement gave the highest official priority to the raising of the Third, Fourth, and Fifth Burma Rifles (often referred to as "Burifs"), which came to be composed mainly of ethnic-Burman, ex-PBF members. Former "Thirty Comrades" Bo Kyaw Zaw, Bo Ne Win, and Bo Zeya, respectively, were appointed commanding officers-designate of these three battalions.

With regard to the officer corps, the Kandy agreement also provided that whenever possible, PBF officers were to be placed in charge of units "originally formed under them, but that this might not be possible in some cases immediately, in the interests of the ultimate efficiency of the Burma Army." At Mountbatten's urging, the PBF delegation agreed to allow British officers to be posted to Burma Army units "to ensure the over-all efficient training of the Burma Army" until they can be replaced by "Burmese officers who are sufficiently trained."[22]

The conference also established a "Joint Board" to "thrash out" the specific details of the amalgamation process.[23] The board was to be made up of representatives from the PBF, British Burma Army (i.e., indigenous minorities), Twelfth Army, and the newly designated Inspector General, Maj. Gen. L. C. Thomas, a career British army officer. It was assigned the tasks of setting up the Enquiry and Registration Centres for the enlistment of personnel, reviewing histories of individual officers in order to recommend rank assignments, and determining how new officers should be trained and where "each officer's military future was likely to lie."[24]

In terms of the broader political environment, the conference also agreed to Aung San's request to hasten the speedy resumption of civil government, which would entail bringing in Dorman-Smith's "Burma government" from India. Given the known hostility of Dorman-Smith—whom Mountbatten called a "reactionary blimp"[25]—and other civilian officials toward Burmese nationalists, Mountbatten later recalled being

> shocked and alarmed when [at Kandy] . . . Aung San and his people came and told me that they would prefer to have Civil Government back in Rangoon, instead of my Military Administration. I was afraid they didn't understand the implications of what they were asking for—and, as a matter of fact, Aung San admitted as much to me later on. But since they had asked for it, I felt I had to

give way, and I allowed the pre-war Civil Government to come back and take over from me in October 1945.

I now think this was a mistake . . .[26]

This decision to return Dorman-Smith's government to Rangoon—at a time when so much of the Burmese population was politically mobilized, had access to weapons, and was suffering the economic hardships of the war—brought Rangoon and other parts of Burma to a near boiling point.

The agreements reached at Kandy probably had less impact on the crisis conditions prevailing in Burma than did the explicit omissions from the Kandy debate and resolutions. Left unaddressed were several issues that PBF leaders considered of the utmost importance, starting with the very basic demand for unit-incorporation, which was only indirectly resolved by the formal establishment of ethnically homogeneous class battalions. Many of Aung San's soldiers rejected continued individual recruitment into the class battalions and refused to report for personal examinations at recruiting centers. They took their guns and left the PBF.

Another unaddressed issue, raised by Aung San, was that of language. In the plenary discussion on the particulars of establishing the Joint Board to determine who was eligible for officers' commissions, Aung San asked that "facilities . . . be given for the use of the vernacular as an alternative medium of expression for purposes of examination" by the Joint Board.[27] This demand got lost in the discussion. The Kandy message was clear: Speak English, or forget career advancement in the new regular army.[28]

Finally, there was also no consideration whatsoever of the PBF and AFPFL demand that a Burmese Defence Minister be appointed when civilian government was reestablished. Instead, at the return of civil government the following month, Governor Dorman-Smith named to the Defence portfolio C. F. B. Pearce, the former head of CAS(B), whom Mountbatten had fired for his anti–AFO/BNA activities in the early months of the reoccupation campaign.

Kandy Fallout

There are few clues in existing sources as to why Aung San, Than Tun, and other Burmese nationalist delegates at Kandy did not insist that these unanswered demands be addressed. Kandy's detailed two-wing army design had met some of the strategic requirements of PBF and AFPFL leaders, who needed to establish a safe structural niche for their followers inside the army and to diminish the prominence of other soldiers suspected to be British loyalists. However, the latter group benefited the most from Kandy, receiving quicker and higher promotions, as well as access to training opportunities and postings that carried real leverage over the army's future.

In fact, the post-Kandy officer selection process was carried out in such a way that it yielded several hundred PBF rejects. The selection board certified only 157 of 600 PBF applicants—less than a third—as eligible for commission.[29] Moreover, the British gave these 157 accepted PBF officers only temporary "emergency" commissions with no assurance of permanence. Aung San wrote: "There is no guarantee that PBF ECOs [emergency commissioned officers] will NOT be demobbed [*sic*] one year after the War (if not sooner) or that they will be commissioned in the *Regular Burma Army* in accordance with the spirit of the Kandy Conference."[30] Former PBF officers also were slighted in the ranks they were assigned by the selection board. Until some kind of permanent officer's commission was authorized in late 1946, no ECO could hold a rank higher than that of second lieutenant, which Aung San argued "greatly handicapped" the careers of former PBF officers.[31] Additionally, PBF ECOs were not among the earliest candidates selected for training abroad, including staff colleges, because of the time-consuming process of raising "new" PBF-based units in the regular army. Only a handful of ranking PBF officers were chosen to attend a "junior officer" training course run by the British at Maymyo in early 1946.[32]

Meanwhile, PBF rank-and-file response to their own recruiting parties had been less than expected, with at least 3,500 former PBF soldiers either not reporting for registration and arms collection or not seeking reenlistment. Consequently, British leaders of the new Burma army determined that no more than 130 PBF officers—a figure considered proportionate to the number of PBF rank-and-file enlistees—should be commissioned in the postwar army. Eventually, Inspector General Thomas and Governor Dorman-Smith upheld the 157 PBF commissions, and they also authorized recruitment from other Burman populations to fill the remaining 43 officer spots that Kandy had allotted to the PBF.[33]

By far the most significant disagreement that arose in the implementation of the Kandy agreement was over the issue of what to do with the hundreds of former PBF personnel deemed "unacceptable" for reenlistment into the postwar army, and how to mitigate the hostility of the hundreds of discharged PBF officers for whom there was no place in the Kandy-designed officer corps. Earlier in the negotiations, Aung San pleaded for the importance of establishing satisfactory arrangements for sending former PBF soldiers and officers back to homes where they were unlikely to have much to eat, much to wear, or anything to do.[34] At Kandy, Aung San proposed forming a territorial army in Burma "for those who want training without becoming regulars and who are not fit for the Regular Army."[35] British negotiators rejected the proposal, ignoring Aung San's concerns about what these armed young men were going to do in a devastated, war-torn economy.

Politics in the Two-Wing Army

The implementation of the Kandy Agreement produced a military organization that was in fact two armies. Each army considered the other a major security threat to the future it envisioned for Burma, and each was preparing to fight the other in the next war. Former PBF officers and soldiers readied themselves to lead yet another campaign against the British in the struggle for political independence. In the other wing, minority officers and soldiers prepared to defend the regime in power under Governor Dorman-Smith. Kandy's elite-level negotiators had intended each wing to be unified and homogeneous (and thus politically reliable), but this was not the case. In each wing, the compromises that underlay the agreement's details created not only distrust and disaffection with the other wing but also divisions within units that quickly undermined the political reliability that ethnic homogeneity was intended to produce.

Mutiny in the Fifth Burifs

Among the newly organized battalions of former PBF fighters, there was serious fallout from the Kandy provisions, especially concerning the agreement to allow British officers to be seconded to PBF/Burma Rifles battalions until former PBF officers were adequately trained. This provision became a source of great tension and in at least one incident threatened to erupt into a mutiny.

On February 1, 1947, a Burman lance corporal allegedly assaulted the Indian manager of the canteen at Fifth Burma Rifles Headquarters (HQ) in Pegu. On February 17, he was tried by a summary court martial and sentenced to three months' rigorous imprisonment. There were rumors circulating throughout the Fifth Burifs that the wrong man had been arrested and punished, and by the morning after the court martial, the soldiers in HQ companies at Pegu "made a strike" against the British battalion commander, Lt. Col. Roper.[36] The mainly Burman, former-PBF companies refused to assemble for parade on February 18, and when Roper ordered indigenous officers to summon their men for parade, the striking soldiers disobeyed these orders.

This incident was labeled a "mutiny" and sent shock waves through the British hierarchy of the Burma Army. Inspector General Thomas immediately ordered an inquiry, wherein it became apparent that tensions between indigenous soldiers and officers, on the one hand, and British commanding officers, on the other, were at the root of the problem that flared up in the canteen incident. However, it was not simply an issue of former PBF members resenting British control of their units. In fact, Lt. Col. Roper, who is remembered by one Burman company commander who joined the strike as a "very good soldier, and strict like the Japanese,"[37] was distrusted not only by the former PBF contingent of the Fifth Burifs. He was also "not popular with the British and Anglo-Burmese officers [in the battalion] for the sole reason that they considered he was Burmanizing the battalion too quickly and giving posts to Burmese officers in preference to them."[38] But in the eyes of the former PBF Burmans in the Fifth Burifs, Roper moved too slowly in promoting indigenous officers. British officers in charge of indigenous units were in a most untenable position. As one former PBF officer wrote in 1947: "The [British] COs [commanding officers] aren't very sympathetic to the Burmans; at the same time they dare not do what they like to the Burma Army."[39]

Inspector General Thomas personally investigated the mutiny incident because of British concerns that it constituted "part of a plan to get rid of British Officers" and may have been instigated by CPB sympathizers who were eager to bring down both the Burma Army and the government. Thomas transferred a more popular British battalion commander from the Fourth Burifs to the Fifth Burifs and then moved the latter battalion to Rangoon to keep an eye on it. He persuaded Aung San to issue warnings about "political activities" going on in army units, and Aung San further reminded members of all Burma Army units that unpopular decisions should be appealed through standard army procedures.[40]

Whether this constituted a true mutiny remains unclear. Former Col. Saw Myint, who was at the time a captain commanding a Fifth Burif company, is to this day unsure how this incident got out of control. He remembers there being a handful of politicized officers throughout the Fifth Burifs. Some were sympathetic to the Socialist Party, others to one of the Communist Party factions. Probably, he thinks, a small number of politicos agitated the troops for the "strike." Saw Myint remembers: "We joined the movement. We thought Bo Zeya [the ranking Burman officer in the battalion] was leading it," and they were surprised to learn afterward that he had not been involved in the boycott.[41] Regardless, the incident demonstrates the degree of mistrust and confusion that characterized army life at this time from the company level up to the Inspector General's office.

Increasing Tensions within the Third, Fourth, and Fifth Burifs

British concerns about "political activities" within the army were based on observations of increasing differences among former PBF members along lines that coincided with growing divisions between the parties that made up the AFPFL, especially the Burma Socialist Party and the Burma Communist Party. Beginning in May 1945, intra-army tensions flared on several occasions between non-communist PBF soldiers and those more sympathetic to or who were members of the CPB. Within the CPB itself, trouble was also brewing. In July 1945, the CPB held its second Party Congress in Rangoon, at which Thakin Than Tun was named chairman of the Politbureau and Thakin Thein Pe its general secretary. Increasingly alienated from the CPB policy advocating peaceful transition to socialism, Thakin Soe split from the party in February 1946 and led his own Red Flag Communist Party—including a handful of members of the army—into rebellion against the British imperialists and the "rightists" in the AFPFL.

These political tensions spilled over into the Third, Fourth, and Fifth Burifs. The Third and Fifth Burifs were mixed in terms of political leanings, comprised of some former PBF officers and other ranks who had received wartime "political" or guerrilla training from Thakin Soe or his right-hand man, Thakin Tin Mya; others who had ties to Thakin Than Tun and/or Thakin Thein Pe; and still others who balked at communist teachings and leaned toward the non-communist Socialist Party. The former PBF Burman officers in the Fourth Burifs were mostly of non-communist persuasion, many having served in the War Office at some point during the Japanese period. This included Maung Maung and Aung Gyi, who were recognized later as leaders of the Socialist faction of the army. Although the Socialist Party never had a major contingent rebel and go underground, it is important to note that there were also bitter rivalries over ideological and personality differences among the Socialists, so even the Fourth Burifs was not seamless in terms of unit loyalty or political persuasion.

Aung San appeared to try to stay out of this increasing factionalism. Shortly after the Kandy conference in September 1945, he rejected the British proposal to appoint him DIG of the Burman/PBF wing of the new regular army. He resigned from the army in October 1945 to pursue a political career. By this time his views had diverged from those of his Communist allies in the AFPFL, and CPB leaders of both factions reportedly tried to persuade him to stay in the army, probably to leave the political stage clear for the Communist Party.[42] Aung San joined no political party, and as leader of the AFPFL managed to maintain at least an image of neutrality and unity for the not-so-united postwar nationalist movement. In September 1946, he was appointed Defence Councilor to the new governor, Sir Hubert Rance. As Defence Councilor, Aung San had an official status to retain his influence over the direction of the postwar army and to try to unify the increasingly politicized and factious troops.

As Burma moved closer to independence, additional layers of political division emerged. Within the leadership of the army, tension emerged when Bo Let Ya, who was named DIG in 1945 when Aung San turned down the position, signed the Britain-Burma Defence Agreement (also known as the Let Ya–Freeman Agreement) with John Freeman, leader of the U.K. Defence Mission, in 1947.[43] The defense agreement negotiations followed the signing of the Aung San–Attlee Agreement of January 1947, which provided for legislative elections to be held in May 1947 and independence to be granted the following January. The Let Ya–Freeman Defence Agreement provided for British military access to Burma and for the establishment of a British Services Mission to oversee training and procurement for the tat-madaw. However, this agreement to maintain British involvement in future Burma Army affairs came in the wake of allegations that British army officers had supplied at least some of the weapons used to assassinate Aung San and other Burmese leaders on July 19, 1947. Hence, for most of the former PBF leaders in the army, it was anathema to allow continued British interference in the army, much less to institutionalize it in the form of the Let Ya–Freeman agreement. Even worse, the agreement provided few concessions to the Burmese, while committing the soon-to-be independent government of Burma to pay the expenses of past, present, and future British oversight of the military of independent Burma.[44] Within the army, Bo Let Ya was castigated as a pro-British "rightist," and several other Burmans who either eschewed party politics or had abandoned the Socialist or Communist Parties were identified as being similarly pro-British and therefore suspect.

The Second Wing: The Minorities

The organizational plan adopted at the Kandy conference worried some minorities within Burma and within the armed forces. Their concerns grew over the next two years as the two-wing army reform plan—that gave minorities status and institutional protections—evolved into what minorities perceived as an AFPFL-British plan to establish a singular, unified Burman-dominated state at formal independence. It is important to remember from chapter 3 that British and U.S. officers sent to organize the minorities to fight with the Allies during the war encouraged them to expect and demand independence from ethnic Burman rule in the postwar era. Dorman-Smith's White Paper (May 1945) and Mountbatten's two-wing plan for the army (July 1945) seemed to confirm the necessity of a future with at least two postcolonial political units occupying the territory mapped into colonial Burma.

On the surface, the Kandy plan seemed simply to spell out Mountbatten's two-wing vision for the postwar army. This was for the most part palatable to the minority officers and soldiers who would compose the so-called loyalist wing because it would keep them from coming under the command of former BNA/PBF—and significantly, ethnic Burman—officers in the new army. However, the Kandy conference also signaled the increasing clout of Aung San's PBF and the AFPFL. The latter organization never had acceded fully to the two-Burma plan, instead opting to press for independence for all of Burma's people and territory in one unitary state. Hence, the Kandy agreement spelled danger to some minority leaders.

Most important for the postwar army, the Karens wasted no time in campaigning against British and Burman plans for an independent Burma in which they would be minority partners in national leadership. Just before the Japanese surrender in August 1945, Karen leaders Saw Ba U Gyi and Sydney Loo-Nee arranged a meeting with T. L. Hughes, who then served as Governor Dorman-Smith's representative at Twelfth Army HQ. They proposed the creation of a new state, "Karenistan" to be included in the "Scheduled Areas" and not in the territory envisioned for independent (central) Burma.[45] Shortly after the Kandy conference in September 1945, a mass meeting of "liberated Karens" was held in Rangoon, where they drafted a memorial to the British secretary of state demanding the creation of the United Frontier Karen States.[46] These demands reflect the dilemma of the Karens, who inhabited geographically scattered areas, most of which were not part of the so-called "Frontier Areas" during the prewar era. Their territory was a no-man's land in the sense that other minorities considered "loyalist" would be covered by British provisions for the second Burma in the "Scheduled" or "Frontier" areas. But the Karen people inhabited territory that was mapped into the portion of Burma likely to gain independence from Britain first and likely to be under AFPFL domination. This geographical conundrum plagued Karen leaders over the next two years, and some of them scaled back their demands for an autonomous Karenistan. However, some combination of confidence (due to their experiences in prewar and wartime western institutions) and fear of mistreatment by the Burman majority kept Karen leaders in the army and in the society from moving toward a compromise with the AFPFL.

For months after the September 1945 Kandy conference, British officials dodged these issues, leaving the Karens caught in the middle of two incompatible futures. After Kandy, British military leaders seemed to be planning the construction of not two wings of a single army, but two distinct armies. The "Frontier" army would be run either by British officers directly or by indigenous minority officers whose loyalty to Britain was secure. Maintaining British influence over the other army, however, was more difficult. The Karens must have been the answer. Almost from the date of his appointment as inspector general, Thomas promoted Karen officers to senior staff and infantry positions, probably hoping that their higher ranks would enable them to wrestle control of the army away from their anti-British, former PBF, Burman counterparts. This strategy proved unworkable, and its faulty logic and faultier implementation helps explain why the majority of British-trained Karen officers and other ranks rebelled against the Burman-dominated postcolonial government in 1949.

Other former levies living beyond the central regions lobbied to be re-enlisted into a new army that excluded the Burmans. As early as mid-June

1945, the commanding officer of the Second Burifs requested that the battalion be designated a "Royal Battalion," or at least a unit under British SOE/Force 136. "The men, Chins, Kachins and Karens" wanted no part of being amalgamated with the BNA. "This is a ticklish business and one it's difficult to sit on the fence about. The men have been fighting them [the BNA] recently during the 'Chindit' operations and on occasions saw some unsavoury work done by this force on their own people."[47] Some of the prewar Burma Army units, like the Chin Hills Battalion, saw the postwar army as "their" army in which their people had served since the turn of the century. They were decidedly unhappy about being treated as juridical equals to those whose military service had been so short.[48]

Violence and the State, 1945–48

The growing divisions inside the two-wing army attracted less attention from the returned civilian regime of Dorman-Smith than did the unprecedented social and economic crises prevailing throughout the territory. Throughout 1945—46 British and Burmese leaders scrambled to try to establish order in a politically mobilized society. Violence became a currency of not only politics but also the economy, largely as a result of postwar scarcity and market paralysis. Because this chaos thoroughly undercut Dorman-Smith's administration, it strengthened the bargaining power of the AFPFL and PBF leaders. However, the same nationalist leaders needed to gain some control over what appeared at times to be random and uncontrolled violence; the AFPFL wanted to create disturbances to destabilize Dorman-Smith's government but also to control the outcomes of these disturbances in order to manage its campaign for political independence. Out of these turbulent conditions came numerous attempts to both spread and contain violence.

Chaos, Strikes, and Violence

The agreement between the Communist Party, BNA, and the PRP that led to the August 1944 formation of the AFO had called for an armed anti-Japanese revolution, followed—if necessary—by armed resistance against any imperialist power threatening the political independence of Burma in the postwar era. Although by May 1945 most AFO and BNA leaders had retreated from hard-line positions backing an armed campaign for independence against the British, there was great concern throughout Burma that the anti-British revolution might have been merely forestalled. Most BNA, AFO, and Karen resistance fighters, as well as other minority levies, did not turn over weapons when ordered to do so by civil affairs personnel in mid-

1945, and probably between thirty and fifty thousand Allied and Japanese weapons were buried or hidden during this period.[49]

From the return of British civil government in October 1945 to its departure in January 1948, government servants out in the districts, and even in Rangoon, doubted that British authority could be fully reestablished. Even the most basic tools of colonial rule were lacking in the postwar period. According to a former colonial bureaucrat with prewar Burma experience who returned to Burma in 1945 as a civil affairs officer, the government had almost no mechanisms for rule in most of Burma.

> It was short of officers. . . . The Government was short of transport; the railway system had been badly damaged, there was no road transport until the Government could bring some in, and this took time. Postal and telegraphic communication was very patchy—in many cases it was necessary to rely upon the Army for the latter. Many Government buildings had been destroyed, both official and residential. There were plans for importing supplies for the civil population, but the organization, storage space, and transport to give effect to these had still to be provided. Stores and equipment for general purposes were lacking.[50]

Dorman-Smith's civilian government was poorly equipped to deal with law and order responsibilities. One British official wrote later that the end of the military administration and return to civil rule caused "an outbreak of violent crime, and by March 1946, it was no longer possible to travel along some sections of the Rangoon-Mandalay road except under armed escort."[51] Donnison, who served as commissioner of the Pegu Division when civil government was restored, wrote that much of his district was "out of hand and on the brink of rebellion."[52] Robbery and dacoity had reached "unprecedented" rates, and local police, village headmen, and "members of the public were terrorized into not giving information" against suspected criminals for fear of retribution.[53]

Set against this state weakness was growing discontent nationwide over economic hardships that seemed to worsen the longer the British were back. By July 1946, the economic situation had deteriorated to the point that government clerks and police officers could not buy enough rice and cooking oil on their salaries to feed themselves and their families. Workers resurrected nascent prewar unions, which attracted members quickly. A number of groups of government services workers held strikes throughout June and July 1946 to demand a cost-of-living adjustment. At the same time, groups of overworked, barely paid police officers in the districts started forming alliances of necessity with local AFPFL politicians to protect themselves from persecution by the many armed, locally based League organizations. In July, police at a Rangoon station refused to accept their inadequate pay in light of the spiraling cost of living and the risks required by their duties. Soon thereafter, police in Rangoon and in many of the upcountry towns and villages went on strike.

The police strike ushered in a nationwide general strike by August 1946, which crippled Burma. The colonial government could not transport rice, had to close ports, railways, and all government offices, and could not control the spread of crime. By this time, British Prime Minister Clement Attlee had sacked Governor Dorman-Smith, replaced him with Sir Hubert Rance, and approved the formation of a new government comprised largely of AFPFL representatives. Oddly enough, it was the strike led by the police—who had long been considered collaborators (or "thudo-Bama") with the British—that brought down the last barriers to nationalists' entry into the government.

The demobilization of British forces and the inability to deploy Indian troops in the service of "internal security" operations left the British state in Burma without its century-old mainstay of coercive power. From the early months of 1946, British army officials pleaded with their own politicians in Burma and in London to consider the very real possibility that Burma could not be held against an AFPFL uprising. In the opinion of British military leaders, the "loyalist" battalions of the postwar Burma Army and the small number of British soldiers on Burmese soil would not be able to protect British subjects in Burma, much less defend the government. In December 1946, the head of the Burma Command wired the War Office in London: "[I] consider [it] imperative that political action be directed towards maintaining a peaceful situation or we may be in [a] serious military position."[54]

The political accommodation reached in January 1947 between Defence Councilor Aung San and British Prime Minister Attlee to effect a peaceful transfer of power within a year did not diminish the disorder prevailing throughout Burma. Governor Rance wrote in August 1947:

A state of nerves exists in Rangoon from nightfall. Every night someone lets off his musket and this is taken up by all and sundry. Last night, when [I was] entertaining Lord Addison and some of his party to dinner, a miniature battle was raging in close vicinity of Government House. [Head of the U.K. Defence Mission] Freeman, whom I had invited to dinner, received warning from the police that it would be unsafe to return to his bungalow, and accordingly spent [the] night here. Battle last night as far as I can ascertain was completely one-sided and was started by one man firing at a shadow. . . . I consider that this state of affairs will continue for some time and may well get worse . . .[55]

Rance wrote these words about a month after a series of assassination attempts against various Burmese politicians had culminated in the massacre of Aung

San and key leaders of the AFPFL on July 19, 1947, at the Secretariat. A rival politician, U Saw, was convicted of organizing the massacre. The collective horror at the loss of the national hero, Aung San, brought some mending of political fences between Burmese communists and socialists, but did not stem the crime wave; if anything, there was an escalation in crime, and assassination would remain an important form of political action for years to come.

Absorbing the Disaffected: The PVO

In British eyes, this violence had been greatly aggravated by the emergence of the People's Volunteer Organisation (PVO) under Aung San after he resigned from the army in October 1945. Originally established in November 1945 as a "welfare organization" to provide assistance to demobilized PBF soldiers as they returned to civilian life, the PVO quickly turned into an alternative army that absorbed thousands of former PBF soldiers and officers and thousands more youths who had been mobilized during the war in mass organizations such as the EAYL.

It is difficult to trace how the idea of establishing the PVO developed. Most likely it was Aung San's attempt to impose central authority over local political and private armies throughout Burma. The necessarily decentralized nature of resistance to Japanese rule had encouraged dozens (maybe hundreds) of local underground leaders to form secret armies of resisters. Many of these leaders were tied in somehow to the Japanese regime, often by membership in the EAYL, Keibotai, or other Japanese-sponsored organizations. These ties allowed local leaders such as Thakin Kyi Shein in Lewe and Hsaya Hti in Meiktila to appropriate some of the resources of these legal organizations for purposes of strengthening their underground cells. These local bosses also ran black market operations that supplied both the Japanese regime and their underground armies. When the war against the Japanese ended, these leaders did not give up their arms or their black market businesses. As the British attempted to reassert political and economic authority throughout Burma, upcountry local leaders occasionally forged working relationships with returning district officers, but were more likely to strengthen their positions as local army bosses by fortifying their forces. Demobilized PBF soldiers were prime recruits for these local armies.

After the Kandy negotiations failed to produce any systematic method of easing army-rejects' reentry into civilian life, Aung San waited only a couple of weeks before launching the PVO. The hierarchy of the PVO mirrored that of the army, with Aung San serving as commander in chief. A uniform was issued, as were badges indicating ranks. In February 1946, Aung San established thirty-two districts and appointed organizers for each to raise money, recruit new members, and provide military training. Initially, only ex-PBF personnel were invited to enroll in the PVO, but PVO branches soon were ordered to expand recruitment by canvassing branches of student unions and other political associations.[56]

It is difficult to ascertain whether Aung San intended right from the start for the PVO to form the core of an army that could wage another war of independence against the British. Other leaders of the PVO, however were quite explicit that this was their intention in joining the organization. For example, in his memoir, *The Battle for Independence*, Bo Thein Swe writes that after the Kandy conference established too much British control over the army, he decided he wanted no part of the British-dominated postwar army. He had served in the wartime BIA, BDA, and BNA. Initially, he had thought his only alternative was to go into politics, but when the PVO was established, he signed up at Rangoon district headquarters and was named deputy chair of that district. He was convinced that a second battle for independence would have to be fought against the British and that the PVO was the only organization that could prepare the people of Burma for this revolution.[57]

The British response to the PVO was surprisingly indifferent at first, not unlike British indecision over the establishment of the nationalist tats in the 1930s (see chapter 1). However, by the time the five-week, seventy-student PVO training course covering "scouting, first-aid and modern tactics of warfare" was completed in Rangoon in April 1946, Governor Dorman-Smith had become very nervous about the existence of PVO branches throughout Burma.[58] He issued orders to police and district officials under the Defence of Burma Rules of 1940 to stop PVO military training, public drilling, and the wearing of uniforms.[59] Local PVO branches in Hanthawaddy district openly defied the order, leading to confrontations between PVO units and police in Insein and Rangoon. The Criminal Investigation Department reported that "defiance of authority spread like measles."[60]

At this point, Aung San told a newspaper reporter that he intended to send a PVO delegation to Governor Dorman-Smith for "negotiations" on this issue, but that if the Governor refused to participate, the latter would be responsible for whatever disturbances resulted throughout Burma. These threats came to a head on May 18, 1946, when police opened fire on a procession of over one thousand unarmed people organized to protest the arrest of eleven local PVO leaders in Tantabin in Insein district, on the outskirts of Rangoon. At least three people were killed, another six severely wounded, and forty others injured. Subsequently, British authorities arrested hundreds of PVO members all around Burma.[61]

The incident galvanized AFPFL political forces. Aung San successfully pressured Governor Dorman-Smith to release most of the arrested PVO members. From this point on, the AFPFL's demands took on a more radicalized, menacing tone, calling for immediate independence for all of Burma, not just central or "Ministerial" Burma. Strikes spread throughout urban areas, which ultimately led to the dismissal of Dorman-Smith and his replacement by Rance in October 1946. The British cabinet directed Rance to defuse the situation at once and bring the AFPFL into the government.

It is important to note that while the PVO organizational structure did provide—on paper—channels for central control over the two hundred or more local armies brought under its aegis, the authority of Aung San and the PVO's national leadership beyond PVO headquarters was more symbolic than real. After Aung San's death in July 1947, even the symbolic authority disappeared. Many PVO branches were simply expanded and renamed versions of the wartime resistance organizations that had sprouted up under local political leaders. Their involvement in illegal economic activities was legendary. There were widespread reports of PVO members selling off land that did not belong to them, running gambling and prostitution rings, and stopping traffic on roads to demand "contributions."[62]

What is most significant about the PVO is that, although it followed the pattern of the prewar tats, it greatly expanded the form and institutional capacity of non- and antistate armies in the postwar period. Like the prewar tats organized by Burman nationalist parties, the PVO was comprised entirely of people ineligible or unsuited for inclusion in the state army. Also like the tats, great permeability existed between the legal political parties and the units of the PVO. This meant that even as the British government tried to limit the activities of the PVO, its manpower and other organizational resources were shifted to the AFPFL, which was growing in both popularity among Burmese and recognition by the British.

In the PVO, this kind of fluid party-army relationship developed into a prototype for party politics in the 1950s. The PVO was the first in a series of well-armed, nonstate and at times antistate armies made up mainly of those kicked out of the state's coercive apparatus or those who had abstained from joining the army for political reasons. Even more significant for the future was the issue of what to do with these armies once their political programs were either defeated or successful. The prewar tats had never been decisively demobilized, only incorporated into the BIA. From 1942–45, formally demobilized BIA soldiers reconstituted themselves into guerrilla resistance cells, which later were incorporated into the AFO, BNA, and PBF. After World War II, demobilized, cast-aside AFO and PBF soldiers carried their weapons secretly to the PVO. Once the PVO's political program—independence—was achieved in 1948, the Union government tried to disarm PVO units, but it failed, and PVO members again were reincorporated into new extrastate, paramilitary organizations. This cycle of armament, failed attempts at disarmament, and subsequent reincorporation into new extrastate armies would continue to make violence the currency of state-society relations in Burma until the army's coup in 1962.

Conclusion

The early months following the British reoccupation of Burma were critical to the development of the parameters for what the postwar and post-colonial army of Burma would look like. The smoke screen that had allowed the Allies and their former enemies (the BNA and AFO) to fight the Japanese together gave way to a situation clear to all involved: The British colonial state would return, and it would not relinquish its coercive arm to these Burmese nationalist "quislings" without a struggle. The negotiations surrounding the postwar disposition of the BNA and PBF were a window on the political future of Burma. At issue was who would hold guns, who would tell whom what to do, and who would have authority over what territory. Beginning with the March 30, 1945, British Chiefs of Staff authorization for Mountbatten's alliance with the plains Burman nationalists, plots and counterplots, claims and counterclaims were bandied about among various British, Allied, and indigenous Burmese leaders in efforts to define, limit, and/or expand the power, nature, and leadership of the postwar state and army.

These struggles led to a number of institutional developments in the armed forces that, once established, carried over into the 1950s and beyond. One of the most significant developments was the further institutionalization of the "two-Burma" vision, which had been initiated administratively during the colonial period and was resuscitated in more concrete, lasting form in the White Paper of May 1945. Although AFO/BNA leaders objected to this kind of division in principle, they nonetheless embraced ethnicity-based structural divisions as a tactic for building an institutional mechanism to protect and preserve BNA forces intact in the reorganized postwar army. Thus, the Burman nationalists backed the establishment of "class" battalions, which remained in existence until the late 1980s.

Perhaps most important was the pattern of social and political fragmentation that emerged as these negotiations periodically broke apart previously united groups on both the British and the Burmese sides. By independence in 1948, the rank and file and officer corps of the Burma army had developed numerous informal factions that would rip apart the army in 1948–49. Karens held the senior army leadership positions, but their total numbers in the army were so small that their leaders' actions were restrained for fear of Burman retaliation. Former PBF members had been polarized along different issues at different times. First was the question of whether to allow themselves to be disarmed; next, whether to join the British-controlled army after the Kandy Conference. The latter issue coalesced around the debate over whether the British would ever really transfer power peacefully to the Burmese or would have to be forced to do so by a revolution. Partisans on either side of this debate ended up joining the army, some because they thought the British would transfer power peacefully, and others because they believed they could use the military training and resources provided by the army to bring down the British regime. Armed nationalists also migrated to the new nonstate army, the PVO. Jealousies raged over the relatively tiny number of officer slots in the new army of the state as more than five hundred wartime officers faced demotion in or removal from the reorganized postwar army. And within both the army and the PVO, cleavages developed along the same lines as those emerging in the AFPFL: between Thakin Soe's Red Flag Communists (who went underground in 1946), Thakin Than Tun's wing of the Communist Party, and the Socialist Party.

During the brief return of British rule, what passed for the "state" was a constantly moving target. At no point during this period did any single group or individual establish unchallenged authority over any significant territory, resources, or persons. As Joel Migdal has argued in his analysis of state-formation processes, at no point was it inevitable "that state leaders [would] achieve predominance for the state."[63] However, in the chaos of the early postwar era, there were moments in which political leaders with armed and determined followings forged ad hoc compromises that resulted in the crafting of institutions that became quite durable in the years to come. The incompatibility of the objectives that mobilized these various armed groups sustained the wartime practices of politics that made violence the currency of power. Political victories came from identifying, disarming, and in some cases destroying enemies, not from accommodating and cooperating with opponents.

5

Insurgency and State Disintegration, 1948–50

I take *Hsaya* San's rebellion as child's play, compared with the present confla-
gration.

Prime Minister U Nu, September 4, 1948

The turmoil that enveloped Burma at the close of World
War II did not abate with the transfer of power from the British to the
Burmese on January 4, 1948. In fact, ethnic, political, and territorial tensions escalated, tearing apart the already thin fabric of the Rangoon-based
national state. Political power became increasingly fragmented, and the
early years of independence saw the emergence of many organizations with
control over substantial violence throughout the country.

Within three months of independence, what remained of the legal Communist Party (i.e., the CPB) launched an armed rebellion against the government. Many of the former PBF soldiers and officers in the tatmadaw deserted in mid-1948 to join the communist rebellion, while at the same time
Karen separatist groups began an armed campaign for an independent
"Karenistan." By early 1949, more than half of government troops had mutinied, and nearly that proportion of its equipment was gone. Important
cities such as Mandalay, Maymyo, Prome, and even Insein (a suburb of Rangoon) fell to insurgent control. Hence by the time Gen. Ne Win assumed
the position of armed forces commander in chief in February 1949, he commanded fewer than two thousand troops, many of whom were of questionable reliability. According to a recent official history, by 1949, 75 percent of

the towns in Burma had fallen to one insurgent group or another.[1] In other words, just as the state became independent from colonial rule, it utterly collapsed.

During the anti-Japanese resistance and the following three years of social and economic chaos under the British, centers of political power had proliferated across the territory, draining Rangoon of any pretense to claim authority even within city limits. With the departure of the British, the AFPFL—victorious in the 1947 parliamentary election—may have held a nominal claim on whatever authority could be mustered, but de facto political power throughout Burma remained beyond the grasp of anyone based in Rangoon. This pattern only deepened over the first two years of independent rule. However, during these two years, the spontaneity and randomness that characterized Japanese- and British-era antistate violence began to give way to patterns of contestation that presaged a potential revival of some form of central state power. Violence became somewhat more regularized, framed in terms of a rightist-versus-leftist elite political struggle for the reins of the postwar state. Embedded in the two-Burma framework that emerged out of negotiations over army reorganization (see chapter 4), this rightist-leftist struggle centered on control over national institutions—the army, the Parliament, the civil service—in Rangoon, but the protagonists in the struggle built alliances with and linkages to powerful forces in the countryside. This knitting together of networks of violence constituted a tenuous but nonetheless productive form of state building. As elites in Rangoon and rural leaders negotiated over how to manage violence and scarce resources, they momentarily appeared to be constructing accommodationist institutions of governance.

Elite-level political conflicts played out in the army as well as in electoral and party politics. Within the tatmadaw, disputes over assignments, promotions, and counterinsurgency strategies reflected the broader struggle over which of the two Burmas institutionalized within the reorganized tatmadaw would inherit the reins of the postcolonial state. As former PBF officers gradually gained ascendancy, this struggle became framed in increasingly durable terms pitting "rightists" against "leftists." This pattern of contestation led initially to an even greater decentralization over the control of violence in Burma as well as further fragmentation of the national state based in Rangoon.

Like the state based in Rangoon, the tatmadaw collapsed during the early months of political independence and could barely be distinguished from the dizzying array of other quasi-state and private armies circulating throughout the country. In immediate postwar Burma, guns were widely available throughout the countryside, where they found their way into the hands of a proliferation of loosely bound groups of former resistance fighters, black marketers, PVO members, farmers, and thugs. All of these postwar, postcolonial armies—including the tatmadaw—were made up of personnel who had been mobilized in the anti-Japanese resistance. Politicians, local warlords, and government officials formed and disbanded new armed units with such frequency and lack of coordination that many of their members did not even know the names of their organizations nor who their allies and enemies were. At no point in the 1948–50 period was it clear that the tatmadaw would evolve into a military that could monopolize political power for longer than any other nation's military in the post–World War II world. At independence, elite-level political struggles in Rangoon—inextricably linked to the violent situation in the countryside—provided an opening for socialist-leaning army officers to eventually acquire enormous power for the tatmadaw within the postcolonial Union of Burma government.

The "Rangoon Government" versus the "Rebels": An Overview of Unrest, 1948–53

In many ways, the three-year interregnum of returned British rule left most of the Burmese countryside in worse condition than the CAS(B) officials encountered upon the departure of the Japanese in 1945. Crime rates skyrocketed in urban areas and their surroundings, where political foes from various resistance era forces squared off against each other. As independence approached, district administrators still struggled to rebuild their headquarters, jails, irrigation systems, courts, hospitals, and police forces. After the civil war began with the revolt of Thakin Soe's Red Flag Communist Party in July 1946, the central government's control over major natural resources and infrastructure slipped even further. Foreign observers began referring to the newly independent regime of Prime Minister U Nu as the "Rangoon government," which signified how far U Nu's de facto authority stretched beyond his office at the Secretariat.

The British interregnum did little to rebuild the war-torn economy. In the 1948–53 period, imports and exports hovered at around one-third of 1938 levels, the government abandoned the operation of passenger trains and cement factories, and forest production levels languished far behind the output of the colonial period. In the countryside, economic conditions were especially unstable throughout the first decade of postcolonial rule. Agricultural indebtedness grew precipitously, while government subsidized loan programs were bled dry by the AFPFL party officials who administered them. Furthermore, table 4 shows the steady decline in the Burmese government's ability to collect its chief source of revenue, land revenue. The steep drops in land revenue demand and collection in 1949–50 mirrored equally steep drops in economywide output, domestic consumption, railway passenger miles, forest production, imports, and exports.[2]

Table 4. Land Revenue Collections in Burma

Year	Demand	Remission	Collection	Outstanding
1945–46	155.30	2.88	47.25	105.17
%		2%	30%	68%
1948–49	283.98	0.97	68.25	214.76
%		0.3%	25%	75%
1949–50	99.23	0.12	12.75	86.36
%		0.1%	13%	87%

Source: Union of Burma Government, "Report on Land Revenue Collections" (n.d., probably 1951), copy in FO 371/83162, PRO.
Note: All figures are in lakhs of rupees.

The Proliferation of Violence

The combination of a devastated economy, a paralyzed government, and a mobilized, uprooted, and armed population meant that social relations in postwar Burma were governed not by paper-pushing district administrators or peace-keeping police but by whomever had the most guns. Throughout the country, farmers, workers, transients, nationalists, refugees, bandits, cattle thieves, and parliamentarians all armed themselves to defend their homes, families, villages, fields, mines, markets, factories, plantations, and political offices. Some of them banded together to take advantage of the chaos in a variety of enterprising ways. While the legal economy remained at a standstill because of the leveled infrastructure, the black-marketing of rice, consumer goods, and guns represented the dynamic economic forces in the country.

A number of the wartime resistance leaders in central Burma continued to rally their local "pocket" armies—such as Bo Tauk Htain's followers in Pyinmana, the Aung Gyi Yandaya Tat in Yedashe, and Thakin Kyi Shein's pocket army in Lewe. In the early years of postcolonial rule, these groups fought alongside tatmadaw units in anti-insurgent operations in those areas while building lucrative black-market networks that undercut the Rangoon government's access to revenues. For example, one district administrator wrote of his attempt to reestablish some measure of law and order in Yamethin soon after independence:

There was one [toll] gate about which I could do nothing. This was on a large, deep stream that crossed the road between Pyinmana and Lewe. To safeguard the bridge against sabotage, . . . guerrilla forces had established an outpost where they were collecting tolls. They had composed a jingle, to the accompaniment of which the collections were made thus adding poetry to pilferage.

Ho, Sir! This is the Aungyi Yandaya Tat!
Garbed in silk and army belts!

Ho, sir! Please do stop!
And pay your mighty kyat [Burmese currency]!

The official added that once the insurgents had moved away from the area, "The police could not take over the bridge, for the guerrillas were politically well-connected. All I could do is turn a blind eye."[3] In other parts of Burma, hard-pressed tatmadaw field commanders encouraged British businesses operating in the country to form their own security forces because the army could not protect them.[4] Throughout many of the former frontier areas, Shans, Kachins, and other minority groups raised their own levies to fight crime and insurrection in their localities.

The disruptions to rural and urban life also created tens of thousands of refugees, who moved into district towns, set up hutment quarters (called *kwet-thit* in Burmese), and looked for a way to make a living in a war-torn economy. Politicians quickly took charge of refugee relief organizations and began recruiting more followers from these uprooted peoples, as well as from dacoit gangs, for their party armies. These *kwet-thit* became indispensable elements of the AFPFL's political machine, particularly in Rangoon. They also became notorious for crime.

Upcountry, some of these locally based armed groups affiliated with cells of one of the two Communist parties fighting against government forces. Others stayed neutral in those battles and instead fought anyone threatening the immediate security of their paddy, homes, villages, livestock, or rackets. And still others floated back and forth between the legal and antistate folds, and among various organized resistance groups. Karen and Kachin levies aligned with some breakaway units of the non-Burman wing of the army and began fighting for some degree of autonomy from the Burman-dominated Union government. Overall, many of these bands of armed men consolidated themselves—however loosely—into one of seven insurgent groups that took up arms against the government between 1948 and 1953.[5] By this point, the then–prime minister remembers that the government "had taken on the appearance of an old house with rotted supports."[6]

Tatmadaw Politics at Independence

The leftist and separatist insurgencies that commenced soon after independence descended from the postoccupation elite struggles in Rangoon and centered on the issue of which Burmese would rule, defend, and pacify the country and its population. The two-Burma conflict was manifest most obviously and most threateningly inside the army, where those who had gained access to privilege and state power based on connections to the

British maintained their status with high ranks in the postcolonial army; those who had been excluded by the British in the prewar era but then elevated by the Japanese found themselves increasingly shut out of positions of authority over army, state, and national resources. The latter group complained of "rightist" domination of Aung San's army; the former worried about the large numbers of "leftists" (PBF Burmans) who swelled the ranks of several infantry battalions. Moreover, Karen and other army leaders worried about the linkages between the leftists in the army and the AFPFL's armed and mobilized following. Throughout 1948, these tensions flared up sporadically with little coordination among opponents. However, by February 1949, this rightist-versus-leftist battle inside the army had shattered its ranks, leaving fewer than two thousand men to fight in the uniform of the Union government.

The "Rightists" in Charge

At independence, Karen and other officers who had never served in the PBF dominated the upper ranks of the postcolonial army. British advisors had appointed Karens as chief of staff of the army (Gen. Smith Dun) and the chief of the air force (Saw Shi Sho); the chief of operations was the Sandhurst-trained Karen, Brig. Saw Kya Doe. The quartermaster general, who controlled three-quarters of the military's budget, was a Karen, Saw Donny. Although the Karen infantrymen who had served with the British during and before World War II had been allotted only three battalions of the reorganized postwar army, Brig. Saw Chit Khin, who was a Karen officer, was appointed to command the first infantry brigade group when it was formed in 1948. Karen officers and other ranks commanded nearly all the supporting services, including the staff, supply and ammunition depots, artillery, and signals corps.[7]

Other minority groups made up four additional infantry battalions, with a majority of those soldiers and officers coming from the ranks of levies that had been recruited by clandestine Allied organizations, some of which had used extensive anti-Burman propaganda in their training. Moreover, Brig. Bo Let Ya, army chief of staff and soon-to-be minister of defence, although a Burman of Thirty-Comrade fame, had shifted his politics rightward and appeared to support continued British influence if not outright command over the tatmadaw. Of the thirty-three senior officers who attended a commanding officers' (COs') conference on January 31, 1949, only four had experience in the PBF. Nine attendees were Karen, four were probably "rightist" Burmans, and the rest were other minorities (mostly Kachins and Chins).[8]

Beyond the army, much of the police force in rural and urban Burma was comprised of Anglo-Burmans, Anglo-Indians, Gurkhas, and Karens who had served the British regime prior to the war. Additionally, Karens who had fought in the anti-Japanese resistance—like guerrillas throughout the rest of Burma—had never given up the arms that Allied organizations had given them during the war. Karen politicians, concerned about safeguarding the interests of Karens as independence approached, established the Karen National Union (KNU) in February 1947; the KNU set up its own militia group, the Karen National Defence Organisation (KNDO), several months later. Hence, both inside and outside the formal state institutions of violence there existed a well-armed and well-trained corps of potential fighters with uncertain loyalty to the AFPFL government.

Early postcolonial AFPFL politics inside and outside the army reflected this concern with the institutional clout of the alleged British loyalists. It is important to remember here that AFPFL politicians and adherents inside the army had mobilized twice to fight the British for independence. Therefore the presence of British "collaborators" in the commanding heights of the army and the government bureaucracy represented a failure of those mobilizations. Throughout 1948, there were widespread fears that Karens and other indigenous groups were conspiring with foreign interests to bring down the AFPFL government; these rumors were reported frequently in the Burmese language press.

Within the military, the Karen leadership's ties to the British Services Mission (BSM) were of particular concern. As provided for in the Let Ya–Freeman Defence Agreement, the BSM advised Burmese military after independence and, more important, vetted all arms purchases sought by the tatmadaw. The former PBF officers in the postwar tatmadaw never entirely trusted the BSM. In addition to their suspicions that some British army personnel were involved in the arming of Aung San's assassins, they still today recall vividly the pro-Karen policies of BSM officers, many of whom had served closely with Karen units during and after the war. In the early postwar era, the main complaint was that the BSM personnel favored Karens for perquisites, promotion, and positions of authority in the reorganized tatmadaw. Former Col. Chit Myaing remembers that the British officers throughout the early postwar era substituted a policy of "Karenization of the Burma Army" for the Burmanization that had been agreed on at Kandy.[9] From their positions in the War Office and quartermaster general's office, Karens also were strategically placed to coordinate the present and future disposition of the army given that all arms purchases would have to be approved by the BSM.

The "Leftists": Former PBF Wing

In contrast, the institutional position of the PBF wing of the postwar tatmadaw, which formed the "leftist" wing of the intra-institutional struggle, was weak. Former PBF officers nominally were in charge of the First,

Third, Fourth, Fifth, and Sixth Burifs, but in fact these Burman officers remained under the command of British counterparts assigned by the BSM. From the BSM's inception, AFPFL and Burman army officers suspected BSM officers of actively trying to sabotage the PBF wing of the postwar tatmadaw. In administrative and supporting arms and services, PBF officers were few and far between, with only a handful capturing positions at the War Office and in field units.[10] As former Brig. Maung Maung noted, "If they [the BSM staff] had had their way, they would have gotten rid of all of us PBF officers."[11] Additionally, the growing political tensions between pro-communist and non- or anti-communist followers among former PBF members was undermining the unity of these battalions, a trend particularly noticeable in the Third and Fifth Burifs. Overall, the pro-AFPFL numbers within the army were small (no more than 25 percent) and on the decline in 1948.[12]

Throughout the 1945–49 period, former PBF leaders and AFPFL politicians attempted to find ways to counter their institutional weakness within the armed forces. Their concern was mainly with the power of the rightists, especially the Karens who had worked with the British throughout the colonial and wartime period. The former PBF leaders inside the army did not consider Communist Party followers inside or outside the tatmadaw to be real threats to the future sovereignty of independent Burma. The best evidence of this anti-rightist, anti-Karen focus of the AFPFL came when the government outlawed the KNDO only four days after its adherents declared full-scale rebellion. By contrast, the CPB, which began its rebellion in March 1948, was not declared illegal until 1953.[13]

Much as in the 1930s, the institutional exclusion or weakness of the former PBF officer corps led to the formation of armed units outside the reorganized army's Karen-dominated chain of command. The PVO was the first postwar manifestation of this solution to the exclusion of mobilized Burman nationalist groups. Aung San was able to organize this pocket army out in the open by construing it as a veterans organization affiliated with the legal AFPFL. He told nervous British officials in 1946 that this welfare organization was not as martially oriented as the tats, which the British allowed to function in the 1930s.[14] Some former BIA, BNA, and PBF soldiers and officers joined Aung San's PVO rather than the postwar army because of concerns about the pro-British and rightward drift of the national military.[15]

With a strength of more than 100,000 at independence in 1948, the PVO began to grow unruly and split into pro-government (called "Yellow Band" PVO) and anti-government ("White Band") factions. All the while, Socialist and other non- (and anti-) Communist leaders of the AFPFL and of the Burma Rifles units began plotting the formation of other paramilitary groups that they could control by placing them outside the chain of command of Defence Minister Bo Let Ya and Army Commander in Chief Gen.

Smith Dun. The space in which these paramilitary forces operated was created initially under the Home Ministry in the form of special police reserves and village defense forces.

Because the Socialist-leaning officers ultimately gained control of the tatmadaw by 1953, it is worth looking in more detail at the way in which these plans developed to counter "rightist"—that is, Karen and pro-British—influence over the armed forces. The 1947 personal diary of then-Capt. Maung Maung (who ten years later rose to be one of the most powerful officers in the military) records frequent informal meetings at the home of Socialist Party leader U Kyaw Nyein. At these meetings, Socialist politicians, former PBF army officers, and government leaders debated a wide range of issues about future political and military plans. Although at the time a split was brewing within the Socialist Party itself, all were united on the necessity of dismantling and reorganizing the rightist-dominated tatmadaw in such a way as to produce "a Burma Army worthwhile having."[16]

The diary of Maung Maung is clear that although there was some concern about "CP [Communist Party] chaps in [the] army," the discussions on army planning focused almost entirely on how to capture control from Karens and pro-British "stooges" (such as Bo Let Ya).[17] By the time of the July 1947 assassination of PVO leader Aung San, the PVO had grown increasingly pro-communist and thus less useful to AFPFL moderates who were trying to counter the institutional power of the rightists in the army. After Kyaw Nyein was named Home Minister on August 1, 1947, the meetings at his house hit on another solution that again reflected the pattern initiated in the 1930s of forming paramilitary pocket armies.

This time, violence was to be organized in the form of special police reserves, which would create an institutional basis for organizing non-communist members of the PVO into a more reliable force and for including those former PBF soldiers who could not pass the entrance examination for the army. Maung Maung reports that he, Kyaw Nyein, Ne Win, Aung Gyi, and Bo Khin Maung Gale met in August 1947 to discuss raising the Union Military Police under Kyaw Nyein's Home Ministry to create a "single military force very loyal to the Government" and *not* subject to the authority of Gen. Smith Dun or the increasingly pro-communist leaders of the PVO.[18] Over the next several months, the AFPFL recruited thousands of supporters into Union Military Police (UMP) units and deployed them on anti-communist and anti-dacoit missions.[19]

Interestingly, this form of political insurance policy was countered almost immediately by Bo Let Ya, one of the "rightist" enemies according to the leftists. Kyaw Nyein claimed that when he went to India for tuberculosis treatment in May 1948, he asked Bo Let Ya to serve as acting Home Minister. Kyaw Nyein left him with instructions to "disarm and demobilize" the civil police who had been "raised during [the] CAS(B) [era] by the British and mainly of Karens and some riff-raffs [*sic*] among Burmans." Instead on his return, Kyaw Nyein discovered that Bo Let Ya had done the opposite. He had transferred these "riff-raffs and Karens" to the UMP.[20]

Counterinsurgency and Mutinies

These intra-army tensions might have resulted in a compromise or power-sharing arrangement had they not occurred in the context of an increasingly threatening civil war. Even before independence in January 1948, the Burma Army found itself fighting the CPB in central and Lower Burma. The returned British colonial state had pursued a counterinsurgency strategy from 1945–48 that was almost purely military and coercive in its campaign to eliminate Thakin Soe's small bands of communist rebels. Upon independence, the Union government and its military inherited this strategy and redeployed this coercive method of addressing insurgent challengers. This approach—which is in direct contrast to the political, incorporative solution championed by the British government in Malaya later in the Emergency—led to the reinvigoration of security institutions within the postcolonial state and to the relative underdevelopment of countervailing domestic political institutions that could check or limit military power. More immediately, however, early anti-communist campaigns brought to the forefront the tensions between the two wings of the army and the two visions of Burma each pursued.

Critics of Counterinsurgency

Former Col. Chit Myaing, then a captain in the Third Burifs who would go on to fight in most of the anti-Karen operations in South Burma, reported that the conduct of the anti-CPB campaigns throughout the 1946–49 period involved a ruthless scorched earth policy. Devised by the British advisors to the army and continued after 1948 by the Karen military leadership, this strategy required the razing of villages suspected of harboring or sympathizing with communists and executing their villagers. Within Chit Myaing's own battalion, which he admits was "known for having many communists," this policy was seen as fratricide. "We didn't believe those killed [in these operations] were really insurgents. These were just men, women, *pongyis* [monks] and children." Chit Myaing remembers pro-communist and non-communist officers and soldiers throughout the rest of the former PBF units in the army criticizing the scorched earth tactics from a practical point of view. "The government would never win the people over to its side with that kind of tactics." Instead, the ruthlessness confirmed the propaganda being spread by Thakin Soe that AFPFL leaders were tools of the imperialists who cared nothing for Burmese villagers.[21]

From the point of view of the rightist wing of the army, as Martin Smith notes, "it is ironic that through these turbulent months the government was only saved by the continued loyalty of the Chin, Kachin and Karen regiments in the Burma Army . . . which gave the government time to reorganise its disintegrating military command and . . . perhaps to prepare secretly for the outbreak of war [in 1949] with the Karen National Union."[22] In other words, ethnic-minority units saved the AFPFL government, which nonetheless continued to harbor suspicions about how loyal the minorities were to the Union government of Burma.

Anti-Rightist Unity

As these tensions escalated between the army's Karen/rightist leadership and the leftist former PBF officers, the latter group organized informal meetings in Rangoon beginning in June 1948 to discuss how to check Karen power within the tatmadaw and to end the communist rebellion. According to one participant, this self-proclaimed "leftist unity" group was comprised of nine members who met nightly from midnight to 3 a.m. The members, all ex-PBF, included then-Brig. Ne Win, commander of the North Burma Sub-District; Col. Bo Zeya, general staff officer (GSO) (1), staff duties; Lt. Col. Ye Htut, commander of the Third Burifs; then-Lt. Col. Tin Maung, company commander in the Sixth Burifs; then-Maj. Chit Myaing, second in command of the Third Burifs; then-Maj. Tun Sein, company commander in the Fifth Burifs; and Maj. Tin U, Sixth Burifs. Initially, the group hoped to forge an alliance with communist rebels, so "we could bring the government, Socialists, Communists, military and AFPFL together on one side."[23] When the Communists rejected their overtures, they changed course in early August and decided that wresting control of the army from the rightists should be their top priority.

This shift in the focus of the former PBF officers led to a split amongst themselves. The split developed over the next two weeks of August 1948, although the chronology of events, the motivations of the participants, and the precise cast of characters involved remains the subject of some speculation. There appears to be consensus on the sequence of some of these events, which probably constituted the first coup attempted in postcolonial Burma.[24] First, there is little doubt that the army's leftist unity committee decided to get rid of Bo Let Ya. Second, at some point in July or early August 1948, Brig. Ne Win and Col. Bo Zeya asked U Nu to replace Bo Let Ya as Defense Minister with one of the leftist officers, and probably it was clear to all involved that the choice would be between Brig. Ne Win and Col. Zeya, who were the most senior of the former resistance fighters in the tatmadaw. Soon after that meeting Bo Zeya returned secretly to U Nu's house to demand that he be awarded the portfolio; Ne Win probably did not know Bo Zeya would do this. And finally, a number of sources confirm that Ne Win learned of Bo Zeya's second visit, which he viewed as a double-cross, and this brought on the split among the former PBF officers that led to two major mutinies.[25]

The Mutinies

Within several hours of his showdown with Ne Win, Bo Zeya and his ally, Bo Ye Htut, tried to round up the First and Third Burif troops they would need to remove the army and governing leadership. While accounts of the First Burifs mutiny are sketchy, former Col. Chit Myaing offers a detailed account of the preparations for a coup and to go underground among the Third Burifs.

First, Ye Htut, commander of the Third Burifs, approached then-Maj. Chit Myaing, who as second-in-command of the Third Burifs had operational control over the only infantry units based in Rangoon at the time. Chit Myaing reports that Ye Htut asked him to let Thein Pe Myint (an active communist politician) or himself address the troops to explain why a coup was necessary. Chit Myaing agreed, on the condition that either Ne Win or Chit Myaing himself be allowed to present the opposing point of view. Ye Htut chose the latter, who informed Ne Win of the plans. On August 9, Ye Htut and Chit Myaing spoke to the Third Burifs. Chit Myaing remembers: "We had a meeting of all officers, warrant officers, and NCOs in the officers' mess building. About eighty to ninety people attended. Ye Htut spoke first, blaming the government for everything. I never defended the government but said that we can't take up arms against a legally constituted government. I think 90–95 percent agreed with me."[26]

Later that night, Chit Myaing learned that rumors spread throughout Rangoon that the Third Burifs was planning a coup. Ye Htut summoned Chit Myaing at 3 A.M. the following morning to a meeting of Thein Pe Myint and twenty to thirty army officers, including Bo Zeya and Bo La Yaung. Chit Myaing remembers, "They asked me to join them; they tried to threaten my life to get me to join." He refused, but warned them that news had spread that they had stolen arms from the training depot and would be arrested if they were still in Rangoon in the morning.

At 5 A.M., Chit Myaing reports that he went to see Ne Win and subsequently Prime Minister U Nu to tell them that he and Ye Htut had decided to split the battalion. "I didn't want to see Ye Htut arrested," he recalls. Ne Win's response to the news of the pending mutiny reportedly was upbeat: "Good. Now we know who is black and who is white."[27]

This remarkably amicable split of the battalion involved two conditions set by Chit Myaing and probably approved by Ne Win. First, Chit Myaing assembled his officers and men and told those who wanted to join Bo Zeya's and Ye Htut's forces that they could take their personal weapons with them but nothing else. And second, all had to agree not to shoot any of their colleagues who either went with them or stayed behind. In return for this concession, Chit Myaing promised not to come after them for seventy-two hours.[28]

The number of deserters and their intent are difficult to ascertain. Probably only a handful of the soldiers who left on the trucks commandeered by Ye Htut understood what was going on. Many were confused as to who was leading them, where they were going, and what their mission was. Additionally, Chit Myaing reports that when he counted the soldiers who had remained loyal and in the barracks, "we still had some fellows whom we didn't want but had stayed behind. But we wanted to get rid of them. We selected them and persuaded them to go with Ye Htut as they would not be happy here. They were worried and said they didn't know where to go, so we gave them maps."[29] In all, 188 out of 800 Third Burifs were declared absent-without-leave on August 10, 1948.[30]

Army "Rightists" Respond

The mutinies did not significantly boost the capacity of the struggling insurgents, but did immediately exacerbate the existing tensions between the remaining PBF officers and the Karen military leadership. On the day after the August 1948 mutinies, Defence Minister Bo Let Ya, Vice Chief of Staff Saw Kya Doe, and the South Burma Sub-District Commander Aung Thinn[31] began drafting plans to disarm the remaining soldiers in the loyal Third Burifs. Ne Win intervened, convincing them not to do so because it would drive even more Burif units underground.[32] Clearly, the political leverage and the numerical strength of the former PBF element inside the army was even further diminished, while sheer numbers appeared to shore up the hold of Karen and other non-AFPFL officers over the infantry and supporting arms and services.

A week after the mutinies, the former PBF officers were further alarmed to learn that Bo Let Ya subsequently convinced Nu to appoint Tun Hla Oung as inspector general of police and U Tin Tut as inspector general of the "Union Auxiliary Forces" (yet another unit of irregular levies raised by the political right) on August 16, 1948; both were given the rank of brigadier.[33] Only two weeks earlier, Tin Tut had delivered public addresses commending the gallantry and efficiency of Brig. Saw Kya Doe in directing the very same anti-communist operations that the former PBF officers believed to be overly cruel and counterproductive in the pursuit of peace.[34]

Additionally, outside the army, Karen leaders found a more sympathetic ear from Prime Minister Nu when they sought arms and recognition for their local defense units operating under the auspices of the paramilitary KNDO. No doubt Nu was eager to defeat the communists and their armed leaders, who had just insulted him in the bungled coup attempt.

The Sitwundan: A New Tat?

The response from the other wing of the army was predictable. The AFPFL and its former PBF officers in the army moved to create and deploy another set of armed levies, out of the chain of command of rightist army leadership. In this case, the leftist-unity group decided to build on the paramilitary organization that had been raised in March 1948—immediately after the CPB rebellion—under Kyaw Nyein's Ministry of Home Affairs and the Burma Police Act of 1945. Vaguely called "Special Police Reserves," this initiative involved establishing linkages between AFPFL and Socialist Party headquarters in Rangoon, Mandalay, and district towns, on the one hand, and the wide variety of local militia already organized by AFPFL politicians upcountry on the other. After the army desertions in August led to an apparent consolidation of Karen control over the army and KNDO control over many parts of the countryside (especially in the Irrawaddy Delta), Socialists inside and outside the army stepped up plans to expand and give status to these special police reserves. They sold the idea to Prime Minister Nu, who asked Bo Aung Gyi—Nu's confidante and parliamentary secretary who was also close to Socialist Party leaders—to take charge of raising these levies, renamed the Sitwundan. On October 1, 1948, Nu transferred authority over the Sitwundan to the War Office, wherein Aung Gyi was assigned the role of inspector general of these levies.[35]

The Sitwundan was yet another party army that found the space to operate inside state institutions. These irregular forces were intended to increase the strength of the former PBF, pro-AFPFL wing of the army by increasing the numbers of troops who would remain loyal to the AFPFL government, rather than the Karen army leadership or the communist insurgents. The army leadership immediately condemned the raising of the Sitwundan, and Bo Let Ya ultimately tendered his letter of resignation over this issue: "Does not the Government trust the army . . . and police? Have not they shown adequate proof of their loyalty?" He went on to criticize the quality of personnel in the Sitwundan: "It was rather surprising to note that the personnel appointed to lead these levies are either dacoits, ex-dacoits or people familiar in police registers. Some of them are either known criminals or political chameleons. . . . What will be the impression of the public to see a criminal or a political chameleon with gazetted rank of deputy SP [special police]?

Sitwundan irregular forces attending military training in Tavoy District, 1948. P(AN56-646) PV(a), DSHRI.

How will police subordinates feel to find a criminal as their senior officer?" He predicted that "there will be a civil war of a large scale between the socialists and anti-socialists if it [the Sitwundan scheme] is not checked in time."[36]

Originally, the Council of Ministers of U Nu's government authorized Sitwundan units to be raised in eighteen districts, at least six of which were KNDO strongholds and ten of which contained communist, PVO, or army deserter guerrillas.[37] The linkage to the former PBF wing of the army was explicit: seventy-six (including officers and other ranks) of Ne Win's Fourth Burifs and ninety-seven of the Fifth Burifs were seconded to the Sitwundan for organizing purposes. Furthermore, as KNDO and Karen army loyalties to the Union government became increasingly suspect, Nu and Aung Gyi quickly expedited its expansion to twenty-six battalions with the possible further expansion to fifty-two. By 1949, there were thirteen thousand Sitwundan levies in twenty-six battalions throughout Burma.[38]

Similar to the earlier pocket armies, which found institutionally secure niches through which to organize violence, the Sitwundan units—once given arms and official recognition—became very difficult for their originators to control. Due to more than twelve hundred defections of Sitwundan to either the Karen or one of the communist rebel groups, the War Office disbanded Sitwundan battalions in nine districts (Pakokku, Magwe, Minbu, Thayetmyo, Myingyan, Mandalay, Meiktila, Sandoway, and Kyaukpyu) by late 1951.[39]

The Two Burmas Collide

The CPB rebellion in March 1948 and army mutinies in July and August 1948 brought to the forefront the incompatibility of the two-Burma framework by identifying the very different visions of who the enemy was for each camp. The Karens and more rightward leaning Burmans who held leadership positions in the army identified the leftist, anti-western claims of the communists—and to an increasing degree, the AFPFL—as the single greatest threat to Burma. Accordingly, these rightward-leaning military leaders directed harsh anti-communist counterinsurgency operations. The institutionally weaker pro-AFPFL elements in the military saw the rightist, pro-western elements as a threat to Burma's continued independence from western domination. The tatmadaw's involvement in counterinsurgency warfare made what had been a fragile balance of power within the institution and the nation no longer tenable.

From Accommodation to Rebellion

In the early months of the rebellion of Thakin Than Tun and his communist followers, it appeared that Karen leaders were still confident that they could work through the existing Union framework to establish "their" postcolonial Burma, or at least a Karen state they could live with inside the AFPFL's Burma. As a number of observers have noted, Karen and Kachin tatmadaw units played key roles in staving off first the communist attacks and then the combined CPB/PVO/army mutineers' offensives against the Rangoon government. However, in May 1948, the AFPFL government made conciliatory offers to communist rebels as part of its formal "Left Unity" proposal. This proposal, an outcome of discussions among former PBF officers still in the army as well as AFPFL politicians, offered amnesty to communist rebels and proffered the possibility of political power-sharing. This initiative must have made it clear to Karen army and political leaders that the two-Burma setup was no longer viable for either side. The Left Unity program threatened to upset the balance of power between leftists and rightists in the government and army.

The first outbreaks of anti-government violence on the part of Karens occurred sporadically in the early months of 1948. Smith Dun, who as head of the army recognized the cross-purposes of trying to deploy the former PBF-dominated infantry units against communist rebels, instead deployed Karen militia units in a number of areas to fight the communists after their insurrection commenced in March.[40] In some cases, however, trailing Burma Rifles troops and irregulars such as Sitwundan and UMP carried out mopping-up operations that brought them into contact with the Karen militia fighting against communist rebels. This led to conflicts between the Burman and Karen units, all fighting at least nominally on the side of the government. Additionally, armed Karen groups who called themselves "Peace Guerrillas" robbed government treasuries in the name of collecting taxes for independence funds. Hence there were intermittent outbreaks of violence between Karen militia and regular and irregular government forces throughout the May-August 1948 period. Beyond these uncoordinated, rather minor skirmishes, the first major sign of rebellion came on August 14, 1948, when Karen UMP irregulars took over Twante near Rangoon, followed by more Karen UMP desertions in Thaton and Kyaikkami a week later. On August 30, the KNDO took over Thaton, and a KNDO-led force aided by Karen UMP deserters took over Moulmein.

More Calls to Arms, More Violence: September–December 1948

It was no coincidence that the government's Council of Ministers expedited plans to raise more irregular levies within days of these events. In fact Nu's September 9 order to reorganize the AFPFL's special police reserves into the Sitwundan and to place Aung Gyi inside the Karen-dominated War Office to take charge of these levies must be seen as preparations by the AFPFL government to fight—and no longer just to marginalize—the Karens in the army, the Karen National Union and the latter's militia, the KNDO. This is not to suggest that the Council's orders to expedite the expansion of the irregular units under AFPFL control were part of some well-thought-out, sinister plan by the Burman-dominated AFPFL to exterminate the Karen race. Instead, the expansion of the Sitwundan looks much like then-Capt. Maung Maung's plans to raise anti-rightist levies (the UMP) the year before. In his diary, Maung Maung recorded that he threw together these plans in less than twenty-four hours. These were on-the-spot solutions to problems as minor skirmishes turned into crises. And if the expansion of the Sitwundan was part of a longer-term plot of any kind, it was one in which the former PBF, pro-AFPFL members of the army were trying to gain greater institutional clout within the state's organizations of coercion.

By September 1948, the chaotic conditions prevailing in independent Burma had polarized remaining "loyal" forces into two politically incompatible camps of armed followers. On one side, the pro-western, "rightist" forces claimed allies in important armed groups, including Karen army leadership; KNDO units (some more centrally tied than others); Karen Peace Guerrillas, who were as likely to be bands of thieves taking advantage of the chaos as they were local defense units; most of the police; and U Tin Tut's levies, called the Union Auxiliary Forces. A number of Karen soldiers defected from the tatmadaw to join these irregular forces. On the other side, the AFPFL had what remained of the former-PBF dominated units of the infantry, which at this point consisted of the Fourth Burifs and a small number of loyal Socialists and AFPFL adherents in the Third, Fifth, and Sixth Burifs; the locally raised, locally armed, and usually locally controlled Sitwundan; and other loosely affiliated village defense units and local political bosses' armies that had in common their reluctance to support communists or rightists.[41]

The strengths of and unity within each camp were much overstated by the proponents and opponents of each. Furthermore, outbreaks of violence that may have been purely locally focused, apolitical, or otherwise insignificant took on far greater gravity as the chaotic conditions made it difficult for partisans of either side to see transgressions as anything but part of the increasingly all-or-nothing, rightist-leftist struggle. In part, this exaggeration was a function of the breakdown of what little communications infrastructure still existed. As the combined communist/PVO/army mutineers' rebellions continued from August through December 1948, their guerrilla attacks shut down the railways, made road travel impossible, and blocked the lines of communication.

These breakdowns not only paralyzed the government but also the KNU, tatmadaw, and AFPFL leadership in their efforts to understand what was going on in the countryside and to coordinate or control their upcountry allies. The vernacular press in Rangoon and Mandalay also stoked the fires of exaggeration. Cases of banditry or political violence often were reported to be evidence of foreign-backed conspiracies, overblown trends, and full-fledged rebellions, thus consolidating a variety of unrelated violence into one category—antistate violence—and grossly overstating the coordination possible under such conditions.[42]

During the last four months of 1948, the numbers of reports of violence escalated throughout the country. The two camps viewed many of these incidents as evidence of growing danger to their visions of Burma's future and their personal safety. AFPFL leaders and former PBF officers within the army grew more convinced that the Karens and rightists had British support for their cause when Alexander Campbell, an ex–Force 136 agent who had trained Karen levies during the war, was arrested in Rangoon carrying letters that suggested he intended to help the Karens overthrow the AFPFL government. Although Campbell had the backing of only a handful of marginal, harmless friends in England, exaggerated rumors of British conspiracies spread throughout the Rangoon and Mandalay press. Additionally, the pro-AFPFL officers in the army were enraged when Smith Dun brokered a November peace deal between U Nu and the Karen rebels holding Twante, Thaton, and Moulmein. The arrangement allowed the KNDO to remain armed and in control of the strategically important Twante Canal, which leads from the Rangoon port to the Irrawaddy River. Soon thereafter, on November 13, 1948, the KNU demanded the establishment of an independent Karen-Mon state that would include the entire Tenasserim and Irrawaddy division and a number of contiguous Lower Burma districts. If established, it would have would surrounded Rangoon. Again the Burmese-language press depicted this initiative as part of a greater plot to wipe out the Union government.

Karen leaders—inside and outside the army and KNU—saw evidence of growing danger to their own survival. Most of their fears revolved around the raising and arming of the Sitwundan. Karen leaders believed this organization was focusing its heaviest recruiting blitzes on Burmans who lived near Karen neighborhoods. Karen officials also told British Embassy staff that in early September, local AFPFL officials demanded that many of the Karen villages in the Irrawaddy Delta surrender any weapons they had, "with the object of reissue to Socialist levies."[43] In December alone, the Karens believed that Aung Gyi and other Socialists had supplied Sitwundan units with as many as 480,000 rounds of .303 ammunition, as well as other weapons and supplies.[44]

On September 19, the day after Campbell was arrested for conspiring to incite a Karen rebellion, U Tin Tut—the head of the rightist levies raised in August who no doubt was viewed as an ally by most Karens—was assassinated in Rangoon. Although the murder case was never solved, it is likely that he was assassinated by a political opponent from the Socialist Party or AFPFL.[45] Karen officers in the War Office told British officials that they were convinced that "Bo Aung Gyi, Deputy Inspector of Sitwundan, was the organiser of the murder."[46]

Finally, by December the violence escalated to outright massacres. On Christmas Eve, a locally raised, ethnic-Burman Sitwundan group threw hand grenades into a Palaw (Mergui district) church, killing eighty Karen Christians in attendance. Over the next month, Sitwundan and other Socialist levies killed hundreds more.[47] KNDO groups retaliated and seized government treasuries in some delta towns. Of course, regular and irregular pro-AFPFL troops retaliated.

The Army Karens Rebel

Until the December massacres, Karen infantry units and Karen officers in the army continued to fight communists on behalf of the Union government. However, everything changed in December 1948 when the Karen Rifles endured extremely difficult battle conditions during their anti-communist operations in Pyinmana. These battles—fought to keep the AFPFL government afloat—were followed by the bloody massacres of Karen villagers by irregular AFPFL forces in the delta. At that point, soldiers and officers in the Karen Rifles began firming up the previously loose linkages between army Karens and Karen political and militia groups. Together, they planned to wage war against the government.

Rightist-leftist violence in the delta escalated and inevitably landed in the suburbs of Rangoon, where Karens and Burmans lived in adjacent quarters. By January 1949, reports from Rangoon suggested the capital itself was surrounded by well-equipped, hostile Karens. KNDO units raided the army's weapons depot in the Karen suburb of Insein in early January. Units of as many as two thousand Karens trained openly on its outskirts. Sitwundan units, reinforced by university students and hooligans from Rangoon, moved into Insein and surrounded the Karen quarters there. From time to time, the Sitwundan and other irregulars fired shots toward Karen quarters in Insein, Ahlone, Kyimendine, and Sanchaung (the latter three located inside Rangoon city limits), which resulted in KNDO leaders calling for reinforcements from outlying districts. KNDO units set up road blocks throughout the Insein area, and skirmishes broke out when they tried to stop vehicles carrying Burman levies or soldiers.

Burmans who lived in Karen-majority neighborhoods lost patience with the government's ability to protect them. They started collecting arms, posting vigilantes, and erecting road blocks of their own all around Rangoon. Buddhist organizations in Rangoon and Burmese-language newspapers sponsored public meetings to call on the government to disarm KNDO forces around the country. These confrontations spread to other towns and communities where Karens and Burmans lived close to one another, mainly throughout the delta.

As tensions escalated in Insein, KNU leader Saw Ba U Gyi contacted an ally in the tatmadaw, Col. Min Maung, commanding officer of the First Karen Rifles at Toungoo, and asked him to create a diversion outside Rangoon.[48] On January 27, 1949, Col. Min Maung's First Karen Rifles seized Toungoo, an important district town lying on the strategically significant Rangoon-Mandalay railway. The next day, Karen troops seized Pyu while Saw Jack, a Karen naval commander who had mutinied, led an unsuccessful attack on Bassein in the western delta. Just outside Rangoon, the Insein skirmishes turned into a full-fledged battle by January 31. The town officially "fell" to the Karens on February 2. KNDO units managed to advance to within four miles of Rangoon before being halted by the government's patched-together forces of regular soldiers, police, militia, Sitwundan, and

General Ne Win, Commander in Chief, Burma Army, inspecting tatmadaw forces at Insein front, June 1949. P(AN90-343) PV(b), DSHRI.

university and high school students armed with *dahs* (knives) and old rifles.[49]

On January 30, the government outlawed the KNDO. Two days later, Nu placed Karen army, navy, and air force leaders "on leave" and replaced Smith-Dun with Ne Win as chief of staff. A few days later Nu named Ne Win "Supreme Commander of All Defence Forces and Police Forces" (hereafter "Supreme Commander").[50] Subsequently, the rest of the Karens in the army either joined the rebellion or were interned in the Armed Forces Rest Camps established on February 7 (South Burma Sub-District) and 8 (North Burma Sub-District).[51] The First Kachin Rifles, led by former anti-Japanese guerrilla leader Naw Seng, joined the rebellion when Ne Win ordered his unit to retake Toungoo from the Karens. Over the next three months, all the major towns from Rangoon to Maymyo—including Prome, Meiktila, and Mandalay—and much of the Irrawaddy Delta fell to one group of insurgents or another (or some ad hoc alliance among them). The government did not retake Insein itself from the Karens until May 1949 and only after both sides had suffered heavy losses. Toungoo was under rebel control until March 1950. Map 5 shows how extensive rebel control of the country was in February–April 1949.

The Post-Karen Tatmadaw

With the bulk of the army leadership either in rebellion or interned in "rest camps" by February 1949, the tatmadaw was decimated. The former PBF officers who landed in vacant War Office positions found depots empty and supplies gone. Army field commanders slapped together patchworks of barely trained soldiers, Sitwundan, local thugs, levies, politicians, and students to launch uncoordinated counterinsurgency campaigns. Aung Gyi, the head of the Sitwundan, remembers deploying soldiers "after only two hours of training" to fight KNDO, CPB, and PVO rebels in early 1949.[52]

The day after the defection of the Karen Rifles, Lt. Col. Kyaw Winn, in his capacity as both quartermaster general and adjutant general in the War Office, undertook a review of who was left in the tatmadaw, as best as that could be determined under the circumstances. He estimated total losses of 11,852 soldiers, more than 4,000 of whom were Karens. Table 5 (p. 138) breaks down the personnel losses by arm or service. A measure of the War Office's desperation can be seen in a Special War Office Council Order, dated February 8, 1949, which reads, "The release [and] discharge of all ranks . . . except on disciplinary or security grounds . . . is suspended until further notice."[53]

While the commanders of the north and south subdistrict headquarters tried to coordinate operations among various armed units, operational control was effectively in the hands of the battalion commanders, who introduced a pattern of local initiative that became institutionalized at the field command level. Local commanders assigned tax collection duties to their men, and whatever was collected was used on the spot to buy rice, guns, telescopes, homemade weapons, and information from local populations across the country. Local commanders also recruited new soldiers—for regular and irregular army units—and in the first two years of the insurrection they alone were responsible for training all new recruits. Little of this unit initiative was ever documented or reported to anyone in Rangoon. The War Office had almost no idea what was going on upcountry. For example, not until April 4, 1950, did a War Office Council Order make official the prevailing practice of local initiative and local responsibility: "As most [field] HQs/Formations/Units are so involved in operational activities or staff

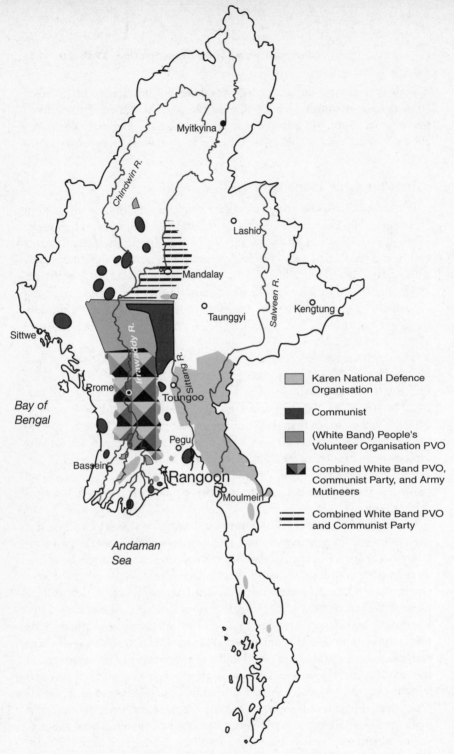

Map 5. Rebel control over Burmese territory, February–April 1949. *Source:* Based on map in Government of the Union of Burma, *Burma and the Insurrections* (Rangoon, 1949), n.p.

Arms captured by tatmadaw from Karen forces, Battle of Insein, 1949. P(AN80-114) PV(a), DSHRI.

work in connection with operations, it is proposed to suspend the submission of Quarterly Historical Reports."[54]

Pocket Armies, Counterinsurgency, and Pacification

Given the disarray in the tatmadaw and rebels' hold over much of the country, how did the "Rangoon government" survive into the 1950s? In fact, the armed forces that managed to regain and maintain control over a large expanse of territory outside Rangoon in the name of the "independent" national government were forces organized *not* under the government's army (the tatmadaw) but instead under local and national politicians with ties to the Socialist Party. These Socialist Party forces pacified most of the country by incorporating local bosses, dacoit bands, and thugs into units loyal enough to the Union government that the elite-

Table 5. Tatmadaw Personnel Losses as of March 19, 1949

Arm or Service	Depletion in Effective Strength
Infantry	6,757
Artillery and Armor	163
Engineers	496
Signals	253
Supply and Transport	920
Ordnance	108
Medical Corps	626
Electrical and Mechanical Engineering	524
Headquarters	308
Training	254
Miscellaneous	416
Education	60
Total	11,852

Source: "Statement Showing the Effective Strength of the Army as at Present 19 March 1949," appendix F to Adjutant-General (Lt. Col. Kyaw Winn), "Manpower Review of the Burma Army," March 1949, DR 1011, DSHRI.

level political struggle in Rangoon stabilized in favor of the AFPFL leadership.

Socialist Debacle at the Center

In February 1949, however, the Socialists appeared to have little chance to endure, much less to thrive in this way. In the wake of the Karen rebellion, the AFPFL government nearly collapsed due largely to the crippling effects of a nationwide civil servants' strike in February–March 1949. On April 1, 1949, all of the five Socialist members of Prime Minister U Nu's cabinet, along with their colleagues who remained from the PVO, resigned their ministries. These resignations probably were the outcome of divisions within elite circles of the AFPFL over what the best strategy was for fighting the Karen, communist, and other insurgents.

Some, including Ne Win, wanted to offer amnesty to communist and other leftist rebels, bring them back into the government's regular and irregular forces, and trounce the rightists. One leading Socialist Party leader argued that Ne Win pressured Nu into forcing the Socialists to resign from the cabinet because they had come to oppose reunification with the communists.[55] Others wanted to fight all the rebels by enlisting the support of conservative forces such as the older politicians who had served in Legislative Councils under the British. This was probably Nu's position, at least in part, since it was clear by April 1949 that Nu had also ruled out bringing the communists into his government. Furthermore, the Socialist politicians in Rangoon had become so unpopular by censoring, threatening, and destroying the urban press establishments critical of them that Nu had to get them out of the limelight, and thus deputed them to return to their home districts to organize counterinsurgency operations.

After the Socialist ministers resigned from the cabinet in April 1949, many prominent Socialist politicians in Rangoon and the PVO members of Parliament returned to their homes outside Rangoon. However, they were "returning" to a countryside that no longer was familiar, inviting, or receptive to them. During the anti-Japanese resistance, the Burmese nationalist leaders—who by 1948–49 had become the principals of the postwar Socialist Party—had chosen deliberately to forgo the cultivation of a mass base in favor of protecting these leaders from Kempetai (Japanese military police) investigation and torture. They hid in plain sight in Rangoon so that they would be able to lead the Burmese to independence when the opportunity arose. This meant that after the war, these leaders—such as Kyaw Nyein, Ba Swe, and Thakin Tin—had escaped relatively unscathed the wartime deprivations of the Japanese, but they also emerged without the mass following that communist leaders such as Thakin Soe had built in the delta.

Immediately after the war and at independence, Socialist leaders stationed themselves in urban elite circles, which probably accounts for their early undoing. Right after the war, the Socialist Party endorsed a mostly conciliatory approach toward the British in the negotiations for independence and argued for compromise over the disposition of prewar British capital. Thus, when the Socialist Party leaders landed ministerial and other significant posts at independence, their moderation ensured that the party would be perceived as having moved to the ideological right of their wartime allies. Furthermore, as ministers, parliamentary secretaries, and district officials, the Socialists early in 1948 became the implementors of state policy, and when the latter was a tax or otherwise extractive policy, they appeared to differ little from officials in the colonial regime.

Given this unpopularity and organizational weakness in 1949, how did Socialist politicians manage to sew together the networks necessary to regain control over much of the countryside? This puzzle is best approached by breaking it down into two questions. First, how did they recruit the armies that bore the brunt of counterinsurgency campaigns? And second, how did Socialist politicians firm up these linkages into networks loyal to the party's leadership?

Recruiting Counterinsurgency Troops

Many former resistance and underground leaders upcountry had held on to weapons used during the war and formed pocket armies to protect local interests from bandits, communists, and other dangers in the chaotic post-war period. In the thick of the Karen crisis, Socialist Party adherents inside the army (such as Maung Maung and Aung Gyi) and the AFPFL (such as Ba Swe and Thakin Kyaw Dun) began visiting these local leaders to try to reestablish ties forged in some cases in the 1936 and 1938 student strikes, in other cases in the BIA and anti-Japanese campaigns, and still others under the auspices of the Japanese-sponsored EAYL. Most of the units that ultimately became labeled "Sitwundan" companies, Socialist "peace guerrillas,"[56] or "territorial forces" already existed when the Karen crisis began and already had engaged in anti-communist and anti-insurgent activities.[57] In some locales, levies had to be raised from scratch, and local politicians, members of Parliament, and local police officers recruited former PVO rebels who had straggled back to rural homes after the July 1948 amnesty; former BDA/PBF soldiers and officers who had been unable to pass the entrance exams for positions in the postwar military; former resistance fighters; schoolboys; unemployed cultivators and workers; and groups of small-time bandits. On the quality of personnel, the head of the Sitwundan frankly described his organization: "It was like a big septic tank."[58]

Many of these groups had experience fighting during World War II as locally based guerrillas and after the war as locally based anti-guerrilla, anti-dacoit units. The key issue was whether local leaders chose to use their weapons to fight against rebels raiding their harvests or against government troops doing the same, both needing food for sustenance. One important consideration that conditioned a pro-government stance for some local militia leaders was their linkage to the Socialist Party that dated back to the networks forged among participants in the 1936 and 1938 student strikes and later in the Thakin Party and the anti-British and anti-Japanese underground resistance.

Furthermore, given the unsettled conditions of postwar Burma, the most sought-after resource in the early civil war period was weaponry, which was readily available to Socialist Party officials throughout the hierarchy via both official and unofficial channels. It is interesting to note that although tatmadaw and government leaders were unable to provide weapons to Burma Army field commanders who sent desperate requests for supplies to Rangoon, Socialist Party leaders in villages, towns, and districts around Burma had little difficulty procuring weapons from their own stores or through the black market operating around the country.[59] In some cases, Ne Win and other tatmadaw leaders ordered their field and staff officers to hand over what few weapons they had to local bosses such as Thakin Kyi Shein and Saya Hti to curb Communist influence in particularly unstable areas. A field commander who led a Burif infantry battalion in an offensive against Thakin Than Tun's forces in Pyinmana 1949 remembers that he had no choice but to share his meager arms with the notorious local political boss (and former Thirty Comrade) Bo Tauk Htain: "We couldn't cover everything, so I had to put him in charge" of a large area of the operation.[60]

From Provincial Pocket Armies to National Power

The above description of the rather mad dash to shore up countryside allegiances to the government explains who was recruited, but it does not explain how national-level Socialist leaders managed to attract and sustain the loyalty of local leaders and local armies. Certainly, these local politicians were not risking life and limb simply out of pure patriotism or devotion to a shaky government that broadcast mixed messages as to what its vision and ideology were and that seemed on the verge of collapse on any given day throughout 1948–49. Initially, these local militia groups were fighting for very local concerns—safety of home, property, paddy, family, and black market niche—and in a number of areas, the government was much less of a threat than the earlier-arriving insurgent groups, who demanded taxes, food, and shelter from villagers and townspeople. Local interests probably had identified the first predators, which were in many locales the insurgent groups, as enemies.[61] By the time the Socialists and other pro-AFPFL adherents arrived to court district towns and villages, the government's claims on the population looked comparatively less invasive and promised a greater degree of local autonomy.

As the insurrection wore on and local pro-government private armies as well as the tatmadaw regained control over more territory, Socialist leaders began revamping the party's corporatist institutions. In many villages around Burma, former underground leaders joined or associated informally or formally with the Burma Socialist Party and the party's All-Burma Peasants' Organization (ABPO). They used these organizational linkages to build political and economic clout. In the early years after independence, the Socialist Party's success at incorporating local leaders around the country into their worker and peasant mass organizations provided a mechanism of ensuring loyalty to the Rangoon government—or at least of ensuring anti-insurgent solidarity—among these local armies.

What did local leaders gain from affiliation with these organizations associated with the Socialist Party? Though the economy had been crippled by war damage, rising debt, and fleeing capital, the government and the Socialists nonetheless had a few resources to parcel out via the party and its mass organizations; these resources included ferry licenses, land grants, reconstruction grants, small loans of capital or materials to cultivators, trading licenses for merchants, Pyidawtha[62] government grants, licenses to operate public transit and alcohol shops, and unofficial promises to ignore the smuggling of teak, rice, gold, and other commodities in the regions controlled by Socialist followers. As early as 1948, former colonial-era land surveyor Furnivall reported that "the distribution of land was mainly in the hands of the Socialists," which gave local leaders an important resource for bargaining with land-hungry tenants.[63] In 1950, a U.S. Embassy official noted that Socialists in rural districts recruited support by manipulating the Consumer Cooperative System (CCS)—"through which essential supplies of food and textiles reach low income groups at a relatively moderate price . . . There is evidence that [CCS] committee members were selected at least as much for their loyalty to the Socialist Party as for their efficiency in the handling of commodities."[64]

Notably, this sketch of Socialist Party patronage upcountry does not suggest that the AFPFL, ABPO, or Socialist Party actually established effective, durable, corporatist-style control by party leaders over party adherents around the country. Instead, despite the fact that these mass organizations did not give a Rangoon-based party headquarters or the government bureaucracy direct control over resources or people outside Rangoon, they did establish a forum for negotiating with local power holders over resources, elections, and administrative affairs. Local officials were able to use these mass organizations to their economic benefit, while Socialist Party leaders were able to use them for their electoral and political benefit.

Conclusion

What emerged in the first few years of postcolonial Burma were state-authorized and often state-armed village, town, and district militias organized under and comprised of party faithful. These locally based, -recruited, and -armed units tipped the balance in favor of the government's reassertion of at least nominal control over much of central Burma. This growing network of counterinsurgency organizations gave the national-level Socialist Party politicians upcountry connections that made possible their gradual consolidation of control over the national government during the next few years. In the 1951–52 legislative and municipal elections, Socialist armies provided "protection" at voting booths throughout the country and ensured through legal and illegal means a strong showing by Socialist and other AFPFL candidates. However, this consolidation of a machine that could deliver municipal and national electoral victories came only by institutionalizing local authority in village and town defense units that grew increasingly autonomous from Rangoon. A journalist from the 1950s noted, "They [Party leaders] couldn't supervise the pocket armies, who did whatever they wanted."[65] One district administrator wrote in his memoirs that when he tried to disarm Thakin Kyi Shein's guerrilla forces in Lewe, "the rogue went down to Rangoon and got a stay order!"[66]

As early as 1948 these local institutions had become the target of opposition party, press, and even government criticism. Throughout the 1948–51 period, scattered newspaper articles suggested that some members of these local militias were responsible for crimes including robbery, dacoity, bribery, and murder in towns and villages around the country. Trying to explain these problems, the BSM noted in late 1950, "Many remote and inaccessible areas have had no stable government for over eight years, and consequently lawlessness flourishes."[67] By the time order was restored throughout enough of Burma for the government to consider holding its long overdue parliamentary elections in 1951–52, the crimes of village defense units, the Sitwundan, and the so-called People's Peace Guerrillas (PPG) accounted for frequent headlines in Rangoon dailies.

The Socialists made some efforts to incorporate existing village armies more formally into a hierarchy with orders emanating from Rangoon, although such a hierarchy was impossible at the time. For example, Socialist Party headquarters laid out plans to register all ြ ောက်ကျား (pyauk-kya; translated, "guerrillas") roaming the countryside in its 1949 *Socialist Party Gazette*.[68] These attempts were not successful, and Socialist politicians, Prime Minister U Nu, and army leaders eventually tried to absorb what they called "respectable" Sitwundan members into expansion units of the tatmadaw and to disband other less reliable pocket armies. Neither strategy worked; for example, Nu's announcement in early 1951 that the PPG would be disbanded during the election campaign of 1951–52 had little impact. Reports of PPG abuses continued for four or five more years.[69] Similarly, although some Sitwundan units were absorbed into the army on schedule, most others held on to their arms. Their legal status was not officially eliminated until 1955.[70] In 1956, when the Sitwundan were formally integrated into the tatmadaw, a new party army—the Pyusawhtis—was inaugurated. By this point, public skepticism about the ability of Rangoon to protect villages and towns from the excesses of the party soldiers ran high enough to force U Nu to establish a Special Tribunal that would investigate crimes committed by Pyusawhtis.

Hence we can see important continuities between the decentralized nature of the anti-Japanese resistance and the state-society relations of the British reoccupation era, on the one hand, and the increasingly imbalanced relationship between the central state based in Rangoon and the many up-country, nonstate authorities armed and skilled in guerrilla tactics and thriving on illegal economic and political activities. The early years of the insurrection saw many of these nonstate local armies either join the insurrection as guerrillas or use their local power bases and guerrilla skills to fight the insurgents. The levies that came to be associated with Socialist Party politicians consisted of experienced guerrillas who turned into counterinsurgency experts with little difficulty. Their success came from their intimate knowl-

Tatmadaw officers meet with villagers during Operation Liberator (October 1951–January 1952) to mobilize them against communist influence. P(AN87-1236) PV(b), DSHRI.

edge over local conditions and their control over local resources. That success was in direct contrast with the faltering central state, which had very little administrative capacity from 1948 to about 1953, and became dependent on these local leaders to reestablish some kind of authority throughout much of the country.

By the time order returned to much of the countryside in the mid-1950s, the state's access to local power holders and rural resources were mediated by leaders of local militia, incipient warlords, and autonomous army field commanders. The alliances between center and upcountry leaders to pacify the countryside led to accommodational processes that began bringing more and more rural and local politicos into Rangoon on a regular basis. Some were elected to the national legislature in the 1951–52 and 1956 elections, while others made the journey purely for business purposes, such as to obtain stay orders to keep district officers out of local commercial enterprises. For the first time in the history of modern Burma, accommodation between power centers in the capital and upcountry was underway.

6

Warfare and Army Building, 1950–53

The Burma Army is *not* fit for War. . . . When it is remembered that the army now consists principally of Burmese and that the Karens, Chins and Kachins, who are the martial races of Burma are either excluded or form a minority of the present Army, it will be appreciated that its fighting value is negligible.
British Services Mission to Burma, June 1951

During the first two years following independence, the nature of domestic warfare and the weakness of the central state gave rise to ad hoc political and military alliances throughout the central region of Burma. These alliances reflected unprecedented political accommodation between Rangoon elites and upcountry political bosses, guerrillas, and black marketers. The remnants of the post-1949 tatmadaw waged piecemeal, uncoordinated operations against small, equally unsystematic antistate rebel groups into the early 1950s.

The character of combat was like that of the anti-Japanese resistance: small units of antistate rebels squared off against the tatmadaw and its locally raised levies in positional warfare against each other, usually over control of an urban center or lines of communication in the central region. To make up for army weaknesses, tatmadaw field commanders knitted together ill-trained, undersupplied groups of soldiers, levies, and youths. These patched-together forces fought to reassert the "Rangoon government's" control over the country. Their "enemy" was a hodgepodge of ex-allies, former classmates, and wartime comrades-in-arms. During this time, the army's institutional boundaries seemed fluid, with many former PBF officers and enlisted personnel reluctant to transform themselves from the courageous champions of the wartime resistance into careerist soldiers in the fledgling army of an increasingly unpopular government based in Rangoon.

As ambivalent army officers improvised counteroffensives against the communists, army mutineers, and Karen rebels, the insurgency in the central region began petering out of its own accord by mid-1950. Over the next couple of years, the increasing stability in central urban areas and the decreasing need to deploy any and all able bodies in tatmadaw uniforms gave way to new rounds of public contestation over what the identity of the army should be. At issue was how the heroic spirit of the wartime resistance could be sustained by a standing, professional army of a national-state.

Civilian politicians, army field commanders, and general staff officers all had very different plans for the postcolonial army. Once again, the debates, negotiations, and tactics over army reorganization set the terms for the manner in which the postcolonial state would be reconstructed. Should the armed forces embrace the organizational imprint of Aung San's dream of a decentralized people's army, thus sustaining its revolutionary roots and connections to the populace? Or should it be reorganized into a more centralized, modern, European-style standing army, with an explicit chain of command emanating from either the elected prime minister or a professional general staff? As in the negotiations between the AFPFL and the British after the end of World War II, at stake in this debate was the question of who would control the institutions and resources of violence, for what purposes, and against whom.

These differences of vision, along with the ad hoc operational style of the army, could easily have continued well beyond the first decade of independence, as they did in post-revolutionary Indonesia.[1] However, in Burma, a new enemy had materialized in 1949 with the potential to threaten not just the popularity of the Rangoon government but also the sovereignty of the country: the Chinese Kuomintang (KMT). In 1949, the People's Liberation Army (PLA) of the newly founded Communist regime in China chased hundreds of KMT deserters across the border from Yunnan province into northeastern Burma. The deserters were soon followed by units of several thousand more disciplined KMT soldiers. Worried that the KMT presence might provoke the new People's Republic of China (PRC) into invading Burma, the tatmadaw initiated counteroffensives against the intruders beginning in 1950. Unable to regain control of any KMT-held territory, army leaders set out to overhaul the institutions of violence.

What emerged from this reorganization process was a military with a strengthened general staff and new formal limits on just how much civilian oversight could be carried out by elected politicians. The reorganization also created an expansive and durable devolution of military authority over anything remotely defined as a security concern. By 1953, the tatmadaw alone claimed responsibility for defining who was an enemy of the state and deciding how enemies and threats would be handled. Along the way, a handful of enterprising, confident staff officers with ties to the Socialist Party managed the reorganization process to create institutional niches that they could use to consolidate their political position within the army.

From the "Rangoon" toward the "Union" Government

During the first year after independence, former PBF field officers who served as field commanders blamed the "rightists" (i.e., Karens, Anglo-Burmans, and "stooges") running the War Office for failures on the battlefield. For its part, the War Office, under the leadership of Smith Dun, was frustrated by the unwillingness of these force commanders to recognize or carry out War Office orders. So weak was Smith Dun's chain of command that the BSM reported in June 1948 that "There is no means of linking infantry battalions administratively." Furthermore, the report noted that the officer in charge of records had a "poor liaison with the War Office" and was "out of touch with Commanding Officers."[2]

Local Autonomy of Field Commanders

Many of the field commanders developed loose alliances with local guerrilla and paramilitary leaders to make up for the support they found wanting from the army administration headquartered in Rangoon. These alliances involved "understandings" as to what territory was to be controlled by the tatmadaw, what territory was to be patrolled and protected by the local politicians' followers, how resources were to be distributed, who could recruit whom, and who had authority over what. For the most part, these understandings were unofficial, and field commanders did not seek or get approval from War Office personnel. Right after independence, these loose alliances were probably the outcome of bet-hedging by these former student union politicians and PBF resistance fighters–turned–field commanders, who were not convinced that the Union's best interests were served by a rightist-run tatmadaw.

By February 1949, most "rightists" had rebelled or been removed from office. The rightist-versus-leftist framework for explaining operational failures and difficulties no longer was germane. At this point, former PBF officers held most of the significant field commands and staff positions in the War Office. When the former PBF officers took over the decimated War Office in February 1949, they allowed their former student union and PBF colleagues in the field free rein to carry out anti-insurgent operations in whatever manner they could. In the field, the loose working relationships with local pocket armies were the key to saving the "Rangoon government." However, these locally autonomous counterinsurgency efforts increased tensions between field and staff officers in the tatmadaw that did not disappear with the removal of the rightists at the staff level.

Weakness in the War Office

In the first year or so after the Karen leadership vanished from the War Office, what little army administration existed came to a standstill as most able bodies were sent out to fight in anti-insurgent operations. The officers and NCOs in the two training companies in Rangoon spent most of 1950 deployed on anti-insurgent operations, and almost no training was conducted anywhere except on an ad hoc basis in the field.[3] The Army Recruiting Organization based in Rangoon had no idea how many soldiers had been recruited anywhere in Burma. What few records did exist at the North Burma Sub-District headquarters were destroyed in the looting that occurred when Maymyo fell into insurgent control in February 1949.[4] In the face of this adversity, the BSM noted among Burmese War Office personnel "a distinct tendency to pander to the opinions and tastes of individual unit commanders on training matters, and a reluctance to insist upon taking adequate measures to eliminate weaknesses exposed by operations."[5]

From the post-Karen War Office point of view, the increasingly autonomous battalion commander presented a major concern not for political reasons (as was the case for the Karen army leadership in 1948) but for organizational and operational reasons. Without any kind of central coordination, major operations were poorly planned and executed, training of new recruits was nonexistent, and discipline "became deplorable," according to an internal army report that evaluated the early counterinsurgency campaigns. In the height of the crisis, the report noted that

> even among the loyal elements, some officers seized moveable property such as motor cars, livestock, etc. which they found in operational areas on the pretext that such property was ownerless. There were also some who engaged on a large scale illicit trade in opium in collusion with professional opium smugglers. A few abused military transport to carry commodities which they bought for the purpose of private trade. Others indulged in unwarranted interference in private quarrels of civilians and in the administrative affairs of the civil authorities. There were still others who openly criticized some actions of the State government in newspapers and on the radio.[6]

Reports trickled back to Rangoon from nervous citizens that off-duty army personnel were "in the habit of going about carrying daggers/knives."[7]

These problems were further aggravated when the War Office in 1949 authorized local commanders to raise new units as quickly as possible. "[M]any undesirable elements crept into the Defence Services," noted one tatmadaw assessment.[8] The hasty efforts to raise minority levy and army units also led to more ethnic tensions. For example, after the Karens occupied Insein, the War Office stepped up efforts to recruit from the Gurkha communities in Burma. A British observer noted that all Gurkhas, regardless of caste, were lumped into the same battalion, producing "considerable difficulties . . . as far as making promotions and feeding were concerned."[9]

The Turning Point

None of these problems between field and staff appeared to either contingent to be insurmountable in light of the fact that as 1950 wore on, the insurrection lost steam. Consequently, the government began to regain at least nominal control over more territory and resources. Government forces, aided by locally raised irregulars, recaptured Toungoo (the KNDO stronghold and seat of their Kawthoolei government) in March 1950 and Prome (a stronghold of one of the communist factions) in May. Soon after, the government offered amnesty to rebels, and six thousand surrendered.[10] In August, government troops killed the Karen rebel leader, Saw Ba U Gyi, in a village near Kawkareik. His death greatly hurt KNDO morale.

By the end of the year, the government had determined that sufficient territory had been recovered to schedule general elections beginning in June 1951.[11] By the following year, even the skeptical British ambassador, Richard Speaight, reported "distinct progress toward restoring law and order and a corresponding lessening of the threat from the insurgents." He noted that insurgents had only interrupted service on the Rangoon-Mandalay railway twice in two months; "indeed a leading British businessman has admitted to me that this line has been interrupted less than was usual in British days during the monsoon, when sections of the track were often washed away." Speaight noted that the road from Rangoon to Mandalay and Maymyo was now "perfectly safe," and that lead and silver mining companies in Lashio and tin miners in Tenasserim reported that they had not been held up by insurgents or bandits in a long time.[12] In addition to decreasing crime rates, customs and other government revenues slowly increased and government leaders began resurrecting ambitious economic and social development programs for the first time since independence.

Army Expansion and New Organizational Tensions

It is important to note that the gains discussed above are probably attributable more to insurgent attrition than tatmadaw successes in combat. In fact, as army ranks expanded and operational efficiency did not improve at corresponding rates, debates developed within the tatmadaw over where the barriers to improvement lay. Two new axes of tension defined the framework that came to structure the internal struggles for power over the institution, at least until the 1962 coup. One axis lay along the experiential divide between the field commanders and Rangoon-based general staff officers, and the other along the ambiguous divide between civilian and military authority over defense macro- and micropolicy.

During this period, the army expanded from a mere eight infantry battalions in 1948 to twenty-six in 1951.[13] With this expansion came both an increase in the army budget's proportion of national expenditures—which rose to 40 percent by 1951[14]—as well as a perception that discipline problems were getting out of control. As a result of these trends, civilian political leaders from the Socialist Party and AFPFL became more active in their efforts to try to control the army. Additionally, inside the tatmadaw, Rangoon-based staff officers in the War Office began trying to rein in their field counterparts and bring them under more centralized control. Field commanders resisted, finding these attempts clumsy and detrimental to operational efficiency.

Civil-Military Tensions

According to the minutes of the 1950 commanding officers' (COs') conference, Lt. Gen. Ne Win's opening speech laid out an agenda that reflected the emerging tensions between military and civilian leaders over internal military affairs. The speech focused on the issue of how to distribute ranks equitably among the three components of the officers corps—"the officers from the old [colonial] army, the officers from the PBF, and the national minority officers." Ne Win instructed the three different "kinds of officers" to sit down and talk to each other about these problems at the conference. However, the minutes of the meeting do not document any serious discussion or resolution of the problems of how to count prewar military, thakin movement, and other kinds of military "service" in the assessment of ranks among three groups with very different service histories.[15]

In interviews in 1992, former PBF officers explained that what was actually at issue here was Prime Minister U Nu's interference in the army promotion process.[16] Soon after the Karen rebellion started in 1949, Nu toured the frontier areas to rally support for the Union government. Along the way, he decided on the spot to promote a Kachin officer to the rank of brigadier-general without consulting the army. The officer, Lazum Tang, had joined the British-sponsored Army of Burma Reserve Organization (ABRO) at the outset of the war, which rendered his loyalties suspect in the eyes of former PBF officers in the postcolonial military. At the time that Nu promoted him, there were only two other brigadiers in the tatmadaw, the heads of the North Burma and South Burma sub-districts; the top general staff officers held no higher than the rank of acting colonel. Prior to the promotion, Lazum Tang had served only five months at the lieutenant-colonel rank as the commander of the Second Kachin Rifles, and then ten months at the acting colonel rank as the commander of the Mobile Tactical Headquarters.[17] Meanwhile former-PBF battalion commanders spent about two years at lieutenant colonel before being considered for promotion. After Nu's announcement, War Office personnel scrambled to find a command suitable for a brigadier's rank. The military secretary—the staff officer in charge of promotions—from the early 1950s reported that the Lazum Tang promotion was his "biggest headache" because other officers were furious about the political, not military, basis for it.[18] Furthermore, some of the former-PBF officers questioned whether the promotion was necessary (as Nu argued) to keep the Kachin state out of rebel hands.[19]

Later in the 1950 COs' conference, Brig. Kyaw Zaw, Commander of the South Burma Sub-District, articulated further concerns about civilians meddling in army affairs. According to the minutes, he castigated unnamed "cabinet ministers" who came up with the "Peace Within One Year" plan. Announced in July 1949, the plan promised to restore all road and rail traffic between Rangoon and Mandalay and to eliminate all pockets of remaining insurgents by July 1950. Kyaw Zaw reportedly criticized the way in which "the plan was set up without consulting the army. . . . There is no plan." Militarily, he argued, this objective was impossible and put tatmadaw units at risk.[20]

The emergence of this civil-military axis of tension was inevitable as the former student union politicians, university hostel mates, and resistance fighters settled into political or military niches in the postcolonial state. Most army officers from the 1950s do not remember choosing to pursue a "career" in the tatmadaw. In fact it was well into the 1950s before the perquisites that go along with a "career" (such as a pension) even existed. Rather, after their experiences in the patchwork of loosely connected resistance groups that fought the Japanese and later formed the AFPFL, they found themselves still fighting well into the postcolonial era.[21]

All the while, army officers watched their old friends and colleagues ascend quickly in the ranks of the nation's political leadership. The politicians had become the government and as such often did things that looked shockingly similar to what the British had done. At the same time, army leaders—especially those in field units—considered themselves somehow more loyal to their heroic revolutionary roots. They believed that they were still fighting for an ideal, while the politicians had already sold out and become careerists and opportunists.

Field-Staff Tensions

Ne Win's opening speech included a second major agenda item—"to make staff officers and brigade commanders consult and discuss with each other the difficulties and problems faced by our forces." Despite the elimination of the Karen officers from the top positions in the War Office, battalion commanders continued to complain bitterly about the lack of support provided to them by the War Office. Ne Win also noted that the same field commanders were reluctant to cooperate with the War Office when the latter asked them to carry out certain procedures.[22]

Among the field commanders' complaints aired at the 1950 COs' conference were concerns that there were not enough permanent, regular units in the military for operational requirements; training was nonexistent; ammunition supplies were dangerously low; and there was no armor support for or telecommunications equipment in most field units. The field commanders also pleaded with the general staff to take better care of their soldiers. Morale was reported to be low. Most battalion commanders did not have enough uniforms or food for their soldiers; the children of soldiers were not entitled to what few rations were available; and the amount of the posthumous award to the families of fallen soldiers was insultingly low. Lt. Col. Tin Maung went on to express frankly his frustration with the War Office: "We want our units' needs filled immediately. The War Office must be reorganized. There are no systematic procedures for relations between the War Office and the commands. . . . We can't help wondering from the field just what the War Office is doing."[23]

Notably, the language and discourse of field commanders changed little over the next two years, as they continued to lodge bitter complaints that housing for soldiers, officers, and their families was woefully inadequate and that rice rations were at a starvation level.

Agenda, Content, and Attendance Changes

In the minutes of the 1951 and 1952 COs' conferences, the reports of Ne Win's opening and closing speeches suggest a growing impatience with the complaints of the field commanders and with their inability to sympathize with the general staff. In 1951, he pointed out that "the present Staff of the War Office was originally meant to serve ten battalions of old Burma Army status." The rapid expansion of the army meant that the "present Staff of the War Office [were] very inadequate and overworked to serve twenty-six battalions." The conference minutes note that Ne Win reminded unhappy field commanders that "it was an age-old tradition in every army that there were always misunderstandings and jealousy between the staff and units. [The] Supreme Commander further stated that our Burma Army was not a ready made Army and as all officers were doing their best with their experiences and as everybody was learning by mistakes only, the unit commanders should give a certain allowance to the staff." Ne Win told the assembled officers that he would like to "shuffle" staff and field officers, but he was worried that "if an officer from a [field] unit be posted to staff now, the unit would suffer and if a staff officer be posted to a unit, the staff would be the sufferer."[24]

In 1952, the focus of the conference expanded beyond trying to improve operational efficiency.[25] Casting the net wider to include more staff officers from the War Office and lower-ranking field commanders, this conference was the first to expand beyond the usual complaint session in which field commanders aired their grievances about supply, welfare, and paperwork with the staff. A variety of speakers including cabinet ministers were brought in to discuss land reform, economic development plans, educational reforms, the "democratization of local administration" legislation,[26] and health planning.

This conference was also the first time the Supreme Commander mentioned concrete proposals to overhaul the army and moved away from sustaining the old practice of improvising ad hoc solutions to problems of operational efficiency. Aung Gyi remembers that this was the conference where the force commanders started treating the general staff with more respect, indeed "as the kingpin of the army."[27] Notably, the shift in content and tone at the 1952 conference led to widespread rumors that the army was preparing to take over the government.[28]

Organizational Tensions, 1950–53

Although an eventual reorganization of the tatmadaw would address some of the field commanders' specific complaints (such as training and unit welfare problems), field commanders continued to arrive at COs' conferences throughout the 1950s bearing a great deal of hostility toward their staff counterparts. There was almost no rotation between field and staff appointments, and both groups were developing a kind of caste mentality with regard to the other.

In the early 1950s, this internal army struggle gained less public attention than did the growing tensions between the war-fighting army and the governing politicians. After Ne Win resigned from the Defense and Home portfolios in September 1950 and was replaced by U Win, this civil-military struggle intensified. U Win, described by the BSM as "a well-educated, middle-aged, moderate Socialist,"[29] immediately began trying to diminish the political influence both of the army and of Ne Win within the army. U Win first tried unsuccessfully to increase civilian control over the military by introducing legislation that would limit the term of the Supreme Commander. He also approached British officials in December 1950 and asked them to provide arms for five to six battalions of police, which he intended to serve as countervailing forces against the growing power of Ne Win and the tatmadaw.[30] However, only a year later, U Win told British officers at the BSM that he had given up on these plans to reduce Ne Win's power, and had instead shifted his efforts to try to appoint "an advisory body of officers who would try to get some better ideas across with him in a tactful way."[31] None of these tactics produced much gain in leverage for civilian politicians.

The KMT and the Tatmadaw

It is no coincidence that the shift toward broader socioeconomic concerns in the 1952 COs' conference came along with reports and promises of an army overhaul. The change in conference agenda and content reflects the army leadership's reluctant realization that the nature of the "enemy" and of warfare had undergone a significant transformation since the eruption of domestic insurgency at independence in 1948. Two factors account for the general staff's emergence at the helm of a new army reorganization movement.

First, the return of Lt. Col. Maung Maung to the War Office staff in August 1951 was a turning point in the development of the general staff. Held prisoner for two and a half years by Karen rebels, Maung Maung returned to the army rather reluctantly.[32] At the prompting of Ne Win and Aung Gyi, he demoted Lt. Col. Hla Aung, an Anglo-Burman, former-PBF officer whom Ne Win apparently suspected of being a "plant" of the Defense Minister, U Win.[33] Soon after, Maung Maung took charge of a recently established entity called the Military Planning Staff (MPS) and from this organizational perch drafted the plans to transform the entire institution from a decentralized, guerrilla (or in this case, counterguerrilla)-style army into a modern, centralized standing army. Most army officers from the 1950s consider Maung Maung to be the "architect" of the modern army. In the process of reorganizing the army, he and Aung Gyi also gained influence over all aspects of internal army affairs, which inevitably led to friction between them and the war-fighting, field commanders outside of Rangoon, as well as politicians trying to use the army for their purposes.

The KMT Threat

But Maung Maung was not a miracle worker, and given the entrenchment of both field and staff officers over their own little fiefdoms, his efforts to remake the army were not enough to shock fellow officers out of their dysfunctional but comfortable habits. The catalyst for reform arrived in north-

Table 6. KMT Troop Buildup in Burma

Date	Total Number of KMT Troops in Burma
January 1950	200
March 1950	1,500[a]
July 1950	2,500
April 1951	4,000
January 1952	8,000
February 1952	12,000

Source: Robert Taylor, *Foreign and Domestic Consequences of the KMT Intervention in Burma* (Ithaca, 1973), pp. 11–13.
[a] In addition to the 1,500 men were 500 of their family members.

eastern Burma just as the Union government had reasserted authority over most of its major cities and control over territory that held key natural resources. In 1949, two thousand Chinese Nationalist army deserters first straggled across the ill-defined border between China's Yunnan province and Burma's Shan states. They burned Shan villages around Kengtung, but did not otherwise pose much of a threat until 1950, when more disciplined, better-organized, and well-armed KMT units entered Kengtung state. These units brought their families with them, which provided the first hint that they were planning to stay. Table 6 shows the steady increase in the number of KMT arrivals into Burma. By 1951, U.S.-supplied air-drops delivered provisions and equipment to the KMT twice a week, and in March 1953, supply planes landed at an airstrip in Monghsat.

In these early years, Gen. Li Mi's KMT forces—with the assistance of the U.S. Central Intelligence Agency (CIA)—geared up to try to retake China from the Communists.[34] However, after two offensives into Yunnan failed miserably in 1951, the KMT began putting down roots inside Burma and preparing for a longer stay. Many of the leaders and rank-and-file of the KMT in Burma became opium smugglers. This lucrative business financed gun purchases for future offensives against the PLA and also made some KMT leaders very wealthy.

By 1953, the KMT had gradually come to control the Kengtung, Manglun, and Kokang states in the Shan states. For all practical purposes, the KMT constituted a foreign occupying force in these regions—and one apparently supported by the United States.[35] As Taylor writes, "They had forced the administration of the government of Burma to flee the area and had themselves assumed the functions of de facto government, including tax collection. They built over one hundred miles of road, seventy in Burma and thirty in Thailand. The KMT, according to the government of Burma, even issued calls for the Burmese to overthrow the central government."[36]

The KMT's aggressive stance became more threatening to the Union government when the KMT made overtures to KNDO rebels, which resulted initially in a "loose alliance" and, by February 1953, coordinated operations.[37] Oddly enough, the KMT situation also may have indirectly benefited the Burmese communist rebels, who had established "joint operational commands" with the KNDO in 1952. That relationship gave the communists access to U.S.-manufactured weapons from their KNDO partners, who had bought them from their KMT partners.[38] (See map 6 for the overall disposition of rebel forces throughout Burma.)

The real threat the KMT posed to the Union government, however, was from the consolidating Chinese Communist regime. Throughout the early 1950s, Burmese politicians, army officers, and the public worried that in the course of trying to stabilize their position in mainland China, the Chinese Communists would need to eliminate the remaining KMT units located on the fringes of China, particularly in Burma. The Nu government, which notably was the first foreign non-communist country to recognize the PRC in 1949, feared that the continuation on Burmese soil of U.S.-backed preparations for a KMT invasion into China would provoke the Chinese Communists into simply annexing all of Burma. Furthermore, with the start of the Korean War, Burmese observers rightfully worried that the United States might be setting up a second front in northeastern Burma.[39]

Military Administration in the Shan States

From the Union government's perspective, the Shan states grew increasingly dangerous in the early 1950s, with a perplexing array of anti-Rangoon forces—ranging from Naw Seng and his Kachin followers, two CPB factions, the KNDO, PVO stragglers, and the KMT—traversing this territory, forming ad hoc alliances, fighting against each other, and competing against both each other and the Rangoon government for resources and opium. When reports filtered back to Rangoon that Chinese Communist troops were building up along the Yunnan border, the government proclaimed martial law on June 24, 1950, in the Shweli River valley area of North Hsenwi state (Shan state). Within two years, military administration had gradually spread to twenty-two of the thirty-three Shan subdivisions.

Many of the Shan traditional leaders, the *sawbwas*, had raised guerrilla forces during the war and continued to maintain bodyguard and levy forces through the 1950s. At the same time, some of the young students who had joined the anti-Japanese resistance mobilized political party resources to try to end what they considered the sawbwas' "feudal" control and bring about democratic reforms. Also, as Silverstein noted, the thirty-three Shan chiefs were divided among themselves over the future of their region and "how to transfer their administrative power to the people and what compensation

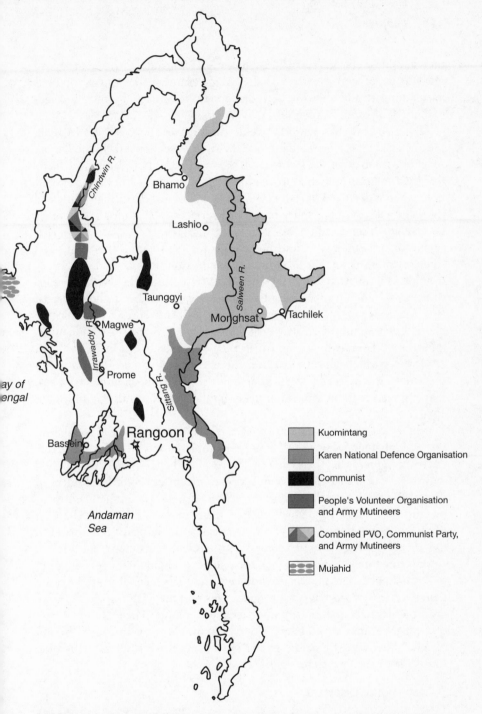

Map 6. Territory held by KMT and other rebel groups, 1953. *Source:* Based on the map "The Civil War in Burma: The KMT Invasion, 1953," in Hugh Tinker, *The Union of Burma: A Study of the First Years of Independence*, 4th ed. (London, 1967), p. 51.

they should receive in return."[40] In the early 1950s, individual and groups of sawbwas negotiated secretly with the Nu government about giving up their local authority and allowing both democratic reforms and tighter linkages with the Union government based in Rangoon.

The sawbwas held a powerful trump card in these negotiations: In 1958, the Shan state was eligible to exercise the right of secession from the Union, a right guaranteed in the 1947 Union constitution. But it seems quite likely that the Nu government improved its bargaining position in these negotiations when it deployed the tatmadaw throughout most of the region and had the army take over tax collection, social services, police forces, and other governmental services previously under the purview of the sawbwas. In fact, as one British embassy official noted after his 1953 trip to the Shan state, "The Burmese claim that this [military administration] was made necessary by the KMT situation, but in fact the areas worst affected by the Chinese insurgency—Kengtung for example—have not been declared under martial law." He concluded that the sawbwas were probably correct to think that martial law was imposed because of "their resistance to the re-shaping of administrative boundaries . . . by which they lose ancient feudal rights."[41] In 1953, the sawbwas and the government arrived at a compromise in which the chiefs would retain their titles and receive compensation from the Union government in return for giving up their administrative authority in 1956.[42]

Whatever the motive for imposing martial law, tatmadaw field commanders suddenly found themselves acting as administrators and not as the heroic guerrilla fighters they had been in the past.[43] Their experience of allying with local Socialist politicians and former thakin pocket army leaders in central Burma during the early insurrection period was nothing like the experience of running local governmental affairs in the Shan states, where no ties to local populations existed. In most cases, the tatmadaw commanders did not even speak the same language as the populations they administered. At the same time, Shan leaders and their subjects found their lives being run by Burman and Kachin tatmadaw officers and their men. During the more than two years of martial law throughout most of the Shan region, the army grew increasingly unpopular among local inhabitants. The embittered wife of a Shan sawbwa wrote later of the "unscrupulous treatment of the hill people." She argued that the tatmadaw "behaved like ruthless occupation forces rather than protectors of the land."[44]

Operational Disasters

The imposition of martial law in the Shan states in 1950 meant that the army was becoming dangerously overcommitted. It was still fighting small cells of KNDO, communist, and other insurgents in central Burma and—

increasingly—in vast stretches of the frontier areas. Moreover, it was facing a possible showdown with the U.S.-backed KMT in extremely difficult terrain, all the while wondering when China would lose patience with its inability to control the KMT.

The stakes involved in fighting the KMT were much higher than anything the tatmadaw had faced to date. The addition of military administration duties, which required greater administrative support from Rangoon, severely tested the abilities and resources of local commanders. For the first time in modern history, army field commanders could not tap into networks of former thakins, student union colleagues, or other old acquaintances to arrange for local support for ad hoc counterinsurgency campaigns.

Given these difficult operating conditions and the lack of militia and other local support, tatmadaw operations failed to regain much territory from the KMT. In 1950, the Union government ordered the KMT to either surrender their arms to Burmese officials or leave the country. When this order was ignored, the comparatively ill-equipped, undermanned tatmadaw launched a counteroffensive in July at Tachilek. Although it appeared at first that KMT troops were retreating into Yunnan, they eventually trickled back into the Shan states, and a second attack (Operation Frost) was launched in November 1951, followed by more piecemeal efforts throughout 1952.[45] It was not until February 1953 that the tatmadaw waged its first full-scale, joint forces counteroffensive against the KMT, called Operation Naganaing (Victorious Naga [mythical serpent]). Superior KMT firepower defeated the operation within a few weeks.[46] According to one Burmese air force pilot who flew air support in the effort, "It was a complete disaster."[47]

Reorganization of the Tatmadaw

The operational failures against a potentially formidable foreign threat made possible and necessary the overhaul of the armed forces. Field commanders, staff officers, and civilian government leaders alike acknowledged the need to transform the institution from its post-resistance, decentralized, guerrilla character into one capable of defending the sovereignty of the Union. In the 1950–53 period, staff officers hatched ambitious plans for the new army, but few came to fruition. Nonetheless, the negotiations, fights, and compromises that characterized the planning process established the broad outlines of a standing army with enormous autonomy to define what constituted "security" and who was an "enemy" of the state. The tatmadaw never gave up this autonomy.

After it became clear that the tatmadaw's piecemeal efforts against the KMT would never succeed, Lt. Gen. Ne Win authorized the formation of a

Spitfire aircraft used by Burma Air Force during operations against the Kuomintang in the 1950s. P(AN91-351) PV(b), DSHRI.

planning committee (later called MPS) under Lt. Col. Aung Gyi to chart "a clear-cut course of military activities" and to advise the government on how to achieve "peace within the State and readiness for national emergency covering all aspects, military, political, social, economic, etc." Ne Win's August 1951 memorandum of authorization spelled out the rationale for the planning committee's formation: "We have been working mostly on an ad hoc or impromptu basis without giving much thought to coordination and correlation of different Departments of State. . . . We are virtually at war and what is worse a more devastating one as any civil war is. . . . I cannot afford to wait for changes in organization and I am immediately in need of a nucleus Planning Staff."[48] The memo emphasized that the War Office was the source of many of the tatmadaw's problems. As a peculiar "hybrid of a Department of State and a military HQ," the War Office was overwhelmed with the details of day-to-day administration and did not have time for longer-term strategizing. "And the result is the dragging on of the frustrating state of affairs in the Union." The memo went on to note that the "need for . . . readiness in case of external aggression is quite apparent," an obvious reference to the KMT menace at the border.[49]

The message of Ne Win's memo was that the time had come to turn the tatmadaw into a first-class fighting force, capable of repelling external aggression. In September 1951, Maung Maung circulated a set of reports to Col. Kyaw Winn, Col. Aung Shwe, Lt. Col. Khin Nyo, Lt. Col. Hla Aung, Lt. Col. Ba Than, Lt. Col. Aung Gyi, Lt. Col. Kyaw Soe, and Lt. Col. Tin Pe—all officers who sympathized with the Socialist Party. The documents included comparative analyses of the organizational structures of the armies of Britain, India, the United States, Australia, and the Soviet Union.[50] Maung Maung argued in his analysis that what separated the early postcolonial tatmadaw from these "progressive" armies around the world was the tatmadaw's organizational weakness at the center and the lack of institutional clout and autonomy for army leadership to plan, carry out, and evaluate strategy and tactics.[51] In other words, the Burma army was still an army of guerrillas. What it needed to become was an army capable of standing up to the KMT and potentially the CIA and the PRC.

Formulation of Doctrine

Maung Maung remembers returning to the War Office in late August 1951 to find that little had been accomplished by MPS.[52] "They were just reading books" and discussing general ideas, but they did not know where to begin. Maung Maung suggested that the planning process had to start with the long overdue formulation of doctrine; without a definition of who the enemy was, the tatmadaw could not devise any strategy for force expansion, reorganization, or deployment. Defining the enemy was simple, according to Maung Maung: "No question about it: It was the Chinese. Indians are not really a problem. The Thais are not strong enough. Realistically, no one is going to invade us from the sea. The only aggressive element was communism. But the Russians can't get here. The only Communists who can come over were the Chinese."[53] The next step was to determine a realistic plan to confront the Chinese threat. Maung Maung proposed that the army plan a defensive strategy of containing Chinese aggression for three months, which was how long he estimated it would take for United Nations (UN) reinforcements to arrive by sea.

The financial support for this plan was crucial. Lt. Col. Aung Gyi conducted a review of defense budgets around the world to determine the funding necessary to build an army to defend the border and proposed that the army would need to command consistently at least 40 percent of the government's budget in order to build capable forces.[54] In his review Aung Gyi focused on the necessity for a swift economic recovery for the nation. According to Maung Maung, "We Socialists—Kyaw Nyein, Aung Gyi and the 'Inner Circle'—figure we have ten years to reconstruct our economy because it will take the Chinese Communists ten years to reorganize their economy."[55] The response from Prime Minister Nu was less than enthusiastic. Maung Maung remembers: "U Nu thinks we can make friends with everybody [including the PRC]. Nu didn't want to spend any money on the army. His friendliness was okay but we have got to have a big stick."[56]

Aung Gyi, the longtime confidante of Nu, was charged with persuading Nu of the necessity for army expansion while Maung Maung forged ahead. He brought into MPS Col. Thein Maung (then attached to the adjutant general's office; ex-PBF), Lt. Col. Ba Than (assistant quartermaster general; ex-ABRO and ex-PBF), and Maj. Yi Aye (staff duties officer, War Office; ex-PBF). Together, they worked out the details of a plan to build an army capable of containing China's PLA at the border for three months. Their plan was to expand to a peacetime army of one division by the end of 1952, with a wartime establishment of two and perhaps three divisions, three armored brigades, three tank battalions, and two motorized infantry battalions. To flesh out the details and requirements of these plans, Maung Maung called daily meetings of most of the senior War Office staff throughout September-October 1951. They were instructed to bring estimates of what their respective departments or directorates would need to sustain the three-month defensive campaign. Air force and navy leadership participated as well.[57]

War Office Reform

Ne Win, Maung Maung, and his cohorts identified as their most urgent objective the transformation of the War Office into a Defense Ministry that would allow civilian control over certain broad policy objectives but would give army officials absolute control over operational and internal military affairs. War Office reform had been discussed three years earlier, when Smith Dun, Bo Let Ya, and other army leaders met five times during the last six months of 1948 to try to straighten out War Office problems. Their efforts, which began only two weeks after the War Office was officially opened in May 1948, "went dormant" after the Karen rebellion in early 1949.[58] Then, as in 1951, army leaders identified the Defense Permanent Secretary's civilian staff as one of the main barriers to improved efficiency. With control over all budgetary decisions, the latter became a choke point on army leaders' initiatives.[59] Smith Dun and Bo Let Ya had not tampered with this system, which resulted in a formal overcentralization of all operational and organizational initiatives, in 1948. In his tenure as Supreme Commander, Ne Win reportedly disliked intensely the civilian permanent secretary, U Ba Tint, and his senior staff officer, Lt. Col. Hla Aung. However, rather than fire or transfer them or reorganize the institution, Ne Win simply ignored them and told his field commanders to come straight to him when they needed anything.[60]

According to Maung Maung, this arrangement was feasible when the tatmadaw was fighting weak, disunited internal insurgents, but it crippled the army's efficiency in preparing to defend the country against more threatening external aggression. Maung Maung and his colleagues did not succeed fully in their plans to streamline army administration in the War Office. However, MPS's efforts to reduce the permanent secretary's influence and to check the power of the "British element" in the War Office were successful. First, MPS delineated more sharply the division of labor between civilian and military leaders. This measure noticeably shrank the civilian secretary's authority over internal army affairs. Second, the reform process provided immediate institutional justifications for moving staff personnel such as Hla Aung out of the War Office and into less important positions.

New Division of Labor

The division of labor between civilian and military leaders was institutionalized in the formation of two policy bodies: the National Defence Committee (NDC) and the Defence Services Council (DSC). The former constituted "an inner War Cabinet and a Sub-Committee of the Cabinet and was empowered to act with the Cabinet's full authority in all defence matters." Its responsibility was to set "broad policy," which would then be passed on to the DSC for implementation. Members of the NDC included the prime minister; the ministers of defense, home affairs, finance, foreign affairs; and one or two other ministers appointed by the prime minister. The chief of staff, defence services, was only an "advisory member." The DSC was to manage all internal military affairs and to be "the mainspring of all activity in the Defence Services."[61] It was to be comprised of the heads of the three services (army, navy, and air force), the adjutant general, the quartermaster general, the defence minister and his parliamentary secretary, and the chief of staff, defence services. The military held the greater share of the influence over DSC decisions.

However vague the distinction between "broad policy" and its "implementation" may appear and however long it took for many of these reorganization proposals to be fully approved by the government, this articulation of separate spheres of responsibility gave Maung Maung, Aung Gyi, and other army leaders the space they needed throughout the 1950s to carry out a wide variety of institution-building activities with little or no civilian oversight or interference.[62] Their plans for expanding military education, sending military missions abroad, and constructing defense industries were managed mainly by the executive committee of the DSC rather than the NDC. In fact, the latter met only twenty-one times between February 1952 and November 1960, whereas the former held five hundred meetings between 1952 and 1962.[63]

MPS pushed through other initiatives—such as the revival of the University Training Corps and the expansion of military education facilities—with similarly little civilian oversight. Furthermore, MPS transferred a number of important functions—such as the all-important control over promotions and appointments—from the civilian Defence Minister's purview to the general staff. The authority to prepare budgets for the army, navy, and air force was reassigned to a new finance section of the revamped Quartermaster General's office. This reform undermined the power of the Permanent Secretary over the tatmadaw's purse.[64]

Unification Command and Loyalties

The second important outcome of these early attempts at institutional reform was that they provided a basis for Socialists inside the army to reassign and in some cases purge personnel whose political loyalties and personal qualifications were suspect. In the War Office, Maung Maung got rid of Lt. Col. Hla Aung by naming him commanding officer of the Third Light Infantry Brigade; later Hla Aung became the head of the Staff College.[65] Maung Maung also used the reorganization to get rid of another senior staff officer, Maj. Ba Ko, an ex-ABRO from the prewar British army. Former PBF, Socialist adherents in the army had resented the extensive authority of Ba Ko over operations. For less political reasons, Maung Maung also transferred Quartermaster General, Col. Aung Shwe, to the command of the Fifth Light Infantry Brigade.[66] He was replaced by Col. Tin Pe, a former officer in the Fourth Burifs, who was recovering from injuries sustained in a car accident.[67] These shuffles further shored up Socialist control over the War Office in Rangoon.

The last two bastions of British sympathizers—or at least those suspected of such sympathies by Ne Win, Maung Maung, and the former PBF officers—were the navy and air force, which were both brought under the strict control of the former PBF element in this reorganization process. In a sense, a unified command already had been established in February 1949 when Ne Win was named Supreme Commander of all defence forces (army, navy, and air force); MPS made the unification of the three services permanent during the 1951–52 planning. The official rationale for this policy was, as Adjutant General Kyaw Winn argued to the DSC in May 1952, that such unification "has now been successfully followed by all progressive countries." Furthermore, he argued, combining procurement and education would reduce costs and allow more operational flexibility. Ne Win told the same meeting that unification was crucial to the conduct of modern warfare. In the past, he told the DSC, navies fought navies and armies fought armies. "Modern warfare means total war," he argued.[68]

What was not discussed on the record at this DSC meeting was the political purge that army leaders were carrying out in the other two services, particularly in the navy. The leadership of the navy was comprised mostly of officers and ratings[69] who were trained by and served under the British in the Burma Royal Naval Volunteer Reserve (BRNVR) before and during the war, although there were also sailors who had remained behind during the Japanese occupation or joined the navy after the war.[70] Many of the BRNVR group, as well as some air force leaders, were Anglo-Burmans whose loyalty to the AFPFL government was considered suspect by army leaders. Although it is difficult to trace exactly what happened, the BSM reported in 1950 that Ne Win had decided that the navy could be useful in joint operations with the army and thus decided to systematically purge its officer corps of those suspected of British sympathies.[71] Former BRNVR Lt. Comdr. Khin Pe Kyi "provided him with a perfect opportunity," when he returned from a Singapore assignment with his official accounts out of order.[72] "This [missing] money, it appears, had been used partly for personal needs and partly to purchase canteen goods and spirits for resale to other naval craft."[73] A year later, Ne Win placed Comdr. Khin Maung Bo, chief of naval staff, on leave when he was held responsible for the "nefarious" conduct of four naval officers serving under him; he stayed on leave until March 15, 1952, when he resigned and was replaced by Comdr. Than Pe (who apparently had ties to Ne Win). In September 1952, a newspaper editorial noted that most of "those who had joined the service [i.e., the navy] prior to the Japanese Occupation and had evacuated to India . . . are now out of the service."[74]

In the air force, there was no corresponding conspiratorial purge, although the attrition rate in operations brought on similar results. At its inception in December 1947, the tiny air force was comprised of two Japanese-trained pilots and six from the prewar, British Burma Volunteer Air Force (BVAF), along with twenty airmen.[75] Because of the necessity of air support in the civil war, the air force had grown to two operational squadrons by the end of 1953. Politically, the divide between the two groups of officers was less significant in the air force than in the army and navy partly because the small size of the force allowed planes, ranks, and resources to be distributed fairly equitably among officers, regardless of when they joined, and partly because of the attrition rate among the former British recruits. Shi Sho, the Karen head of the air force, went into hiding in January 1949 and, like other Karen officers throughout the armed forces, was placed on "special leave" for several years after that.[76] In June 1950, another former BVAF recruit, Wing Commander Selwyn Khin, died in an air crash over Kengtung.[77]

Education, Training, and the End of the BSM

Perhaps the most remarkable result of these early efforts at military reform was the ambitious project launched in late 1952 to reorganize existing
educational and training institutions and to establish a number of new ones,
including the West Point–style Defence Services Academy (DSA). These
training establishments eventually became the core institutions that produced the officer corps of the world's most politically powerful military, although most of the MPS-planned project did not come to fruition for a few
years. However, the zeal with which the educational reforms were pursued
produced one immediate and unanticipated outcome: the downfall of the
British Services Mission to Burma.

In the early days of the insurrection, education and training were very low
priority for an army trying to keep the state afloat. Furthermore, under the
terms of the Let Ya–Freeman Defence Agreement of 1947, BSM personnel
ran most in-country training facilities, which made them unlikely assignments for former PBF officers. Not surprisingly, the post-Karen War Office
sent far fewer officers for training, even in local courses. From 1948, when
the army leadership was dominated by Karens, to 1949, the number of officers being trained in local military courses dropped from 270 to 59.[78]

As part of the September–October 1951 MPS review process that formulated the new doctrine, Maung Maung and the War Office's training staff
also reviewed the training and educational status of the officer corps.[79] The
expansion of the army from eight infantry battalions in 1948 to twenty-six
in 1951—along with an increasing number of support units—and the never-
ending demand for the small number of officers to serve in an operational
capacity "placed a great strain" on the existing officer corps, as noted in a
February 1952 War Office directive. "As a result, most of the major units
are under strength as regards officers and can ill afford to send officers on
courses of instruction within Burma and abroad."[80] At the time, it was found
that there were still 606 commissioned officers who had never attended an
Officers' Training School (OTS) course or an equivalent. Furthermore, this
directive noted that the tatmadaw would need a minimum of 458 staff officers by the end of 1952; in February of that year, there were only 244 who
had completed any kind of staff training, including the elementary Pre-staff
and Staff Learners' courses.[81] The directive called for "a large number of officers and NCOs . . . [to be] trained in a short period of time" and for officers to be released by units for training both in Burma and abroad.[82]

As a result of these deficiencies, the War Office issued a new training policy to accomplish two goals generated under the new doctrine. One was to
train infantry officers in the conduct of modern—and not just guerrilla—

warfare so that the expanding regular units would be capable of defending against an external aggressor. The second was to have tatmadaw officers take over the training institutions previously run by BSM personnel. With Burma squeezed between the two sides of the Cold War, the BSM's presence in all of the tatmadaw's training facilities was a magnet for criticism from the Chinese.

To attain these objectives, the War Office immediately increased the intake at OTS from 120 to 360 per batch and the frequency of intakes from two to three in 1952.[83] However, given local constraints, the key to modernizing and indigenizing the tatmadaw lay in securing enough slots at established British and other foreign schools so that competent indigenous officers would return to teach at Burma Army schools.

The appeal for foreign training became a source of great friction between the War Office and the BSM when the War Office asked for more slots in courses crucial to the reorganization of the army and the BSM was unable to deliver. For example, in 1952, the War Office's bid for vacancies in U.K. courses for infantry commanders nearly triple the number of slots requested the previous year. The BSM was barely able to offer half the number of requested slots.[84] The number of officers given staff training in the United Kingdom or in Commonwealth countries was still minuscule, despite BSM recognition of the weaknesses in local staff training. It is unclear who in the British bureaucracy trimmed the number of allotments for the tatmadaw, but as the numbers of unmet requests increased, the War Office reportedly requested seventy-two places in Australian defense courses for officers and other ranks.[85] The irritated staff at the BSM gave the Australian embassy "our comments on this demand," which apparently resulted in the Australians offering only one slot. In 1953, the War Office also requested 252 vacancies in the United States for training forty-three officers and sixty-eight other ranks; the United States offered only a single slot.[86]

The issue of course allotments proved to be the undoing of the BSM to Burma. Criticism of the BSM was not new: Over its four years of existence, army leaders (especially former PBF officers) had criticized the BSM for blocking arms procurement and for sympathizing with the Karen rebels and other rightists. However, it so happened that the BSM's original contract came up for renewal for the first time at the end of 1952,[87] just as the disagreements over course allotments reached a critical stage.

In December 1952, then-Col. Maung Maung was negotiating course bids with the BSM. When allotments came back thirty-two slots short of the War Office request, he reportedly told BSM personnel that the War Office would lobby against extending the BSM's contract unless it increased its training commitment. He remembers explaining in great detail why all the requested slots were crucial to meeting the demands associated with the new doctrine and strategy, only to be rebuffed by the BSM, which argued that MPS's plan was overly ambitious.[88]

Shortly thereafter, the NDC met in December to discuss the BSM contract renewal and to review the army's reorganization plans. At the meeting, Maung Maung and then-Lt. Col. Ba Than presented the new doctrine and reorganization plans, which included a budget projection for the next few years. "I told the Council, 'If we renew with the British Services Mission, then they must accept our plan and give what we need at the rate we need.' " Prime Minister Nu was unreceptive and, according to Maung Maung, stormed angrily out of the meeting after expressing his reluctance to spend so much money on an army that could defend the country for only three months. After Nu left, Kyaw Nyein and Defence Minister Ba Swe took over the meeting, which proceeded to vote to give twelve months' notice to the BSM.[89] The BSM closed up shop on January 1, 1954.

The Defence Services Institute

Finally, it is worth noting another institutional innovation that came out of field-staff tensions voiced at COs' conferences. To meet the welfare needs of the field units, especially those in remote areas, staff officers started a NAAFI-like business in September 1950 to replace the inefficient, unworkable unit-run canteens.[90] When colonial rule ended in 1948, British army officials had turned over remaining supplies to the postcolonial Civil Supplies Board, which in turn contracted out to a local firm to supply and run canteens for the army. By July 1948, "owing to certain irregularities on the part of the contractor," the contracted canteen system was abolished and unit commanders were forced to improvise to meet the daily needs of their soldiers. During the height of the insurrection in 1949, field commanders had little time to devote to "procuring goods from the black market," the main source for unit canteens. At this point, the War Office began looking into taking over these services.[91]

Then-Maj. Aung Gyi was named the head of the new canteen outfit, which became known as the Defence Services Institute (DSI). It was registered as a business although it was not intended to earn profits. According to its authorization memorandum, "It was to cater for the welfare and needs of troops and for the maintenance of morale."[92] To get the welfare service started, in 1951 the Ministry of Defence loaned it six hundred thousand kyat (approximately U.S.$126,000 at the time), which was paid back within two years.[93]

The first DSI store opened in Rangoon in May 1952, undertaking "bulk sale of goods such as milk, sugar and beer" to soldiers and the public. Within two months, it had expanded to handle "both bulk and retail sale of all consumer goods." A year later, a Mandalay store opened, followed by shops in Maymyo, Meiktila, and Taunggyi.[94] By 1960, Aung Gyi and his colleagues were running banks, shipping lines, and the largest import-export operation in the country under the auspices of the DSI.

Notably, the creation of DSI coincided with a campaign led by Aung Gyi to root out corruption, black-marketing, and indiscipline among field officers and other ranks. Whether or not DSI was intended to undermine the growing autonomy of locally based unit commanders and their civilian allies upcountry, the reform had the effect of removing an important source of their income and influence. The establishment of DSI transferred some of the economic power previously held only by field commanders and Indian and Chinese business operators to War Office personnel. With its tax-exempt status, DSI could not help but make substantial profits, which gave the tatmadaw a source of money and resources outside the purview of civilian legislators and Ministry of Finance bureaucrats.

Conclusion

During the 1950–53 period, the decimated tatmadaw laid the foundation for its eventual consolidation of authority within the state. This is not to suggest that what occurred during this period was part of a deliberate, conspiratorial plan by militarists or Socialists inside the army to take over the country. Instead, the expanding institutional clout of the army within the national state was a by-product of the decades-long struggles over how power would be constituted, by whom, in whose name, and across what territory. Just as the postcolonial state making or -remaking process took an accommodationist turn in the early insurgency years (1948–50), the arrival on Burmese territory of a new type of enemy, the KMT, created the conditions for a fundamentally more threatening kind of warfare. This change in the nature of the state's enemy opened up a range of possibilities for staff officers intent on building a politically and militarily stronger tatmadaw.

The military's centralization of administrative power was by no means an inevitable outcome. In fact, the internal political consolidation brought about by the elimination of Karen "rightists" in the army leadership did not remove all sources of friction in the postcolonial tatmadaw. In the difficult conditions under which the infantry waged counterinsurgency operations—with shortages of personnel, resources, and ammunition—two axes of tension emerged that framed much of the internal debate over state violence for the next decade. These two axes had a common reference point: a division between those who were no longer war-fighters and those who were.

One axis marked a split between civilian politicians and army leaders, both vying for control over operations and broader defense policy. Although both contingents had "fought" imperialists together during the war and the resistance, by the early 1950s, only the tatmadaw remained "uncontaminated" by the journey beyond these heroic revolutionary roots. The other axis delineated a growing intramilitary divide between those who were actually fighting and those who were organizing, administering, and fantasizing about fighting. Field commanders found War Office personnel to be irresolute and unresponsive to their needs. Staff administrators in Rangoon began to view many unit commanders as arrogant, corrupt barriers to the development of a modern, efficient fighting force.

The shifting intersection of these two axes of tension led to institutional realignments and innovations aimed at either lessening the tensions or moving the axis in a direction favorable to one side or another. For example, when civilian interference in internal army affairs such as promotion harmed morale in the officers corps (particularly in field units), the MPS included in its reorganization plans a number of provisions that stripped civilian authorities of control over these decisions. At the same time, as will be shown in chapter 7, the War Cabinet's control over all-important budget allocations for defense resulted in some creative and cunning War Office attempts either to hide money or to court cabinet officials' support for expanding the army's share of the national budget.

Moreover, field-staff disagreements that were aired at annual COs' conferences led to War Office innovations that ultimately limited the influence of both civilians and field commanders in the shaping of the future tatmadaw. For example, when field commanders complained to Gen. Ne Win that their units' welfare needs were not being met, Col. Aung Gyi stepped into the picture and set up DSI, the new canteen operation. Not only did DSI ultimately control much of the import-export business in Burma, but it also gave the general staff extensive resources and leverage in internal military politics. Only a few years after airing their complaints, those same field commanders greatly resented Aung Gyi's growing clout in economic, political, and military affairs. This resentment deepened this axis of discontent between field and staff officers and probably led to the original coup plot in 1958, as will be shown in chapter 7.

The change in the nature of the threat to the young nation-state transformed the army: The accommodationist style of war fighting and state building that developed in the early civil war period (1948–50) soon gave way to the establishment of the army as a mediator between the country and the world, the citizen and the state, and the consumer and the supplier. After civilian political leaders failed to mobilize UN support to fend off the KMT occupation, the decentralized, improvisational nature of military operations threatened the sovereignty of the country and led to the remaking of the army into a modern, European-style standing army. The reorganization process was a messy one, creating winners and losers in Rangoon and throughout the central region. Vested interests coalesced across the civil-military and field-staff axes of tension over the issue of how to defend the nation. As these tensions played out in the early 1950s, a handful of energetic, inventive staff officers gradually laid the foundation of new military and economic institutions capable of mobilizing resources, weapons, and soldiers across the territory. Warriors had commenced on a path that would make them state builders.

7

Warriors as State Builders, 1953–62

This concept of a government of the people, by the people, for the people is certainly out of place presently in Burma. Because we now face an anomalous, if not ridiculous, situation where a man who was a rebel until two months ago . . . can now become a minister and even the head of the Government . . .
Tatmadaw Directorate of Education and Psychological Warfare,
October 1958

If the army has to intervene again, democracy in Burma may not recover for generations, if at all.
Richard H. S. Allen, British ambassador to Burma, April 1960

In the 1950s, the changing nature of warfare in Burma prompted the Military Planning Staff's ambitious overhaul of the tatmadaw. The new, more alarming threat, the KMT, required a reorganized national military capable of defending national sovereignty. To fight the more dangerous enemy, military leaders claimed scarce material resources, human capital, and political leverage. Gradually, military-building activities expanded into the realm of state building. This transformation of warriors into state builders was neither smooth nor unchallenged, nor was it the outcome of any rationalized planning process or sneaky conspiracy. Throughout the 1950s, the transformation of the army into a militarily and politically powerful force was the product of the day-to-day, ad hoc decisions, whims, and fantasies of field and staff officers, as well as elected civilian leaders.

By the late 1950s, the formerly self-sustaining, isolated tatmadaw units combined forces to channel national resources and energy into achieving victory over sophisticated, well-armed enemies. In 1962, this new tatmadaw boasted fifty-seven infantry battalions, five regional commands, and more than one hundred thousand soldiers,[1] a considerable expansion from the twelve battalions and five thousand men at independence, and the paltry three to four battalions and two thousand soldiers who wore tatmadaw uniforms during the early civil war period. Although the development of many of the supporting arms and services lagged behind infantry growth, other institutional innovations signaled the remarkably fast progress made toward the goals of the MPS. For example, by 1962, the third class of the four-year, degree-granting Defence Services Academy had graduated, and the army's other educational and training institutions had developed a wide range of sophisticated specialty courses that rivaled those found in the west.

Meanwhile, joint air force, army, and navy operations—coordinated from both Rangoon and brigade headquarters—began to make headway against entrenched insurgent groups. As historian Hugh Tinker noted, the 1954 Operation Bayinnaung against the KMT represented "the first time large-scale operations [in Burma] were carried out by an army and not by an assorted number of battalions."[2] The numbers of anti-government insurgents dropped from twenty-five thousand in 1953 to about ten thousand in 1962. These remnants roved mainly in small bands and no longer posed an immediate danger to the Union government. Moreover, the threat from the KMT was greatly reduced by the military's success in Operation Mekong in 1961.

The process of building this modern army was a highly political one, and was entangled with the postcolonial project of creating a durable national state in the territory that the British had mapped into "Burma" a century earlier. Army-building and state-building processes were characterized by ongoing struggles among civilian politicians, military field commanders, and staff officers over what that state should look like, who could claim legitimacy at its helm, and who its enemies were. Twice these conflicts produced coups d'etat, in 1958 and 1962, as segments of the armed forces sought to consolidate power against other contenders for national power. Intra-elite struggles over different visions of national defense continued to track along the civil-military and field-staff divides that had emerged in the early 1950s (see Chapter 6).

Along the way, the same citizens who had been potential recruits for various sides in these elite struggles in the earlier part of the decade gradually became objects of distrust and potential enemies in the eyes of military leaders. The citizenry had failed to mature into dedicated defenders of the Union, and influential army leaders viewed this failure as a threat nearly as dangerous as the KMT occupation of northeastern Burma. To counter all these threats, military leaders continued their structural reforms

Arms and ammunition captured by the tatmadaw from Kuomintang forces, 1961. P(AN90-17) PVI.

along paths that transformed war fighters into state builders preoccupied with remaking the citizenry. This transformation brought about the institutionalization of the most durable military governance in the postwar world.

Burma Army tanks in transit for Operation Tabinshweti against communist insurgents, 1962.
P(AN78-447) PV(b), DSHRI.

Experimentation and the National Army

The Burma army experienced a veritable explosion of institution building
in the mid-1950s that seems understated even by the impressive increase in
personnel noted above. During nearly every month from 1951–58, the army

archives' "Administrative History" documents the raising, authorization, or reorganization of at least one new army education, training, psychological warfare (psywar), counterinsurgency, intelligence, counterintelligence, special forces, or engineering unit.[3] Admittedly, some of these new units barely got beyond the authorization stage. However, by the late 1950s, army leaders had constructed many important tatmadaw facilities, initiated specialized services, and laid down organizational policies—all of which elevated the military's position among the array of organizations that would be vying for political authority in Burma for decades to come.

After the near-collapse of the tatmadaw in 1948–49, early War Office attempts to rebuild it had sputtered ahead slowly. The leaders of this standing national army in the 1950s had come of age as anti-government resistance fighters. The lessons they had learned about warfare became obsolete when they were called on to construct a state—rather than antistate—army. The art of building the armed forces of a sovereign state was one that had to be learned, and the early postwar period was an optimal time for such an education.

Shopping for the National Army

How did the former antistate, guerrilla fighters at the helm of the postcolonial tatmadaw learn how to construct the bureaucratized army of the late 1950s? A large part of the answer may be found in the "shopping" trips of various tatmadaw leaders around the world in the mid-1950s. Prior to 1951, the main foreign destination of military purchasing and study "missions" from Burma was the United Kingdom. The paternalistic officers of the BSM in Rangoon and their counterparts at the Ministry of Defence in London carefully managed these trips. However, in 1952, in the wake of U Nu's failure to obtain UN condemnation of the KMT presence in Burma, the tatmadaw began shopping elsewhere.

Destinations for study and purchasing missions expanded to include not only India, Pakistan, Australia, and other Commonwealth countries, but also Yugoslavia, France, Israel, Germany, and the People's Republic of China (PRC). For example, from Israel, the tatmadaw lifted a civil defense plan and the structure of the women's auxiliary force; from Yugoslavia and England, army leaders copied the formula for constructing a Historical Section and a national army museum; and bits and pieces of the Defence Services Academy were lifted from Sandhurst (U.K.), St. Cyr (France), Dehra Dun (India), and West Point (U.S.).[4]

Organizational Commitment and Corporate Identity

The more than fifteen military missions sent overseas from 1951–58 had two important effects on the emerging corporate identity of the expanding tatmadaw. First, the act of representing one's country and military to foreigners gave officers new bases for their commitment to careers in the military. Most of the army officers who took part in these trips were going overseas for the first time in their lives. Since many of them had not joined the postwar army to pursue a military "career," their reception by British, Israeli, U.S., Yugoslav, and German military counterparts reinforced their role as representatives of a military institution. Furthermore, mission participants filed reports on their return to Burma in which they sound increasingly confident about the quality and in some cases the superiority of the Burma army and officer corps when compared with those of the visited nations.[5]

Second, in the military mission reports, military officers exhibited a sophisticated form of comparative analysis as they tried to decide who could teach Burma the most appropriate lessons about building a national army. It appears that the burning questions for these travelers were, "Who is most like us, who do we want to be most like, and who has done everything wrong?" The model most frequently identified as suitable for the tatmadaw of the 1950s was Yugoslavia. A 1955 mission report included a section called, "Yugoslavia—Similarity with Burma," which noted the geographical, political, and geopolitical similarities between the two countries. Yugoslavia's population of "18 million being formed into one social unity and country out of many racial entities and five states such as in the Union of Burma and in the stage of social and economic development on perhaps more vigorous and pronounced socialist economic lines and having on the north and eastern borders the satellite states of the militant Soviet block."[6] In terms of intra-army policies and practices, mission reports of the 1950s identified the Yugoslav and Israeli armies as role models for bringing together the two contradictory thrusts of the reorganizing tatmadaw—one drawing on the guerrilla warfare skills army leaders acquired in wartime resistance and the other emphasizing the construction of coordinated, standing formations capable of withstanding foreign aggression. According to a 1955 mission report, without sacrificing its army's roots in a patriotic guerrilla movement, Yugoslavia quickly had become "for its size and population . . . the best prepared nation to defend its independence."[7]

Moreover, the reports also suggest a growing certainty about which countries were negative models, albeit useful contacts in terms of arms procurement or slots at educational institutions. For example, in 1952, then-Col. Maung Maung led a three-month study mission to India and Pakistan. The mission report was quite critical of the "professionalism" of the postcolonial Indian Army and the corresponding neglect of the "cultivation of military spirit and fighting qualities such as a Burmese Army officer would desire." The report goes on to note that despite political independence from Britain, Indian Army officers were becoming more Europeanized "in their manners and . . . even to excel [beyond] the Europeans in their own ways of social conduct." In contrast, the mission found more to admire in the "fighting spirit" of the junior officers in the Pakistan army. That army had become "one of the first class fighting forces in the world" largely because "the junior officers [became] convinced that the old Indian and British Army professionalism and their staid and fossilised traditions are things to be avoided."[8]

Army Advantages in Experimentation

These shopping trips allowed army leaders to go abroad, identify "products" to add to the tatmadaw, and then return to organizational perches that in many cases allowed fairly extensive latitude in experimenting with new ideas. The army, more so than civilian political leaders who also were shopping overseas for policy products, held important advantages in their excursions. At the most basic level, army leaders were courted extensively by foreign weapons' manufacturers who—in the hopes of generating a new client in Southeast Asia—generously bankrolled many of the trips.

Furthermore, tatmadaw journeymen were remarkably successful at "purchasing" or lifting policies, units, and practices from foreign countries, returning home, and translating them into immediate authorizations. Their record stood in marked contrast to their civilian counterparts' efforts. Although cabinet ministers also made many foreign visits, they were notoriously ineffectual at implementing the reforms they learned about on their overseas study missions. Two reasons account for this difference. First, the endeavors of the MPS to reorganize the tatmadaw from 1951–52 included efforts that effectively moved most internal military issues off of the civilian-controlled agenda of the National Defence Committee. As long as army leaders could sell their reforms to their two hundred or so colleagues at the annual COs' conferences, they could move ahead with implementing changes. By contrast, civilian leaders' reforms had to pass through the legislative arena and press scrutiny, which meant that economic, administrative, and social reform proposals had to create few enough disenchanted voters to ensure reelection of those backing the reforms.

Additionally, the position of an official, national army in the postcolonial, Cold War context of the 1950s privileged it vis-à-vis other state power contenders in terms of its opportunities to expand domestic political and economic influence. For the most part armies—rather than parties or bureaucracies—in the new nation-states of the Cold War era became the mediators between world power politics and (often) young domestic political institutions and practices and, in some instances, between the world economy and the domestic economies. This role was foisted on armies by the increasingly interconnected and inflexible global system of nation-states. As Robert Jackson and Carl Rosberg have shown with regard to postcolonial African states, this system had an interest in preserving the state-ness of its components in order to preserve the legitimating principle of statehood for the international state system as a whole.[9] Once the nation-state became the modus operandi of all large organized societies, systemic preservation of state-ness and statehood placed national armies at key "intersections between domestic sociopolitical orders and the transnational relations within which they must maneuver for survival and advantage in relation to other states."[10]

The positioning of armies rather than other domestic political organizations at these key intersections can only be explained by reference to the context of the Cold War in the 1950s. For example, from the files of the U.S. and U.K. embassies in Rangoon, we can see that at the root of "balance-of-power" politics lay the issue of which side each nation-state's army would fight on in the next world war. Would the army in question, such as the tatmadaw, fight for or against communism? In the 1950s, if the answer was unclear, the competing superpowers and their weapons manufacturers moved into the business of pitching their worldviews to the political and military leaders of neutral or undecided countries. Both blocs tried especially hard to sell or give away their weapons and military expertise so as to have some idea of what to expect from and how to influence that sought-after army. Political leaders were also courted, but a careful look at Burma in the 1950s suggests that the hard sell went to the military. The United States, the Soviet Union, and the PRC dealt with Prime Minister U Nu primarily as an afterthought.[11]

This mediational position of armies in new nation-states gave the kind of institution-building process occurring inside the tatmadaw a broader impact in Burma more generally. Many of the tools of army building were the administrative tools of state building. The army was creating channels through which the central state's power radiated out of the capital city and into remote regions of the country. These tools also created army-centered stories and histories of a "Burma" through the authorization of research on an official army history and the creation of a military museum. Moreover, army building increased linkages between juridically distinct territories when the army sent plains Burmans into the Shan states, Arakan, and other frontier regions to teach Burmese, deliver salt, and pay salaries to local officials. These interactions certainly generated friction between the army, the minorities, and rural populations. However, despite the tensions generated, the modular tools of army building in the postcolonial, Cold War era also provided the first postwar institutional basis for territorial integration and state building throughout the broad geographical expanse of Burma.

COs' Conferences: Shifts in the Axes of Friction

The ideas and products assembled from the military's foreign journeys often were displayed first at COs' conferences. For example, military missions returning from Israel presented national service proposals to an annual meeting of the senior officers long before the Constituent Assembly (the national legislature) ever debated the issue; those returning from Yugoslavia reported on ethnic integration inside the army and defense industries there.[12] Moreover, as military officers traveling abroad came back convinced of the need not just to reform the military but also the state, the annual COs' conference became a forum for debating broader national policy alternatives. The agendas of the annual three-to-five-day meetings reflected this expansion of scope. Morning and afternoon sessions were filled with seminars and lectures on the economy, local governance, ideology, military discipline, arms procurement, psywar, training, and education. Officers and civilians presented drafts of policy and research papers focused on these issues. Attendees were also sent on field trips to nearby government factories and industries.

Changing Tones and Tensions

In the mid-1950s, the conference interactions between civilian lecturers and military listeners became decidedly antagonistic. At the 1953 and 1954 COs' conferences, the prime minister and other cabinet ministers gave one- or two-hour, informative speeches to the two hundred or so gathered officers. Characterized by cordial, solicitous tones, these speeches were opportunities for cabinet ministers to rally support for their causes. For example, in 1953, Prime Minister U Nu charged them to "free the Union from the ravages of both internal and external enemies" as part of their duties to assist with his Pyidawtha economic plan.[13] The following year, he lectured the officers on "War and its Consequences" and explained the moral and practical basis for the government's neutral foreign policy.[14]

By 1955, however, the tone of the civil-military exchanges had changed dramatically, and there were a number of reports of officers heckling and verbally attacking cabinet ministers during and after their presentations. In one case, after Minister for Industries Kyaw Nyein lectured about industrial and economic development, Col. Aung Gyi—then vice chief of staff, army—reportedly attacked him "and threatened that unless the Anti-Fascist People's Freedom League [AFPFL] could make a better showing of running Burma's affairs, the army would have to intervene."[15] Finance Minister U Tin also was asked to explain why the Defence Services would be required to endure major budget cuts.[16] Prime Minister Nu's speech to the assembled officers revealed his growing unease about the army's increasing organizational clout. On the one hand, he congratulated the officers on successfully transforming the army "from the position of stooges without backbone, at the beck and call of this or that organization [to] dependable custodians of the Union Constitution." Only moments later, he chided them: "With the increase in numbers and the brief period of reorganization, it is inevitable that there may be certain elements both in the officer and private ranks of all racial denominations who swagger with revolvers dangling on their belts or with rifles in their hands, dizzy with newly-acquired power and arrogant in dealing with people."[17] By 1957, his criticism was even less veiled, when he warned officers at the conference to make sure they were a "people's tatmadaw" and not a politician's "pocket army."[18]

Two developments account for the change in the tone of exchanges between civilian and military leaders at these conferences. First, as many observers have pointed out, from about 1954 on, the AFPFL itself was wracked by internal division.[19] Thus, the hostility that characterized the speeches of U Nu and other civilian leaders reflected the increasing strain of trying to hold together the united-front governing coalition. But these explanations overlook the manner in which the growing sense of corporate identity amongst army officers created yet another source of strain for the governing party. As army officers traveled the world, returned home to fight communists, the CIA, and the KMT, and came together at national and regional-level conferences to share their experiences, they began to see themselves as distinctively different from their former comrades-in-arms who had become cabinet ministers in the postcolonial era. Army leaders, with mentoring from role models like Israel and Yugoslavia, hoped their reorganization efforts would institutionalize the tatmadaw's "purer" revolutionary spirit. By contrast, politicians appeared to be moving further and further from their revolutionary roots.[20] Indeed the expanded agendas of COs' conferences—which covered almost every major national policy debate— suggested that this was a forum at least as significant as AFPFL executive committee meetings or the Constituent Assembly for working out the problems of governance.

The Civil-Military Divide Spreads Upcountry

Another source of civil-military tension was aired in the 1955 COs' conference. Participants reported lengthy discussions about the inadequacies and corruption of district and urban police, as well as of the local pocket armies of upcountry politicians.[21] The conference debated and approved two initiatives to address these problems. One proposed that the army set up garrisons in all major towns throughout the country. The second established a new kind of village defense unit under joint civil and military control, with local brigade commanders assuming direct operational control over the units.

These initiatives indicate that army leaders in Rangoon and in some of the field commands were ready to try out ideas learned in Israel and Yugoslavia about organizing territorial forces and civil defense. In so doing, they intended to eliminate private armies operating outside the tatmadaw's chain of command. The plan to garrison soldiers in every major town did not materialize (because of logistical and recruiting problems), but the War Office did raise the new village units—the Pyusawhtis—within two weeks of COs' conference approval.

The 1955 formation of the Pyusawhtis, named after a hero who eliminated dangerous beasts plaguing Pagan in the year 551 (Buddhist era), represented the first attempt to bring local militias under the control of the War Office since Aung Gyi joined the Karen-dominated War Office in 1948 to raise the Sitwundan. However, it is significant that the Pyusawhtis plan came directly from the War Office and not out of a party "inner circle" or executive committee meeting, as had the Sitwundan plans of August 1948. Originally, the Pyusawhtis were set up under the National Defence Committee and in principle were to be overseen by the army field commanders in the areas where the militia were raised.[22] The army leadership's intention was to free up the army from the tedious work of trying to wipe out pockets of rebel guerrillas and roaming bands of dacoits. Field and general staff officers alike were worried that insurgents would step up their activities as the 1956 general elections approached.[23] As the army's planning memo on the Pyusawhtis spells out, "The Union since its conception in 1948 has been . . . plagued by the modern 'Great Tiger,' 'Great Bird,' 'Great Flying Squirrel,' and the 'Vicious Bitter Bottle Gourd plants'[that similarly had plagued Pagan]. The present situation is analogous to that of the reign of King Thamudirit at Pagan. The people are living in constant fear of being robbed, and killed any day. The farmers have been unable to plough the fields peacefully, the traders have not been able to move about freely for trading purposes."[24]

From the inception of the Pyusawhtis, however, the logistical difficulties of recruiting "new" militia meant that the army was forced to rely on district party personnel for recruiting and training levies.[25] Hence, the Pyusawhtis were manned in most instances by the same levies who had been armed under local political bosses during the previous decade. When an intra-AFPFL split developed in Rangoon and spread to the districts, Pyusawhti units became targets for constituency raising, which exacerbated the already unsettled conditions upcountry.

Psywar, Ideology, and Civil-Military Tensions

The 1956 COs' conference constituted a watershed in postwar Burmese history in that the conference proceedings were dominated by the relatively small, but increasingly powerful Directorate of Psychological Warfare (Psywar Directorate), the successor to the MPS. Its prominence was most clearly seen in the Directorate's 1956 presentation of the first draft of what became the official ideology of the post-1962 Socialist government.[26] Written under the direction of Col. Aung Gyi and Lt. Col. Ba Than, the head of the Psywar Directorate from its founding in 1952, the ideological statement was the culmination of several years of psywar programs aimed at politically isolating enemies of the Burmese state. The activities of the Psywar Directorate are worthy of greater consideration here, given that it oversaw the military's shift from a purely conventional approach to fighting insurgents to one that required military officers to embrace explicitly political tactics. This shift in counterinsurgency strategy prompted the tatmadaw's expansion into nonmilitary national affairs, most of which was managed and overseen by officers connected with the Psywar Directorate.

After barely a year in existence, the MPS was transformed into the "Psychological Warfare Branch" and Lt. Col. Ba Than was transferred from the assistant adjutant general's office to be director. The specific impetus for the transformation of MPS into a psywar office came when Prime Minister U Nu scolded MPS leaders, Cols. Maung Maung and Aung Gyi, for requesting too much of the national budget for their army reorganization plans (see chapter 6). The solution, according to Maung Maung, was to promise Prime Minister Nu to modify the plans to take into account a "pet project" of Nu's—psychological warfare.[27] Thus emerged the Psywar Directorate with Nu's close friend Col. Aung Gyi unofficially at its helm.

Aung Gyi gave Lt. Col. Ba Than great latitude in designing programs to win over the hearts and minds of the Burmese population, domestic insurgents, and soldiers of the tatmadaw. Over the next decade, psywar initiatives included establishing the Defence Services Historical Research Institute and sponsoring *pwe* (traditional variety show) performances, radio shows, and pamphlet publication and distribution.[28] Ba Than and Aung Gyi moved quickly into the commercial magazine market, launching their *Myawaddy* magazine in 1952 "to provide balance" in a market dominated by anti-government publications. According to Aung Gyi, the most popular magazine of the time was *Shumawa*, which contained many cartoons and articles penned by leftist artists and authors who criticized the tatmadaw. Aung Gyi remembers: "We were defenseless. This is democracy." Over the next few years, *Myawaddy* carried numerous articles by "famous Communist writers" who had either returned to the legal fold or who had never formally rebelled. "In psywar," Aung Gyi explained later, "you cannot do only one-sided propaganda." He stole *Shumawa*'s writers by offering them a little more money per story; he undercut *Shumawa*'s advertising rates and increased *Myawaddy* revenues; and he put together "better covers with prettier girls." Four years after *Myawaddy* was started, *Shumawa*'s editor quit and *Myawaddy*'s circulation rose to eighteen thousand.[29]

The Psywar Directorate also sponsored projects aimed at convincing tatmadaw officers and soldiers that they were part of a legitimate national army fighting for a just cause.[30] It was toward this goal that Aung Gyi, Maung

Maung, and Ba Than organized preliminary meetings in 1956 to prepare an ideology for the armed forces. They invited former communists and socialists to draft an ideological statement synthesizing communism and socialism within the context of a Buddhist society. U Saw Oo (editor of the Socialist *Mandaing* newspaper), U Chit Hlaing (former communist follower of Thakin Soe), and Ba Than prepared the draft, which was submitted to the 1956 COs' conference. The presentation of the ideology ran four hours at the conference. Over the next two years, Psywar Directorate leaders Aung Gyi and Ba Than presented revised drafts of this ideological statement, which branched out to include ambitious proposals for Philippine-style civic-action programs and plans to open a Psywar School at Mingaladon with its first class to graduate in 1958.[31] Emphasizing the importance of ideology in warfare, the Psywar Directorate pleaded with the officers at these conferences to take charge of remaking Burma's population into modern citizens; if the military did not do this, the communists likely would, and the Union would never endure.

As was the case in the early 1950s, the civil-military axis of tension—which divided the war-fighting army from the governing politicians—gained more attention from army officers, politicians, journalists, and foreign observers. The content, conduct, and attendance of the annual COs' conferences suggest that tatmadaw staff and field officers alike pressed for greater and more direct military control over resources, territory, perquisites, and responsibilities and for less civilian interference in these matters. However, this is not to suggest that all was harmonious within the army and that field-staff tensions had faded away. The increasingly broad, policy-oriented focus of annual COs' conferences had shifted the conference spotlight off of—but not eliminated—field-staff tensions. Field officers lost their national forum for airing grievances against the general staff. In a sense, expressions of these field-staff tensions, which continued to be felt, were only temporarily quieted, while the ongoing friction was partially responsible for the form of the 1958 coup.

The 1958 Coup

Scholars usually point to civil-military tensions as the cause of the coup of September 1958.[32] In April 1958, the AFPFL formally split into two separate, bitterly opposed parties, pitting the new "Clean AFPFL" led by Prime Minister U Nu and Agriculture Minister Thakin Tin against the "Stable AFPFL" led by Ba Swe and Kyaw Nyein. Subsequently, the leadership of each faction launched frantic campaigns to line up national- and local-level supporters as well as to court Pyusawhtis and other local militias in Rangoon and in the countryside. This process greatly exacerbated the already unsettled conditions in the districts.[33]

The Civil-Military Angle

The AFPFL split spilled over into the army, although most officers were sympathetic to the Stable faction. Many army leaders had long-running, personal ties to Kyaw Nyein and especially Ba Swe that either were based on family connections or dated back to student union politics in the 1930s. This alignment was quite problematic for Nu, whose performances at the 1955 and 1957 COs' conferences had already shown his hostility toward the army's growing autonomy, clout, and arrogance. As journalist Sein Win reported, "The Nu-Tin Government could not possibly suspend all these [pro-Stable] forces on suspicion of Swe-Nyein bias. So it tried to remove the suspected Swe-Nyein sympathizers from important positions and replace them with their trusted personnel in the UMP, the police and Civil Service; and it also tried to discredit the Army, Navy and Air Force before they too could be tackled likewise."[34] For the first time since the January 31, 1949, COs' Conference, conflicts over political loyalties inside the army became an issue not only for internal debate but also for nationwide, public debate in the press, in tea shops, and on the radio.

When U Nu's Clean AFPFL held its party congress from August 31–September 2, 1958, district representatives from Moulmein, Hanthawaddy, and Sandoway districts publicly named army field commanders who allegedly favored Stable politicians, threatened Clean ones, and provided protection and ceremonial welcomes only for Stable members of parliament on their district visits. According to a journalist present at the time, "The delegate from Hanthawaddy declared the Army, 'Public Enemy Number One.' "[35] These accusations infuriated field commanders. Clean AFPFL leader and Prime Minister U Nu tried unsuccessfully to control the damage by giving a series of halfhearted speeches lauding the tatmadaw for staying neutral and protecting the nation.[36]

The accusations against tatmadaw field commanders by Clean representatives came at a time when rumors were rife around the country that the Nu-Tin faction was on the verge of bringing communist political leaders into the government and—more important—their guerrilla fighters into the tatmadaw. Furthermore, mass surrenders and amnesties for at least fifty-five hundred rebels in 1958 brought the total number of former antigovernment rebels-turned-voters to forty thousand.[37] Given that the U Nu government barely survived a June no-confidence motion in the Constituent Assembly and elections were scheduled tentatively for later that year, the rebels-turned-voters probably constituted Nu's only chance to solidify his majority in the legislature. Rumors that Nu's bargain with rebels included integration of their forces into the tatmadaw infuriated military leaders, who had risked their lives on battlefields fighting these very rebel forces.

Soon after the conclusion of the Clean AFPFL congress on September 2, Home Minister Bo Min Gaung (a Clean supporter) further alienated army field commanders by unilaterally transferring Union Military Police (UMP) units out from under the authority of brigade commanders, moving them to Rangoon locations under his direct command. This move followed Nu's July 30 announcement ordering army leaders to reduce the number of Pyusawhtis in the districts by one-half.[38] It is not clear what Bo Min Gaung intended to do with the UMP troops; there is speculation that he was preparing either an anti-Nu or an anti-army coup.[39] Regardless of his intentions, however, his and Nu's actions were unquestionably aimed at reducing the numbers of soldiers at the disposal of army field commanders. Journalist Sein Win described the shuffling and buildup of armed forces in this period: "The situation then resembled the international politics where world powers justify their armaments as precautionary measures for defence."[40]

The Field-Staff Angle

According to former field commanders as well as officers involved in carrying out the coup on September 26, concerns about these anti-tatmadaw and especially anti-field-commander moves of the government led to informal discussions among field commanders. These secret meetings were attended by then-Col. Aung Shwe (Northern Commander), Lt. Col. Chit Khaing (then the GSO(1) directly under Aung Shwe), and Lt. Col. Kyi Win (then CO at Kyauk Brigade Headquarters).[41] It is unclear exactly what occurred in these meetings, but it seems likely that plans for some kind of anti-Clean offensive or coup d'etat were discussed. These officers later approached Col. Maung Maung and other staff officers to complain of ill treatment by the Clean AFPFL and to elicit support for their still-vague plans to remove the government. Although there are conflicting reports from those involved in these discussions with Maung Maung, the latter probably did not object to their complaints or their proposed solution. His lack of reaction may have appeared to the field commanders to be a nod of support.[42] Maung Maung claims that Ne Win ordered him not to halt the field commanders' orchestrations.[43]

Word of these meetings got back to both Prime Minister U Nu and Gen. Ne Win. Pro-Nu cabinet ministers immediately stepped up efforts to transfer Forest Guards, loyal Pyusawhtis, and more UMP into Rangoon. In the first week of September, Nu met with Cols. Aung Gyi, Maung Maung, and Tin Pe and offered to defuse the situation by appointing the three of them plus Gen. Ne Win as cabinet ministers. According to Maung Maung, "This made me very angry. The field commanders would think we had been bribed by Nu" if he and his colleagues accepted the portfolios.[44]

The Counter-Coup

Maung Maung and Aung Gyi—two of the three officers ultimately responsible for the actual takeover on September 26, 1958—report that this meeting was a turning point in civil-military and field-staff relations. The prime minister's offer showed how little Nu understood the delicate balance between field and staff officers inside the tatmadaw. He may have read the tensions between the two camps as a battle between equals in which he could tip the balance in favor of the staff officers to whom he offered portfolios. However, no matter how close Maung Maung and Aung Gyi may have been to Ne Win or how much power they thought they held within the tatmadaw, they knew they could not make a move that would infuriate their field counterparts. Unlike the field commanders, Maung Maung, Aung Gyi, and the general staff directly controlled only a few troops and fewer resources throughout the country. Maung Maung's and Aung Gyi's refusal of the portfolios shows how seriously the Rangoon-based staff officers had come to treat the demands of the field commanders.

But that did not mean that Maung Maung and Aung Gyi were going to sit back and allow their field counterparts to march to Rangoon, dethrone U Nu, and take charge of the country themselves. Maung Maung reports that after coming out of the meeting in which U Nu offered the ministerial positions, he went back to his office and began planning his own coup. "I didn't want their coup," Maung Maung remembers, referring to the still-nascent plans of the field commanders. "So we decided to make our coup."[45] The range of options was somewhat limited if they were going to stave off a possible backlash from the fractious field commanders. The solution had to involve getting U Nu and the Clean AFPFL out of the picture. The general staff had direct operational control over Col. Kyi Maung's Rangoon Command, which the War Office had deliberately placed outside of the Northern and Southern Commanders' operational purview in order to give the War Office secure control over the capital. Maung Maung also contacted the 104 and 106 special forces battalions, which had been established in 1955 as light infantry, mobile units "on call by the army sub-district commands or the brigade in whose area they are stationed."[46] Maung Maung also remembers calling in Rangoon-based commanders of support services such as the Signal Corps and putting them on alert duty.

By September 22, troops from the 106 Battalion, supporting arms and services, and the Rangoon Command were placed strategically throughout the capital, including one contingent that surrounded the cabinet ministers' compound in Windemere. At this point, Maung Maung remembers that he did not want to use force and "this was just a contingency plan to prevent the field commanders from taking the initiative" against the UMP, Forest Guards, and other irregular troops assembled by the Nu-Tin faction.[47] Nu returned that day from a trip upcountry and learned from Bo Min Gaung and Bohmu Aung that an army coup was imminent. Nu's personal secretary, U Ohn, who lived in the same house as Maung Maung, probably confirmed the speculation.

On September 23, Cols. Maung Maung and Aung Gyi visited Nu to apprise him formally of the increasing danger of violence in Rangoon. According to Aung Gyi, "I told him, 'I am a general staff officer and I will suppress the [field commanders'] coup if I get the order from you. But there will be a lot of casualties.' " Maung Maung remembers telling Nu in this meeting, "We will try to control the boys [in the field commands]." By the next day, the two colonels returned to Nu with news that rumors were spreading that Nu-Tin followers were planning to assassinate army leaders and that the general staff no longer could control the army. Later that day, Maung Maung and Aung Gyi met U Ohn and came up with a compromise solution to have Nu transfer power to a cabinet comprised of non-politicians. Gen. Ne Win, they agreed, must be named prime minister to ensure army loyalty.

Nu found out about the suggestion and summoned Cols. Maung Maung, Aung Gyi, and Tin Pe on the morning of September 26. Nu agreed to transfer power, although he tried unsuccessfully to limit the new administration to three months. Nu and the three officers drafted letters that morning to be exchanged between Nu and Ne Win formalizing the transfer without a specific time limit. The new arrangements were to be called the "Caretaker government," although most Burmese referred to it as the "*Bogyoke* [General] government," pointing to the titulary role of *Gen.* Ne Win.[48]

Implications of the Coup

The way in which the coup transpired—progressing from an escalation of tensions along factional party lines, along the civil-military axis of tension, and along the field-staff axis—had an enormous impact on political and army developments for decades to come. The immediate winners were Gen. Ne Win, and Cols. Maung Maung, Aung Gyi, and Tin Pe, who had navigated successfully the treacherous minefield that lay around Rangoon in September 1958. They managed to find a solution that did not lead to further aggravation of internal army tensions, at least for the moment. The field commanders, however, had made a formidable enemy in U Nu. His only direct challenge likely came in February 1961 when ten of them were purged from the armed forces. Nu's more general antipathy toward the army also surfaced in frequent campaign speeches in 1960.

The general staff who were involved in planning the official transfer slated for October 28 soon unleashed a barrage of contempt for the existing parliamentary system. Within three weeks of the September 26 coup, the army's Directorate of Education and Psychological Warfare circulated a critique not only of the political machinations behind the events of 1958, but more importantly of the fundamental tenets of the Union's Constitution. Entitled "Some Reflections on Our Constitution," the critique was presented at the tatmadaw conference that Gen. Ne Win called on October 20–21 in Meiktila to explain the specifics of the transfer of power.[49]

Herein we can find the first extended articulation of the army leadership's profound distrust of the population, democracy, and especially the "misconstructed" constitutional provisions guaranteeing freedoms of speech and association. On the subject of the Burmese people, the paper criticizes "the general apathy of the electorate," which leaves them "at the mercy of skillful propaganda" of rebel groups. It suggests that a major flaw in Burmese democracy lay in the deficient character of the masses, "being left in the grip of their instincts alone, which generally are not of too high standards, viz., egoism, personal interest and continuation of existence or survival at any cost whatsoever."[50]

The Psywar paper lists a number of "anomalous" conditions that result from "allowing every adult citizen [to be] equally free to express his views and desires upon all subjects in whatever way he wishes," including allowing rebels to preach anti-government rhetoric in public. The paper concludes:

> These [observations] should rightly give rise to some suspicions on our part as to the adequacy of the Constitution. We venture to say that there might be many more such or similar flaws, weaknesses and contradictions which can be more fully observed and explained by those who have more specialized knowledge and experience regarding the Constitution. What we dread most is that unscrupulous politicians and deceitful Communist rebels and their allies may take advantage of these flaws, weaknesses, contradictions and inadequacies in the Constitution and bring about in the country gangster political movements, syndicalism, anarchism and a totalitarian regime.

The paper recommends the establishment of a commission to review constitutional flaws and the immediate adoption of a draconian "Anti-Subversion Ordinance" to give the government the tools necessary to crack down on its opponents.[51]

The significance of this paper cannot be overstated. Prior to this 1958 Meiktila conference, references to the Union Constitution in the papers and discussions at COs' conferences generally came in the form of the Psywar Directorate chastising officers for not knowing it and for not teaching their soldiers about the fundamental principles enshrined therein. By 1958, the Constitution was no longer sacred. The tatmadaw's language, tone, and message in this critique of parliamentary democracy have been echoed in subsequent actions and policies throughout the last forty years. This reproachful tone was repeated in Ba Than's official army history, *The Roots of the Revolution* (1962), and came to dominate army policy papers, military leaders' speeches, and even the themes of the Defence Services Museum that opened in Rangoon in 1994. Given how busy the general staff was in the weeks following the September 26 exchange of letters between Nu and Ne Win, it seems likely that a draft of or the critical mass behind this critique already existed before the coup. The critique was undoubtedly an outcome of the growing tensions between civilian and military leaders observed in the COs' conferences of the 1950s. The tatmadaw's reading of Burma's first decade of postcolonial rule was that elected political leaders could not be trusted with holding the Union together, and citizens were potential enemies because the Constitution allowed subversives to brainwash them into destabilizing the country.

The Bogyoke Government, 1958–60

The transfer of power from U Nu to Gen. Ne Win provided in many ways the perfect solution for the ambitious leadership of the tatmadaw to ameliorate both civil-military and field-staff tensions. Gone were the pesky civilian politicians who cut army budgets and interfered with the military's internal security operations. Meanwhile, field commanders were mostly satisfied with the dismissal of the Nu-Tin cabinet ministers and the elevation of Gen. Ne Win to prime minister. According to Col. Hla Maw, then CO of the Eleventh Brigade, "We were happy with the 1958 coup." The fact that Ne Win's deputies, Cols. Maung Maung, Aung Gyi, and Tin Pe and not the field commanders themselves had seized the moment, did not trouble him: "Remember—we were not even thirty-five [years old] yet. It was hero worship of Ne Win."[52]

New Opportunities Neutralize the Field-Staff Divide

The formation of the Bogyoke government decreased the tensions that had come to divide field and staff personnel in the previous decade in three ways. First, the huge expansion of posts available to both field and staff officers eliminated the friction over scarce resources and choice assignments. At the same time, army officers from field units moved to Rangoon, where they worked together for the first time with general staff officers in bureaucratic and political roles. Second, this expanding range of opportunities gave all army officers the chance to make extra money (legally) from the programs of the much-expanded Defence Services Institute. And third, after the mass surrenders of rebels and the shift of the field commanders' focus toward Rangoon, most army leaders on both sides of this divide became less concerned with operations.

After Nu officially transferred power to Gen. Ne Win on October 28, 1958, the army wasted no time in shuffling officers into every major ministry and department of the government. Although the cabinet ministers themselves were civilians, "colonels, lieutenant-colonels, majors and even captains were soon running the responsible offices of government," according to an American lecturer at Rangoon University.[53] By mid-December, ninety-four army, navy, and air force operators had been seconded to civil government positions.[54]

More than one-third of those officers taking on civil responsibilities came directly from field assignments to Rangoon offices. For example, the combat-seasoned Seventh Brigade commander, Col. Chit Myaing, took over National Registration efforts aimed at establishing records of all citizens and immigrants in the country. Many field officers were placed in departments and ministries where they worked alongside general staff officers for the first time in their careers. The Ministry of Labour was a case in point. Of the sixteen tatmadaw officers assigned to this ministry, half came from staff duties, half from field assignments.[55] Furthermore, some of the general staff officers found themselves in roles that required extensive duties outside of Rangoon. For example, Col. Maung Maung's assumption of command over internal security operations took him out of Rangoon and into the districts for substantial periods of time. The expanded military role in governance ended the long-running practice of tracking the career paths of field officers separately from those of staff officers, only to bring them together at the annual COs' conferences.

The Bogyoke government also was a "bonanza" for the Defence Services Institute (the canteen outfit organized in 1951), according to U Thaung, a journalist of that era. By 1960, DSI had opened or bought banks, an international shipping line, an import-export business, the single coal import license, a hotel company, fisheries and poultry distribution businesses, a construction firm, a bus line that carried thirty thousand passengers daily in Rangoon, and the biggest department store chain in Burma. All the while it retained its tax-exempt and customs-exempt status. U Thaung recalled: "It had become the most powerful business organization in the nation." Furthermore, DSI began to offer lucrative perquisites to army officers. U Thaung provided an illustration: "For the military officers to start a small business, the DSI introduced new three-wheeled cars to run as taxicabs. The DSI imported hundreds of Mazda three-wheelers and sold them to all the military officers above the rank of captain, to encourage them to do business on the side. Officers who could not afford the cost of the car were issued loans from the [DSI-owned] Ava Bank for the opportunity to start a business."[56]

Field Commanders

While the removal of the Nu-Tin leadership resolved civil-military tensions at least temporarily in favor of the new army governors, the field commanders also got what they perceived as their due. During the Bogyoke government, counterinsurgency operations were lower priority probably because so many of the seasoned senior field officers now held administrative posts on the civil side of the government. The officers who filled their empty command spots in the field units gained a great deal more autonomy from Rangoon in their conduct of operations. Brigade and regional commanders dispensed with attempts at large-scale operations in favor of company and even platoon-strength units operating with a minimum of supporting arms. According to the British military attaché at that time, "These [small-scale] fighting patrols enable the Army to 'hunt' down the insurgents by pursuing them and so preventing their escape into the jungle."[57] The decreased emphasis on large-scale operations was reflected in the 1959 COs' conference schedule, which allotted just over two hours of the three-day conference to the discussion of operations and tactics; in contrast, five hours were devoted to a discussion of the latest draft of army ideology.[58]

During the Bogyoke government, brigade commanders were placed in charge of regional "security councils," which brought all law and order affairs under their control. An elaborate hierarchy linked local security councils to a national one. They became the organ through which the army attempted to dismantle the AFPFL's—and especially the Nu-Tin (clean) AFPFL's—machinery of political control outside Rangoon.[59] Regional security councils disarmed Pyusawhtis, Forest Guards, and unruly UMP units. Furthermore, security councils took charge of mass organizations of workers and peasants.

Moreover, the security councils worked hand in hand with Col. Chit Myaing's National Registration teams to ensure that "no person should be left unregistered." In its previous eight years of existence, the National Registration Department had registered only 4.1 million people out of the 18 million residents of the Union; by contrast, in the first three months of the Bogyoke government, the department registered 1.3 million. The department's report to the 1959 COs' conference shows why the army saw this as a higher priority than did the previous civilian government:

> With the completion of the national registration work within the Union, movements of the people, especially of bad hats, can be effectively checked in the districts. They won't be allowed to move about without any . . . hindrance. The chances of miscreants committing crime, political or otherwise, are becoming poorer, for their identity cards shall be examined by the security authorities and, if suspected, they can be kept under surveillance.[60]

These expanding opportunities for field and staff officers alike reduced tensions between the two camps. In the districts, field commanders received far more resources and responsibilities than they had under the civilian regime. The inauguration of the Bogyoke government formalized the transformation of war fighters into state builders, and this transformation alleviated internal military tensions, at least for the short term.

Is Trust Vindicated?

The tatmadaw's efforts went a long way toward restoring law and order and preparing for free elections—the army's official mandate for taking over the government. The reorganization of district law and order personnel under the security councils probably brought about the steep drop in violent crime from 1958 to 1960. Other evidence of improvement can be seen in the fact that for the first time since independence, fully 95 percent of the country's electoral districts were able to conduct the February 1960 elections. Furthermore, local security councils arrested many of the upcountry racketeers and gangsters.[61]

In Rangoon, Col. Tun Sein fired many senior personnel in the city government, reorganized the corrupt municipal police, and mounted his "Sweat Campaign" to clean up the city. He deployed "sweat brigades" of civil servants, students, teachers, and other residents to the streets to clean up the messes that had accumulated after a decade of internal refugee resettlement. Rangoon resident Trevor Dupuy described the situation before Tun Sein took over as mayor:

> Garbage was overflowing the gutters of Rangoon streets; not even hundreds of thousands of pariah dogs could keep these mounting piles of filth under control. Squalid squatters' huts were crowding streets, parks and any open area that the masses of unemployed, or partially employed, could find. The [Nu] government apparently lacked both the ability and the will to cope with the mounting threats of lawlessness, pestilence and disease in Rangoon.[62]

Tun Sein's "cleansing operation" was carried out on 25 successive Sundays with approximately 100,000 persons participating and 11,154 tons of refuse collected for disposal. Tun Sein also oversaw the construction of the first two satellite towns north of Rangoon, Okkalapa and Thaketa; 167,000 people from nearly 25,000 "hutments" were moved to these satellite towns between January and May 1959.[63] Elsewhere, the Shan sawbwas signed a "Renunciation Treaty" with the Bogyoke government in April 1959, formally ending their legal authority in their states in return for hefty pensions.

As might be expected, the Bogyoke government stepped up psywar efforts, targeting populations susceptible to communist overtures. The crew that had penned the early drafts of the army's ideology produced this government's major psychological offensive, "The Dhammarantaya" ["Buddha's Teachings in Danger"].[64] This was a caustic attack on the antireligious, anti-Buddhist communists. More than one million copies were printed in Burmese, Mon, Shan, and Pao languages, while a less Buddhist version was translated into Urdu for distribution to the Muslim community. Yet another Psywar critique, *The Burning Question*, was aimed at the Christian community and was translated into Sgaw and Pwo Karen, Chin, Kachin, and English.[65] Although the Bogyoke government pronounced the religious war on communism a success, Martin Smith rightly questions "the effectiveness of such anti-communist campaigns. . . . All political parties, above and underground, tried to enlist the religious argument on their side in the civil war, but with mixed results."[66] However, what is significant is that the psywar officers in the army were convinced that they could do it much better than the religiously pious U Nu or other civilian political leaders and organizations.

These efforts, along with the activities of most of the major government departments, are described in great detail in the Bogyoke government's, *Is Trust Vindicated?* The book, written in English, includes chapters on various army initiatives to clean up Rangoon, increase agricultural output, improve food distribution, and so forth. The volume reads like a high school yearbook and brims over with the military's pride about its accomplishments. It also censures civilian leaders of the previous decade for their corruption, irresponsibility, and incompetence.

New Sources of Civil-Military Strain

The army's methods of governing Burma during the Bogyoke government reflected the harsh tone of the Psywar Directorate's 1958 critique of the Constitution. As the British ambassador—an order-conscious supporter of the more "efficient" army government—wrote in April 1960: "Both the moral and physical cleansing of the country have been carried out at a cost which liberal-minded people found excessive. The freedom of the Press suffered heavy encroachments; even minor criticisms of the Government were severely punished."[67] As proposed in the 1958 critique, the army often dispensed with the constitutionally guaranteed rights of citizens. Hundreds of political prisoners were arrested "on the flimsiest evidence" and sent to a new "concentration camp" built on the Coco Islands in the Martaban Sea, where they awaited trial, in some cases for years.[68] As the British ambassador noted in April 1960, "In the early stages [of the Bogyoke government] the arm of the law fell more heavily on U Nu's supporters than those of his rivals."[69]

With regard to information dissemination, the government amended the Press Registration Act of 1876 to strengthen government control over an "irresponsible press."[70] The amendment allowed the government to trace the origins of publishers' finances and required all publishers of newspapers, magazines, and books to pledge their loyalty to the Constitution by printing the statement "We shall not advocate a dictatorial system" in their publications. Under Col. Maung Maung's internal security team, the Psywar Directorate conducted something of a witch hunt for leftists among the press corps, shutting down five or six newspapers and imprisoning numerous editors, publishers, and reporters for alleged communist sympathies.[71] An onerous British-era public order law, the Public Order Preservation Act, Section Five, was also used to arrest as many as four hundred government critics, including Aung San's brother, U Aung Than.[72]

The Return to the Barracks

One of the mysteries of postcolonial Burmese politics is the question of why the Bogyoke government scheduled the 1960 elections when it had already become clear that the army's popular appeal was on the wane and the chances were diminishing for the electoral victory of the Stable AFPFL political party backed by the army. The official explanation was, of course, that the army respected democracy. However, given that Burma's chaotic democratic practices helped push the army toward the 1958 coup in the first place, this account leaves much unexplained. Some analysts suggest Nu was a brilliant, powerful force, one that could not be kept out of office any longer.[73] Others suggest that the army leadership recognized how unpopular it had become and also recognized the structural limits to the economic and social reforms it had initiated; hence military leaders wanted to get out of office before the tatmadaw's reputation was tarnished.[74] A number of military officers interviewed for this project concurred with this latter account.

The most likely scenario in late 1959, when the Bogyoke government announced the pending elections, was that a combination of factors contributed to the return to the barracks. One factor was the army's growing unpopularity. The second was the increasing friction between field and staff officers, which was greatly exacerbated when staff officers began hinting at the possibility of returning the government to elected civilians.

A glance through the records of the September 1959 COs' conference reveals evidence that the tatmadaw leaders at all levels were fully apprised of the army's unpopularity. Among the papers distributed for discussion at that conference are five extensive reports on a survey carried out by the Psywar Directorate to determine public opinion about the tatmadaw and the Bogyoke government.[75] Complaints against the tatmadaw included concerns about the overpoliticization of the officer corps; the "haughty, self-esteemed, inconsiderate" attitudes of soldiers; army corruption at fisheries auctions and in the black market; and the rampant disrespect shown civilian officials by army personnel.[76] While the Psywar surveys also included sixty pages of positive feedback on the tatmadaw,[77] it seems likely that the public's criticisms would have had a dampening effect on the army's enthusiasm about continuing in office, regardless of how profoundly the officer corps had come to distrust the populace.

Resurgent Field-Staff Tensions

During the Bogyoke government, many observers interpreted the army's move into the government in 1958 as an indication that a return to civilian rule was many years away. The British and U.S. embassies were convinced that Cols. Maung Maung and Aung Gyi would never allow a return to civilian rule, especially if there was a chance the Nu-Tin Clean AFPFL Party could win the general elections. Interestingly, diplomats believed the only powerful figure in the Bogyoke government advocating the return to the barracks was Bogyoke Ne Win himself, which seems rather ironic given the twenty-six years of Ne Win rule that followed the next coup in 1962.[78]

The Rangoon-based diplomats completely missed the resurgence of field-staff tensions outside the capital. To be fair, although the axis of friction had lurked ominously behind the expansion of the tatmadaw's political power throughout the 1950s, the increasing range of opportunities afforded to both groups during the Bogyoke government seemed on the surface to have ameliorated the conflicts. However, new concerns emerged as the tatmadaw leadership began to plan for a return to the barracks. Many of the field commanders who had been seconded to new administrative jobs had left their combat units in the hands of more junior officers, who subsequently had carved out niches for themselves. By 1960, the field commanders of 1958 had been replaced. Additionally, one field commander who had remained at a brigade CO position throughout the period noted that the projected return to the barracks would also mean a return to the possibility of civilian interference in army affairs and civilian attacks on the conduct of the field commanders.

Due to these concerns, a number of field commanders, including Chit Khaing, Aung Shwe, Hla Maw, Tun Sein, Kyi Win, Kyi Han, and others, met at Chit Khaing's house to discuss contingency plans in case the Nu-Tin faction won the 1960 election.[79] While the details of the discussions in these meetings are difficult to uncover, it is clear that these field commanders were unhappy about the return to the barracks and debated whether to do something about it. Significantly, as a field commander pointed out, staff officers Maung Maung and Aung Gyi had been deliberately excluded from these discussions.[80]

Free and Unfair Elections

By all accounts, the election of February 1960 involved a fair amount of cheating by army and party people alike. According to U Thaung, "soldiers were posted near the ballot boxes and aimed guns at the voters while they were voting."[81] Many critics of army rule in Burma have attributed this widespread cheating to an armywide conspiracy hatched by Gen. Ne Win, Col. Maung Maung, and Col. Aung Gyi. If these army leaders had hatched such a conspiracy, however, Nu's Pyidaungsu Party (Union, the new name of the Clean AFPFL) would never have won the election. In fact, the fairly widespread election abuses were quite "amateurish," according to a district officer in Pegu Division at the time.[82]

What little evidence exists does not reveal a systematic plot to fix the election. More likely, local army units acted on their own initiative and Rangoon-based army leaders decided to look the other way. For example, on the day of the elections, a former intelligence officer serving under one of the field commanders who attended the meetings at Chit Khaing's house remembers his unit seizing the moment "to make sure we won the elections." His unit was sent to Pa-an to ensure electoral victory. "We stole votes from [ballot] boxes. They were kept overnight in the police stations and we just moved all the votes into the Stable box. Of course, the Stable Party candidate there won."[83]

Furthermore, "the army" was not universally pro-Stable, which created some on-the-spot, intra-army frictions on election day. For example, former Col. Mya Thinn, who was in Arakan with his 104 (special forces) battalion, remembers that on election day, the head of the Arakan Force discovered Mya Thinn's unit was mostly pro-Union Party. The Force commander sent his Fourteenth Regiment to surround Mya Thinn's troops. According to Mya Thinn, "We told them we were neutral and told them if they didn't leave immediately there would be some shooting. Some negotiations followed and they left."[84]

In spite of (or perhaps because of) these machinations, Nu's Pyidaungsu Party won the election. Afterward, the new Constituent Assembly was called, Prime Minister Nu was sworn in with his new Pyidaungsu Party cabinet, and all but a handful of officers still finishing up duties in civil offices returned to the barracks. Their return was lauded around the world as a giant step forward for democracy. The international community showered Gen. Ne Win with praise. He was even awarded the Magsaysay Award for "his conscientious custodianship of constitutional Government and democratic principles in Burma through a period of national peril."[85]

Civilian Rule and Army Transformation

Within weeks of regaining office, Nu's Pyidaungsu Party split, pitting the "U-Bo's" against the *thakins*. The former included younger politicians and professionals (the "U's") and older resistance fighters (the "Bo's"), all of whom favored a conservative approach to party politics and government policy. The older thakins, veterans of the trade union and mass movements of the 1930s, favored a Socialist orientation to policy. Nu appeared indecisive, and his decision to retreat to Mt. Popa for forty-five days of meditation in the midst of heightened political tensions made his administration look "disorganized."[86] Many authors writing about this return to civilian rule focus on the internal division of the Nu's Pyidaungsu Party, which is said to have paralyzed the government. The chaotic return to civilian rule, along with Nu's ill-advised move to dismantle many of the organizations put into place by the Bogyoke government and to reverse many of the policies that *Is Trust Vindicated?* cited as crowning achievements, are usually considered to have invited the next military coup in 1962.

However, as with existing explanations of the 1958 coup, these interpretations focus on the disarray in civilian politics and overlook the concurrent consolidation of power within the military. When the tatmadaw returned to the barracks in April 1960, it was not there even a year before Gen. Ne Win and a newly ascendant cohort of officers completely restructured it. These changes effected the most dramatic transformation of the tatmadaw since the MPS-directed house-cleaning of 1951–52.

The Purge of Maung Maung

In February 1961, U Nu's government announced the purge of nine brigade commanders, one regional commander, and Brig. Maung Maung (then director of military training). Initially reports circulated that the dismissals were a reaction to a conspiracy hatched among all these officers to eliminate Ne Win as head of the armed forces.[87] In fact, the purge of Maung Maung and those of the field commanders were actually unrelated, and sprang from different sources of tension with Gen. Ne Win and U Nu.

Gen. Ne Win probably fired Maung Maung because he did not approve of Maung Maung's close working relationship with U.S. officials, particularly those from the CIA. In 1958, then-Col. Maung Maung formed a "research unit" under his Directorate of Education to initiate counterintelligence activities in the tatmadaw. By his and then-Col. Aung Gyi's accounts, authorization for the unit had come from Gen. Ne Win himself in a meeting of the three officers. Therein Aung Gyi told Ne Win about his trip to the Philippines in 1958, where he had been much impressed with the way the Philippine army had been trained in intelligence and counterintelligence by the CIA.[88] According to Aung Gyi, Maung Maung and Ne Win agreed that the army's intelligence corps was nearly useless, in large part because it had been trained poorly by the British. Maung Maung initiated plans to set up his research unit for the purpose of training handpicked army, navy, and air force officers in counterintelligence. A CIA contact at the U.S. embassy helped organize the unit, providing typewriters, air conditioners, and trainers to teach Maung Maung's cadets "how to shadow, . . . put microphones in walls, etc."[89] According to Maung Maung, Ne Win not only authorized the formation of his counterespionage unit but actually inspected it several times.

So why was Maung Maung forced to resign? Two possibilities seem likely.[90] First, he got caught up in a personal rivalry with Director of Military Intelligence Bo Lwin. As one former intelligence officer pointed out, "The both of them were doing intelligence. They clashed." Aung Gyi reports that Bo Lwin was angry when Maung Maung passed him over and instead appointed Myint Swe as head of his well-funded research unit. For years, Bo Lwin had reported intelligence about insurgent activities and army happenings to Ne Win directly. Bo Lwin may have used this channel to lead Ne Win to believe (perhaps rightly so) that Maung Maung was allowing the CIA too much influence in tatmadaw affairs.[91]

Maung Maung's anti-communism is the second possibility. His personal rivalry with Bo Lwin probably became significant only because of the way Maung Maung got caught in the Cold War squeeze. He had become unpopular with many left-leaning officers in the tatmadaw because of his fervent anti-communist stance.[92] This stance was palatable in 1958, when U Nu was believed to be inviting Burmese communists to take over the tatmadaw. The environment had changed by 1961, when U Nu and even Gen. Ne Win were making strong overtures to the PRC to settle the long-running border dispute and to obtain Chinese foreign assistance. Furthermore, in the 1960–61 dry season, a major tatmadaw offensive foundered against the resurgent KMT forces, who were armed with U.S.-manufactured weapons. The tatmadaw's Ninth Brigade then teamed up with units of the Chinese People's Liberation Army to expel most of the KMT from Burma.[93] This was not an opportune moment for Maung Maung to be identified as an ally or mole of the CIA inside the army. Such an identification was especially significant given that Maung Maung was widely considered to be the second or third most powerful officer in the tatmadaw. Bo Lwin's jealousy and alleged rumor-mongering may have fueled Ne Win's fears that Maung Maung might try to mount a CIA-backed coup against him.

The Purge of the Field Commanders

Maung Maung's "resignation" was announced in the Rangoon press on February 6, 1961, effective on February 1. On February 6, just as Gen. Ne Win was convening the annual COs' conference in Rangoon, the press also reported that nine brigade commanders and the southern regional commander had relinquished their commands.[94] Only five commands out of eighteen were left untouched by the purge (table 7). Maung Maung and five of the field commanders were sent out as military attachés, four field commanders were "retired," and Southern Commander Brig. Aung Shwe was sent to Australia as ambassador.

The official reason later given for this purge was that these officers had disobeyed Ne Win's orders not to interfere with the 1960 elections. Even though Ne Win had announced over megaphones to troops that they were to stay out of the elections, these field commanders "probably thought that [announcement] was just for public consumption," according to a district officer then serving in Pegu.[95] It was widely thought that Prime Minister Nu had encouraged and possibly ordered Ne Win to terminate these field commanders, who had planned quite brazenly to overthrow his government in 1958 and then tried to sabotage his reelection campaign.[96]

Given that this purge removed two brigade commanders from ongoing operations (Col. Tun Sein from the anti-KMT offensive and Col. Thein Doke from the increasingly threatening Shan insurgency) and replaced only one of them with a seasoned field commander, it seems unlikely that the election interference a year earlier was Ne Win's only grievance. Indeed, Ne Win and his newly ascendant cohort worried that the mass dismissal of most of the army leadership might provoke a formidable backlash. On February 9, just after Ne Win closed the annual COs' conference, newspapers reported that strict new security arrangements had been set up at the Burma Broadcasting Station, a standard tactical move to stave off coups.[97]

Some foreign observers believed that the purged officers were all pro-west and anti-China; the purge was said to be a result of a power struggle over Burma's position in the Cold War.[98] This Cold War interpretation is questionable because some officers with pro-U.S. leanings remained safely ensconced in lower-level field commands. Furthermore, this view is often based on the idea that because Ne Win was "of largely Chinese origin," he was pro-PRC. In fact, his position toward China was not always favorable throughout the postwar period.

Another explanation popular at the time was that all the field commanders were plotting a coup against Ne Win and the government.[99] Former Col. Hla Maw, who was stripped of his Fifth Brigade Command and posted to Belgrade as military attaché, believes that the meetings among field com-

Table 7. Tatmadaw Infantry Commands before and after the 1961 Purge

Field Unit	CO, Pre-Purge	CO, Post-Purge
1 Infantry Brigade	Col. Lun Tin	Col. Lun Tin
2 Infantry Brigade[a]	Lt. Col. Aye Maung[b]	Lt. Col. Aung Pe
3 Infantry Brigade[a]	Lt. Col. Aung Pe	Lt. Col. E.A. Sinclair[c]
4 Infantry Brigade[a]	Col. Thein Doke	Lt. Col. Gwan Shein[c]
5 Infantry Brigade[a]	Col. Hla Maw[b]	Lt. Col. Mya Thaung[c]
6 Infantry Brigade	Col. Maung Shwe	Col. Maung Shwe
7 Infantry Brigade[a]	Col. Kyi Win[b]	Lt. Col. Tan Yu Saing[c]
8 Infantry Brigade[a]	Col. Sein Mya[b]	Lt. Col. Thein Han[c]
9 Infantry Brigade[a]	Col. Tun Sein[b]	Col. Ba Shwe
10 Infantry Brigade[a]	Lt. Col. Kyaw Myint[b]	Lt. Col. Aung Zin[c]
11 Infantry Brigade[a]	Col. Ba Shwe	Lt. Col. Van Kuhl[c]
12 Infantry Brigade[a]	Col. Tin Maung[b]	Lt. Col. San Kyi[c]
13 Infantry Brigade[a]	Lt. Col. Ba Phyu[b]	Lt. Col. Tin U
Rangoon Command	Col. Kyi Maung	Col. Kyi Maung
Arakan Force[a]	Lt. Col. Tin U	Lt. Col. Ye Gaung[c]
1 Infantry Division	Lt. Col. Khin Maung Kyaw	Lt. Col. Khin Maung Kyaw
Northern Command	Brig. San Yu	Brig. San Yu
Southern Command[a]	Brig. Aung Shwe[b]	Col. Sein Win[c]

[a] Change in the commanding officer (CO) in 1961
[b] Forced to relinquish command in February 1961
[c] Newly elevated to command position (i.e., not shifted from previous high-level field command)

manders around the time of the election, in which they discussed alternatives to returning to the barracks, had probably raised Ne Win's ire. Hla Maw believes that one of the attendees, probably Tun Sein, must have reported the discussions to Ne Win.[100]

However, Hla Maw also suggested that the reason for the purge was not so much the content of those discussions as it was simply the convening of discussions among field commanders and *only* field commanders. Some years later, he came to the conclusion that the history of tensions between his field colleagues and the Rangoon-based leadership—especially Maung Maung and Aung Gyi—was more likely the decisive factor in Ne Win's calculations.[101] Field commanders had become too influential in their areas of operation for Ne Win to allow them to start scheming about national-level affairs, especially without input from staff personnel in Rangoon. Moreover, after the end of the Bogyoke government, there were more field commanders than there were command billets. Competition for commands undoubtedly stoked rumors of coups led by senior officers who were denied the posts they desired.

Army Reorganization

The interpretation that the purges resulted from field-staff tensions is supported by Ne Win's campaign over the next several months to reorganize the command structure of the tatmadaw. The Northern and Southern Regional Commands were abolished and replaced by five division commands, each led by a brigadier general with a colonel as deputy commander. In addition to these five divisions, four independent brigades were established in Arakan, the Kachin state, the Naga Hills, and the Chin Hills, all under the direct control of the Ministry of Defence. As one observer pointed out at the time, the reorganization gave the Ministry of Defence staff "tighter control over all military activities" by eliminating the powerful northern and southern commanders "who might (if disaffected) be in a strong position to stage a military coup." Field units were dispersed across five senior divisions, none of which had enough troops to constitute a potential threat to Rangoon.[102] Of the five divisional commands, three were involved in extensive counterinsurgency activities and were heavily dependent on the Defence Ministry for logistics and support for their operations. Only the Northwestern and Central Commands had enough nonoperational time to even consider any kind of move against Rangoon, and it is no surprise that the two commanders appointed to these commands were Brigs. San Yu and Sein Win, whose loyalty to Ne Win was unquestioned.

The Definitive Coup of March 1962

On March 2, 1962, tatmadaw units occupied all key transport routes and communication facilities in Rangoon. Unlike the coup that established the Caretaker or Bogyoke government in 1958, this was a military operation that deployed troops and tanks in an overt seizure of power. As in the case of the 1958 coup, analyses of the 1962 military coup tend to stress nonmilitary causes, focusing on events immediately preceding the coup that are said to have pulled and pushed the allegedly "militarist" Ne Win back into office. In fact, these extramilitary, environmental "pulls" and "pushes" existed throughout the 1950s but did not drive the army into interventionist mode until 1958, and again in 1962. Instead, the long-term, structural causes of both coups lie in the shifting fortunes of political and military elites along the civil-military and field-staff axes of tension. The way these struggles played out created winners and losers, rulers and ruled, citizens and enemies.

Existing analyses of the 1962 coup argue that U Nu and his Pyidaungsu government "pulled" or somehow forced the tatmadaw back into office and that the tatmadaw's taste of power in 1958–60 made it trigger-happy in the face of an increasingly unstable political environment. Many analysts accept at face value the explanation proffered immediately after the coup by Brig. Aung Gyi. He proclaimed that U Nu's sympathy to ethnic-minority calls for

political reform threatened the territorial integrity of the Union.[103] This al-
legation came out of Nu's agreement in mid-February 1962 to meet Shan
and Karenni (also known as Kayah) state representatives in Rangoon; these
two states enjoyed the constitutional right to secede from the Union.[104] At
this meeting, which became known as the Federal Seminar, ethnic-minority
representatives discussed proposals ranging from moderate constitutional
amendments to more radical secessionist demands. During these proceedings, army leaders seized the moment to take over the government once
more. Early in the morning of March 2, the army arrested fifty leading government ministers and officials (including the president, prime minister,
and chief justice) and the attendees of the Federal Seminar.[105] Despite army
pronouncements to the contrary, few observers watching the Federal Seminar at the time believed that Nu was planning to reconfigure the Union's
territory. Wrote the British ambassador at the time: "U Nu's Government
had shown no signs of being ready to make any major concessions to the
federalists."[106]

What may have been more significant was that the Federal Seminar had
given Shan leaders a forum not just to discuss their reform efforts but also to
air grievances against the tatmadaw that dated back to the 1950 establishment of martial law in parts of the Shan states. Shan leaders also had more
recent complaints against the army, as the British air attaché pointed out at
the time: "The Army and Shans have been at loggerheads ever since General Ne Win stripped the Sawbwas of their feudal powers in 1959."[107] As in
1958 at the Clean AFPFL's party congress, U Nu again sponsored a forum
that entertained public criticism of the army and probably specifically of the
field commanders who had run campaigns and military administration in
the Shan state since 1950.[108]

Unlike in 1958, the field commanders, tank commanders, Ne Win, and
other staff and administrative personnel were all brought on board for this
coup. Units took up strategic positions not only around Rangoon but in key
upcountry locations as well. This was a coup that bore the stamp of a unified, bureaucratized military, in which orders issued from Rangoon were
followed with remarkable regularity throughout the territory.

This unity may well explain why this coup brought civilian rule to such a
definitive end. In 1958, the army had demonstrated that it could take over
the government, but not that it could do so for the long term. By 1962, the
internal consolidation of the tatmadaw after fourteen years of intramilitary
struggle brought the army full circle from its weak, decentralized state of
1949. At that time, to the degree that any representatives of the Union government held any kind of authority beyond Rangoon, it was the local field
commanders, who ran virtual fiefdoms in many parts of the country. While
the War Office and civilian AFPFL government were forced to look the

other way, local field commanders forged informal agreements with black marketers, weapons dealers, opium smugglers, and local political bosses. Crackdowns by the 1958–60 Bogyoke government weakened the capacity of many nonmilitary social forces in both rural and urban areas. By the time of the 1962 coup, the army had become a standing, bureaucratized, and centralized institution, capable of eliminating such challenges to its claims over state power.

A final note regarding this coup: Many authors attribute the success of this coup to Ne Win's extraordinary charisma and almost spell-like hold over army personnel. While there is no doubt his rapport with the troops helped him to carry out both the coup and various army and political reforms, the previous decade of institution building is probably more important for explaining the 1962 coup and the peculiar path taken by army rule in postcolonial Burma. Among Burma scholars and journalists, there is a tendency even today to hold up Ne Win as the residual explanation behind Burma's unusual policies and politics. However, Ne Win's charisma alone could never have pulled off either the 1962 coup or the radical reforms that followed had the MPS not laid the framework that allowed him to issue orders in March 1962 that he could be sure would be carried out throughout the Union. No similar kind of bureaucratic regularity of command had been established in any other institution in Burma. Ne Win faced no serious challenges.

Conclusion

Burma's postcolonial state was engaged in warfare from its earliest moments of independence from Britain. None of the threats faced in the 1950s could be blamed on easily identifiable, geographically containable populations, which led battalion commanders and military planners almost inevitably into broader programs aimed at reordering, reeducating, and redefining the population throughout the country. War fighters became state builders.

However, war fighters in other similarly unstable, new nation-states did not necessarily assume the reins of state power as a result of security crises. In fact, most of the postcolonial nations of South and Southeast Asia were engulfed in regime-threatening civil warfare for a decade or more following independence, and yet only a few of these states—such as Burma and Indonesia—came to be dominated by armed forces. In other regimes under fire—Malaya (later Malaysia) and the Philippines—state armies fought against serious threats but remained largely under civilian control. What explains this variation in outcome?

One possible answer lies in the different counterinsurgency combat strategies pursued by governments in the years surrounding transitions to independence. Nearly all South and Southeast Asian states faced serious internal insurgencies in the 1950s. Most governments initially responded with purely military approaches to eliminating antiregime forces. But in Malaya and the Philippines, the governments quickly abandoned the coercive, military approach and opted for accommodation strategies to incorporate and co-opt the opposition; this was a strategy aimed at winning over the hearts and minds of regime opponents and the population. As in the development of parliamentary institutions in early modern Europe, citizens of newly independent (or soon-to-be independent) Asian states as well as critics of ruling elites had to be offered incentives to cooperate, which often entailed power-sharing arrangements or institutional reforms that allowed for more inclusive politics. This political strategy required the concurrent bureaucratization, centralization, articulation, and empowerment of both nonmilitary and military institutions of governance.

In Indonesia and Burma, by contrast, the states experimented with accommodationist strategies but never really budged from the purely military approach. The pursuit of this military strategy led to the development of powerful centralizing militaries and the concurrent withering of civil services and political parties that provided direct channels of input from the populace. Moreover, in both countries, it was the armies—not civilian bureaucracies—that experimented with political counterinsurgency strategies (such as Burma's psywar operations in the 1950s) to co-opt internal populations that otherwise might support insurgents. In Burma and Indonesia, this state-making process created parallel structures of governance that regulated the country's political, social, and economic life. One limp structure lay in the civilian realm; the other, more robust structure in the military bureaucracy. In neither Burma nor Indonesia did civilian groups or institutions ever possess the dynamism or influence of civilian counterparts in Malaysia or the Philippines.

This comparative insight should not be taken to suggest that political counterinsurgency strategies inevitably produce the kinds of governing institutions that might be called "democratic." Malaysia's counterinsurgency experience created a political system that is hardly representative or open in any sense of the terms, and the civic action campaigns of the 1950s Philippines laid the groundwork for the emergence of Marcos' most undemocratic revolution. However, the comparison does suggest a more limited, nonetheless significant, finding. States that pursue coercion-intensive, military solutions to internal security and political crises will likely see their militaries take on a range of functions—law enforcement, economic regulation, tax collection, census taking, magazine publishing, political party registration, food aid distribution, and so on—that have little to do with traditional defense responsibilities. In Alfred Stepan's terms, this involves a transformation of the "military-as-institution" into the "military-as-government."[109] In independent Burma's most serious security crises, this transformation went even further. Because the civil war and KMT crises coincided with and were exacerbated by the breakdown of the state machinery, the movement of military-as-institution into nonmilitary affairs could take place only with an overhaul first of the military itself and then of the state. Internal military reform in the 1950s involved resource mobilization, administrative centralization, and territorial expansion, all of which became benchmarks of the subsequent military-led, state rebuilding process. In a sense, the military solution to internal crises crowded out other potential state reformers, turning officers into state builders and military-as-institution into military-as-state itself. In this solution, citizens became barriers to the army's consolidation of political power and national sovereignty.

Epilogue

The Armed Forces, since its formation as an organized and disciplined force, has never evaded its responsibilities even in the face of great odds and great sacrifice. . . . [I]t should be noted that the leaders, at every level, are always personally involved in all tasks in the interest of the nation and the people—no task is ever too small for care and attention.

"Development Projects and the Uplift of Morale,"
Myanmar Perspectives, September 1997

Only the army is mother,
Only the army is father,
Don't believe what the surroundings say,
Whoever tries to split us, we shall never split.
We shall unite forever.

Tatmadaw slogan, appearing on billboards
and in print media in the 1990s

In the four decades since it took political power, the Burmese tatmadaw has created a choke hold on political power unrivaled in the world. A decade and a half after establishing the latest incarnation of military rule in a bloody crackdown on a nationwide pro-democracy movement in 1988, today's generals have barely been touched by the suspension of international economic assistance, the imposition of an arms embargo, and bans on new investment in Burma by U.S. and European firms. Throughout more than forty years of military rule, rumors of intramilitary splits among officer factions, elite infighting ("hard-liners vs. soft-liners"), infantry mutinies and foot soldiers' desertions, and the inevitable demise of the regime have been notable both for their frequency and their inaccuracy. All around them, Burma's generals witness the crumbling of authoritarian regimes. But in Burma, military rule endures.

The visitor to contemporary Burma senses the military presence everywhere, from the soldiers guarding the airport runways and downtown markets, to the menacing propaganda billboards littering cityscapes and rural roadways. These red and white signs tell us (often in English): "Crush all destructive elements," "Only when there is discipline will there be progress," and "Down with the Minions of Colonialism." Straight out of Fort Bragg psychological warfare manuals from the 1950s, the propaganda campaign seems anachronistic, more suited to the Cold War–era counterinsurgency campaigns that clumsily appropriated Maoist techniques to rally populations. On the surface, little has changed since 1958, when military leaders hankered for "more skillful propaganda" to snap the masses out of "the grip of their instincts alone, which generally are not of too high standards, viz., egoism, personal interest," and so on.[1] From the late 1950s on, the military has continuously preached discipline and responsibility to a citizenry that— in military eyes—has responded with little better than indifference.

The Legacy of Distrust

The military's distrust of the population, first fully articulated in 1958, was reinforced on a number of occasions, starting two years later when the electorate voted against the military-backed political party in the 1960 elections. The new U Nu government disassembled the top-heavy, security-focused Bogyoke government of 1958–60. Chaotic political conditions ensued. After cleaning house inside the army, Gen. Ne Win wasted little time before leading the ultimate offensive against civilian parliamentary rule in March 1962.

Socialist Warfare and State Building

As in 1958, the military took direct control of the state in 1962, but this time the ruling officers organized themselves into a "Revolutionary Council" aimed at completing the heroic revolution that began with the anticolonial struggle. Much like Latin American militaries did in the same era, this junta outlawed all other political parties and invoked emergency measures to justify the repression of civil rights. In surprising contrast to other military regimes, however, the Revolutionary Council proclaimed a Marxist state ideology—the "Burmese Way to Socialism"—and established a single legal political party, the Leninist-style Burma Socialist Program Party

(BSPP). With its Burmese Way to Socialism, the BSPP attempted to impose a centralized, command economy and to eliminate foreign control over business in Burma.

The leftist turn of the tatmadaw confused most foreign observers. The United States and other non-communist countries initially embraced military "antipolitics" for its elimination of destabilizing, personalistic, and leftist political forces in Burma. However, the attempt to implement radical social and economic restructuring left the non-communist world wondering if Ne Win had turned Burma into another falling domino. In fact, Ne Win's move to make Burma into a socialist country was simply a revival of the rhetoric of the anticolonial nationalist movement of the 1930s and 1940s. Officers from the Psywar Directorate had been arguing since 1956 that without an ideology, the AFPFL government would never keep people in the countryside from helping the communist rebels, whose ideology successfully harkened back to the heroic resistance. The Revolutionary Council's move to the left also represented a very clever tactical decision: if the greatest military threat to Burma was the People's Republic of China, the latter could hardly justify aggression against Burma after it proclaimed the socialist revolution in 1962.[2]

In the twenty-six years of socialist rule that followed, state building and warfare mapped into two distinctly different zones for the tatmadaw and the BSPP. In the central regions, or what the British colonizers had called "Ministerial Burma," the regime offered amnesty to most of the communists and other ethnic-Burman insurgents, driving those who refused out of the central regions into what the British colonial regime had designated the "Frontier Areas." In the mostly pacified central region, the military's activities involved the overt use of force only in rare political crises, such as the urban, anti-government demonstrations that surrounded the 1974 funeral of former UN Secretary-General U Thant. Police generally handled disorder, while soldiers helped with development, propaganda, and infrastructure projects. The tatmadaw was a willing partner in the BSPP's project to transform the "apathetic" public (as described in the army's 1958 critique of the Constitution) into a new socialist citizenry. As a fighting force, however, the military was almost invisible in the central regions.

The bulk of army activity transpired in the frontier areas, where eventually more than a dozen (mostly) ethnic-minority organizations would take up arms against the socialist government in Rangoon. Seeking reforms that ranged from cultural autonomy within a federal system to outright secession, these groups waged effective guerrilla warfare against the government for four decades. Pursuing a strategy called the "Four Cuts" (cutting the enemy off from sources of food, funds, intelligence, and recruits), the tatmadaw engaged in brutal counterinsurgency campaigns. As one opposition group noted, the military's strategy was based on the assumption that "the best way to destroy these [rebel] groups is to destroy the ability of the civilians to support them."[3] Martin Smith estimates that five hundred thousand people, most in the frontier regions, have died in Burma's four decades of civil strife.[4]

Tatmadaw field units earned a reputation among Burma's neighbors for excellence in combat despite their serious shortfalls in materiel and armaments.[5] Most of today's senior officers were promoted based on their performances on these frontier battlefields. Many of them remember a growing sense of alienation from higher circles of political decision making during the 1970s and 1980s. In interviews with the author in the 1990s, former infantry officers complained that the BSPP was too busy dispensing patronage resources to its followers in the 1970s and 1980s to pay attention to the dangerous insurgencies festering in Burma's frontier regions. In fact, most of those career warriors think that the tatmadaw could have unified Burma and ended the civil wars twenty years ago had the BSPP committed the resources to the objective. While fighting in the frontier areas far away from Rangoon, the priorities of war fighters had been edged off the agenda of the BSPP.

The Restoration of Direct Military Rule

When the BSPP collapsed in the face of widespread social protests in 1988, the military once again took direct political power and formed a new junta, the State Law and Order Restoration Council (SLORC). In the decade to follow, SLORC not only took charge of the political system but also embarked on the most ambitious army transformation program since the 1950s. SLORC suspended the 1974 constitution and abolished all of the national governing institutions from the former single-party state. Under SLORC's orders in August–September 1988, the crack troops of the armed forces put an abrupt end to popular pro-democracy demonstrations, killing thousands of unarmed civilians in the process. SLORC distributed cabinet portfolios to senior military officers. Senior Gen. Saw Maung assumed the offices of prime minister and defense minister and renamed the country "Myanmar." Martial law was declared, and all gatherings of more than three people were declared illegal. SLORC enacted economic reforms aimed at opening the market, but the regime refused to make any serious structural or currency reforms for fear of generating politically explosive hardships. Since its inception, the junta has systematically intimidated political opposition, and all media have been censored in an effort to control public opinion.

The military regime held elections in 1990, and its political party (the National Unity Party) suffered a crushing defeat when it won only ten seats. Opposition to the regime and its policies coalesced around Aung San Suu Kyi (daughter of Aung San) and her party, the National League for

Democracy (NLD). Despite junta attempts to hamper opposition efforts, the NLD swept the elections, winning 392 of the 425 seats it contested. SLORC's subsequent refusal to honor the election results, the arrests and flight of many successful opposition candidates, the house arrests (1989–95 and 2000–2) of Suu Kyi, and the numerous restrictions on party activities over the last decade have all but decimated Aung San Suu Kyi's loosely organized, populist NLD party.

Similar to the earlier era of the KMT crisis, the crisis conditions of 1988 spawned an army reorganization and the initiation of a wide range of state-building programs, once again emanating from the tatmadaw. With the BSPP gone, SLORC began to rebuild the collapsed state almost from scratch. It did so with the only tools it considered reliable—its military personnel. In asserting central control over political and economic affairs throughout the country, the junta constructed a government that made the maintenance of stability and order its highest priority. This state-rebuilding campaign entailed a massive expansion of the armed forces. From 1988 to 1996, the tatmadaw grew from 186,000 to more than 370,000 soldiers. The junta spent over $1 billion on 140 new combat aircraft, 30 naval vessels, 170 tanks, 250 armored personnel carriers, as well as rocket launch systems, anti-aircraft artillery, infantry weapons, telecommunications surveillance equipment, and other hardware.[6]

In addition to improving the weaponry available to combat forces, the regime also reformed the tatmadaw's command and control structure in order to increase the high command's authority throughout the country. The Ministry of Defence was reorganized in 1990, and the central Bureau of Special Operations took charge of most combat units. The reorganization led to a proliferation of new army units, including two mobile light infantry divisions, specialized engineer battalions, and armor and artillery units. New army garrisons were erected in towns and villages throughout the country, and the numbers of naval and air force bases were also increased.[7] The military's industrial base expanded as well, and the regime launched an import substitution program in the critical area of arms manufacturing.[8]

This expansion and modernization of the military was accompanied by the establishment of an array of welfare, health, and educational facilities that insulate members of the tatmadaw, creating an "exclusive social order" of privilege for active-duty and retired soldiers.[9] Modern hospitals and clinics were built to serve military families. The regime co-opted private businesses to make regular "donations" to army welfare organizations (which, like the *yayasan* foundations in Indonesia, provide support services to armed forces personnel).[10] Subsidized, scarce commodities such as high-quality rice and cooking oil were made available to most soldiers and officers. Finally, the regime greatly expanded military higher education facilities, while keeping civilian universities closed for much of the time after 1988.[11]

As in the 1950s, the remaking of the military led to the concentration of state-rebuilding initiatives and resources under one military department or another. In the 1990s, the Office of Strategic Studies (OSS) and the regional commanders have been the most prominent agents of military state building. Founded in 1994 under the Directorate of Defence Services Intelligence (DDSI), the OSS evolved into an organization that was credited with near omnipotence in Burma's political realm.[12] Like the Military Planning Staff in the 1950s, OSS departments coordinated and perhaps even initiated policies in areas as significant as the drug trade, the economy, ethnic minority affairs, and foreign relations.[13] Although the OSS was officially dissolved in late 2001, its departments and personnel were transferred directly into DDSI and continue to wield significant influence over policy making.

While OSS formulated and coordinate regime policy on everything from archaeological digs to foreign affairs, the junta delegated the day-to-day responsibilities for state rebuilding throughout the countryside to its regional commanders.[14] As a result, political authority throughout the country came to rest not with the junta but with the regional commanders. Three new regional commands were established (bringing the total to twelve), and regional commanders were given de facto authority over all political and economic affairs in their areas of operation. (See map 7 for the territory covered by each command.) Although there was variation among regions, the junta asked regional commanders to eliminate political dissent, dismantle the old socialist state and party, and negotiate new or transformed administrative and economic arrangements. Accordingly, regional commanders built roads, housing, suburbs, and markets; rearranged urban and rural populations to accommodate tourism and other industries; and expanded surveillance and crowd-control capabilities. Along the way, they amassed enormous wealth and power.

How was this extension of the geographical and functional reach of the state financed? In the 1950s, military expansion and state-building activities were funded and facilitated almost entirely by external sources. In the 1990s, the sources of funding were more complicated. Some of the military modernization program was paid for by government revenues, and most observers estimate annual spending on the military during the 1990s at between 40 and 60 percent of the national budget. Although it is impossible to know precisely how much of the government's cash came from the "whitening tax" on foreign exchange profits from the opium and methamphetamine trade, there is no doubt this off-budget revenue provided capital for arms purchases.[15] Additionally, early purchases of arms and ammunition were financed by soft loans from China. Other weapons suppliers included Pakistan (until 1991), Singa-

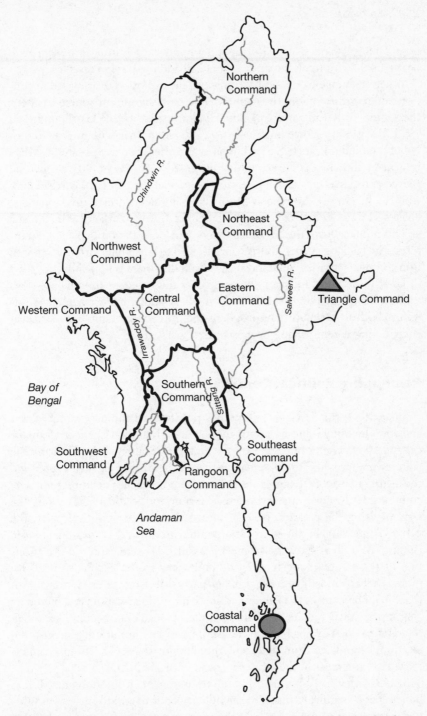

Northern
Command

Northeast
Command

Chindwin R.

Northwest
Command

Central
Command

Eastern
Command

Salween R.

Triangle Command

Western Command

Irrawaddy R.

Bay of
Bengal

Southern
Command

Sittang R.

Southwest
Command

Southeast
Command

Rangoon
Command

*Andaman
Sea*

Coastal
Command

Map 7. Tatmadaw regional commands, as of 2001. *Source:* Based on maps displayed in the Defence Services Museum, Rangoon, Burma.

pore, Israel, Poland, North Korea, and a number of European private arms dealers, paid with funds from the regime's dwindling foreign reserves.[16]

Other off-budget revenues have financed the explosion of army-led institution building throughout the country. The most significant source has been the Union of Myanmar Economic Holdings, Ltd. (UMEH). Founded in 1990, UMEH has grown into the largest indigenous firm with registered capital of ten billion kyat (U.S.$1.4 billion at the official exchange rate). UMEH is owned jointly by the Directorate of Defense Procurement (40 percent) and retired and active-duty defense services personnel (60 percent). UMEH controls the lucrative gem trade in Burma, and all major foreign investors must engage UMEH in a joint venture to enter the Burma market. UMEH and a second military firm, the Myanmar Economic Corporation (MEC), hold interests in banking, gems, tourism, trade, real estate, transportation, power, iron and steel factories, and foodstuffs. Given that there is no public reporting of UMEH or MEC finances, the companies thus operate an immense slush fund on behalf on military leadership, who have undoubtedly channeled profits into both arms acquisitions programs and the dozens of initiatives aimed at constructing the tatmadaw's new privileged social order.[17]

Remapping Political Conflict

Since 1988, the SLORC regime has transformed the geography of war and state building. The nature of the threat to Rangoon changed dramatically in 1989, when opposition leader Aung San Suu Kyi began touring the country and crossing the boundary between the mostly pacified center and the insurgency-prone frontier areas. In trips and speeches to ethnic-minority communities, she canvassed this "new" terrain for political allies, along the way inspiring the creation of local incarnations of her political party, the NLD. Appearing at times in ethnic-minority apparel—a Karen *htamein* (sarong) or a Shan *khamauk* (conical peasant hat)—she captured the attention of populations long-ignored by politicians in the pacified central regions. Perhaps most evocative was her party's decision to use a drawing of that Shan khamauk as the ballot pictogram indicating a candidate's membership in the NLD.[18] The symbolism of the khamauk connecting Aung San Suu Kyi to populations beyond the center was lost on no one. In the 1990 election, candidates from nineteen ethnic minority parties won parliamentary seats, and most of the victors were allies of the NLD.

SLORC viewed Aung San Suu Kyi's experiment in interethnic coalition building as a significant threat to the military's power and to Burma's continued existence as a unitary state. In the aftermath of the bloody, divisive 1988 uprising, military leaders correctly calculated that the army lacked the capacity to fight battles in border regions and Rangoon alike, should an alliance develop between the NLD in central Burma and armed, ethnic-minority rebels beyond the center. Accordingly, Lt. Gen. Khin Nyunt initiated cease-fire negotiations with ethnic rebel groups in 1989. Over the next several years, seventeen of the twenty-one major anti-government forces (with as many as fifty thousand troops) concluded cease-fire agreements with SLORC.

In the regions where cease-fires were concluded, the junta has deployed the Ministry for the Development of the Border Areas and the National Races (later renamed the "Ministry for the Progress of Border Areas and National Races and Development Affairs") to build roads, Burmese-language schools, hospitals, power plants, telecommunications relay stations, and other institutions aimed at both modernizing and subjugating former rebel-held territory. These border-areas projects, which are on a scale unprecedented in Burmese history, are carried out by soldiers, officers, and local residents conscripted into labor gangs by the tatmadaw.[19]

Distrust and Historiography

At the heart of the junta's state-rebuilding campaigns was a deeper national reinvention program, which the junta rooted in a series of historiographical and cultural projects aimed at remaking national identity. After twenty-six years of rewriting history to explain the teleology of Burmese socialism, the Rangoon regime launched a new growth industry in writing tatmadaw-centered history in 1989. One of the first projects that the junta assigned the Committee for the Compilation of Authentic Data of Myanmar History was to oversee research on a history of Burma's chaotic experiment in democracy in the 1950s. Not surprisingly, the resulting four volumes, which are based on archival sources and extensive interviews carried out by historians at the universities of Rangoon and Mandalay, emphasize the divisiveness of domestic politics and the dangerous geopolitical position of Burma in that period. Also, the archivists and research staff from the DSHRI have written seven volumes of army history.[20] Throughout all of these histories runs a narrative that emphasizes the stabilizing role of the military in times of crises.

In its attempt to remake history, the regime did not stop at producing books. After 1988, science, cultural, and national and local history museums popped up all over Rangoon and the rest of the country. Built by particular ministries, regional commands, or armed forces directorates, all of them revere the tatmadaw as central to the narrative of progress and national history. In 1994, the military finally opened the Defence Services Museum, four decades after the Psywar Directorate authorized its creation.[21] Compared to military museums in other Southeast Asian nations, Burma's army museum is unequaled in both its size and the deliberateness with which it places the tatmadaw at the center of all aspects of national history.

Defence Services Museum exhibit honoring the "great unifying" kings of Burmese history. Mary Callahan, February 2002.

Located in central Rangoon on a plot of land that connects two major urban arteries, the 200,000–square-foot museum reads like a primer on the tatmadaw's views of itself and of Burmese society. The junta's self-portrait depicts that tatmadaw as a "people's army" that has kept the nation alive and intact in the most dangerous of environs. It likens the tatmadaw to the "great unifying" kings of the past (e.g., Alaungpaya, Bayinnaung, and Chansittha). Throughout the museum, more than half the display captions are presented only in Burmese, which suggests that the target audience is probably the domestic citizenry. They are expected to tour hundreds of displays—which are organized in what the museum personnel call "showrooms"—and leave with a sense that nothing good in contemporary Burma came to pass without the hard work of the tatmadaw. Amid the displays of tanks, rifles, combat photos, and military leaders throughout history are three-dimensional, diorama models of paper mills, spice factories, fish farms, railway lines, Buddhist pagodas, airports, golf courses, and suburban housing developments. The history that Burmese citizens become part of here in this crowded museum has no room for alternative meanings or interpretations.

In the museum, history is told and retold throughout the displays as a history of progress against great odds. Against the superior firepower of first the British, then the Japanese, then the U.S.-backed KMT, then the Chinese-backed communist insurgents, the martial spirit of the Burmese people—led by and embodied in the tatmadaw—held the country together and allowed for Burmese culture to survive intact and flourish.

The Defence Services Museum claims that it has as many as ten thousand visitors a month during school season, and about a hundred or so are foreign visitors. The museum's creators envision it functioning like a gas station on the road to citizenship: Schoolchildren and adult trainees "fill up" on their tatmadaw history, and that "gas" powers the engine of citizenship and national unity.

The Limits of Military Modernization and State Rebuilding

As in the 1950s, state building in the 1990s has been neither smooth nor without setbacks. Military initiatives to extend the geographic and functional reach of the state have produced at least four consequences that run fully counter to these objectives. First, by working through its regional commanders, this junta has built a rickety yet (so far) enduring state apparatus that is at least for now beholden to the whims of regional commanders. Anyone who travels outside Rangoon can see the mansions, luxury cars, and royalty-like treatment of these officers. On several occasions, the Rangoon-based junta has tried to curb the incipient warlordism of the regional commanders. One such effort came in the November 1997 reorganization of the junta into the State Peace and Development Council (SPDC).[22] The reshuffle allowed the junta's top four leaders to purge most corrupt cabinet ministers (some of whom had launched their illicit empires while serving as regional commanders), to "demote" most of the regional commanders by assigning them ministerial portfolios in Rangoon, and to place relatively junior general officers in regional commands and in the junta itself for the first time in the decade.

In the future, the ongoing tensions between the junta and the upcountry commanders may not be resolvable by cabinet and command reshuffles. If the center demands greater control over upcountry resources and the commanders balk, the Rangoon regime—whether it is this junta or a democratic government—will have to find some kind of compensation or incentive for field commanders to give up their power and wealth. To date, the Rangoon-based junta has tried different mechanisms to entice regional commanders to toe the regime line, but none have seriously chal-

Entrance to the Eastern Regional Command shrine in the Defence Services Museum, Rangoon. Mary Callahan, February 2002.

lenged the organizational setup that devolves power to military commanders upcountry.

The second unforeseen consequence of this military-led state-building process is that in establishing extraordinary army dominance of national affairs, it also created the worst discipline problems across the ranks since the chaotic moments that surrounded independence in 1948. In its efforts to enlist nearly 200,000 more soldiers, the regime ordered village and town leaders to furnish quotas of recruits to serve as foot soldiers. Local leaders have not sent their most promising youths off to the army. Instead, the massive recruitment has swelled the ranks with young hoodlums, ruffians, and criminals. Discipline and morale appear to be at an all-time low.

Moreover, in the upper ranks, senior officers have helped themselves to unprecedented spoils from their positions as cabinet ministers and regional commanders. On several occasions, senior officers have refused to cut back on the "fees" and "gifts" they exact from businesses, foreign investors, and ordinary villagers, and the standoffs between the junta's top three to four

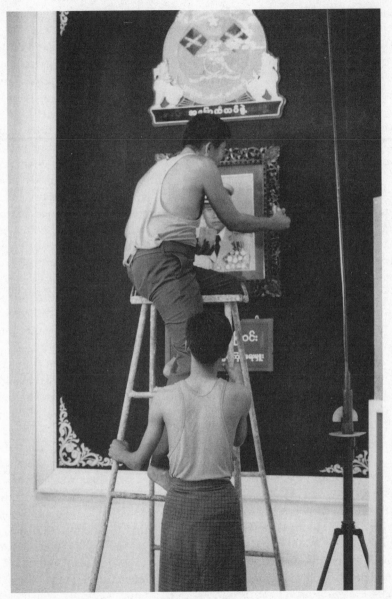

Regional Command shrine under revision after the 2001 reshuffle of senior officers. Mary Callahan, February 2002.

leaders and their unrepentant colleagues have appeared to threaten the regime. In early 2002, for example, two high-ranking generals allegedly conspired with relatives of former dictator Ne Win to protect their vast illicit empire by plotting a coup against the junta. These recalcitrants were arrested and charged with treason. Regime leaders have also purged other corrupt ministers who refused warnings to cut back on their ill-gotten gains.

Third, this redirection of military objectives to state-building programs rather than combat has created an unprecedented experiential gap between army leadership and young soldiers. This gap results directly from SLORC's successful campaign to obtain cease-fire agreements with minority insurgents between 1989 and 1996; seventeen were signed during this period. Thus, for the first time in this army's history, the "military" experiences of officers commissioned over the last ten or fifteen years are unlikely to include extensive combat. In fact, officers as high-ranking as majors and in some cases lieutenant colonels today probably have less experience fighting wars than trying to build roads. This is not to suggest that road building is a new job for the tatmadaw. The senior officers in today's tatmadaw were also involved in infrastructure and civic projects in the 1970s, but these projects were part of the counterinsurgency war effort. They were aimed at keeping the officers and their defense academy classmates alive during hard-fought battles with dangerous rebels. Today's junior officers conscript villagers to build roads that many admit are more likely to wash away with the next rains than to contribute much to Burma's economic development efforts.

The end of hostilities in the frontier regions produced the fourth unanticipated consequence of the state-rebuilding process in the 1990s. In addition to a temporary, ad hoc cessation of hostilities, the agreements also have allowed some of the former ethnic insurgent groups to retain their arms, police their own territory, and use their former rebel armies as private security forces to protect both legal and illegal business operations. Tatmadaw units are often disarmed at the entrance to territory patrolled by these ethnic armies; upon exiting the territory, they receive their weapons again. Even in Rangoon, Wa and Kokang leaders freely move about the capital with armed guards wearing the uniforms of drug barons' armies and paying little attention to the law enforcement officers they inevitably encounter.

These four unintended consequences of the SLORC/SPDC state-rebuilding process in the 1990s suggest that the armed forces are not the omnipotent, fully unified organization that contemporary political debate implies. Significant dilemmas internal to the military command at least as much of the attention of tatmadaw leaders as do concerns about Aung San Suu Kyi and the political opposition. These internal military problems do not make the downfall of the regime a foregone conclusion. But it is necessary to take them into account to comprehend the full range of the complexity underlying the current political deadlock. Much of the debate about Burmese politics today assumes that the regime's intransigence on liberalization measures comes out of a position of strength and arrogance. In fact, the state-rebuilding project undertaken in the 1990s has created as many sources of weakness for the military as it has strengths, and the weaknesses probably account as much for the regime's unyielding behavior.

Making Enemies: War and State Building in Modern Burma

More than a century of war-induced state building in Burma has solidified what Crawford Young calls the "command relationship" between state and society.[23] From the arrival of the modern bureaucratic state with the British colonizers in the late nineteenth century through to today, the relationship between rulers and ruled has been one mediated by profound distrust and the constant threat of violence. Citizenship in modern Burma has never been about the rights of individuals to make claims on the state or about the obligations of the state to treat the population in fair or standardized ways. Instead, coercion and the threat of violence have been the enduring features of state-society relations.

In the colonial era, the state had to pacify the population and prevent what it considered natural tendencies to obstruct the accumulation of profits by European firms. The top-heavy security apparatus was indigenized violently by the process of two extended campaigns in World War II. The one moment in modern history when Burma's political system began developing channels for social forces and individuals to make claims on the state was in the early years following independence. After the patched-together tatmadaw cleared Rangoon of former resistance-colleagues-turned-rebels in 1949, politics followed an accommodationist path. Army and political leaders of the newly independent government provided state resources and privileges to social elites around the country, who offered their local intelligence and private armies to help government forces in the waning civil war.

But the situation changed in the early 1950s, when thousands of KMT troops and their U.S. "advisors" arrived on Burmese soil. They constituted a threat that was exponentially more dangerous than the early mutinies and rebellions. Army leaders considered it likely that the fledgling People's Republic of China would invade any territory occupied by its enemy, the KMT. The growing hostilities of the Cold War made the China threat so palpable to those in the War Office that they came to see the increasingly accommodationist style of politics in the central regions as a threat to national sovereignty and defense.

As it became apparent that the army could not count on the United Nations or civilian political leaders to eliminate the China threat, senior staff officers in the War Office began an overhaul of the military and the state that transformed war fighters into state builders. Neither smooth nor inevitable, this transformation created army institutions that could mobilize resources, weapons, and soldiers throughout the territory. In the difficult political and economic circumstances of the 1950s, these army institution-building processes took resources and capabilities away from other nascent, nonmilitary national institutions, such as the Parliament, judiciary, bureaucracy, and political parties.

In the 1950s, war fighters resurrected the once-despised, coercive tools of colonial rule and took them one step further. Instead of simply aiming to pacify a population that threatened to interfere with state objectives, the tatmadaw's leaders built a coercion-intensive state that aimed to mobilize those pacified citizens into modernity. Among the tools resurrected were the colonial state's draconian internal security and public order laws that allowed any and all critics of the government and army to be treated as enemies of the state. Military intelligence and psychological warfare teams traveled the countryside and urban areas, compiling lists of subversives and research on threats to the integrity of the Union of Burma.

But the military did not just round up, threaten, and eliminate those considered dangerous to the state. Instead, in the 1950s, the military enthusiastically embraced trendy psychological warfare programs, aimed at remaking the "apathetic" public in the central regions into ardent defenders of the Union and, later, turning ethnic minorities outside the central regions into Burmese-speaking, "modern" people. The military's objective was to do more than just pacify the population. It wanted to mold the Burmese people into a disciplined, dependable citizenry of a modern nation-state. To this day, as the epigraphs to this epilogue show, these twin objectives still animate the state's relationship with its citizenry: pacifying potential enemies of the state, and turning them into disciplined defenders of the realm.

Imbued with this modernist optimism that the population can and must be remade, the tatmadaw's command relationship with society is simultaneously more benign and far more menacing than that of politically powerful militaries in Argentina in the 1970s and early 1980s, Chile in the 1970s and 1980s, Guatemala from the 1960s to today, the Philippines in the 1970s; and Indonesia (on Java in the 1960s and in East Timor from the 1970s until the late 1990s). At least in the central regions, the Burmese army did not carry out ongoing campaigns of slaughter in the name of counterinsurgency; other military-dominated regimes carried out state terror with more regularity.

This is not to say there has been no violence in central Burma. In moments the military itself defined as "crises," the tatmadaw did not hesitate to deploy maximum force against often unarmed fellow citizens. These "crisis" moments included the army's 1962 bombing of the Rangoon University Student Union and its bloody crackdowns on unarmed, urban protestors in 1974 and 1988. But in contrast to the Philippine Army's torture squads, Burmese soldiers have not spent a significant portion of their careers murdering fellow citizens who looked like themselves, spoke the same language, and came from the same social circles. Perhaps this difference goes a long way in explaining why most Burmese in the central regions considered the villains of the repressive, pre-1988 socialist state to be not the army but the police, whose corruption and heavy-handedness made them the target of widespread disgust.

Beyond the central regions, however, the tatmadaw's activities have been far from benign. In these frontier areas, soldiers' careers depended on their performance in ongoing, treacherous combat against fellow citizens. However, unlike the people of central Burma, these fellow citizens often spoke other languages and looked physically different. Starting in the 1960s, the military's "Four Cuts" counterinsurgency strategy officially aimed at cutting enemies off from sources of food, funds, intelligence, and recruits. But in practice, as a recent study by Hazel Lang shows, the main goal of the tatmadaw in these regions was simply to depopulate them.[24] Since it was impossible to determine which Shans, Karens, or Arakanese were rebels and which were peaceful citizens, the easiest solution was to force everyone out of their homes, and in many cases across a flimsy border with a neighboring state such as Thailand or Bangladesh. The costs to the tatmadaw of failing to depopulate the frontier were huge: probably at least fifty thousand soldiers and officers of the tatmadaw were killed or disabled in the civil war. This underfunded, technologically backward military carried out a different geography of slaughter than that pursued by their Guatemalan and Indonesian counterparts (who killed citizens in or around their capital cities). The displacement and killing of citizens in Burma's frontier regions occurred mostly off the radar screen of the population residing in the central regions. When Voice of America and the British Broadcasting Corporation broadcast Burmese-language reports of army atrocities in border regions, few in the center ever questioned the rectitude or necessity of the tatmadaw's actions. Nor did anyone ever consider that in this kind of counterinsurgency warfare, the tatmadaw construed all citizens as potential enemies of the state. In the frontier areas, enemies had to be eliminated at all costs.

Even more menacing than the records of murderous militaries in Argentina, Chile, Guatemala, Indonesia, and the Philippines is the comparative durability of the tatmadaw's command relationship with its society. In the other countries, direct military rule was always short-lived, and the brutal and repressive institutions of military "antipolitics" were remarkably easily dismantled by subsequent regimes.[25] Nonmilitary, social forces—such as nongovernmental organizations (NGOs), mass organizations, class-based groups, etc.—in these countries managed to survive the shorter periods of repression and provided rallying points both to bring down military regimes and to mobilize resources to rebuild a less repressive, more liberal state. Along the way, regime critics often found allies from within the military who had become unhappy with the marriage of power, coercion, and bloodshed.

In Burma, no one in the central regions ever questioned the morality or efficiency of the tatmadaw's counterinsurgency campaigns in the ethnic-minority regions. The idea that minority citizens were potential enemies became orthodoxy for ethnic-majority Burmans committed to holding the Union together. Only in 1988, when the tatmadaw rethought the terrain of this strategy and made citizens in the center potential enemies as well, did any debate over the use of force occur.[26] By then, the military's power over state and society had been institutionalized over a period of three-and-a-half decades, rather than just months or a few years. And in contrast to the militaries of the authoritarian eras in Argentina, the Philippines, and perhaps Indonesia, there are no reports that anyone inside the tatmadaw is questioning the propriety of treating citizens as enemies.

Beyond Enemies: Citizens in a Demilitarized Burma

There is no easy solution to the problem of dissembling this security-obsessed state and constructing a new one that treats citizens with dignity and accountability. The removal of the handful of top generals and colonels from the government, and their replacement with elected officials, will not transform overnight the century-old command relationship between state and society. Breaking the political deadlock between the opposition and the SPDC will only be the first tiny step in the direction of demilitarizing this polity. Two very serious institutional dilemmas stand in the way of that task: the unworkable nature of federalism in this multiethnic society and the widespread intolerance for any forms of political dissent.

Minority Rights in a Demilitarized Burma

The first dilemma is prickly both for the military and advocates of democratic political reform. In some respects, through its seventeen cease-fires, the SLORC/SPDC constructed a novel approach to federalism. By providing extensive local autonomy for minority groups along the border areas, this junta conceded the most central control over Burmese territory in modern history, even more so than U Nu's 1962 plans to grant statehood to the Mons and Arakanese and to consider seriously Shan and Karenni efforts to exercise their secession rights.

Moreover, former SLORC chairman Sr. Gen. Saw Maung promoted an ill-conceived ethnic policy dividing the dozen or so major national ethnic groups into what he claimed were 135 races. This reclassification represented a typical counterinsurgency tactic to divide potential opponents into smaller and smaller groups and set them against each other. This strategy backfired on the junta and reportedly halted progress by the National Convention charged with drafting a new constitution. Explaining why no constitution has been produced since the Convention opened in 1993, one member of a committee assigned to deal with the ethnic problem in the constitution, reported that the document has stalled over federalism: "We have to accept the 135 races theory, but now all 135 want their own states."[27]

The difficulty of ensuring minority rights within a sovereign national state would not go away if a democratically elected government were to take over the regime. How would a democratic government be able to collect taxes or implement social or economic policy in—for example—the Kokang region, where local elites are profiting greatly from the noninterference of the Rangoon government under the junta? Without access to economic resources such as gems and teak from the border areas, how would a democratic regime be able to alleviate the suffering of frontier populations who are trying to find their way out of two generations of war? Some ethnic minority leaders question whether a democratic government based in central Burma would really commit national resources to development programs for the border areas. As one ethnic Pao leader told Smith: "The issue of democracy is often put before ethnic nationality questions, but in our view it [the ethnic question] needs to come first."[28] With the world focusing on Aung San Suu Kyi and her party, some minority leaders worry that the needs of their people are not being taken into account by the NLD or by democracy supporters around the world.

For any kind of meaningful political integration, a future regime might need to try some of the tactics of consociationalism, a form of governance that aims to integrate culturally diverse societies by ensuring minorities' rights. Tactics might include providing for mutual veto in decision making; education and mass media in minority languages; and army, university, and bureaucracy recruitment and promotion practices that favor previously excluded minorities.[29] However, these kinds of policies face a major obstacle in Burma. Elsewhere, they have generally been successful in countries where there is a ruling ethnic group (of either majority or minority status) that for some reason has been pressured to give up its privileged position and to commit itself to proportionally fewer demands on national resources in the future (e.g., contemporary South Africa); other instances of consociational success have come in societies where there is no clear single majority group (e.g., Lebanon from 1943–75). In the current environment it seems unlikely that ethnic Burmans—most of whom have never had access to reliable information about the plight of Karen, Kokang, Shan, or other minority groups and have developed little in the way of cross-ethnic empathy—will be content to give up university places, officer commissions, or other opportunities to recruits from ethnic-minority groups.

Dissent, Dialogue, and Difference

Regarding the second dilemma—historical intolerance of any form of dissent—the five decades since independence have not given Burma any real experience with political institutions that allow, accommodate, and incorporate dissent, dialogue, and difference. The current regime clearly is unwilling to risk reforms in this regard. The NLD, too, exhibits characteristics that seem intolerant of and inimical to the development of democratic processes. For example, in January 1997, the NLD expelled Than Tun and Thein Kyi, two elected members of the never-convened Parliament, for insubordination when they refused to sign a mandate giving the NLD's Central Executive Committee full power to act on behalf of the party. Than Tun and Thein Kyi claimed after the expulsion that their differences with party leaders occurred in the debate over whether to compromise in the process of bringing SLORC to the negotiating table. According to Than Tun: "We are trying to put up these different ideas and ways for the NLD to survive through these difficult times. . . . We must get dialogue first. . . . [T]he SLORC is ignoring us all the time. They [the NLD] want to stick to principles. To get compromise you must not always stick to principles."[30] Given the nature of censorship of political information, it is difficult to know whether the NLD's actions were representative, justified (i.e., if the NLD had evidence that the two members were SLORC plants, as some diplomats have suggested), or taken out of context. However, anti-government student groups and political parties over the last decade have also shown a distinct tendency either to expel critics (who then form their own party or group) or to fragment around leaders with uncompromising positions.

The tendency toward intolerance also extends to ethnic-minority groups which—as one such group noted—have been guilty of "relentlessly persecuting racial, regional and religious minorities within their own populations while demonising the Burmans, thereby preventing the very understanding among peoples which is so necessary to bring an end to military rule."[31]

Some might suggest that intolerance for dissent is an immutable cultural flaw in the Burmese personality. However, it is important to remember that in the 1950s, democratic practices, institutions, and dissent were not completely lost causes. While in practice, the elections, constitutionalism, and civilian rule proved untenable in the crises of the 1950s, Burmese culture did not impede the emergence of such promising developments as loyal opposition (even under great repression), an independent judiciary, and a mobilized electorate. Instead of cultural pathology, there may be a more historically discrete factor that accounts for institutionalized intolerance across the generations of "democratic," "socialist," and SLORC/SPDC–ruled Burma.

Under colonial, parliamentary, socialist, and post-1988 military rule, conflicts over views, visions, and policies have always been framed as winner-take-all battles of "good guys" ("us") versus "bad guys" ("them" or "the enemy"). Because most national-level leaders, including the NLD executive committee in early 1997, have conceived of themselves as fighters against an evil old regime or imperialism or authoritarianism, they have behaved as though the only answer to conflict was to eliminate it. Accordingly, the only way to eliminate conflict was to enforce absolute unity and solidarity. The future of Burma will continue to look bleak until its leaders develop organizational frameworks that can manage and moderate conflict.

This last dilemma appears to paralyze governmental and opposition leaders of contemporary Burma and to make the prospects of sustaining any kind of democratic reform very doubtful. As political theorist Bonnie Honig writes, democracy cannot exist without contest and contestation and without differences in opinions, outlooks, dreams, and demands:

> To take difference . . . seriously in democratic theory is to affirm the inescapability of conflict and the ineradicability of resistance to the political and moral projects of ordering subjects, institutions and values. Moreover, it requires that we recast the task of democratic theory, and move it beyond that of simply orchestrating multiple and conflicting group needs and toward a new responsiveness to that first task's propensity to involve democratic cultures and institutions in violent and resentful dynamics of identity/difference. It is to give up on the dream of a place called home, a place free of power, conflict, and struggle, a place—an identity, a form of life, a group vision—unmarked or unriven by difference.[32]

Common to both the SLORC and the NLD is an overarching emphasis on unity and solidarity that is inimical to the development of institutional mechanisms that can accommodate the needs and demands of the broad range of social forces that exist throughout the country.

This political quandary could have come right out of the debates of 1946–47, when Aung San was attempting to rally disunited forces to stand up to the British one more time for the cause of independence: "We must take care that 'United we stand' not 'United we fall' [*sic*]. . . . Unity is the foundation. Let this fact be engraved in your memory, ye who hearken to me, and go ye to your appointed tasks with diligence."[33] This unified show of force was probably critical in moving the British to grant independence. However, unity became an end in itself, and by virtue of historical habit, Burmese politics has never matured beyond this phase.

Notes

Introduction

1. Dorothy Hess Guyot, "The Burma Independence Army: A Political Movement in Military Garb," in *Southeast Asia in World War II: Four Essays*, ed. Josef Silverstein (New Haven, 1966), p. 51. Other scholars use this characterization to explain why the military has maintained political power for three decades. This is probably the most cited phrase in studies of modern Burmese politics.

2. *Coercion, Capital, and European States, A.D. 990–1990* (Oxford, 1990).

3. I was not able to obtain permission to research the post-1962 period in Burmese military archives. Given that the rest of this book is based on carefully documented archival research—always checked and countered by alternative sources of information—I have chosen to place the necessarily more tentative and speculative arguments about the way warfare played out in post-1962 state-society relations in the epilogue. This more recent period is woefully underdocumented in alternative archives (such as the U.S. National Archives or British collections). Moreover, there are no reliable military histories available, and only a handful of political histories are based on primary sources.

4. Anne Judson, *Memoir of Anne Judson*, compiled by James D. Knowles (Boston, 1854), p. 162; Father Sangermano, *The Burmese Empire a Hundred Years Ago as Described by Father Sangermano* (Delhi, 1893).

5. Robert H. Taylor, *An Undeveloped State: The Study of Modern Burma's Politics*, Working Paper no. 28 (Melbourne, 1983), p. 27.

6. *Politics, Personality and Nation-Building: Burma's Search for Identity* (New Haven, 1962).

7. *Nationalism as Political Paranoia in Burma: An Essay on the Historical Practice of Power*, rev. ed. (Copenhagen, 1999).

8. *Colonial Policy and Practice: A Comparative Study of Burma and Netherlands India*, rev. ed. (New York, 1956).

9. See Leach's "The Frontiers of 'Burma,'" *Comparative Studies in Society and History* 3 (1960): 49–68; and *Political Systems of Highland Burma: A Study of Kachin Social Structure* (Boston, 1968). Manning Nash also presented a compelling analysis of village society in central Burma in the 1950s that suggests that culture was as much affected by local politics (as well as the intrusion of global forces in local markets) as vice versa. See *The Golden Road to Modernity* (Chicago, 1965).

10. Michael Aung-thwin, "Divinity, Spirit, and Human: Conceptions of Classical Burmese Kingship," in *Centers, Symbols, and Hierarchies: Essays on the Classical States of Southeast Asia*, ed. Lorraine Gesick (New Haven, 1983), pp. 45–85.

11. Ibid., p. 50.

12. *Culture and Imperialism* (New York, 1993), p. 35.

13. *The State in Burma* (London, 1987), p. 12.

14. Guyot, "Burma Independence Army," p. 51.

15. Howard G. Brown, *War, Revolution, and the Bureaucratic State: Politics and Army Administration in France, 1791–1799* (Oxford, 1995); Victor Lee Burke, *The Clash of Civilizations: War and State Formation in Europe* (Cambridge, 1997); Thomas Ertman, *Birth of the Leviathan: Building States and Regimes in Medieval and Early Modern Europe* (Cambridge, 1997); Anthony Giddens, *The Nation-State and Violence* (Berkeley, 1987); Otto Hintze, "Military Organization and the Organization of the State," in *The Historical Essays of Otto Hintze*, ed. Felix Gilbert (New York, 1975); Kalevi J. Holsti, *The State, War, and the State of War* (Cambridge, 1996); Michael Howard, *War in European History* (London, 1976); Michael Mann, *The Sources of Social Power*, vol. 2 (Cambridge, 1983); Bruce Porter, *War and the Rise of the State* (New York, 1994); Karen A. Rasler and William R. Thompson, *War and State Making* (Boston, 1989); Charles Tilly, "Reflections on the History of European State-Making," in *The Formation of National States in Western Europe*, ed. Charles Tilly (Princeton, 1975), "War Making and State Making as Organized Crime," in *Bringing the State Back In*, ed. Peter Evans, Dietrich Rueschemeyer, and Theda Skocpol (Cambridge, 1985), and his *Coercion, Capital, and European States, A.D. 990–1990* (Oxford, 1990). For accounts of the impact of different kinds of war on non-European state-building processes in the twentieth century, see Paul B. Rich and Richard Stubbs, eds., *The Counter-Insurgent State: Guerrilla Warfare and State Building in the Twentieth Century* (New York, 1997); Eiko Ikegami, *The Taming of the Samurai: Honorific Individualism and the Making of Modern Japan* (Cambridge, Mass., 1995); and Jeffrey Herbst, "War and the State in Africa," *International Security* 14, no. 4 (1990): 117–39.

16. Holsti, *The State, War, and the State of War*, p. 61.

17. Thompson, *War and State Making*, p. 183.

18. Crawford Young, "The African Colonial State and its Political Legacy," in *The Precarious Balance: State and Society in Africa*, ed. Donald Rothchild and Naomi Chazan (Boulder, Colo., 1988), pp. 25–66, 51.

19. On India, see Stephen P. Cohen, *The Indian Army: Its Contribution to the Development of a Nation* (Delhi, 1990); Stephen Peter Rosen, *Societies and Military Power: India and Its Armies* (Ithaca, 1996). On Indonesia, see Ruth McVey's two articles on the institutional genesis of the Indonesian military in the late 1950s: "The Post Revolutionary Transformation of the Indonesian Army," pts. 1 and 2, *Indonesia* 11 (1971), and *Indonesia* 12 (1972).

20. Joel Migdal, *Strong Societies and Weak States: State-Society Relations and State Capabilities in the Third World* (Princeton, 1988), p. 31.

21. Florencia E. Mallon, "Reflections on the Ruins: Everyday Forms of State Formation in Nineteenth-Century Mexico," in *Everyday Forms of State Formation: Revolution and the Negotiation of Rule in Modern Mexico*, ed. Gilbert M. Joseph and Daniel Nugent (Durham, N.C., 1994), pp. 69–106, 69.

22. *Democracy and Authoritarianism in South Asia: A Comparative and Historical Perspective* (Cambridge, 1995), p. 7.

23. Vivienne Shue, *The Reach of the State* (Stanford, 1988); Elizabeth Remick, "Cadres, Clerks, and Tax Farmers: State Building in Rural China, 1927–1937 and 1982–1992" (Ph.D. diss., Cornell University, 1996).

24. Taylor, *The State in Burma*, p. 26. See also the extensive literature on premodern, Indic states in Southeast Asia: Clifford Geertz, *Islam Observed: Religion and Development in Morocco and Indonesia* (New Haven, 1968), pp. 36–39; Geertz, *Negara: The Theatre State in Nineteenth-Century Bali* (Princeton, 1980); Soemersaid Moertono, *State and Statecraft in Old Java: A Study of the Later Mataram Period, 16th to 19th Century* (Ithaca, 1968); and S. J. Tambiah, *World Conqueror and World Renouncer* (Cambridge, 1976), chap. 7.

25. Taylor, *State in Burma*, p. 48.

26. William J. Koenig, *The Burmese Polity: Politics, Administration, and Social Organization in*

the Early Konbaung Period (Ann Arbor, Mich., 1990), p. 118; Victor B. Lieberman, *Burmese Administrative Cycles: Anarchy and Conquest, c. 1580–1760* (Princeton, N.J., 1984), chap. 3.

27. No serious effort to collect accurate statistics on the ethnic composition of the population has been attempted since the colonial government carried out a deeply flawed census in 1931. According to Martin Smith, "Present-day statistics are even more contentious. No reliable figures have been collected or released since independence and those that are published appear deliberately to play down ethnic minority numbers." *Burma: Insurgency and the Politics of Ethnicity*, 2d ed. (London, 1999), p. 30.

28. Taylor, *State in Burma*, p. 223.

29. Youssef Cohen, Brian R. Brown, and A. F. K. Organski, "The Paradoxical Nature of State Making: The Violent Creation of Order," *American Political Science Review* 75 (December 1981): 902.

30. The junta's Secretary-1, Lt. Gen. Khin Nyunt, initiated the cease-fire negotiations with ethnic rebel groups in 1989 after the Communist Party of Burma collapsed. Since 1989, seventeen of the twenty-one major antigovernment forces have agreed to cease-fire arrangements with the junta. Martin Smith, "Burma at the Crossroads," *Burma Debate*, November–December 1996, 4–13, 7.

Chapter 1. Coercion and the Colonial State, 1826–1941

1. Before the third Anglo-Burmese war, Crosthwaite had studied indigenous forms of local administration in Burma and concluded that the defective indigenous system needed to be replaced by the Indian-style village system in order to bring Burma into the modern era. See his *Pacification of Burma* (1912; reprint, London, 1968). See also Daw Mya Sein, *Sir Charles Crosthwaite and the Administration of British Burma*, (Rangoon, 1938); John Cady, *A History of Modern Burma* (Ithaca, 1958), pp. 176–78; D. G. E. Hall, *A History of South East Asia*, 3d ed. (London, 1969); John S. Furnivall, *Colonial Policy and Practice: A Comparative Study of Burma and Netherlands India*, rev. ed. (New York, 1956).

2. Furnivall, *Colonial Policy*, p. 77.

3. G. E. Harvey, *British Rule in Burma, 1824–1942* (London, 1946), p. 40.

4. Carl Trocki, "Political Structures in the Nineteenth and Early Twentieth Centuries," in *The Cambridge History of Southeast Asia*, ed. Nicholas Tarling, vol. 2 (Cambridge, 1992), pp. 79–130, 120. Actual martial law regulations were in effect only until 1890.

5. Cady, *History of Modern Burma*, pp. 129–30. A detailed characterization of the violence is found in Ni Ni Myint, *Burma's Struggle against British Imperialism* (Rangoon, 1983). See also Dorothy Woodman, *The Making of Modern Burma* (London, 1962), chaps. 15–17. Regimental histories also provide details on the violence; see Lt. Col. W. L. Hailes, *The Jat Regiment: A History of the Regiment, 1803–1907* (Bareilly, 1967), pp. 66–69; and Col. H. C. Wylly, *History of the 3rd Battalion, the 2nd Punjab Regiment* (Aldershot, 1927), pp. 36–41.

6. Cady, *History of Modern Burma*, p. 133.

7. Nigel G. Woodyatt, *The Regimental History of the 3rd Queen Alexandra's Own Gurkha Rifles from April 1815 to December 1927* (Simla, n.d.), p. 50.

8. Sir Reginald Hennell, *A Famous Indian Regiment, the Kali Panchwin, 2/5th, formerly the 105th, Mahratta Light Infantry, 1768–1923* (Delhi, 1985), p. 134.

9. Cady, *History of Modern Burma*, pp. 125–37. The official history of the tatmadaw has somewhat higher numbers: "In the fighting against Burmese rebels, the British used its infantry, cavalry, navy, artillery and other forces, bringing their strength to 50,000." However, no primary sources are cited. တပ်မတော်သမိုင်း၊ ၁၈၂၄-၁၉၄၅၊ တွဲ [*Tatmadaw History, 1824–1945*, vol. 1] (Rangoon, 1994), p. 44.

10. Cady, *History of Modern Burma*, pp. 135–37.

11. "Notes on the Land Forces of Burma," L/WS/1/276, India Office Records (hereafter IOR).

12. Jendayi Frazer, "Sustaining Civilian Control: Armed Counterweights in Regime Stability in Africa" (Ph.D. diss., Stanford University, 1994), p. 59. See her discussion of this development in British colonies in Africa, especially Kenya, pp. 59–63, 123–33.

13. Taylor, *State in Burma* (London, 1987), p. 160.

14. "Notes on the Land Forces of Burma."

15. Note that the term *Burman* refers to the ethnolinguistic majority group in modern Burma. The term *Burmese* refers to those who are or have been citizens or subjects under a government in the territory now known as Burma. *Burmese* carries no ethnolinguistic connotation.

16. Furnivall, *Colonial Policy*, p. 75.

17. Ibid.

18. John Leroy Christian, *Modern Burma: A Survey of Political and Economic Development* (Berkeley, 1942), p. 152. According to Harvey (*British Rule in Burma*, p. 38.): "England and Wales, with 40 million people, have 140 murders a year; Burma, with only 15 million, had 900."

19. F. S. V. Donnison, *Public Administration in Burma: A Study of the Development during the British Connexion* (London, 1953), p. 42.

20. Furnivall, *Colonial Policy*, p. 139. Furnivall derived his statistics from the "Annual Report on the Administration of Burma," Rangoon, from 1877–78, 1910–11, and 1914–15.

21. "Annual Report on the Administration of Burma," Rangoon, 1920–21, quoted in Furnivall, *Colonial Policy*, p. 139.

22. Albert D. Moscotti, *British Policy and the Nationalist Movement in Burma, 1917–1937* (Honolulu, 1974), p. 37.

23. Bisheshwar Prasad, *Official History: Defence of India, Policy and Plans* (Bombay, 1963), p. 42.

24. Christian, *Modern Burma*, p. 161.

25. Term borrowed from Crawford Young, "The African Colonial State and Its Political Legacy," in *The Precarious Balance: State and Society in Africa*, ed. Donald Rothchild and Naomi Chazan (Boulder, Colo., 1988), pp. 25–66, 28.

26. Furnivall's characterization of the "laissez-faire" nature of the British colonial state in Burma has never really been challenged. It is beyond the scope of this book to analyze the full nature of state-society relations in the colonial era, but simply looking at the state's lack of welfare policy—as Furnivall does—misses the more hands-on approach taken to issues of social and crime control. It is hard to understand how a state that destroys a centuries-old traditional social system, imports more than three hundred thousand coolies from India to serve as laborers, and maintains law and order by resort to armed force in most situations can be characterized as laissez-faire.

27. Robert H. Taylor, "The Relationship Between Burmese Social Classes and British-Indian Policy on the Behavior of the Burmese Political Elite, 1937–1942" (Ph.D. diss., Cornell University, 1974), p. 94.

28. Ibid., p. 94. The British undertook the separation of Burma from India to free up India from the Burma problem. Taylor observes: "The problems of an Indian federation were great enough without complicating them by trying to maintain Burma as part of India." British interests tried to do whatever it took to move their flagship colony, India, toward Dominion status within the Commonwealth. Ibid., pp. 90–94, 93.

29. Donnison, *Public Administration in Burma*, pp. 96–97.

30. This is basically the argument of all postcolonial "official histories." See တပ်မတော်သမိုင်း၊ တွဲ ၁ [*Tatmadaw History*, vol. 1]; တိုင်းရင်းသားလူမျိုးများနှင့်၁၉၄၇အခြေခံဥပဒေ [*The Indigenous Races and the 1947 Constitution*] (Rangoon, 1991); and Ba Than, *The Roots of the Revolution* (Rangoon, 1962), p. 2.

31. တပ်မတော်သမိုင်း၊၊ တွဲ ၁ [*Tatmadaw History*, vol. 1], pp. 20–22; Furnivall, *Colonial Policy*, pp. 178–84.

32. Ibid., pp. 180–81. Smith-Dun recounts the story of this battalion of Karen military police and the "regrettable" incident at Monywa that led to its dissolution. See his *Memoirs of the Four-Foot Colonel* (Ithaca, 1980), pp. 103–4.

33. Government of India, Census Commissioner, "Census," Rangoon, 1911.

34. Furnivall, *Colonial Policy*, p. 178.

35. Stephen Cohen details the policy debate that went on in the aftermath of the 1857 mutiny over the shift from territorially based recruitment to the new system based on race and caste, adopted in 1892. The British used the term *class* to refer to one particular ethnic group or caste recruited into the army; hence this system came to be known as class recruitment, and the resulting units were called class regiments and class battalions. Cohen, *The Indian Army: Its Contribution to the Development of a Nation* (Delhi, 1990), pp. 35–45.

36. Furnivall, *Colonial Policy*, pp. 178–84.

37. Bisheshwar Prasad, ed., *Official History of the Indian Armed Forces in the Second World War, 1939–45: Expansion of the Armed Forces and Defence Organisation, 1939–45* (India, 1956), p. 84.

38. တိုင်းရင်းသားလူမျိုးများ၊ တွဲ ၁ [*Indigenous Races*, vol. 1], p. 46.

39. Do (တို့) can be translated as either "our" or "we." *Bama* (ဗမာ) refers either to the collective identity of all persons in the territory of Burma, or more narrowly to the ethnic-majority group. *Asiayone* (အစည်းအရုံး) is translated as "union," "association," "organization," or "league."

40. The Dobama's song became (in slightly different versions) the national anthem during the Japanese occupation and at independence in 1948. The following are the original lyrics of the song (with my translation):

ဗမာပြည်သည် – တို့.ပြည်။	Burma is our country.
ဗမာစာသည် – တို့.စာ။	Burmese literature is our literature.
ဗမာစကားသည် – တို့.စကား။	Burmese language is our language.
တို့.ပြည် ချစ်ပါ။	Love our country.
တို့.စာ ချီးကျူးပါ။	Award [or praise] our literature.
တို့.စကား လေးစားပါ။	Respect our language.

From appendix 1 of Daw Khin Kyi's *The Dobama Movement in Burma: Appendix* (Ithaca, 1988), p. 1.

41. Kei Nemoto, "The Concepts of *Dobama* (Our Burma) and *Thudo-Bama* (Their Burma) in Burmese Nationalism, 1930–1948," *Journal of Burma Studies* 5: 1–16.

42. During the colonial period, *thakin* became the equivalent of *sahib* in India; in other words, it was used as a respectful form of address to Europeans. Nationalists appropriated the title to show that they considered themselves to be masters.

43. *Tat* (တပ်) is translated as "armed forces," "troops," "military," or "group of people assembled for collective action." These groups are often referred to in English-language histories as "volunteer corps," which was the translation some of the 1930s politicians proffered to camouflage their activities. I prefer to use "tat" throughout because none of the concepts in English translation carry the same range of ambiguity between "a group assembled for collective action" (with no connotation of violence) and "armed forces."

44. U Maung Maung, *From Sangha to Laity* (New Delhi, 1980), p. 76.

45. The *galon* is a mythical bird; *Galons* was the name of Hsaya San's forces during the peasant uprising of 1931–32. U Saw was one of the attorneys who defended Hsaya San and was trying to remind the Burmese population of his association with the martyred hero.

46. Taylor, "Burmese Social Classes," pp. 188–89.

47. It is important to note that the fascination with Hitler's fascist ideology and practice was based on a superficial understanding of it. These nationalists were trying to figure out how to fight an extremely powerful imperial apparatus, and the idea of mobilizing the masses in the cause of independence—as Hitler had done in the cause of national socialism—was appealing.

48. Robert Taylor's analyses of British "Monthly Intelligence Summaries" on Burma in 1940–41 reveal that there were 743 "total live units" of "volunteer corps" operating in Burma in June 1941. Taylor notes that some of these "never got beyond the 'paper' stage" and many units were not active. "Burmese Social Classes," p. 189.

49. In *From Sangha to Laity* (p. 256, n. 32), U Maung Maung reports that the Galon Tat of U Saw was particularly inflammatory. He cites an article in U Saw's newspaper, *The Sun*, on May 28, 1938, in which U Saw proclaimed he would build his army to a strength of one hundred thousand, and it would be made available to Britain in the coming war in return for a promise of independence. He also published a column in *The Sun* throughout the month of July 1938 listing the names of youths who had joined the Galons in different towns throughout Burma. Taylor reports that U Saw called himself "commander in chief" and publicly announced his plans in 1938 to establish a Cadet Officers' Training Institution; he tried unsuccessfully to purchase an airplane and seaplane for instructional purposes. "Burmese Social Classes," pp. 189–91. See also Robert H. Taylor, "Politics in Late Colonial Burma: The Case of U Saw," *Modern Asian Studies* 10, no. 2 (1976): 161–93, 168–69.

50. "Burma's Challenge, 1946," in *The Political Legacy of Aung San*, ed. Josef Silverstein, rev. ed. (Ithaca, 1993), pp. 74–161, 121.

51. S. V. Donnison, *The Changing of Kings: Memories of Burma, 1934–1949* (London, 1985), p. 131.

52. Donnison, *Public Administration in Burma*, p. 99.

53. Taylor, "Burmese Social Classes," p. 188.

54. The constitution is reproduced (in Burmese) in full in Daw Khin Kyi, *Dobama Movement in Burma: Appendix*, pp. 113–47.

55. Tony Mains, a British intelligence officer posted to Burma in 1941, argues that the legal reclassification of military authority in Burma from an "Independent Military District of India" to the "Burma Command" did not represent any significant change in actual authority relations. "[T]o say that the Government of Burma, in 1942, was responsible for defence, was complete nonsense." *Retreat from Burma: An Intelligence Officer's Personal Story* (London, 1973), p. 35.

56. Maung Maung, *Burma in the Family of Nations* (Amsterdam, 1954), p. 90; Taylor, *State in Burma*, pp. 100–101.

57. FO 643/140, p. 40, Public Record Office (hereafter PRO).

58. Taylor, *State in Burma*, p. 101.

59. Furnivall, *Colonial Policy*, p. 183.

60. *State in Burma*, pp. 100–101.

61. See Edith Piness's analysis of exceptions to this rule, found mainly in the middle levels of the bureaucracy, in "The British Administrator in Burma: A New View," *Journal of Southeast Asian Studies* 14, no. 2 (September 1983): 372–78. Eleven of the first fourteen chief commissioners or lieutenant governors of Burma were appointed from India never having set foot in Burma.

Chapter 2. The Japanese Occupation, 1941–43

1. Dorothy Guyot, "The Political Impact of the Japanese Occupation" (Ph.D. diss., Yale University, 1966), p. 98.

2. Guyot, "Political Impact," pp. 97–98; Tony Mains, *The Retreat from Burma: An Intelligence Officer's Personal Story* (London, 1973), pp. 40–42; Leslie Glass, *The Changing of Kings: Memories of Burma, 1934–1949* (London, 1985), p. 138.

3. Guyot, "Political Impact," p. 108.

4. Joyce Lebra, *Japanese-Trained Armies in Southeast Asia: Independence and Volunteer Forces in World War II* (New York, 1977), p. 47. Aung San actually left Burma to solicit assistance from Chinese Communists for Burma's struggle for independence. However, probably by mistake, he got on a boat sailing for Amoy, which had only recently been occupied by the Japanese; upon arrival he could not find any communists to talk to. See တို့ဗမာအစည်းအရုံးသမိုင်း: [*History of the Dobama Asiayone*] (Rangoon, 1976), pp. 520–21 and 527–29.

5. Izumiya Tatsuro, *The Minami Organ*, trans. U Tun Aung Chain, 3d ed. (Rangoon, 1991), p. 30. Izumiya was a member of the Minami.

6. In a last-minute reversal of strategy, army officials in Japan sent orders to Suzuki in Bangkok to detain the trainees aboard ship and send them back to Tokyo. However, "Suzuki, angry at this reversal and unwilling to disappoint the Burmans after so many months of training," sent back a cable that the trainees had already disappeared into the Siamese jungle, which was not true. Ibid., p. 59.

7. ဗိုလ်ဗလ၊ လွတ်လပ်ရေးခရီးတစ်ထောက် [Bo Ba La, *A Journey to Independence*] (Rangoon, 1974), pp. 265–66; Sawamoto Rikichiro, "A Short History of the Burma Army," unpublished manuscript, September 1955, DR 255, Defence Services Historical Research Institute (hereafter DSHRI); as a major general in the Japanese Burma Area Army, Sawamoto served as chief advisor to the Burma National Army (a later incarnation of the BIA) from 1943 on.

8. See the biography of Bo Ba Too, which tells the story of how Ba Too, as a labor leader among mineworkers in Tenasserim, joined the BIA on its arrival there. သိပ္ပံစိုးရင်၊ ဗမာတော်လှန်ရေး အာဇာနည် ဗိုလ်မှူးကြီးဗထူ: [Theippan Soe Yin, *Martyr of the Burmese Revolution: Bo Ba Too*] (Insein, 1969), pp. 23–31. See also Bo Ba La, ဗိုလ်ဗလ၊ လွတ်လပ်ရေးခရီးတစ်ထောက် [*Journey to Independence*], pp. 284–92, and ဗိုလ်သံတွိုင်၊ လွတ်လပ်ရေးအရေးတော်ပုံမှတ်တမ်း၊ တွဲ ၁ [Bo Than Daing, *Record of the Independence*

Revolution, vol. 1] (Rangoon, 1967), pp. 1–14. Bo Thein Swe, a former member of the UTC and the Thanmani Tat, lists all of the early bogyokes (generals) from the Thanmani Tat of the Rangoon University Students' Union; they include Bo Yan Naing (who later became a "Thirty Comrade"), Ko Chit Myaing (who was known as one of the finest field commanders in the postwar army; he retired at the rank of colonel), and Ko Maung Maung (who was Aung San's aide-de-camp during the war and later the mastermind behind the 1952 reorganization of the tatmadaw; many people consider him the "architect" of the postwar army). From ဗိုလ်သိန်းဆွေ၊ လွတ်လပ်ရေးတိုက်ပွဲ [Bo Thein Swe, *Battle for Independence*] (Rangoon, 1967), p. 110; see also pp. 121–28, for his memories of the prewar underground.

9. (Former Brig.) U Maung Maung, *Burmese Nationalist Movements, 1940–1948* (Honolulu, 1990), p. 32.

10. At opposing poles were Suzuki, ever loyal to "his" BIA, and Col. Ishii Akiho, senior staff officer of the Southern Area Army, who was far more concerned with the military exigencies of holding Burma, extracting her resources, and moving on to fight the more important battles for China and perhaps India. In January 1942, Suzuki proposed to the Southern Area Army to proclaim immediately an independent Burmese provisional government; however, Ishii was convinced an independent Burmese government would interfere with Japanese prosecution of the war, and instead established a new Administrative Section in Fifteenth Army Headquarters. The task of the Administrative Section was to prepare to establish military administration in Burma. For a number of complicated reasons, Ishii ultimately held sway, and Suzuki's last-ditch effort to establish a Burmese administration in April 1942 under thakins he trained at San-ya survived only three months. See Won Z. Yoon, "Military Expediency: A Determining Factor in the Japanese Policy Regarding Burmese Independence," *Journal of Southeast Asian Studies* 9, no. 2 (1978): 248–67; Lebra, *Japanese-Trained Armies*, pp. 43, 64–68.

11. Guyot, "Political Impact," pp. 129–30.

12. Ibid., p. 156. Note that this discussion covers only those towns administered by BIA committees, which Guyot estimates to be 80 percent of the total number of townships. In a few small towns that were first occupied by Japanese forces, Japanese company commanders appointed local administrators. They tended to choose older, more conservative members and bypass thakin candidates.

13. Ibid., p. 163.

14. Ibid., p. 151. Tekkatho Sein Tin also discusses the collapse of the British order in the countryside in his biography of Major Aye Cho; ဗိုလ်မှူးအောင်ဆန်းသူရိယအေးချို [*Bohmu Aung San Thuriya Aye Cho*] (Rangoon, 1990), pp. 203–4.

15. Given the rather loose structure of the BIA and the Japanese army's inability to bring it into any kind of centralized chain of command, it is difficult to arrive at an acceptable estimate of the size of the BIA. Many Burmese sources use the high figure of fifty thousand (see, e.g., Dr. Maung Maung, *Burma's Constitution* (The Hague, 1961), p. 55, and တပ်မတော်သမိုင်း ၁၈၂၄–၁၉၄၅၊ တွဲ ၁ [*Tatmadaw History*, 1824–1945, vol. 1] (Rangoon, 1994), chap. 5. Won Z. Yoon (*Japan's Scheme for the Liberation of Burma: The Minami Kikan and the Thirty Comrades* [Athens, Ohio, 1973]) conservatively estimates the figure to be closer to ten thousand, and Trevor Nevitt Dupuy (*Military History of World War II: Asian and Axis Resistance Movements* [New York, 1985], p. 51) gives the lowest estimate in the literature: four thousand. Joyce Lebra (*Japanese-Trained Armies*, p. 65) suggests an estimate of twenty thousand, although she does not cite her source for this number. In his analysis of Japanese military administration documents, Frank Trager arrives at a figure of 23,500 ("Introduction," *Burma: Japanese Military Administration, Selected Documents, 1941–1945*, ed. Frank Trager [Philadelphia, 1971], p. 11).

16. Guyot, "Political Impact," p. 118.

17. Technically, there were channels and policies to establish such a line of command, but Colonel Suzuki chose to flout orders and, in order to protect "his" BIA from the predations of the Japanese army and navy, set himself up as the only liaison between the BIA and Japanese army authorities. Ibid., p. 126.

18. Ibid., p. 122.

19. Naw Angelene, "Aung San and the Struggle for the Independence of Burma" (Ph.D. diss., University of Hawaii, 1988).

20. See, e.g., Aung San, "Burma's Challenge, 1946," in *The Political Legacy of Aung San*, ed. Josef Silverstein, rev. ed. (Ithaca, 1993), pp. 74–161, esp. 86–87; (former Brig.) U Maung Maung, *Burmese Nationalist Movements*, chaps. 3–4; ဗိုလ်မှူးချုပ်ကောင်း၊ အနှစ်နှစ်ဆယ် [Bohmu Chit Kaung, *Twenty Years*] (Rangoon, 1969).

21. See his လွတ်လပ်ရေး အရေးတော်ပုံ မှတ်တမ်း၊ တွဲ ၁ [*Record of the Independence Revolution*, vol. 1], pp. 75–117.

22. Dorothy Guyot, "Political Impact," p. 121.

23. See Kiyoshi Aonuma, "An Analytical Study of Educational Administration in the Japanese Occupation of Burma, 1942–1945," in *Japan in Asia, 1942–1945*, ed. William H. Newell (Singapore, 1981), pp. 104–18.

24. Order cited in Saw Rock Top, "The Development and Role of Army in Burma, 1941–1962" (Ph.D. diss., University of Tokyo, 1988), p. 69.

25. This is not to suggest that Aung San or any other Burmese army leaders had any clear notions in July 1942 that the reduced numbers could lead to this outcome. In fact, Aung San later wrote that he considered his position at this point to be untenable, and suggested that he knew he had no choice but to acquiesce in whatever the Japanese authorities demanded and to try to make the best of a bad situation. (See Saw Rock Top's analysis of the range of factors that went into Aung San's decision to concede the dissolution of the BIA, ibid., pp. 66–67.) Naw Angelene argues that the potential benefits of this reorganization were unclear to Aung San in July 1942 and that the stress involved in this difficult period was one important factor that led to his collapse and hospitalization for a month. From her "Aung San and the Struggle," pp. 152–53.

26. See Bo Than Daing's chapter on the Pyinmana orientation session, in his လွတ်လပ်ရေး အရေးတော်ပုံ မှတ်တမ်း၊ တွဲ ၁ [*Record of the Independence Revolution*, vol. 1], pp. 160–94.

27. ဗိုလ်မှူးကြီး၊(ဟောင်း)တင်မောင်၊ ဂျပန်ခေတ် စစ်ပညာတော်သင်တစ်: [(Former) Col. Tin Maung, *A Military Trainee in the Japanese Era*] (Rangoon, 1973), pp. 51–62; and ဗိုလ်မှူးချွပ်ဝင်းအုန်း၊ ဖက်ဆစ်ဝါဒီများအား ၁၉၄၅ခုနှစ်တွင် တိုက်ထုတ်စဉ်က [Brig. Khin Ohn, *While Fighting against the Fascists in 1945*] (Rangoon, 1993), pp. 22–24.

28. ဗိုလ်မှူးချုပ်ကောင်း၊ ၊ အနှစ်နှစ်ဆယ် [Bohmu Chit Kaung, *Twenty Years*], p. 22.

29. Saw Rock Top, "Development and Role of Army," pp. 117–18.

30. Later, some of the recruiting was done through the channels of the corporatist-style political party—Dobama Sinyetha—established by Dr. Ba Maw in late 1942. Ibid., p. 75. However, Guyot argues that party attempts to gain control over the army "by requiring that all volunteers for the army apply through their local party" were abandoned when the army refused to go along with this requirement. Guyot, "Political Impact," p. 283.

31. Saw Rock Top, pp. 69–70; Brig. Khin Ohn wrote that after the EAYL was established, its local chapters also screened recruits for the army. ဖက်ဆစ်ဝါဒီများအား ၁၉၄၅ခုနှစ်တွင် တိုက်ထုတ်စဉ်က [*Fighting against the Fascists*], pp. 23–24.

32. From ဗိုလ်သိမ်းဆွေ၊ လွတ်လပ်ရေးတိုက်ပွဲ [Bo Thein Swe, *Battle for Independence*], pp. 168–69.

33. This is often referred to as "*Japan-khit-siq-tekkatho*," which is translated, "Japanese-era War College." In some materials it also is referred to as "The Military Academy" in English. The Japanese term is transliterated, *Kambukohoseitai*.

34. Guyot, "Political Impact," p. 321.

35. တပ်မတော်သမိုင်း၊ တွဲ ၁ [*Tatmadaw History*, vol. 1], p. 227. See also ဗိုလ်မင်းညို၊ ဂျပန်ခေတ် စစ်တက္ကသိုလ် [Bo Min Nyo, *Japanese-Era War College*] (Rangoon, 1969), pp. 1–4.

36. Ibid.

37. Most authors seem to assume that because 300 places were authorized under these two categories, in fact 300 cadets enrolled. Saw Rock Top ("Development and Role of Army," chap. 2), Dorothy Guyot ("Political Impact," p. 321), and တပ်မတော်သမိုင်း၊ တွဲ ၁ [*Tatmadaw History*, vol. 1], p. 228, make this mistake. However, Bo Min Nyo lists the names of only 134 students in the first batch at OTS in his ဂျပန်ခေတ် စစ်တက္ကသိုလ် [*Japanese-Era War College*], pp. 9–14. Lebra (*Japanese-Trained Armies*, p. 70) writes that "the first class consisted of two to three hundred men." The only real evidence that any of Dr. Ba Maw's appointees enrolled at OTS is the account of Bon-bauk Tha Kyaw, who wrote that he was admitted to the first batch at Mingaladon based on the recommendation from Dr. Ba Maw; in ဘုံပေါက်သာကျော်၊ တော်လှန်ရေး ခရီးဝယ်၊ တွဲ ၁ [*On the Revolutionary Journey*] (Rangoon, 1973), p. 106.

38. Commander of the Hayashi Army Group, "Summary of the Establishment of the Burma Defense Army," August 9, 1942, trans. Won Zoon Yoon and reprinted in Trager, ed., *Burma: Japanese Military Administration*, p. 108.

39. ဗိုလ်မင်းညို၊ ဂျပန်ခေတ် စစ်တက္ကသိုလ် [Bo Min Nyo, *Japanese-Era War College*], pp. 127–28; တပ်မတော်သမိုင်း၊ တွဲ ၁ [*Tatmadaw History*, vol. 1], p. 229. Bo Than Daing wrote of being slapped in the face whenever he uttered a word in Burmese; from his ဗိုလ်သံတိုင်၊ လွတ်လပ်ရေး အရေးတော်ပုံမှတ်တမ်း၊ တွဲ ၁ [*Record of the Independence Revolution*, vol. 1], p. 25. See also (former) Col. Tin Maung's memories of face-slapping incidents, in ဂျပန်ခေတ် စစ်ပညာတော်သင်တန်း [*Military Trainee in the Japanese Era*], pp. 132–40.

40. Ibid., pp. 102–10.

41. Jan Becka, *The National Liberation Movement in Burma during the Japanese Occupation Period (1941–1945)* (Prague, 1983), p. 148. See also Thein Pe's description of Bo Tu's experience at OTS: "While studying there and receiving the slaps of the Japanese teachers, he met with Communist cells and went to secret Communist classes." စစ်အတွင်းခရီးသည် [*Wartime Traveler*] (Rangoon, 1953), p. 263. Furthermore, Tin Win Nyo, who attended the junior cadets' course at Mingaladon during the war, remembers that most evenings were spent "in discussions with Communists. They bribed us with cigarettes, which couldn't be smoked freely or we would be beaten." Interview, May 8, 1992, Rangoon. All interviews in this book were conducted by the author unless otherwise noted.

42. Chit Kaung, a student in the second OTS batch, reports that first-batch graduates advised and assisted him and his classmates through difficult times; အနှစ်နှစ်ဆယ် [*Twenty Years*], p. 25. See also the memoir of Col. Tin Maung, a graduate of the first OTS batch who briefly served as instructor to the second batch; ဂျပန်ခေတ် စစ်ပညာတော်သင်တန်း [*Military Trainee in the Japanese Era*], pp. 147–63.

43. "Summary of the Establishment," p. 106.

44. Saw Rock Top, "Development and Role of Army," p. 74.

45. Ibid., p. 75.

46. ဗိုလ်မှူးချစ်ကောင်း၊ အနှစ်နှစ်ဆယ် [Bohmu Chit Kaung, *Twenty Years*], pp. 38–39.

47. Almost all references in the secondary literature on this AYRG can be traced to Ba Than's semi-official history, *The Roots of the Revolution* (Rangoon, 1962), pp. 43–44. From interviews with a number of the principals involved in what later came to be known by this name, I do not believe the nineteen "energetic and . . . rather reckless" young officers Ba Than claims formed this organization ever gave it a name or considered it to have the kind of integrity that has been attributed to it by scholars citing uncritically the Ba Than book. These young officers had two things in common. First, they were not members of the Thirty Comrades, and hence did not have the same ties to and fears of the Japanese as their counterparts trained at Hainan. Second, many were members of the prewar People's Revolutionary Party (PRP), which had been started in 1939 as a Marxist-leaning party that was an alternative to the Communist Party; as such, most of these nineteen were allied with PRP politicians including Ba Swe and Kyaw Nyein. However, political loyalties were fluid during the war, and it cannot be said that the War Office was dominated by the PRP since there were a number of Burmese there who had attended or were attending secret Communist Party–sponsored politics courses. Bohmu Chit Kaung's memoirs give a convincing account of the fluidity of political positions at the War Office during this era; အနှစ်နှစ်ဆယ် [*Twenty Years*], pp. 33–42.

48. DSHRI, "An Administrative History of the Armed Forces in Burma," vol. 1, unpublished manuscript for internal circulation (Rangoon, n.d.), p. 165.

49. Interview, former Brig. Maung Maung, February 16, 1993; Thakin Nu, *Burma under the Japanese: Pictures and Portraits*, trans. J. S. Furnivall (London, 1954), p. 104.

50. Khin Myo Chit writes about her experiences as a "special messenger" taking copies of *Reuters News* (which the War Office started receiving in 1944) to Thakin Than Tun, who lived near her, and Kyaw Nyein, who worked with her husband. From her "Many a House of Life Hath Held Me," unpublished manuscript, n.d., MSS Eur D 1066, IOR.

51. သခင်တင်မြ၊ ဘုံဘဝမှာဖြင့် [Thakin Tin Mya, *A Life of a Commune*] (Rangoon, 1971); U Maung Maung, *Burmese Nationalist Movements*, pp. 126–27.

52. ဗိုလ်မှူးချစ်ကောင်း၊ အနှစ်နှစ်ဆယ် [Bohmu Chit Kaung, *Twenty Years*], pp. 37–38.

53. Later in his memoir, Chit Kaung mentions studying and discussing "anti-Japanese

materials" that he and his friend Ko Chit Hlaing read in the dim light behind the Halpern Road brothel, established by Burmese army leaders. Ibid., p. 39.

Chapter 3. Resistance and the United Front, 1943–45

1. In his official history, F. S. V. Donnison writes that the remote border regions inside Burma that were not occupied by the Japanese became known by this term. *British Military Administration in the Far East, 1943–1946* (London, 1956), p. 131. This term was used throughout Mountbatten's *Report to the Combined Chiefs of Staff by the Supreme Allied Commander, South-East Asia* (London, 1951).

2. Jan Becka, *The National Liberation Movement in Burma during the Japanese Occupation Period (1941–1945)* (Prague, 1983), p. 339.

3. The conference delegated administration of "liberated" areas of Burma to the Civil Affairs Service (Burma) (CAS[B]), which was almost entirely recruited from prewar Burma Civil Service personnel.

4. Donnison, *British Military Administration*, p. 13.

5. Figure cited by Mountbatten in September 1945; Minutes of the Supreme Allied Commander's Meeting, Kandy, Ceylon, September 6, 1945, R/8/20, p. 48, IOR. The same figure appears in Ian Morrison, *Grandfather Longlegs: The Life and Gallant Death of Major H. P. Seagrim* (London, 1946), p. 148; Louis Allen, *Burma: The Longest War, 1941–1945* (London, 1984), p. 578.

6. The results of this review cannot have been surprising to Slim, given that an earlier review of intelligence operations in the area had been conducted in 1942 which turned up eight functionally autonomous "organizations engaged in the collection of intelligence." See Memorandum by General Headquarters, India, General Staff Branch, New Delhi, to Brig. E. T. L. Gurdon (Eastern Army), Brig. J. Aldous (Fourth Corps), and Brig. Scott (Fifteenth Corps), August 24, 1942, in R/8/21, IOR.

7. "Introduction: Marxism," in *Marxism and Resistance in Burma, 1942–1945*, ed. Robert Taylor (Athens, Ohio, 1984), p. 18.

8. Ibid., p. 13.

9. *Last and First in Burma, 1941–1948* (London, 1956), p. 231.

10. "Race and Resistance in Burma, 1942–1945," *Modern Asian Studies* 20, no. 3 (1986): 483–507, 500.

11. Leslie Glass, *The Changing of Kings: Memories of Burma, 1934–1949* (London, 1985), p. 180. Propaganda quoted in Becka, *National Liberation Movement*, p. 188.

12. Charles Cruickshank, *SOE in the Far East* (Oxford, 1983), p. 3.

13. နေညွန့်ဘဆွေ၊ "ပြည်သူ့အရေးတော်ပုံ ပါတီ ၁၉၃၉–၁၉၄၆" [Ne Nyunt Ba Swe, "The People's Revolutionary Party, 1939–1946" (M.A. thesis, Rangoon University, 1984)], pp. 12–13.

14. သခင်သိန်းဖေမြင့် စစ်အတွင်းခရီးသည် [Thein Pe Myint, *Wartime Traveler*] (Rangoon, 1953) and ဗိုလ်မှူးချစ်ကောင်း၊ အနှစ်နှစ်ဆယ် [Bohmu Chit Kaung, *Twenty Years*] (Rangoon, 1969), p. 43.

15. Dorothy Guyot, "The Political Impact of the Japanese Occupation" (Ph.D. diss., Yale University, 1966), p. 287.

16. Guyot (ibid.) reports that the Keibotai membership peaked at around eight thousand men. This was a mostly urban, youth organization established in February 1943. There are no existing studies of the Keibotai and its influence on the resistance movement, but its significance probably lay in the organization's rolling ten-day training sessions that brought young urban nationalists together for weapons and defense training, beginning in August 1943. မြန်မာ့အလင်း၊ ၈၊ ၈၊ ၁၉၄၃ [*Light of Burma* (newspaper), August 8, 1943].

17. AFO organizers decided on "Anti-Fascist Organization" as the English translation of "ဖက်ဆစ်တိုက်ဖျက်ရေး၊ တပ်ပေါင်းစုကြီး၊ ပြည်သူ့လွတ်လပ်ရေးအဖွဲ့ချုပ်" which more literally would be translated "Fascist-Destruction (or Eradication), People's Freedom League."

18. Further meetings between BNA officers and PRP and CPB politicians in the delta the following month established a unified "တော်လှန်ရေးတပ်ဦး" (pronounced "taw-hlan-yeh tat-u"), which was translated the "Vanguard of the Revolution." The Tat-u created one single party, still to be known as the CPB, out of the existing PRP and CPB. Thakin Soe convinced Kyaw

Nyein, Ba Swe, Ne Win, and Aung San to serve as members of the CPB's central committee. However, due to lack of coordination, there were almost no real changes in the makeup of local branches of the communist and PRP underground, and Thakin Soe declared the Tat-u dead in December. See Becka, *National Liberation Movement*, pp. 169–74.

19. From the declaration of the Vanguard, signed by the CPB on October 3, 1944; this declaration is reprinted in သခင်တင်မြ၊ ဖက်ဆစ်တော်လှန်ရေးဌာနချုပ် နှင့် တိုင်း(၁၀)တိုင် [Thakin Tin Mya, *Anti-Fascist Headquarters and Its Ten Divisions*] (Rangoon, 1968), pp. 25–30.

20. လွတ်လပ်ရေးတိုက်ပွဲ သမိုင်းဝင်စာတမ်းများ [*Historical Documents from the Battle for Independence*] (Rangoon, 1978), pp. 5, 15–16.

21. Selth, "Race and Resistance," p. 491.

22. Saw Tha Din, quoted in Martin Smith, *Burma: Insurgency and the Politics of Ethnicity*, 2d ed. (London, 1999), p. 62.

23. Bo Thein Swe, *Battle for Independence*, pp. 174–75; Smith, *Burma: Insurgency*, p. 63; "Nominal Roles of the Patriotic Burmese Forces of Zones 2 and 3," DR 603, DSHRI. Unfortunately, soon after the uprising, Kya Doe was captured and interned by the Japanese. သခင်တင်မြ၊ ဖက်ဆစ်တော်လှန်ရေးဌာနချုပ် [Thakin Tin Mya, *Anti-Fascist Headquarters*], pp. 181–216.

24. Morrison, *Grandfather Longlegs*, p. 164. See also Cruickshank, *SOE in the Far East*, pp. 166–67, and the odd collection of reminiscences, correspondence, and official reports compiled by the wife of a deceased British agent who organized Karen guerrillas in the eastern hills; in Geraldine Peacock, *The Life of a Jungle Wallah: Reminiscences in the Life of Lt. Col. E. H. Peacock, D.S.O., M.C.* (Devon, 1958), pp. 67–128.

25. Raymond Callahan provides a detailed analysis of the failure of the 1943 offensive into Arakan in his *Burma: 1941–1945* (London, 1978), pp. 32–67. See also Bisheshwar Prasad, ed., *Official History of the Indian Armed Forces in the Second World War, 1939–1945; The Arakan Operations, 1942–1945* (Delhi, 1954).

26. The Arakanese resistance forces are much overlooked in the literature on the anti-Japanese uprising in Burma, generally, and even in histories of the Arakan operations. The best source on this is သခင်တင်မြ၊ ဖက်ဆစ်တော်လှန်ရေးဌာနချုပ် [Thakin Tin Mya, *Anti-Fascist Headquarters*], pp. 115–23. Donnison's *British Military Administration* is also useful, as is Mountbatten's *Report to the Combined Chiefs of Staff*, pp. 107–13, 124–30. Note the lack of consideration given the Arakanese resistance forces in Prasad, *Arakan Operations*.

27. Vum Ko Hau, *Profile of a Burma Frontier Man* (Bandung, 1963), p. 33.

28. Morrison, *Grandfather Longlegs*, p. 113; Louis Allen, *Burma: The Longest War*, pp. 576–77.

29. Cruickshank, *SOE in the Far East*, p. 166; Field Marshall William Slim, *Defeat into Victory* (New York, 1961), pp. 424–25; Mountbatten, *Report to the Combined Chiefs of Staff*, p. 143.

30. Cruickshank, *SOE in the Far East*, p. 169.

31. Glass, *Changing of Kings*, p. 188.

32. Taylor, "Introduction: Marxism," p. 29.

33. Donnison, *British Military Administration*, pp. 348–49.

34. Glass, *Changing of Kings*, pp. 186–87. Glass wrote that SOE's Mackenzie had deceived the civilian Burmese government officials at Simla "as long as he could" so that his plans for co-operation with Aung San could not be stymied by critics. Mountbatten confirms this deception in his *Report to the Combined Chiefs of Staff*, p. 198.

35. *SOE in the Far East*, p. 173.

36. Dorman-Smith and other civilians at Simla frequently used this phrase, "respectable elements" to refer to prewar Burmese politicians loyal to the colonial regime. These "respectable elements" were distinguished from the "quislings" and "traitors" with whom SOE proposed to ally.

37. Mountbatten to British Chiefs of Staff, telegram, March 27, 1945, L/WS/1/993, IOR.

38. Ibid.

39. Supreme Allied Command, South East Asia, to AMSSO, telegram, March 31, 1945, L/WS/1/993, IOR.

40. Glass, by this time, had joined the staff of CAS(B) and was observing closely the activities of Force 136 in the campaign. "Old stager" refers to those working for CAS(B) who had served as civil servants or businessmen in Burma in the prewar era. He contrasted the "old

stagers" with the "young [Force 136] officers, full of rosy liberal, and some even of Communist, sentiments, and generous with 'simple' solutions to problems of which they little understood the complexity." *Changing of Kings*, p. 195.

41. Taylor, "Introduction: Marxism," p. 34. Taylor based this conclusion on his interview with (former) Maj. Tim Carew.

42. Mountbatten, *Report to the Combined Chiefs of Staff*, pp. 170, 173.

43. Ibid., pp. 200–1.

44. Hilsman, *American Guerrilla*, pp. 212–13. For a similar reaction reported among Karen levies, see Morrison, *Grandfather Longlegs*, pp. 157–59.

45. The writings of (former Brig.) U Maung Maung (*Burmese Nationalist Movements*, pp. 135–76) and Hugh Tinker ("Introduction" to *Burma: The Struggle*) deliver excellent analyses of these developments.

46. Robert Taylor, "The Burmese Communist Movement and Its Indian Connection: Formation and Factionalism," *Journal of Southeast Asian Studies* 14, no. 1 (1983): 95–108, 104.

47. သခင်သိန်းဖေမြင့်၊ စစ်အတွင်းခရီးသည် [Thakin Thein Pe, *Wartime Traveler*], p. 24.

48. Ibid., pp. 250–51.

49. Thein Pe Myint, "Toward Better Mutual Understanding and Greater Co-operation" (unpublished document), quoted in Robert H. Taylor, "Introduction: Marxism and Resistance in Wartime Burma," in *Marxism and Resistance in Wartime Burma, 1942–1945*, ed. Robert H. Taylor (Athens, Ohio: Ohio University Press, 1984), 1–94, 23.

50. Taylor, "Burmese Communist," p. 104.

51. သခင်တင်မြ၊ "ဘဲ့ဘဝမှာဖြင့်"၊ မြဝတီ ၁၈၊ ၂ (၁၉၆၉) [Thakin Tin Mya, "A Life of a Commune," *Myawaddy* 18, no. 2 (1969)].

52. U Maung Maung, *Burmese Nationalist Movements*, p. 143.

Chapter 4. Making Peace and Making Armies, 1945–48

1. Minutes of the War Cabinet, India Committee I (45), March 29, 1945, CAB 91/2, PRO. See also Chiefs of Staff to SAC, telegram, March 30, 1945, R/8/20, IOR, pp. 232–34, in which the chiefs of staff reiterated their concerns about the dangers of allying with the nationalists in central Burma.

2. The weapons estimate comes from B. R. Pearn, "Burma: Political Developments, 1945–1948," May 9, 1955, FO 371/117029, PRO, p. 72.

3. Htin Fatt, "The *Yebaw* Story," *The New Burma Weekly*, August 23, 1958.

4. Ibid.

5. Advanced Headquarters ALFSEA to SAC, South-East Asia, telegram, May 9, 1945, WO 203/59, PRO. From the available documentation, it appears that Pearce attempted to secure Aung San's arrest without Mountbatten's knowledge.

6. Hugh Tinker, ed., *Burma: The Struggle for Independence; Documents from Official and Private Sources*, vol. 2 (London, 1983–84), pp. 1059–62.

7. The White Paper's section on the frontier regions is explicit: "We consider that when self-government is established in Burma proper [i.e., central Burma], the administration of the Scheduled [i.e., frontier] Areas . . . should remain for the time being the responsibility of His Majesty's Government, until such time as their inhabitants signify their desire for some suitable form of amalgamation with Burma proper." From War Cabinet, "Policy in Burma," April 30, 1945, War Cabinet Paper WP (45)275, IOR M/3/1573.

8. As early as December 1944, the government-in-exile established the First Battalion Kachin Rifles, absorbing into it the Kachin levies that had been operating under British command. Three weeks later, the Second Battalion Burma Rifles came into being; it reunited a number of prewar members of the Burma Army in a mixed ethnicity battalion. In March 1945, the First Battalion Chin Rifles was organized, and a second battalion of Chins was established on April 1. Also on that date, the Second Battalion of Kachin Rifles was established. By June, two battalions of Karen Rifles were organized out of the Karen guerrillas who had been trained and armed by SOE/Force 136 agents. Additionally, more ex-soldiers from the prewar army

were recruited into the First Battalion Burma Rifles when it was authorized in June. Tinker, *Burma: The Struggle for Independence*, p. 1060.

9. Chiefs of Staff to SAC, South-East Asia, telegram, May 22, 1945, WO 203/4874, PRO.

10. "Blue Print for Burma," in *The Political Legacy of Aung San*, ed. Josef Silverstein, rev. ed. (Ithaca, 1993), p. 21.

11. Ibid., p. 24.

12. The "Programme of 'National Reconstruction through National Service' " called for an intensive propaganda campaign in which leaflets and posters would be distributed by AFO groups. Lectures, mass meetings, and dramatic performances would be held to disseminate appropriate teachings to the people. Copy in R/8/20, IOR, p. 117.

13. Minutes of the SAC's Meeting, Government House, Rangoon, July 15, 1945, R/8/30, IOR, p. 224. Note that British usage reverses the terms *Burmans* and *Burmese*; the latter is the ethnic group and the former is the broader (non-ethnic) category of those residing in Burma or claiming citizenship there.

14. Maj. Gen. Aung San, "Memorandum on the Proposed Reorganisation of Burma Patriotic Forces," appended to ibid., pp. 86–87.

15. Minutes of Conference to Discuss Certain Points Regarding the Enrollment of PBF into the Burma Army and the Handing in of Arms by Those Not Immediately Required for Operations, July 11, 1945, Rangoon, R/8/30, IOR, pp. 19–22.

16. Gen. Aung San to Lord Louis Mountbatten, August 21, 1945, copy to Governor Dorman-Smith, WO 203/2370, PRO.

17. "Resolution Passed at the Conference of Area Commanders of the Patriotic Burmese Forces Held at Rangoon on 12 August 1945," Annex D to Minutes of the SAC's Meeting, Kandy, Ceylon, September 6, 1945, R/8/20, IOR, p. 68. See also လူထုဦးလှ၊ သတင်းစာများပြောပြတဲ့စစ်တွင်းဗမာပြည်၊ တွဲ ၄ [Ludu U Hla, *Newspaper Accounts of Wartime Burma*, vol. 4] (Rangoon, 1968), pp. 226–59; and တက္ကသိုလ်စိန်တင်၊ ဖက်ဆစ်တော်လှန်ရေးသမိုင်း [Tekkatho Sein Tin, *History of the Fascist Revolution*] (Rangoon, 1969), pp. 573–76.

18. CAS(B) Intelligence, "Weekly Intelligence Summary," August 25, 1945, M/4/1239, IOR.

19. The following year, Prime Minister Jawaharlal Nehru wired Aung San directly to emphasize his government's desire to get Indian troops out of Burma. See reference in Lord Pethick-Lawrence to Sir Hubert Rance, telegram, October 10, 1946, reproduced in Tinker, *Burma: The Struggle*, vol. 2, document 59.

20. Minutes, September 6, 1945, pp. 53–54.

21. SAC HQ, "Agreed Conclusions Reached Between the Supreme Allied Commander, South East Asia and Major General Aung San at a Meeting Held at HQ SACSEA, Kandy, on Friday 7 September 1945," enclosed in letter from Adm. Lord Louis Mountbatten to Bogyoke Aung San, September 7, 1945, WO 203/5240, PRO. This list of conclusions became known as the "Kandy agreement."

22. Ibid.

23. This was Aung San's terminology in the conference meeting in which the Joint Board was discussed. From HQ, SAC, Minutes, September 6, 1945, p. 60.

24. SAC HQ, "Agreed Conclusions" (Kandy Agreement). Disagreements between board members over any of these decisions were to be referred to the SAC, Mountbatten, until military administration ended, and thereafter to the civilian governor of Burma.

25. Philip Ziegler, *Mountbatten: The Official Biography* (London, 1985), p. 317.

26. Mountbatten, quoted in John Terraine, *The Life and Times of Lord Mountbatten* (London, 1968), p. 121.

27. Ibid., p. 58.

28. SAC HQ, "Agreed Conclusions" (Kandy Agreement).

29. Maj. L. C. Thomas, Burma Command, "Commissioning of 200 P.B.F. Officers," May 8, 1946, enclosed in letter from Lt. Gen. H. R. Briggs, HQ Burma Command, to C. F. B. Pearce, Councilor to Governor Dorman-Smith, May 8, 1946, R/8/34, IOR, pp. 34–37.

30. Aung San to Lt. Gen. H. R. Briggs, January 19, 1946 (drafted December 29, 1945), R/8/34, IOR, pp. 49–53, 50. This letter was copied to Governor Dorman-Smith, SAC Admiral Mountbatten, and Maj. Gen. L. C. Thomas, Inspector General of the Burma Army.

31. Ibid.

32. See Secretary of State for Burma, London, to Burma Office, Rangoon, telegram, November 4, 1947, FO 643/106/GSO, PRO; this telegram offered six slots at Sandhurst for a course beginning in August 1948. Other telegrams in this PRO file (FO 643/106/GSO) include requests from Burma Army leaders for a number of vacancies at technical courses in Britain, which were all turned down.

33. Minutes of Meeting Between Inspector General, Burma Army, and Representatives, Patriotic Burmese Forces, Kandy, Ceylon, September 7, 1945, R/8/20, IOR, p. 33.

34. Aung San brought this issue to Slim's attention at the very first installment of negotiations on the future of the army on May 16, 1945; see Field Marshall William Slim, *Defeat into Victory* (New York, 1961), p. 519.

35. Minutes, September 6, 1945, p. 62, R/8/20, IOR. The Kandy agreement provided for a minimum of 5,200 slots for the 9,000 PBF soldiers and 200 slots for the 750 PBF officers. Aung San estimated that one-third of the soldiers would be uninterested in reenlistment or found ineligible, meaning that roughly 6,000 should be considered eligible. If his estimate was accurate, as many as 800 willing and able PBF soldiers could be turned away from the new army, and 550 officers would have to be demoted or discharged.

36. This was the phrase used by former Col. Saw Myint, a company commander in the Fifth Burifs, in an interview, April 27, 1992.

37. Ibid.

38. Maj. Gen. L. C. Thomas, Inspector General Burma Army, to Aung San, February 25, 1947, L/WS/1/699, IOR.

39. Capt. Maung Maung diary, April 14, 1947, CD 874, DSHRI. Maung Maung (May 10, 1947) notes that the British officer assigned to his Fourth Burma Rifles unit in 1947 had "undermined the discipline of the battalion" by "inciting the CO against Bo Ne Win."

40. Message from Bogyoke Aung San, Defence Councilor to Government of Burma, to All Units of the Burma Army, March 1, 1947; L/WS/1/669, IOR.

41. Interview, April 27, 1992.

42. Naw Angelene, "Aung San and the Struggle for the Independence of Burma" (Ph.D. diss., University of Hawaii, 1988), p. 220.

43. For the text of the agreement, see "Britain-Burma Defence Agreement," August 29, 1947, PREM 8/412, PRO.

44. Debt repayment and a release from financial liability for the defense of independent Burma were the main concerns of the British negotiators. Almost none of the discussion on the defence agreement engaged Burmese representatives' concerns about what form the future army would take in the postcolonial era.

45. T. L. Hughes, Governor's Representative to the Twelfth Army, to H. N. C. Stevenson, Governor's Secretary, August 15, 1945, M/3/1676, IOR.

46. The territory designated included Tenasserim (entire), a portion of the Pegu district, and territory in eastern Burma stretching into Siam.

47. Lt. Col. J. A. McKay, Command, Second Battalion, Burma Rifles, June 16, 1945, to H. N. C. Stevenson, Secretary to the Governor of Burma, Simla.

48. See "A Brief History of the Chin Hills Battalion, 1894–1949," n.d. [probably 1949], MSS Eur E 250, IOR, p. 360.

49. This figure includes Allied arms dropped to Karen levies operating secretly in the Irrawaddy Delta and in the eastern hills; arms supplied to Allied-sponsored hill levies; arms handed out to Arakanese resistance fighters in the early weeks of the Burma campaign in 1944; and arms dropped in to the BNA/AFO guerrillas in March and April 1944. Throughout Burma, villagers also collected thousands of weapons first in 1942 from the retreating British and Indian troops and later in 1945 from the retreating Japanese forces.

50. From the memoir of F. S. V. Donnision, MSS EUR E 362/4, IOR.

51. Pearn, "Burma: Political Developments," n.p.

52. Donnison, memoir, January 4, 1946.

53. Ibid.

54. General Officer Commanding, Burma Command, to WO, telegram, December 13, 1946, M/4/2621, IOR.

55. Sir Hubert Rance to the Earl of Listowel, telegram, August 19, 1947, M/4/2501 IOR.

56. Although English-language representations of the organization's objectives tended to stress the "welfare" aims of the PVO, it was from its inception much more than a veterans' welfare organization. For one thing, the name of the organization in Burmese was Pyithu Yebaw Tat, which literally translates to "People's Comrades' Tat." The term *tat* connotes an armed force, while the term *yebaw* ("comrade"), indicates the political and especially leftist orientation of the organization. The official English name of the group—the People's Volunteer Organisation—sounded far more innocuous.

57. ဗိုလ်သိန်းဆွေ၊ လွတ်လပ်ရေးတိုက်ပွဲ [Bo Thein Swe, *The Battle for Independence*] (Rangoon, 1967), pp. 195–203.

58. DIG of Police, Criminal Investigation Department, "History of the *Pyi-Thu-Yebaw Tat*," May 31, 1946, M/4/2619, IOR.

59. "Report of the Tantabin Incident Enquiry Committee," May 10, 1947, M/4/2619, IOR. See also ၁၈-၅-၄၆-ထန်းတပင်မြို့, လူထုအင်အားပြပွဲ၌ သေနတ်ပစ်ခတ်မှုကိစ္စနှင့် ပတ်သက်၍ - ဖဆပလ - ဦးစီးအဖွဲ့ချုပ်မှဆေလ္လွတ်လိုက်သော စုံစမ်းရေးအဖွဲ့၊ ၎င်း၏ ဒုတိယအစီရင်ခံစာ။ [Enquiry Committee, AFPFL Headquarters, Second Report on Shooting Incident at Public Assembly in Tantabin, May 18, 1946].

60. DIG of Police, "History of the Pyi-Thu-Yebaw Tat."

61. "Report of the Tantabin Incident."

62. See, e.g., E. C. V. Foucar, *I Lived in Burma* (London, 1956), p. 192.

63. Joel Migdal, *Strong Societies and Weak States: State-Society Relations and State Capabilities in the Third World* (Princeton, 1988), p. 31.

Chapter 5. Insurgency and State Disintegration, 1948–50

1. ဦးစံငြိမ်း နှင့် ဒေါက်တာမြင့်ကြည်၊ ၁၉၅၈-၁၉၆၂ မြန်မာနိုင်ငံရေး၊ ၁ တွဲ ၁ [U San Nyein and Dr. Myint Kyi, *Myanmar Politics from 1958 to 1962*, vol. 1] (Rangoon, 1991), p. 95.

2. The most reliable data on economic performance is found in the Central Statistical and Economic Department, Government of Burma, *Quarterly Bulletin of Statistics* (various issues). According to David Steinberg (*Burma: The State of Myanmar* [Washington, D.C., 2001], p. 21), it was not until 1976 that Burma rebuilt its economy to the standards of the immediate pre–World War II period.

3. From Balwant Singh, *Independence and Democracy in Burma, 1945–1952: The Turbulent Years* (Ann Arbor, 1993), p. 149.

4. A. P. Ruddy, High Speed Steel Alloys Mining Co. Ltd., Tavoy, to Consul-General, British Embassy Rangoon, September 6, 1950, FO 1041/5, PRO.

5. The number of armed groups generally—either insurgent, criminal, village protection, party-affiliated, or otherwise—is probably untraceable. Even the number of insurgents identified as "rebels" is difficult to calculate given the chaotic conditions prevailing, but probably totaled between thirty and sixty thousand. One set of government figures that appears in numerous publications is an estimate of rebels actively fighting against the government in 1949: twelve thousand KNDOs, ten thousand Communists, six thousand PVOs, and two thousand (combined) Taungthus, Mujahideen, and fighters from the Mon National Defence Organisation.

6. U Nu, *Saturday's Son: Memoirs of the Former Prime Minister of Burma* (New Haven, 1975), p. 163.

7. The head of the Burma Artillery was Maj. Aung Sein; the head of the Burma Army Training Depot was Lt. Col. Saw Leder; the head of the Burma Regimental Center was Lt. Col. Saw Calvin Ogh. All were Karens.

8. ၁၉၄၉-ခုနှစ်၊ ဇန်နဝါရီလ-၃၁ရက်နေ့ တပ်မှူးညီလာခံအစည်းအဝေးမှတ်တမ်း [*Minutes of the Commanding Officers' Conference*, January 31, 1949], DR 859, DSHRI.

9. Interview, September 8, 1994.

10. The list of twelve attendees to the first staff training course held in 1948 included only

four with PBF backgrounds. That four Karens were enrolled is significant given that Karens already had been overrepresented in the spaces allotted for overseas staff training during the 1945–48 period. Those officers most in need of staff training were the former PBF officers. Notably, by the publication of the "Burma Army List" (DR 1535, DSHRI) in May 1952, none of the four Karen trainees were on active duty. The list of staff course attendees is found in War Office Council Order, "Course Result: Burma Army Staff College No. 1 of 1948," no. 18/49, DR 1043, DSHRI.

11. Interview with U Maung Maung, May 9, 1992.

12. BSM to Burma, "British Services Mission Preliminary Report," February 9, 1948, FO 371/69481, PRO.

13. This contrast is pointed out in Martin Smith, *Burma: Insurgency and the Politics of Ethnicity* (London, 1991), p. 116. Furthermore, the PVO was not officially banned until July 19, 1951.

14. See Aung San's "Burma's Challenge, 1946," in *The Political Legacy of Aung San*, ed. Josef Silverstein, rev. ed. (Ithaca, 1993), pp. 74–161, 121.

15. For example, Bo Thein Swe's malaria kept him from reporting for re-enlistment into the postwar army. Once he had recovered from the illness, however, he reports that he was disgusted with the rightward drift of the army and instead opted for membership in the PVO. See ရိုလ်သိမ်းဆွေ၊ လွတ်လပ်ရေးတိုက်ပွဲ [Bo Thein Swe, *The Battle for Independence*] (Rangoon, 1967), p. 197.

16. Capt. Maung Maung diary, May 25, 1947, CD 875, DSHRI. Among those recorded as present at these meetings from March through September 1947 were Kyaw Win, Aung Gyi, Ba Swe, Ba Swe Lay, Ba Hla Zan, Bo Kyin, Tin Pe, and Bo Khin Maung Gale.

17. March 13, 1947, entry ibid.

18. August 24, 1947, entry ibid. A British Embassy secret dispatch in February 1948 confirms that the new UMP was intended to replace the PVO as the AFPFL's loyalist army; Amb. James Bowker, British Embassy, Rangoon, to Foreign Office, London, dispatch, February 26, 1948, FO 371/69481, PRO.

19. It is difficult to estimate the actual numbers of UMP recruits given the lack of paperwork generated by this organization. However, the first BSM report filed in 1948 suggested that the tatmadaw was "weaker in bayonets than the projected Union Military Police." In BSM to Burma, "Preliminary Report," FO 371/69481, PRO.

20. U Maung Maung interview with Kyaw Nyein, September 28, 1984; transcript on file at IOR.

21. Interview with former Col. Chit Myaing, September 8, 1994. Hugh Tinker also argues that former PBF officers were galled by the sight of Karen soldiers killing their former resistance-comrades-turned-communists; in his *Union of Burma: A Study of the First Years of Independence*, 4th ed. (London, 1967), p. 38; see also Smith, *Burma: Insurgency*, p. 115.

22. Smith, *Burma: Insurgency*, p. 109.

23. Interview with former Col. Chit Myaing, September 8, 1994.

24. For an extended analysis of existing primary and secondary accounts of these events, see Mary P. Callahan, "The Origins of Military Rule in Burma" (Ph.D. diss., Cornell University, 1996), pp. 344–47.

25. U Nu, *Saturday's Son*, pp. 156–57; interview, Chit Myaing, September 8, 1994; interview, U Maung Maung, May 12, 1992.

26. Interview with former Col. Chit Myaing, September 8, 1994.

27. Ibid.

28. Ibid. Others confirmed the terms of the agreement, including former Col. Sein Tun [interview, April 30, 1992] and Aung Gyi [interview, May 14, 1992].

29. Interview, September 8, 1994.

30. Ibid. The tatmadaw's official explanation of this mutiny was that Thein Pe Myint, a founding member of the Burma Communist Party, had duped the mutineers into rebellion, promising to join them only to stay safe, comfortable, and legal in Rangoon. See Directorate of Education and Psychological Warfare, "Newspapers [*sic*] Analysis," November 26, 1959, CD 358, DSHRI.

31. Aung Thinn was an Anglo-Burman who appeared to be pro-Karen, pro-British, and pro–Bo Let Ya.

32. Interview with former Col. Chit Myaing, September 8, 1994.

33. Accordingly, the first battalion of Union Auxiliary Forces was raised in Rangoon as of August 16, 1948, the same day Tin Tut left the Foreign Minister's job to become inspector general of the UAF. (DSHRI, "An Administrative History of the Armed Forces in Burma," vol. 2, unpublished manuscript for internal circulation [Rangoon, n.d.], p. 750.) U Tin Tut told reporters that afternoon that he intended to recruit men with previous military experience who could be deployed immediately to fight the insurrection. (*The Times*, August 16, 1948). He clearly had in mind recruits who had served with the British in the prewar or wartime eras.

34. U Tin Tut's press statement entitled, "Tribute to Army, Police and Village Levies," is carried in full in *The News Bulletin*, no. 25, July 31, 1948; copy on file in DR 698, DSHRI. Aung Gyi and Khin Nyo recalled that Tin Tut recruited only Anglo-Indians, Anglo-Burmans, and Gurkhas. Interview, May 14, 1992.

35. According to Aung Gyi, authority was transferred to the War Office because "as police, our supplies were limited; but more was available [when the Sitwundan were put under] the army." Interview, May 8, 1992.

36. Brig. Bo Let Ya, Special Commissioner, North Burma, "Weekly Report for Week Ending August 28, 1948," cited in British Embassy, Rangoon, to Foreign Office, telegram, September 5, 1948, FO 371/69485, PRO.

37. Ibid. The government authorized each battalion to be made up of two companies, each to consist of 105 men. WE no. 149/1/49; quoted in "Corps of Sitwundan: From Levies to Sitwundan," (n.d., probably 1958), DR 8117, DSHRI. See especially this report's appendix E: "Statement Showing Effective Strength of Arms (Artillery, Infantry and Engineers)."

38. "Corps of Sitwundan."

39. Ibid. In his 1975 memoir (*Saturday's Son*, p. 176), Nu reports ambivalence about the formation of the Sitwundan in hindsight. After the Karens had snubbed his efforts at conciliation, he must have been desperate for any kind of answer to the threats to the government. Aung Gyi and the Socialists' solution—the Sitwundan—no doubt appealed to him more than letting the communists back into the AFPFL and the government.

40. Smith Dun, *Memoirs of a Four-Foot Colonel* (Ithaca, 1980), p. 86.

41. Most rural militia were less pro-AFPFL than they were anti-communist and anti-rightist. Those local bosses who were running black market operations had much to fear from communists and rightists (both of whom wanted to either take over or put a stop to racketeering, smuggling, and other local operations). As a result, they probably threw in their lot with the less threatening AFPFL.

42. သမဂ္ဂသတင်းစာ [*The Tribune*] and ဦးဝေသသတင်းစာ [*Oway*] newspapers carried these kinds of inflammatory reports throughout 1947–49.

43. Ambassador John Bowker, British Embassy, Rangoon, to Foreign Office, London, telegram, September 7, 1948, FO 371/69485, PRO.

44. BSM to Burma, Rangoon, to Foreign Office, London, telegram, January 8, 1949, FO 371/75661, PRO.

45. The murder was investigated both by the police and an army court of inquiry. A young journalist at the time, Guardian Sein Win remembers that U Aung Chein, Rangoon police commissioner, told him that he was fired because he had discovered who the murderer was and that the culprit was from the Socialist Party. Interview with Guardian Sein Win, April 23, 1992.

46. BSM to Burma, Rangoon, to Foreign Office, London, telegram, January 8, 1949.

47. Bo Sein Hman, formerly a cabinet minister, led one of these massacres on a Karen village near Taikkyi in which more than 150 Karens were killed. *The Nation* (January 16, 1949) reported that Bo Sein Hman "commanded a punitive force of 200 men which converged upon the village from all sides and . . . opened fire on the houses and all moving objects."

48. Smith, *Burma: Insurgency*, p. 138.

49. For example, to fight the KNDOs, the army commandeered Sherman tanks sold as scrap by the Allies to a Burmese merchant; army mechanics got them running again. *The Nation*, October 26, 1949.

50. Special War Office Council Order, "Appointments—Officers," March 17, 1949, no. 11/S/49, DR 1043, DSHRI, and Special War Office Council Order, "Appointments—Officers," February 19, 1949, no. 6/S/49, DR 1042, DSHRI.

51. DSHRI, "Administrative History," vol. 1, p. 821.

52. Interview with Aung Gyi, May 8, 1992.

53. Special War Office Council Order, "Release/Discharge of All Ranks from Regular/Emergency Engagement," February 8, 1949, no. 4/S/49, DR 1042, DSHRI.

54. War Office Council Order, "Submission of Quarterly Historical Reports," April 4, 1950, no. 33/50, DR 1030, DSHRI. Lt. Gen. Ne Win, Chief of General Staff, signed the order.

55. U Kyaw Nyein reported that Ne Win addressed a meeting of Socialist Party politicians just before their resignations and told them that he would no longer "be your house guard dog." After the defection of the Karen army personnel, the First and Third Burifs, half the PVO, and the communists, Ne Win "was unwilling to fight" on behalf of the Socialists, whom he said were blocking progress toward peace. He pressed them to resign and offered to form a government with the CPB. Kyaw Nyein also reports that Nu told him in 1949 that Ne Win had met with Nu to ask him to appoint Thakin Than Tun and some of his Communist Party colleagues to the cabinet. U Maung Maung interview with Kyaw Nyein, September 26, 1984; transcript on file at IOR.

56. Since the beginning of the anti-British underground, there were armed and unarmed units all over Burma calling themselves "ပြောက်ကျား" (guerrillas). From 1945–48, the British had authorized the Karens to organize village defense units, many of which called themselves, "Peace Guerrillas." Later, other guerrilla, village defense, and dacoit leaders called their armed followers "Peace Guerrillas" or "People's Peace Guerrillas" to add a note of legitimacy to their undertakings. In general, when not referring to Karen groups, the term peace guerrillas referred to armed units that had a connection to the Socialist Party, either through a local Socialist politician or through the local peasant union representative.

57. A more detailed analysis of development of the Socialists' irregular forces is found in Mary P. Callahan, "The Sinking Schooner: Murder and the State in 'Democratic' Burma," in *Gangsters, Democracy, and the State in Southeast Asia*, ed. Carl Trocki (Ithaca, 1998).

58. Aung Gyi, who was inspector general of the Sitwundan, confirmed the mediocrity of levy leadership, some of whom had failed to pass the army entrance exam on several occasions. Interview, May 8, 1992.

59. Col. Khun Nawng, for example, pleaded for supplies from the War office. See his letter to Lt. Col. Ba Han, War Office, August 9, 1949, DR 8101, DSHRI. See also Nu, *Saturday's Son*, pp. 185–87.

Former PBF officers in the postcolonial military considered the biggest obstacle to weapons procurement and distribution to be the British Embassy and the BSM. The Let Ya–Freeman Defence Agreement made Britain the main supplier for the tatmadaw and the BSM the arbiter of all arms purchase requests made by the Burmese military.

60. Interview with former field commander, February 1993.

61. Interviews with Thakin Kyi Shein, February 10, 1993; Widura Thakin Chit Maung, February 23, 1993; and former field commander, February 1993.

62. The Pyidawtha ("Happy Land") program was an all-encompassing scheme of economic and social welfare policies first introduced in 1952. Local Pyidawtha committees distributed subsidies and loans to indigenous business owners and cultivators. Party hacks usually controlled the committees.

63. John S. Furnivall to C. W. Dunn, July 4, 1948, box 1: vol. 1, Furnivall Correspondence, School of Oriental and African Studies Library, London.

64. Edward W. Martin, Charge d'Affaires, U.S. Embassy, Rangoon, to Secretary of State, February 20, 1950, 790B.00/2–2050, Record Group 59, U.S. National Archives.

65. Interview, Guardian Sein Win, April 23, 1992.

66. Singh, *Independence and Democracy in Burma*, p. 158.

67. BSM to Burma, "Fourth Quarterly Report, 1950," December 31, 1950, FO 371/92170, PRO.

68. See the final article in ပြည်ထောင်စု ဆိုရှယ်လစ်ပါတီဌာနချုပ်၊ ပါတီတွင်းပြန်တမ်း၊ [Union Socialist Party Headquarters, Party Gazette] (Rangoon, 1949?).

69. For examples of robberies and other crimes reportedly committed by the PPG and other levies after they were supposedly disbanded, see the လူထု [*The People* newspaper], May 7, 1953; *The Nation*, May 15, 1954 and May 16, 1955.

70. See the rather quiet way in which the legislation to extend the Sitwundan for another six months was pushed through the Parliament in ဟံသာဝတီ [*Hanthawaddy* newspaper], September 25, 1954. For the list of War Office orders relating to the Sitwundan, see DSHRI, "Administrative History," pp. 763–64.

Chapter 6. Warfare and Army Building, 1950–53

1. Ruth McVey, "The Post Revolutionary Transformation of the Indonesian Armed Forces," parts 1 and 2, *Indonesia* 11 (1971) and *Indonesia* 12 (1972).

2. BSM to Burma, "Second Quarterly Report, 1948," June 30, 1948, FO 371/69483, PRO.

3. BSM to Burma, "Second Quarterly Report, 1950," June 30, 1950, FO 371/83176, PRO.

4. A 1951 Army Recruiting Office report calls for reforms to require local units to forward enrollment forms to the Records Office, Burma Army, "so we can have accurate data." See "Recruiting Report for the Period May 5, 1949, to March 31, 1951," April 12, 1951, DR 399, DSHRI.

5. BSM, "Second Quarterly Report, 1950."

6. Maj. Ba Thike, "The Importance of Discipline," (n.d., probably 1956–58), DR 8117, DSHRI.

7. Special War Office Council Order, "Discipline," July 18, 1950, no. 19/S/50, DR 1030, DSHRI.

8. Maj. Ba Thike, "The Importance of Discipline."

9. Lt. Col. R. G. A. Campagnac, "Brief Review of the Characteristics, Religion, History and Fighting Spirit of the Burma Gorkhas [*sic*]" (n.d., probably early 1950s), DR 411, DSHRI.

10. Amb. Richard Speaight, British Embassy, Rangoon, to Foreign Office, London, despatch, November 15, 1950, FO 371/83108, PRO.

11. Elections were held in three phases (June, August, and October 1951) to allow the government to relocate forces from one region to the next to protect polling places.

12. Amb. Richard Speaight, British Embassy, Rangoon, to R. H. Scott, South-East Asia Department, Foreign Office, London, despatch, September 13, 1952, FO 371/101003, PRO.

13. BSM to Burma, "Fourth Quarterly Report, 1951," December 31, 1951, FO 371/101024, PRO. See also ၁၉၅၁-ခု မတ်လ ၂၈-၂၉-၃၀ ရက်နေ့, စစ်ရုံးမှာကျင်းပသောတပ်မှူးညီလာခံ အစည်းအဝေးမှတ်တမ်း [Minutes of the COs' Conference, War Office, Rangoon, March 28–30, 1951], CD 349, DSHRI.

14. *The Nation*, September 2, 1950.

15. ၁၉၅၀-ခု ဇန်နဝါရီလ ၂၀-ရက်နေ့,စစ်ရုံး၌ ကျင်းပသော တပ်မှူးညီလာခံ အစည်းအဝေးမှတ်တမ်း [Minutes of the COs' Conference, January 20, 1950], CD 350, DSHRI.

16. Interviews with former Brig. Maung Maung, April 11, 1992; and former Brig. Aung Gyi and former Col. Khin Nyo, May 4, 1992.

17. "Burma Army List," May 1952, DR 1535, DSHRI.

18. Interview with former Col. Khin Nyo, May 4, 1992.

19. Interview, former Brig. Maung Maung, April 11, 1992. What is significant here is that the former PBF officers were angry about Nu's interference and stayed angry for years; whether Maung Maung's interpretation of the pointlessness of the promotion is accurate is open to debate.

20. ၁၉၅၀ တပ်မှူးညီလာခံမှတ်တမ်း [Minutes, COs' Conference, 1950].

21. For example, former Col. Chit Myaing reported:

I had decided not to rejoin the army in the postwar period. I was going back to college. Bohmu Aung told me, "Aung San wants you to join the army." But I had given away my uniform. Then Bo Sein Hman gave me a khaki shirt. . . . I went to see Aung San the next day. He said, "I need you." I told him okay, I would join the army and fight for independence. Then we didn't think we would get independence from the British. But I didn't want to join the army under them [the British]. I am not a mercenary.

Two days later, when he was called before the officers' Selection Board, he met many of his reluctant colleagues from the PBF in the waiting room. Interview, September 8, 1994.

22. Quoted in ၁၉၅၀ တပ်မှူးညီလာခံမှတ်တမ်း [Minutes, COs' Conference, 1950].

23. Ibid.

24. ၁၉၅၁ တပ်မှူးညီလာခံမှတ်တမ်း [Minutes, COs' Conference, 1951], CD 349, DSHRI.

25. ၁၉၅၂-ခု ဇူလိုင်လ-၁၂ရက်နေ့.မှာ ကျင်းပသောတပ်မှူးညီလာခံအစည်းအဝေး မှတ်တမ် [Minutes of the COs' Conference, July 12, 1952], CD 351, DSHRI.

26. In February 1949, the Parliament passed a bill that provided for popular election of local government councils, which were given administrative and judicial authority. The Democratisation of Local Administration program was piloted in a few districts but never really got off the ground.

27. Interview, May 14, 1992.

28. See Ne Win's denial of these rumors in *The Nation*, July 27, 1952.

29. BSM to Burma, "Third Quarterly Report, 1950," September 30, 1950, FO 371/83176, PRO.

30. Amb. Richard Speaight, British Embassy, Rangoon, to Foreign Office, London, despatch, FO 373/83108, PRO.

31. Speaight's evaluation of this strategy: "A forlorn hope indeed!" Amb. Richard Speaight, British Embassy, Rangoon, to Foreign Office, London, despatch, September 21, 1951, FO 371/92137, PRO. Socialist Party leader, U Ba Swe, replaced U Win as Defence Minister. Notably less energetic and less contentious than U Win, Ba Swe gave army leaders a great deal of autonomy over internal army affairs. However, this did not eliminate civil-military tensions, which by this point had penetrated throughout the ranks of both the AFPFL and the army.

32. During his captivity, a Catholic priest visited Maung Maung frequently and brought him religious books to read. When he was rescued in Operation Linyaung (led by Col. Saw Myint, Fifth Burifs), he converted from Buddhism to Catholicism and intended to study to be a priest. Church officials advised him to take the conversion slowly and soon his former student-union and resistance colleagues convinced him to reenter the army.

33. Interviews, Maung Maung, May 9, 1992, and February 18, 1993. According to Maung Maung, Hla Aung (also known as Henry Smythe) "was PBF, but was not recruited until 1943," and before the war he was Superintendent of Land Records for the British in Burma. Maung Maung implies that his loyalty was dubious.

34. On CIA involvement, see Robert H. Taylor, *Foreign and Domestic Consequences of the KMT Involvement in Burma* (Ithaca, 1973); Charles D. Ameringer, *U.S. Foreign Intelligence: The Secret Side of American History* (Lexington, Mass., 1990), chap. 19; Fred Branfman, "The Secret Wars of the CIA," in *Uncloaking the CIA*, ed. Howard Frazier (New York, 1978), pp. 90–100; Bertil Lintner, *Burma in Revolt* (Boulder, Colo., 1994), chap. 4; Alfred W. McCoy, *The Politics of Heroin: CIA Complicity in the Global Drug Trade* (New York, 1991); Ralph W. McGehee, *Deadly Deceits: My 25 Years in the CIA* (New York, 1983); Christopher Robbins, *Air America* (New York, 1979); Andrew Tully, *CIA: The Inside Story* (New York, 1962), chap. 14; David Wise and Thomas B. Ross, *The Invisible Government* (New York, 1964), chap. 7.

35. U.S. advisors openly trained and lived among the KMT in the Shan states. Moreover, the bodies of three white men fighting alongside KMT troops against the Burma Army were discovered in 1953; diaries and notebooks listing their addresses in the United States were found on these bodies. The U.S. embassy claimed that they were Germans, but there was little evidence to support this. See Lintner, *Burma in Revolt*, p. 113.

36. Taylor, *Foreign and Domestic Consequences*, pp. 15–16.

37. The objective of these operations was to clear a transit route from the Shan states all the way to Moulmein, so that supplies and heavy weapons could be brought in by sea. See Martin Smith, *Burma: Insurgency and the Politics of Ethnicity*, 2d ed. (London, 1999), p. 153.

38. Taylor, *Foreign and Domestic Consequences*, p. 39. Based on interviews with KNDO members of that era, Lintner disputes Taylor's claim. *Burma in Revolt*, p. 109.

39. Ibid., p. 98.

40. Josef Silverstein, "Politics in the Shan State: The Question of Secession from the Union," *Journal of Asian Studies* 18, no. 1 (1958): 49.

41. K. R. Oakeshott, British Embassy, Rangoon, to R. W. Selby, South-East Asia Department, Foreign Office, London, despatch, June 17, 1953, with attached report of British Consul from Maymo on his conversation with the Special Commissioner of the Shan State, the Sawbwa of Hsenwi, FO 371/106682, PRO.

42. Silverstein, "Politics in the Shan State," p. 54.

43. Interview with former field commander, February 1993; (later Dr.) Maung Maung, *Grim War against the KMT*, pp. 60–61.

44. Inge Sargent, *Twilight over Burma: My Life as a Shan Princess* (Honolulu, 1994), p. 143. See also Shan criticisms of army conduct in the "Statement Issued by the Revolutionary Council, Shan State Independence Army" (n.d.), CR 107, DSHRI.

45. Lintner, *Burma in Revolt*, pp. 95–100 and chap. 4.

46. In fact, most of the former army, navy, and air force officers interviewed for this book referred to the operation by a nickname that became popular after its failure, "Naga-shoun" (Loser-Naga).

47. Interview, former Col. Tin Maung Aye, April 2, 1992.

48. Memorandum by General Staff Department, War Office, Government of the Union of Burma, "Formation of a Military Planning Staff at the War Office," August 28, 1951, DR 4768, DSHRI.

49. Ibid. This paper trail on the formation of MPS is probably misleading in that it assigns Ne Win with more of a role in its formation than he actually had. For months, Ne Win had been distracted by romantic scandals and their fallout. In fact, he was officially on leave when this order was signed. Maung Maung and Aung Gyi, the principals involved in starting the MPS, provide different stories as to who was behind its formation. Maung Maung suggests that it was the Socialist "inner circle," which was worried that Ne Win was allowing "the British element" in the War Office to control too much of army affairs (interview, April 11, 1992). Aung Gyi claims that U Win created MPS as part of his campaign to develop institutional niches from which he could chip away at Ne Win's and the army's power (interview, Aung Gyi, May 8, 1992).

50. These analyses are attached as appendices to Memorandum by General Staff Department, War Office, Government of the Union of Burma, "Organization of the War Office and Formation of an Army Council," September 23, 1951, DR 4768, DSHRI.

51. Ibid.

52. The formulation of doctrine is difficult to trace because there is almost no documentation of the process. Given that Maung Maung was not known for his patience or lack of confidence, it seems likely that he returned to the War Office to find staff officers there trying to pull together the reorganization plans. Drawing on his staff training in England, he probably chastised them for trying to reorganize without any formulation of doctrine and subsequently proposed his rather simple doctrine. Given the force of his personality, it seems unlikely that he faced opposition from colleagues, who were indifferent or reluctant to stand up to him.

53. Interview, Maung Maung, April 11, 1992. Of course, MPS had only been in existence a few days when Maung Maung took it over.

54. Interview, Aung Gyi, May 8, 1992.

55. Interview, Maung Maung, April 11, 1992.

56. Ibid.

57. Ibid.

58. DSHRI, "An Administrative History of the Armed Forces in Burma," vol. 2, unpublished manuscript for internal circulation (Rangoon, n.d.), p. 431.

59. Ibid.

60. Interviews with former field commander, February 1993, and with former Brig. Maung Maung, May 12, 1992.

61. Memorandum by DSC, Government of the Union of Burma, "Reorganisation of the War Office into a Ministry of Defence," September 19, 1952, copy reproduced in DSHRI, "Administrative History," pp. 641–58.

62. For example, the War Office was not officially reorganized into a Ministry of Defence until January 1, 1956 (WE no. BA100/2/56); copy reproduced in DSHRI, "Administrative History," pp. 722–23.

63. Ibid., pp. 614 and 661.

64. "Reorganisation of the War Office," September 19, 1952.

65. Former PBF officers in the postcolonial tatmadaw identified Hla Aung as an U Win *ta-byay* (follower). Interestingly, the British ambassador described him as an "anti-British Anglo-Burman." Amb. Richard Speaight, British Embassy, Rangoon, to Foreign Office, London, despatch, December 17, 1952, FO 371/101025, PRO.

66. Interviews with former Brig. Maung Maung, April 11, 1992 and May 12, 1992. "The Burma Army List," May 1952, confirms these shuffles.

67. Interview, former Brig. Tin Pe, May 16, 1992.

68. All of these remarks are recorded in Minutes of the Meeting of the Defence Services Council, May 13–14, 1952, copy reproduced in DSHRI, "Administrative History," pp. 616–38.

69. *Ratings* are the naval equivalent of "other ranks" in the army and "airmen" in the air force.

70. The strength of the navy in 1951 was 135 officers and 1,599 ratings. From "The Navy," (n.d., probably 1956–58), DR 8117, DSHRI.

71. Lt. Comdr. J. G. Brookes, Head of Naval Element, BSM to Burma, to Secretary of Admiralty, London, despatch, March 24, 1950, FO 371/83179, PRO.

72. Khin Pe Kyi had also served as an aide-de-camp to Smith Dun, which no doubt further increased suspicions of his unreliability.

73. Brookes to Secretary of Admiralty, March 24, 1950.

74. From *The Nation*, September 27, 1952.

75. During the war, the Japanese recruited ten graduates of the Mingaladon OTS to attend air force training in Japan. They arrived in Japan in April 1944 and enrolled as cadets in the Army Air Force Academy. They completed their training there in October and joined a fighter training school at Argayno, which was completed on May 21, 1945. They were repatriated to Burma in August 1945. Of the ten cadets, there were still six in the air force in the mid-1950s. From "Short History of the Japanese-Trained (10) Air Force Officers," (n.d., probably 1955), DR 5855, DSHRI.

76. According to Col. (retired) Tin Maung Aye, formerly of the Burma Air Force, Shi Sho subsequently was reinstated in the mid-1950s and sent to Australia as military attaché. He later returned to Burma and became a staff officer in operations and research; from this position he retired (interview, April 2, 1992).

77. According to the obituary in *The Nation* (June 16, 1950), Khin had logged several hundred flying hours over Germany on secondment to the Royal Air Force during World War II. He was the first Burmese pilot to bring down a Messerschmidt over the English Channel.

78. "War Office Training Directive No. 1," February 28, 1952, DR 4771, DSHRI.

79. This committee was comprised of Col. Maung Maung (as chair), Lt. Col. Thaung Kyi (then GSO[1]-Operations and Training; a former PBF officer out of the Third Burifs), and Lt. Col. Kyaw Soe (Commandant, Burma Army OTS; former PBF officer out of the Fourth Burifs). From "Training of the Burma Army: The Past and the Future" (n.d., probably 1956–1958), DR 8117, DSHRI.

80. "War Office Training Directive No. 1."

81. Ibid.

82. Ibid.

83. This figure comes from the syllabi ("Burma Army Officers Training School, Maymyo: Organization of Instruction and Syllabus") of the training courses held from 1950 to 1953. In DR 3027, DSHRI.

84. The army War Office requested slots for thirteen infantry commanders' training in 1951 and thirty-four in 1952. Statistics come from BSM, "Details of Training Courses Provided by the Army, 1951, 1952 and 1953" (n.d., probably 1954), FO 371/106711, PRO.

85. The number of slots requested from the War Office did not change much from 1951 through 1953 (138 in 1951; 131 in 1952; and 149 in 1953) but the number of slot requests that were refused doubled over the period from sixteen in 1951 to thirty-two in 1953. The areas of deficiency changed from year to year. For example, the infantry requests were considerably underallotted in 1952 (as noted above); in 1953, the major shortfall came in military intelligence and methods of instruction courses. From "War Office Training Directive No. 1."

86. From BSM, "Periodic Report, 1st August–31st November 1953," FO 106719, PRO. That year, the United States offered only one slot, although it was a prestigious one at Fort Leavenworth U.S. Army Command and General Staff College. See ၃-စိလ်မှူးကြီးသောင်းထိုက်၊ ဖိုလ်လီဗင်ဝပ်သ် အမေရိကန်စစ်ဦးစီးစီးတက္ကသိုလ် [Lt. Col. Thaung Htike, *The American Staff College at Fort Leavenworth*] (Rangoon, 1987).

87. As mandated in the Let Ya–Freeman Defense Agreement.

88. Interview, former Brig. Maung Maung, April 11, 1992.

89. Ibid. At the time, Kyaw Nyein's and Ba Swe's control over the Socialist Party in Rangoon and upcountry was crucial to the AFPFL's control of the government. If Maung Maung's account is accurate, this might explain their willingness to make this decision in Nu's absence and also Nu's choice to both walk out of the meeting and not challenge the decision.

90. Navy, Army, and Air Force Institutes (NAAFI) were the British military organizations responsible for providing food service and inexpensive consumer items to military members and families.

91. From Maj. Kyaw Soe (last name in unreadable type), "The Defence Services Institute" (n.d., probably 1956–58), DR 8117, DSHRI.

92. Memorandum by Quartermaster General's Department, September 11, 1950, no. 6-Q2B(CS) 43, quoted in ibid.

93. Ibid.; Interview, U Aung Gyi, May 4, 1992.

94. Maj. Kyaw Soe, "The Defence Services Institute."

Chapter 7. Warriors as State Builders, 1953–62

1. From ကာကွယ်ရေးဦးစီးချုပ်ရုံး(ကြည်း) အစီရင်ခံစာ၊ ကာကွယ်ရေးဝန်ကြီးဌာန။ ၁၉၆၂-ခုနှစ် တပ်မတော်ညီလာခံ [Chief of Staff (Army), Report to Defence Ministry, Tatmadaw Conference, 1962], CD 341, DSHRI. This number includes officers, other ranks, and Union Constabulary forces (which were being absorbed into new army units).

2. *The Union of Burma: A Study in the First Years of Independence*, 4th ed. (London, 1959), p. 331.

3. DSHRI, "An Administrative History of the Armed Forces in Burma," vol. 2 (Rangoon, n.d.), unpublished manuscript for internal circulation.

4. On the civil defense plan and the women's auxiliary forces, see H. B. Martin, wing commander and air attaché, British Embassy, Tel Aviv, to War Office, London, "Visit of Burmese Mission to Israel," despatch, July 19, 1954, copy in FO 371/112005, PRO. On the necessity for a museum and historical office, see Commodore Than Pe, Col. Tin Pe, and Col. Maung Maung, "Report by the Burmese Armed Forces Mission to Yugoslavia and Visit to France, West Germany and Israel, 23 April to 16 August 1955," CD 26, DSHRI. The DSA charter's assessment of why Burma needed such an institution was simple: "Every nation has one." From "The General Charter of the Defence Services Academy" (n.d., probably 1952). See also "စစ်တက္ကသိုလ်သမိုင်း ၁၉၄၇ခုနှစ်မှ ၁၉၉၀ပြည့်နှစ်ထိ" ["History of the Defence Services Academy, 1947–90," Maymyo, 1990].

5. See, e.g., "General Report of the Burma Army Military Mission on the Military Establishments of India and Pakistan, 19 June to 14 September 1952," CD 1486, DSHRI.

6. Commodore Than Pe et al., "Report by the Burmese Armed Forces Mission to Yugoslavia and Visit to France, West Germany and Israel." At that time, the population of Burma was around eighteen million as well.

7. Ibid. There can be little doubt that Tito's generosity toward the Burma army—which ranged from putting up officers at his home during their visits to Yugoslavia's to donating the equipment for a brigade of mountain artillery—also reinforced this identification.

8. "General Report of the Burma Army Military Mission on the Military Establishments of India and Pakistan."

9. Robert H. Jackson and Carl G. Rosberg, "Why Africa's Weak States Persist: The Empirical and Juridical in Statehood," *World Politics* 35 (1982): 1–24.

10. Theda Skocpol, introduction to *Bringing the State Back In*, ed. Peter Evans, Dietrich Rueschemeyer, and Theda Skocpol (Cambridge, 1985), p. 8.

11. An illustration of this point can be found in the varying treatment of Burmese army and political leaders by the United States in the 1950s. Prime Minister U Nu tried desperately to obtain an invitation to visit Washington, D.C., in the mid-1950s, even writing a personal request to President Eisenhower in 1954. Nu never received a response. In contrast, Gen. Ne Win, just back from a mission to Peking, was invited in 1956 to the United States, given a tour of military and industrial installations nationwide, and greeted at the Pentagon's front doors by a camera crew and Gen. Maxwell Taylor where Taylor awarded the Legion of Merit to the embarrassed Supreme Commander. *The Nation*, June 3, 1956.

12. "တပ်မတော် ညီလာခံ၊ ၁၉၅၄-ခုနှစ်" [Tatmadaw Conference, 1954], CD 99, DSHRI, and "တပ်မတော် ညီလာခံ၊ ၁၉၅၇-ခုနှစ်" [Tatmadaw Conference, 1957], CD 13, DSHRI.

13. Nu's speech is translated and reprinted in *Burma Weekly Bulletin*, September 22, 1955. On the Pyidawtha plan, see chap. 5, n. 62.

14. ၁၉၅၄ခုနှစ်၊ စက်တင်ဘာလ (၁၃)ရက်နေ့၊တွင်၊ မေမြို့မှာ ကျင်းပသော ဗမာ့တပ်မတော် တပ်ရင်းမှူးကြီးများ အစည်းအဝေးတွင် နိုင်ငံတော်ဝန်ကြီးချုပ်၏ ပြောကြားသော မိန့်ခွန်း [Prime Minister's Speech, Delivered to the Meeting of Commanding Officers, Maymyo, September 13, 1954], DR 4755, DSHRI.

15. K. R. Oakeshott, British Embassy, Rangoon, to Rt. Hon. Harold MacMillan, despatch, October 21, 1955, FO 371/117082, PRO. Oakeshott quotes from a report filed by Col. Berger, military attaché at the British embassy, regarding his conversations with Col. Aung Gyi and U Thi Han, director of Procurement at the War Office.

16. ၁၉၅၅-ခုနှစ် ဆဋ္ဌမအကြိမ်မြောက်-တပ်မတော်ညီလာခံ၊ စစ်သေနာပတိချုပ် မဟာသီရိသုဓမ္မ ဗိုလ်ချုပ်ကြီးနေဝင်း၏မိန့်ခွန်း [Speech by Commander in Chief Gen. Ne Win to the Sixth Annual Tatmadaw Conference, 1955], DR 1134, DSHRI.

17. From "၁၉၅၅-ခုနှစ် စက်တင်ဘာလ ၁၆ ရက်နေ့တွင်၊ ဗမာ့တပ်မတော် တပ်ရင်းမှူးကြီးများ၏ညီလာခံတွင် နိုင်ငံတော်ဝန်ကြီးချုပ်၏ပြောကြားသောမိန့်ခွန်း" [The Prime Minister's Speech Delivered to the Burma Tatmadaw COs' Conference, September 16, 1955], DR 4765, DSHRI.

18. "ဗမာ့တပ်မတော် တပ်ရင်းမှူးကြီးများ၏ညီလာခံတွင် နိုင်ငံတော်ဝန်ကြီးဦးနု၏ ဩဝါဒမိန့်ခွန်း" ၉-၉-၅၇ [Prime Minister U Nu's Advisory Speech to the Burma Tatmadaw COs' Conference, September 9, 1957], DR 1389, DSHRI.

19. See John F. Cady, *A History of Modern Burma*, rev. ed. (Ithaca, 1969), supp.; Guardian Sein Win, *The Split Story* (Rangoon, 1959); Maung Maung, "Burma at the Crossroads," *Indian Quarterly* 14, no. 4 (1958): 380–88; Josef Silverstein, *Burma: Military Rule and the Politics of Stagnation* (Ithaca, 1977), chap. 7; and Frank N. Trager, "Political Divorce in Burma," *Foreign Affairs* 37 (1959): 317–27.

20. I am not arguing that either contingent had rightful claim on the "purity" of their revolutionary roots, but rather that tensions between civilian politicians and army leaders were framed along these lines.

21. Oakeshott to McMillan, despatch, October 21, 1955, FO 371/117082, PRO; and British Embassy, Rangoon, to Hon. Harold MacMillan, London, despatch, October 12, 1955, FO 371/127030.

22. It is difficult to find reliable sources on any local militia, even the highly publicized Pyusawhtis. The best sources on the Pyusawhtis are: DSHRI, "An Administrative History," vol. 2, pp. 135–45; War Office, Government of the Union of Burma, memorandum, "Pyusawhti Planning," October 1955–June 1956, DR 8517, DSHRI; and ဗဟိုကော်မတီ၊ ဗမာပြည် ကွန်မြူနစ်ပါတီ "ပြူစောထီး စီမံကိန်း"၊ ၁၉၅၅ခုနှစ်-ဒီဇင်ဘာလ(၂၀) ရက်နေ့။ [Central Committee, Burma Communist Party, "Pyusawhti Planning," December 20, 1955], DR 5423, DSHRI.

23. Interview, former Brig. Maung Maung, February 18, 1993.

24. War office, Government of the Union of Burma Government, "Pyusawhti Planning."

25. See the AFPFL's memorandum by Thakin Tha Khin issued two weeks after the army authorized the formation of the Pyusawhtis; it charges local party leaders with the responsibilities of organizing and arming the Pyusawhtis. သခင်သာခင်၊ ဖဆပလ အဖွဲ့ချုပ်၊ "ပြူစောထီးနှင့် ပတ်သက်သော ညွှန်ကြားရေးလွှာအမှတ်-၁၅"၊ ၁၃၊ ၁၀၊ ၅၅ [Thakin Tha Khin, "Directive on Issues Related to Pyusawhti Planning," October 13, 1955, AFPFL Executive Committee], CII(c), microfilm, Historical Research Department, University of Yangon.

26. This is not to suggest that the draft writers were plotting the ultimate takeover of the government six years later. In fact, Aung Gyi's famous 1988 letter suggests that once this ideology

had gone through several drafts and was published as "The National Ideology of the Defence Services" for the 1958 COs' conference, it took on a life of its own. After Ne Win took over in 1962, his ideas about the kind of socialism he wanted to pursue in Burma were rather ill-formed, and he fell back on this document as the basis for much of what came later to be associated with the "Burmese Way to Socialism." See Aung Gyi's widely circulated Letter to Bo San Yu, Bo Aye Ko, Bo Sein Lwin, Bo Maung Maung Kha, Bo Hla Han, Bo Kyaw Htin, Bo Tun Tin, and former members of the Revolutionary Council, May 9, 1988.

27. Interview, former Brig. Maung Maung, May 9, 1992. Nu had a long-running fascination with pop psychology and even translated Dale Carnegie's *How to Win Friends and Influence People* into Burmese.

28. According to a report on psywar activities submitted to the 1958 COs' conference, in that year alone the directorate had published 145 posters, sponsored seven different radio shows 81 times, and sponsored 26 "returning to the light" (i.e., surrender or amnesty) ceremonies. From စစ်ဦးစီးချုပ်ဌာန၊ "၁၉၅၈–ခုနှစ် တပ်မတော်ညီလာခံ၊ စစ်ဦးစီးချုပ်ဌာန အစီရင်ခံစာ" [General Staff Department, "Report of the General Staff Department to the Tatmadaw Conference," 1958], CD 1, DSHRI.

29. Interview, Aung Gyi, May 8, 1992. In 1958, the Psywar Directorate started publishing ခေတ်ရေး (*Khit-yeh*), a magazine geared toward rural readers. Its stories read far more like propaganda than the *Myawaddy* magazine, and even though it was free it was notably less popular.

30. Toward that end, Ba Than launched two magazines, published by the Psywar Directorate, for army personnel in the 1950s: စစ်နှလုံးတပ်မတော် ဂျာနယ် (*Sit-hna-loun Tatmadaw Journal*) was first published in July 1953, distributed to all units, and aimed at junior officers and NCOs; the second, စစ်ပညာဂျာနယ် (*The Military Science Journal*) was published four times a year beginning in 1956. The latter's objectives were laid out in its introductory issue: "Throughout history, military science has progressed and changed on a day-by-day basis. As we in Burma have sometimes ignored these changes and not improved our military science, we have been in danger of becoming another's slave. Therefore it is not only every soldier's responsibility to keep on top of developments but also every citizen's responsibility." From "စစ်ပညာဂျာနယ်၏ ပေါ်လစီနှင့် ရည်ရွယ်ချက်များ"၊ စစ်ပညာဂျာနယ် ၁၊ ၁ (ဇွန်လ ၁၉၅၆–ခုနှစ်) ["The Objectives and Policies of the Military Science Journal," *Military Science Journal* 1, no. 1 (1956): 1].

31. Discussions of the updated ideology draft at the 1958 COs' conference also included papers on "psychological preparedness," see စိတ်ဓာတ် ညွှန်ကြားရေးမှူးရုံး၊ "စိတ်ဓာတ်ရေး ကြံ့ခိုင်မှုအတွက် ပြင်ဆင်ထားခြင်း"၊ ၃၀–၈–၅၈ [Psychological Warfare Directorate, "Paper on Psychological Preparedness," August 30, 1958], CD 172, DSHRI.

On the civic-action proposal to "stimulate, motivate and sustain by morale action the public interest and belief in the ultimate triumph of democracy and socialism and the public participation in the fight for democracy and socialism," Ba Than reported at length to the 1957 COs' conference about his observations during a study mission to Manila. See ၁၉၅၇–ခုနှစ် တပ်မှူးများညီလာခံ၊ စိတ်ဓာတ်စစ်ဆင်ရေး ဟောပြောပွဲနှင့် ဆွေးနွေးပွဲတွင် မြွက်ကြားချက်များ [Public Lecture and Discussion of Psychological Warfare Operations, COs' Conference, 1957], CD 1, DSHRI; see also "The Report of the Morale Sub-Committee," Rangoon, June 18, 1957, CD 232, DSHRI.

The plan for the first eight-week psywar course in 1957 was sketched out in Directorate of Education and Psychological Warfare, Ministry of Defence, "Proposed Plan and Syllabi of Instruction of the First Psychological Warfare Officers' Course," August 19, 1957, CD 232, DSHRI.

32. The best sources on how the AFPFL split spilled over into the army are Sein Win, *Split Story*; Maung Maung, "Burma at the Crossroads"; and Trager, "Political Divorce in Burma."

33. See Martin Smith's eloquent description of this chaotic situation in *Burma: Insurgency and the Politics of Ethnicity*, 2d ed. (London, 1999), chap. 10.

34. Sein Win, *Split Story*, p. 74.

35. Ibid., p. 75.

36. "Burma Owes a Debt of Gratitude to the Defence Services," translation of Prime Minister U Nu's speech delivered on September 4, 1958, over the Burma Broadcasting System; copy DR 7619, DSHRI. Later, Nu emphasized that reports of the district delegates criticizing the army were "exaggerated by our political enemies" and claimed he had no knowledge of the two days of army-bashing that went on at his party's congress. In Sein Win, *Split Story*, p. 76.

37. Smith, *Burma: Insurgency*, pp. 168–70.

38. Probably Nu hoped to weed out pro–Swe Nyein supporters and to send a message to field commanders that their pro-Stable leanings would not be tolerated.

39. Bo Min Gaung, as a former member of the Thirty Comrades, apparently hoped that he "would be able to wield considerable influence over the armed forces personnel" (Sein Win, *Split Story*, p. 73). However he had not seen active service since the war nor had he developed much influence inside the tatmadaw.

40. Ibid., p. 70.

41. None of these former field commanders would meet this author for an interview because of their involvement in recent politics. However, a number of other sources, including a former field commander close to all three (interview, February 1993), identified these three officers as core members of the discussion.

42. Maung Maung denies ever assenting to their plans (interview, May 6, 1992). However, former Brig. Aung Gyi and former Col. Khin Nyo reported that Maung Maung was open to the idea of deposing U Nu because of his long-standing battle with the prime minister over army budget requests. Also, Nu's attempt to name Buddhism the state religion greatly irritated the Catholic Maung Maung (interview with Aung Gyi and Khin Nyo, May 14, 1992).

43. Interview, former Brig. Maung Maung, May 6, 1992.

44. Ibid. Aung Gyi confirms that the offer was made and that it angered him as well; interview, May 14, 1992. Sein Win's story is slightly different. He writes that Nu offered to form a "six-man Inner Circle with three Army Bosses and three from his faction to take a joint helm of the State" (*Split Story*, p. 76). Although the details are murky, Nu probably offered army leaders some kind of power-sharing arrangement.

45. Interview, former Brig. Maung Maung, May 6, 1992.

46. Maung Maung, *To a Soldier Son* (Rangoon, 1974), p. 99.

47. Sein Win (in *Split Story*) estimates that around five hundred UMPs sneaked into Rangoon in mufti at the last minute and that there were about five thousand well-armed Pyusawhtis in Tharrawaddy, three thousand in Insein, and twenty-five hundred in Prome on standby.

48. Interview, Aung Gyi, May 14, 1992; interview, former Brig. Maung Maung, May 6, 1992; and interview, former Brig. Tin Pe, May 16, 1992.

49. Directorate of Education and Psychological Warfare, Ministry of Defence, "Some Reflections on Our Constitution," October 17, 1958, CD 172, DSHRI.

50. Ibid. Some hints of this attitude were published only days after the coup in the army's *Khit-yeh* magazine. See ခေတ်ရေး၊ ၁၊ ၅။ ၃၀-၉-၅၈ [*Khit-yeh* 1, no. 5 (September 30, 1958)].

51. Attached to the Psywar Directorate's "Some Reflections" is a copy of the draconian "Anti-Subversion Act of the Republic of the Philippines, Republic Act No. 1700," which was to serve as a model for the proposed ordinance.

52. Interview, former Col. Hla Maw, February 21, 1993.

53. Trevor Dupuy, "Burma and Its Army: Contrast in Motivations and Characteristics," *Antioch Review* 20, no. 4 (1961): 428–40.

54. "List of Officers Seconded to Civil Government, as at 17 December 1959," CD 213, DSHRI. Many more officers were seconded to civil positions in February 1959 when the Constituent Assembly extended Ne Win's term.

55. Ibid.

56. U Thaung, "Army's Accumulation of Economic Power in Burma, 1940–1990," *The Burma Review* (1991): 17–22.

57. H. M. Military Attaché, British Embassy, Rangoon, "Annual Appreciation for the Period 1st June 1958 to 30th April 1959," FO 371/143888, PRO.

58. Conference schedule found in CD 105, DSHRI. The discussion of ideology was based on a paper submitted to the conference: "နိုင်ငံတော်ဝါဒရေး၊ ပေါ်လစီစာတမ်း (မူကြမ်း)၊ တပ်မတော်ညီလာခံ၊ ၁၉၅၉ခု၊ စက်တဘာလ(၁၅)ရက်။ ["National Ideology Policy (Draft)" (paper presented to Tatmadaw Conference, September 15, 1959)], CD 105, DSHRI.

59. ၁၉၅၉-ခု၊ ဧပြီလ ၂၁၊ ၂၂၊ ၂၃ ရက်နေ့များတွင် ရန်ကုန်မြို့ တပ်မတော်ကပွဲရုံကြီး၌ ကျင်းပသော လုံခြုံရေးကောင်စီများညီလာခံကြီး၏ မှတ်တမ်း [Minutes of the Security Councils' Conference, Tatmadaw Theater, Rangoon, April 21–23, 1959], CD 216, DSHRI.

60. From အမျိုးသားမှတ်ပုံတင်ဌာနနှင့် သန်းခေါင်စာရင်းဌာန၊ "မှတ်ပုံတင် လုပ်ငန်းရပ်များ တင်ပြချက်၊" ဗမာ့တပ်မတော် တပ်မှူးများညီလာခံ ၊ ၁၉၅၉ခုနှစ်၊ စက်တင်ဘာလ (၁၇)ရက်။ [National Registration and Census Department, "Report on National Registration Efforts" (paper presented to the Tatmadaw COs' Conference, September 17, 1959)], CD 105, DSHRI.

61. See the report on the Internal Security Press Conference, *The Guardian*, May 13, 1960; and British Embassy, "The Achievements of the Ne Win Government."

62. Dupuy, "Burma and Its Army."

63. Corporation of Rangoon, "Half-Yearly Report, 1 December 1958–1 June 1959," copy in DR 2313, DSHRI.

64. According to Martin Smith, the text probably was written by U Chit Hlaing, the former follower of Thakin Soe who was one of the writers of the first version of army ideology in 1956. *Burma: Insurgency*, p. 180.

65. Fred Von Der Mehden, "Burma's Religious Campaign Against Communism," *Pacific Affairs* 33, no. 3 (1960): 290–99.

66. Smith, *Burma: Insurgency*, p. 181.

67. British Embassy, "The Achievements of the Ne Win Government."

68. Amb. Richard Allen, British Embassy, Rangoon, to Selwyn Lloyd, Foreign Office, London, despatch, December 20, 1958, FO 371/135729, PRO. The "concentration camp" comment is from U Thaung, *A Journalist, A General, and An Army in Burma* (Bangkok, 1995), p. 41.

69. British Embassy, "The Achievements of the Ne Win Government."

70. It should be noted that the elected government of U Nu also tolerated very little criticism from the "irresponsible press," and journalists often were arrested for criticizing the government.

71. The only journalist identified as a communist in the Directorate of Education and Psychological Warfare's "Newspapers Analysis" [November 26, 1958; in DSHRI: CD 358] who was not arrested was U Thaung, a fairly vocal critic of the Bogyoke government.

72. Smith, *Burma: Insurgency*, p. 180.

73. See Dupuy, "Burma and Its Army."

74. See, e.g., Willard Hanna, "Re-Revving a Revolution," *American Universities Field Staff Reports Service*, Southeast Asia Series 11, no. 4 (1963).

75. "နိုင်ငံတော်အစိုးရ အပေါ် ပညာဗဟုသုတ ရှိသူများ၏ ယေဘုယျသဘောထား အကြမ်းပြင်စပ်ပြု သုတေသနစာတမ်း" ["The General Views of Knowledgeable Persons Regarding the National Government, Random Sample Survey" (n.d., probably 1959)]; "တပ်မတော်အပေါ် ပညာဗဟုသုတရှိသူများ၏ ယေဘုယျ သဘောထား၊ အကြမ်းပြင်စပ်ပြု သုတေသန စာတမ်း" ["The General Views of Knowledgeable Persons Regarding the Tatmadaw, Random Sample Survey" (n.d., probably 1959)]; "ပြည်အတွင်း အနှံ့အပြားမှ ပညာဗဟုသုတရှိသူ ၂၀၀ကျော်ထံ မေးမြန်း၍ သိရှိခြင်း၊ တပ်မတော်သား အချို့အပေါ် မကြိုက်သောအချက်များ အတွိချုပ်၊" ၁၉၅၉–ခုနှစ် တပ်မတော်တပ်မှူးညီလာခံ ["Summary of the Views of 200 Knowledgeable Persons Regarding What They Do Not Like About Some Military Personnel" (paper presented to the COs' Conference, September 1959)]; and "ပြည်မအတွင်း အနှံ့အပြားမှ ပညာဗဟုသုတရှိသူ ၂၀၀ကျော်ထံမေးမြန်း၍သိရှိခြင်း၊ တပ်မတော်သားအချို့အပေါ် ကြိုက်သောအချက်များ အတွိချုပ်)၊" ၁၉၅၉–ခုနှစ် တပ်မတော်တပ်မှူးညီလာခံ ["Summary of the Views of 200 Knowledgeable Persons Regarding What They Like About Some Military Personnel" (paper presented to the COs' Conference, September 1959)]. All of these documents are found in CD 168, DSHRI.

76. " ၂၀၀ကျော်ထံ မေးမြန်း၍ သိရှိခြင်း၊ (တပ်မတော်သား အချို့အပေါ် မကြိုက်သောအချက်)" ["Views of 200 Knowledgeable Persons Regarding What They Do Not Like."]

77. Some of the positive comments read like verbatim army propaganda:

"The Burma Army is now an organized and disciplined body, serving as a steel wall against insurgency and foreign aggression."

"There is a fine spirit of cooperation between the armed forces and complete lack of departmental jealousies, thus leading to achievement of results."

"Senior Army Officers have full understanding of capabilities of their juniors and do not indulge in over-supervision."

"The Burma Army will always stay a beacon of democracy whatever the situation may be."

"The Burma Army is an aid to Civil Power."

"Army personnel are known for 'loving kindness to all law-abiding villagers on their visits.'"

From "၂၀၀ကျော်ထံ မေးမြန်း၍ သိရှိခြင်း (တပ်မတော်သား အချို့အပေါ် ကြိုက်သောအချက်များ)။" ["Views of 200 Knowledgeable Persons Regarding What They Like."]

78. See, e.g., Allen to Lloyd, despatch, December 20, 1958, FO 371/135729, PRO.
79. Interview, former Col. Hla Maw, February 21, 1993.
80. Ibid.
81. U Thaung, *A Journalist*, p. 47.
82. Interview with retired district civil servant, February 1993.
83. Interview, anonymous former intelligence officer, May 8, 1992.
84. Interview, February 1993.
85. The quote is from the statement issued by the Magsaysay Awards Foundation board of governors; quoted in *The Nation*, August 4, 1960. Ramon Magsaysay was president of the Philippines from 1953–57. According to the official web site of the award, the foundation honors every year individuals who "perpetuate his [Magsaysay's] example of integrity in government and pragmatic idealism within a democratic society" (from "History," Magsaysay Awards website, http://www.rmaf.org.ph/about.html, accessed January 15, 2003). On August 17, Ne Win turned down the award—for which he would have received $10,000—because of Magsaysay's personal connections to the CIA as well as the foundation's reputed CIA backing. Ne Win reportedly was outraged that the foundation had leaked the story to the international press before he had a chance to reject the award. The British Foreign Office reported that Ne Win "feels that to accept so valuable a prize as this could be considered as a reward for following pro-Western policies." Memorandum by C. W. Squire, "Foreign Office Minute," August 8, 1960, FO 371/152253, PRO.
86. This is Frank Trager's description; from *From Kingdom to Republic* (London, 1966), p. 198. See also Richard Butwell, "The Four Failures of U Nu's Second Premiership," *Asian Survey* 2, no. 1 (1962): 3–11, and his *U Nu of Burma* (Stanford, 1963); Lucian Pye, "The Army in Burmese Politics," in *The Role of the Military in Underdeveloped Countries*, ed. John J. Johnson (Princeton, 1962); and Jon Wiant and David Steinberg, "The Military and National Development," in *Soldiers and Stability in Southeast Asia*, ed. J. Soedjati Djiwandono and Yong Mun Cheong (Singapore, 1988).
87. For example, on February 9, 1961, the British military attaché reported, "We now have reason to believe that . . . he [Aung Shwe] and two or three other brigade commanders have been actively plotting a coup to displace Ne Win, and presumably thereafter to take over the Government." Although he admitted that Maung Maung's role in this plot was unclear, the attaché suggested the latter must have been implicated because of his friendship with Aung Shwe. Col. F. M. Shaw, Military Attaché, British Embassy, Rangoon, to Brig. A. P. Block, War Office, London, "General Ne Win," despatch, February 9, 1961, FO 371/159777, PRO.
88. Interviews with former Brig. Maung Maung, May 9, 1992, and former Brig. Aung Gyi, May 14, 1992.
89. Interview, former Brig. Maung Maung, May 9, 1992. This was not the tatmadaw's first cooperation with the CIA, in spite of the CIA's assistance to the KMT in northeastern Burma. In 1956, Col. Aung Gyi, Col. Maung Maung, and other officers visited the United States to meet Pentagon officials to discuss weapons sales. After a luncheon hosted by CIA Director Allen Dulles, the Burmese officers were told that their weapons requests could be paid for out of "discretionary funds." Maung Maung and Aung Gyi claim that they did not discover until later that this "discretionary" money came from the CIA. Additionally, some officers had been trained at the CIA's intelligence course at Okinawa.
90. A journalist of that era reports that Maung Maung had offended Ne Win deeply by not updating him on the development of the research unit. He reports that Maung Maung told the unit commander, Myint Swe, "Don't tell anybody" about the activities of the unit. When Ne Win called Myint Swe in for questioning, the latter refused to tell him anything because of his orders from Maung Maung. Interview, Guardian Sein Win, April 7, 1992.
91. Interview, anonymous former intelligence officer, May 8, 1992; interview, Aung Gyi, May 14, 1992. When asked why Ne Win would believe Bo Lwin over Maung Maung, Aung

Gyi pointed to an incident that he believed drove a wedge between Maung Maung and Ne Win: In 1960 or 1961, the tatmadaw captured a Chinese lieutenant-colonel. Maung Maung took charge of the case. Aung Gyi remembers that Ne Win was furious when he learned that Maung Maung allowed the CIA to interrogate the Chinese officer.

92. Aung Gyi attributes the virulence of Maung Maung's anti-communist stance to his conversion to Catholicism. Interview, April 28, 1992.

93. This was a highly controversial move at the time, and the government stridently denied widespread reports of the temporary alliance. However, a number of intelligence sources as well as a tatmadaw field commander (interview, February 1993) involved in the operation confirm the joint operation. See, e.g., H. M. Military Attaché, British Embassy, Rangoon, "Annual Appreciation of the Burma Army for the Period 1 May 1960 to 30 April 1961," FO 371/159777, PRO.

94. *The Nation*, February 6, 1961.

95. Interview, anonymous, February 1993.

96. Amb. R. H. S. Allen, British Embassy, Rangoon, to F. A. Warner, South-East Asia Department, Foreign Office, London, despatch, February 9, 1961, FO 371/159777, PRO.

97. Ibid.

98. Robin Sanders, "Peking's Burma Friends," *The Observer*, July 15, 1962.

99. Allen to Warner, despatch, February 9, 1961.

100. Interview, Hla Maw, February 21, 1993.

101. According to Hla Maw, "I finally realized afterward that if you are against Maung Maung and Aung Gyi then you are against Ne Win." Ibid.

102. H. M. Military Attaché, British Embassy, Rangoon, "Annual Appreciation of the Burma Army for the Period 1 May 1961 to 30 April 1962," FO 371/166395, PRO.

103. Aung Gyi explained, "We had economic, religious and political crises with the issue of federalism as the most important for the coup. . . . A small country like Burma cannot afford division." In *The Guardian*, March 8, 1962.

104. Chapter 10 of the 1947 constitution guaranteed to the Shan and Karenni states the right to secede from the Union no earlier than ten years after independence. In order to invoke this clause, the state had to pass a secession resolution by two-thirds of the members of the State Council (the state legislature), after which the president of Burma would order a plebiscite to be held to poll the people of the state.

105. On the morning of the coup, a soldier shot Mye Thaike, the son of Shan sawbwa Sao Shwe Thaike, in the head. The Hsipaw sawbwa, Sao Kya Seng, also disappeared after being stopped by soldiers in Taunggyi. He was never seen again. (See the moving memoir by Kya Seng's wife, Inge Sargent, *Twilight over Burma: Memoirs of a Shan Princess* [Honolulu, 1994].) Most of those arrested spent the next five years in detention. For excellent accounts of the events of early March, see Bertil Lintner, *Burma in Revolt* (Boulder, Colo., 1994), chap. 6; and David Steinberg, "Burma Under the Military: Towards a Chronology," *Contemporary Southeast Asia* 3, no. 3 (1981).

106. Amb. Richard Allen, British Embassy, Rangoon, to Secretary of State, Foreign Office, despatch, March 7, 1962, FO 371/166369, PRO. On the same day the British air attaché wrote:

> On the evidence available, this [explanation that federalism necessitated the coup] hardly stands up to scrutiny, since U Nu had shown no signs of being ready to make any major concessions to the federalists. The Shans, as those most concerned, had no hope of imposing their will on the rest of the country, and it was clearly U Nu's idea, and a logical one at that, to take the heat out of the issue by having it properly ventilated.

From Memorandum by Group Captain P. W. Cook, Air Attaché, British Embassy, Rangoon, to Air Ministry A.D.I.2., "Military Coup d'etat–Union of Burma," March 7, 1962, FO 371/166369, PRO.

107. Ibid. A few weeks later, the British ambassador reported that Brig. Aung Gyi had mentioned numerous times that the "foreign intervention" in the Shan state (i.e., U.S. assistance to the KMT) was another reason for the coup. Amb. Richard Allen, British Embassy, Rangoon, to Secretary of State, Foreign Office, despatch, April 4, 1962, FO 371/166370, PRO.

108. Perhaps Ne Win feared a repeat of the 1958 Clean AFPFL Congress, which spent two days criticizing the army in public view. That congress led to the first documentable moves by field commanders to plan anti-government and maybe anti–Ne Win action.

109. Alfred C. Stepan, *Rethinking Military Politics: Brazil and the Southern Cone* (Princeton, N.J., 1988).

Epilogue

1. Directorate of Education and Psychological Warfare, Ministry of Defence, "Some Reflections on Our Constitution," October 17, 1958, CD 172, DSHRI.

2. The argument that the move to the left was a tactical one rather than an ideological one was reinforced in interviews with some of the major players. Former Brig. Tin Pe, who became Ne Win's advisor on ideology, remembers being surprised when Gen. Ne Win ordered him to produce a viable leftist ideology in a matter of days. Tin Pe recalls driving a truck to the university library, collecting every book on Marxism on the shelves, and spending seven days working his way through them. "What did I know about ideology?" Tin Pe recalled in an interview (May 16, 1992). He is still today remembered by many as "the Red Brigadier," the nickname he earned for this endeavor.

3. Karen Human Rights Group, *Suffering in Silence: The Human Rights Nightmare of the Karen People of Burma*, ed. Claudio O. Delang (Parkland, 2000), p. 15.

4. Martin Smith, *Burma: Insurgency and the Politics of Ethnicity*, 2d ed. (London, 1999), pp. 100–101.

5. Andrew Selth, *Transforming the Tatmadaw: The Burmese Armed Forces Since 1988* (Canberra, 1996), p. 7.

6. Micool Brooke, "The Armed Forces of Myanmar," *Asian Defence Journal* (January 1998): 13; Anthony Davis and Bruce Hawke, "Burma: The Country That Won't Kick the Habit," *Jane's Intelligence Review* (March 1998): 26–31.

7. Andrew Selth, "The Future of the Burmese Armed Forces" (paper presented at Burma Update Conference, Australian National University, Canberra, August 5–6, 1999), p. 11.

8. Davis and Hawke, "Burma."

9. Selth, "Future of the Burmese Armed Forces."

10. Robert Lowry, *The Armed Forces of Indonesia* (Sydney, 1996), pp. 139–41.

11. In July 1999, 112,000 students out of nearly 400,000 passed the entrance examinations for university. They joined 300,000 students who passed the exams from 1996–98 and awaited the reopening of civilian universities, which had been closed since early December 1996. Reuters, July 26, 1999.

By contrast, the expansion of military higher education facilities has been dramatic. An army spokesman told a conference in 1998 that the Defence Services Academy was being expanded to accommodate intakes of 1,000 cadets per class. In the 1980s, DSA intakes were probably around 150–200 for each class (Col. Thein Swe, "Human Resource Development in Nation-Building: The Role of the Armed Forces," *Myanmar Perspectives* [July 1998]. Available online at http://www.myanmar.com/gov/perspec/7-98/hum.htm, accessed May 14, 1999). The new Military Technology College in Maymyo reportedly has 5,000 students enrolled. (Kyaw Zwa Moe, "Students Sentenced to Death," *The Irrawaddy [Online]* [June 10, 2002]; available online at http://www.irrawaddy.org/news/2002/june10.html, accessed July 25, 2002).

12. Bertil Lintner, "Velvet Glove," *Far Eastern Economic Review*, May 7, 1998.

13. OSS was probably founded in 1994 for two reasons: to create a new four-star general billet so that there would be one to justify Lt. Gen. Khin Nyunt's promotion to General, and to create a semi-academic institution similar to strategic studies think tanks elsewhere in the Association of Southeast Asian Nations (ASEAN), thus giving Burma a "one-and-a-half-track" seat at ASEAN gatherings. See Andrew Selth, "Burma's Intelligence Apparatus," *Burma Debate*, September–October 1997.

14. In part, this delegation of authority from the junta to the regional commanders eased intra-elite tension among senior military leaders. At the time of the September 1988 coup d'etat,

the junta members held lower ranks than the regional commanders and occupied positions that reflected those lower ranks. The ranks of the regional commanders gave them greater status and claim to power in the reorganizing regime, and their resulting rise to incipient warlordism no doubt reflects this rank differential. Note that the junta attempted to address this imbalance by raising the rank status of positions in the newly reorganized Ministry of Defence and the high command by one or two ranks; most junta members were summarily promoted.

15. U.S. Department of State, Bureau for International Narcotics and Law Enforcement Affairs, *International Narcotics Control Strategy Report* (Washington, D.C., 1998).

16. Selth, *Transforming the Tatmadaw*, pp. 22–26.

17. David I. Steinberg, *Burma: The State of Myanmar* (Washington, D.C., 2001), chap. 5; Gustaaf Houtman, *Mental Culture in Burmese Crisis Politics: Aung San Suu Kyi and the National League for Democracy* (Tokyo, 1999); and Investor Responsibility Research Center, *Multinational Business in Burma* (Washington, D.C., 1997).

18. Pictograms representing each party appeared on the ballot, in recognition of the population's multilingual nature and the serious problem of illiteracy nationwide.

19. On forced labor, see the International Labour Organization, "Forced Labour in Myanmar (Burma): Report of the Commission of Inquiry Appointed under Article 26 of the Constitution of the International Labour Organization to Examine the Observance by Myanmar of the Forced Labour Convention, 1930," July 2, 1998. Available online at http://www.ilo.org/public/english/standards/relm/gb/docs/gb273/myanmar.htm, accessed July 25, 2002.

20. ဦးစံငြိမ်းနှင့်ဒေါက်တာမြင့်ကြည်၊ ၁၉၅၈–၁၉၆၂၊ မြန်မာနိုင်ငံရေး၊ ၄ တွဲ [U San Nyein and Dr. Myint Kyi, *Myanmar Politics, 1958–1962*, 4 vols.] (Rangoon, 1991); တိုင်းရင်းသားလူမျိုးများနှင့် ၁၉၄၇ အခြေခံဥပဒေ [*The Indigenous Races and the 1947 Constitution*] (Rangoon, 1991); တပ်မတော်သမိုင်း၊ ၇ တွဲ [*Tatmadaw History*, 7 vols.] (Rangoon, 1994–2002). Scholars and activists have tended to discount the "official histories" published by writers associated with the Historical Commission, the Universities Historical Research Centre, and the Defence Services Historical Research Institute (DSHRI). However, careful readings of their Burmese-language histories reveal data never publicly circulated under the Socialist regime. See, e.g., U San Nyein's and Daw Myint Kyi's မြန်မာ့နိုင်ငံရေး [*Myanmar Politics*] insightful discussions of the plots and counterplots that preceded the 1958 coup d'etat. Additionally, the extensive footnotes in the official histories provide useful guides to scholars who wish to pursue archival research in the future.

21. No serious attempts to physically build the museum occurred until the military took direct control of the government in 1988. Between the 1950s and the 1990s, a skeletal staff of archivists, librarians, and support personnel dedicated themselves to collecting artifacts and historical documents and displaying them in a public exhibition hall once a year for Armed Forces Day (March 27). They worked for the DSHRI out of makeshift quarters, first in a small colonial-era building in central Rangoon, and later in part of a complex originally intended to become the headquarters of the BSPP in the northern Rangoon suburb, Gon-Myin-Tha. SLORC began construction of the museum in 1990, and the staff, exhibits, and archives moved into the current location in central Rangoon in 1994.

22. Although the reorganization may have redistributed power among military leaders, the SPDC has not shown any serious deviation from previous policies of SLORC. Herein, I call the junta by the name "SLORC" when referring to particular policies or activities of the regime from 1988–97; I use "SPDC" to refer to the same after 1997. When discussing the entire period of this junta's rule, I use the clumsy moniker "SLORC/SPDC," since the reorganization represents little more than a change in name.

23. Crawford Young, "The African Colonial State and Its Political Legacy," in *The Precarious Balance: State and Society in Africa*, ed. Donald Rothchild and Naomi Chazan (Boulder, Colo., 1988), pp. 25–66, 51.

24. *Fear and Sanctuary: Burmese Refugees in Thailand* (Ithaca, 2002).

25. Brian Loveman and Thomas M. Davies Jr., eds., *The Politics of Antipolitics: The Military in Latin America* (Wilmington, Del., 1997).

26. Notably, among regime critics in the center, there was little outcry when the regime began massive forced relocations of villages in the Karenni, Shan, and Karen states (where a few small rebel groups continue to fight the government). As the Karen Human Rights Group

reported, "Many of the villages ordered to move do not even have any contact with opposition groups, but they fall within an area where the SPDC believes the opposition can operate." Karen Human Rights Group, *Suffering in Silence*, p. 17.

27. Interview, army colonel, September 22, 1997.

28. Khun Okker, foreign affairs spokesperson for the National Democratic Front, quoted in Martin Smith, "Burma at the Crossroads," *Burma Debate*, November–December 1996, 4–13, 4.

29. Arend Lijphart, *Democracy in Plural Societies* (New Haven, 1977), pp. 25–52.

30. Reuters, February 4, 1997.

31. Karen Human Rights Group, *Suffering in Silence*, p. 25.

32. Bonnie Honig, "Difference, Dilemmas, and the Politics of Home," in *Democracy and Difference: Contesting the Boundaries of the Political*, ed. Seyla Benhabib (Princeton, 1996), pp. 257–77, 258.

33. From "Bogyoke Aung San's Address at the Convention Held at the Jubilee Hall, Rangoon, on the 23rd May, 1947," in *The Political Legacy of Aung San*, ed. Josef Silverstein (Ithaca, 1993), pp. 151–61. The last sentence apparently is a translation of a Pali proverb.

Index